LEARNING FROM THE

SECRET
PAST

LEARNING FROM THE

SECRET PAST

Cases in British Intelligence History

ROBERT DOVER

and

MICHAEL S. GOODMAN

Editors

Georgetown University Press / Washington, D.C.

Georgetown University Press, Washington, D.C. www.press.georgetown.edu

Library of Congress Cataloging-in-Publication data

Learning from the secret past: cases in British intelligence history / Robert Dover and Michael S. Goodman, editors
        p.cm.
Includes bibliographical references and index.
ISBN 978-1-58901-770-2 (pbk.: acid-free paper)
1. Intelligence service—Great Britain—History—20th century. 2. Intelligence service—Great Britain—History—21st century. 3. Intelligence service—Great Britain—Case studies. 4. Military intelligence—Great Britain—Case studies. 5. Great Britain—Foreign relations—1945. 6. Great Britain—Military relations. I. Dover, Robert, 1977-
II. Goodman, Michael S.
  JN329-I6L43 2011
  327.1241—dc22

                                                                    2010051651

♾ This book is printed on acid-free paper meeting the requirements of the American National Standard for Permanence in Paper for Printed Library Materials.

15   14   13   12   11   9   8   7   6   5   4   3   2   First printing

Printed in the United States of America

Historia est vitae magistra
—Cicero, *De Oratore*

Contents

Preface

Learning lessons from history is the most important task of security professionals in the early part of the twenty-first century. While the current threats to our nations and way of life seem radical and new, they are all part of established patterns and have all—in one way or another—been dealt with before. But intelligence failures have been the defining aspect of the post–9/11 world. The failures identified in the American and European intelligence communities have been varied: political interference, bureaucratic processes, and the failure to look in the right places and come to the right conclusions. The organizing principle behind this book is that the failure to appreciate historical lessons is a widespread problem in all aspects of political and social life, and particularly within intelligence communities. The reasons for this are relatively clear; the pressure of time on officers, the necessarily insular nature of intelligence agencies, and the turnover of staff means that historical lessons are easily forgotten. The British agencies, in light of the problems with the intelligence about Iraq prior to the 2003 invasion, have been anxious to review their historical lessons, and have put internal processes in place to do so. Professor Christopher Andrew, the official historian of MI5, has talked about "historical attention span deficit" disorder—in his words, the inability of those studying intelligence to learn from prior examples. The rationale for this book is to attempt to ameliorate this situation. By commissioning leading experts in the field to produce a series of "lessons learned" case studies, we intend to bring to the fore an awareness of what has gone on in the past, and the crucial need to learn from historical precedents.

There are eleven contributions in this volume, and the authors are leading specialists in their fields. The approach we have taken is novel for several reasons, and these are clear from the remit for each chapter: a description of the historical event, its context and significance, and a discussion of the lessons that emerge. Therefore, this is not simply a historical account of different episodes: it is an attempt to place events in their historical context (and explain their contemporary relevance), and to view them as more than just discrete examples. We have not aimed exclusively at a practitioner or academic audience; our aim is to provide a collection of essays that could be usefully accessed by knowledgeable and inquisitive general readers, by scholars of intelligence, and by those working in this professional field.

The book is arranged in thematic order, and the lessons that are drawn cut across the chapters. David Omand emphasizes in his chapter that learning from history is a key element of the work of intelligence analysts. Michael Herman and Peter Gill provide the chapters in the first section, which deals with the organization and oversight of intelligence. In Michael Herman's chapter a distinguished former secretary of the Joint Intelligence Committee reconsiders that organization's origins. Peter Gill's chapter provides an interesting and instructive account of what is meant by oversight and its limitations in a liberal democracy.

Rob Dover and Mark Phythian focus on political interference in the intelligence process, when it can go wrong at the analytical stage or when levels of political interference are too strong. Dover tackles the thorny issue of what intelligence can reveal about the less savory areas of government licensing of military equipment for sale to other governments, as revealed in the Scott Report. Phythian, on the other hand, uses his chapter to explore directly the problems of politicization. Although markedly different in their substantive focus and approach, these two chapters bring home the tensions placed upon the intelligence process.

Matthew Jones, Richard Aldrich, and Eunan O'Halpin explore the important issues of counterinsurgency and counterterrorism, which include consideration of ethics, accountability, and oversight, both in a legal and political framework and in the context of information gathering. Ethics has become a large issue surrounding (and overshadowing) intelligence in the Western world, mostly as a result of the so-called rendition programs run by the United States (and supported secretly by Western Europe). The often violent and sudden, officially sanctioned, kidnapping of terrorist suspects brought into sharp relief the limits of government activity abroad (or the lack of such limits). The problematic cases were those where the suspects were then proved to be entirely innocent of any wrongdoing, and the alleged instances of outsourced torture merely made the critiques stronger. Aldrich tackles the subjects of interrogation techniques and forms of internment head on, through a Northern Irish case study, to provide some historical and practical lessons for governments of today. Matthew Jones and Eunan O'Halpin consider the lessons that emerge from past counterinsurgency and counterterrorist efforts, especially the role and value of intelligence in these campaigns. Jones deals with the British response to the Malayan emergency, and O'Halpin focuses on the personality politics of intelligence in Northern Ireland. The lessons that can be learned from these moments in history are not necessarily direct—the character of the insurgencies is very different now, as are the participants—but there are valuable lessons to be drawn from these case studies, particularly about the use of intelligence in counterinsurgency and the management of human sources.

Finally, Gill Bennett, Len Scott, and Michael Goodman take on the thematic point of avoiding surprises, and a subsidiary focus on the uses of intelligence—the value of placing too much reliance on a single source and of the need to place decisions based on intelligence within a wider, international context. Gill Bennett, the former chief historian at the Foreign Office, considers a well-trodden subject—the Suez crisis of 1956—but in a new context. The majority of accounts tend to ignore what else was going on, and neglect to show how the British decision to intervene was based on a far wider-ranging interpretation of international events than a simple desire to overthrow Nasser. Len Scott, as a long-time observer of the Cuban missile crisis, tackles the use, value, and impact of human intelligence in his chapter and explores—in particular—the role of Colonel Oleg Penkovsky, frequently described by some as the "spy who saved the world." As the official historian of the Joint Intelligence Committee (JIC), Goodman uses the files that have been released into the public domain to discuss the Nicoll Report, which was a pivotal but undernoted moment in British intelligence history.

This is a good moment to analyze the lessons that can be learned from intelligence history. There is an appetite among security officials to make the best use of historical analyses, and this collection of essays aims to provide a snapshot of the sort of lessons that can be learned from careful analysis of single documents.

Acknowledgments

We would like to thank the King's College London's Teaching Fund, without which this project would not have been possible. We would also like to thank all of the authors for their timely, original, and excellent contributions, and Don Jacobs at Georgetown University Press for his professionalism and for making the publication process as trouble-free as it is ever likely to be. Rob would like to thank Mike for being an excellent collaborating partner—it is always a pleasure. He would also like to thank Chrissie for putting up with his long stints in the study and Jessica, Sophie, and Charlotte for reminding him that there are more important things in life. Mike would like to thank, as usual, Rob, who has made this project easy, straightforward, and enjoyable. He would also like to offer his heartfelt thanks to his lovely wife Denise for her continuing support, and to his gorgeous son Oliver, who has brought so much joy, laughter, and wonder to their lives.

Abbreviations: Acronym Key

BND	Bundenachrichtendienst
CEP	Captured Enemy Personnel
CID	Criminal Investigation Department
CIG	Current Intelligence Group
COS	Chiefs of Staff
CS	Cipher School
DF	Direction Finding
DIS	Defense Intelligence Staff
DTI	Department for Trade and Industry
ECHR	European Convention on Human Rights, European Court of Human Rights
EIS	Egyptian Intelligence Services
EOKA	Ethniki Organosis Kyprion Agoniston
FAC	Foreign Affairs Committee
FCO	Foreign and Commonwealth Office
FIC	Federal Intelligence Committee
FO	Foreign Office
GC&CS	Government Code and Cipher School
GCHQ	Government Communications Headquarters
GKKNIR	State Committee for the Coordination of Scientific Research Work
GLCM	Ground-Launched Cruise Missile
GOC	General Officer Commanding
GRU	Glavnoye Razvedyvatel'noye Upravleniye or General Staff of the Russian Armed Forces
HMG	Her Majesty's Government
IED	Improvised Explosive Device
IIC	Industrial Intelligence Center
IMF	International Monetary Fund
IOCA	Interception of Communications Act
IRA	Irish Republican Army
IRBM	Intermediate-Range Ballistic Missile
IS(O)	Intelligence Section (Operations)

ISB	Intelligence Services Bill
ISC	Intelligence and Security Committee
ISTD	Interservice Topographical Department
JCHR	Joint Committee on Human Rights
JIB	Joint Intelligence Board
JIC	Joint Intelligence Committee
JIS	Joint Intelligence Staff
JPS	Joint Planning Staff
JTAC	Joint Terrorism Analysis Centre
KGB	Komitet gosudarstvennoy bezopasnosti or Committee for State Security
MBFR	Mutual and Balanced Force Reduction
MCP	Malayan Communist Party
MEW	Ministry of Economic Warfare
MNLA	Malayan National Liberation Army
MPAJA	Malayan People's Anti-Japanese Army
MRBM	Medium-Range Ballistic Missile
MSS	Malayan Security Service
NATO	North Atlantic Treaty Organization
NGO	Nongovernmental Organization
NPIC	National Photographic Intelligence Centre
NSC	National Security Council
PFIAB	President's Foreign Intelligence Advisory Board
PIRA	Provisional Irish Republican Army
PM	Prime Minister
PUS	Permanent Undersecretary
PWE	Political Warfare Executive
RUC	Royal Ulster Constabulary
S and T	Scientific and Technical Intelligence
SAC	Strategic Air Command
SALT	Strategic Arms Limitation Talks
SAS	Special Air Service
SEATO	South East Asia Treaty Organization
SEP	Surrendered Enemy Personnel
SIGINT	Signals Intelligence
SIS	Secret Intelligence Service (MI6)
SOE	Special Operations Executive
START	Strategic Arms Reduction Treaty
TNA	The National Archives
UDR	Ulster Defence Regiment
UMNO	United Malays National Organization
UVF	Ulster Volunteer Force
WMD	Weapons of Mass Destruction

Learning from the Secret Past

DAVID OMAND

The ability to learn from history is a key attribute of intelligence analysts. There are useful parallels to be drawn between the approach of the analyst tackling the secrets of the present and that of the historian trying to reconstruct the secrets of the past.

My first point is an analytical one. Intelligence work rests on a form of historiography. It rests on a sense of past as well as of present and future events; that is, on an interpretation of the relevant history. Suppose a secret report comes from a well-placed agent who has access to circles in which interesting topics are likely to be discussed. The case officer responsible for that source will have to judge whether his reporting chain is robust, and whether the information is valid. Does the source, for example, feel under pressure to report a positive finding on the subject? Is the source seeking to curry favor, perhaps for financial gain or to gain assistance for his family (as may have been the case with *Curveball*, the German Intelligence Service [BND] source on Iraqi biological warfare programs who appeared to have been fabricating part of his story)? Is it possible that the source is being controlled by a hostile intelligence service or in some way is acting as a double agent? The information may have come from a casual contact, or a new source still on trial whose reliability has not been fully tested. Even having endorsed the bona fides of the individual agent, can the case officer be satisfied that the information being reported was itself valid and not just palace gossip or a document deliberately put in the way of the agent in order to deceive? Such questions become even more pressing when the source is relying on subsources not known personally to the case officer, or when the information has been taken from internet chat sites when the participants may have suspected they were being monitored.

Similar questions have to be asked about every kind of intelligence access. Was the intercepted conversation between terrorist suspects carried out by the parties knowing that it might be eavesdropped or intercepted? Does, for example, an agreement between them to "meet at noon with the spare parts," mean "noon to repair the car," or is it a prearranged code to mean "two hours earlier and with the detonators" (a potential example of the difference between evidence and intelligence)? Is what is shown on the aerial photograph a real structure, or is the

1

intention to deceive (including the deliberate hiding of activity, for example during the known pass time of a low earth orbiting satellite)? Does the country concerned have a history of deception and historical motives that might end up being reflected in our intelligence, for example, Saddam Hussein's desire to convince Iran that his weapons of mass destruction programs were still operational?

The questions to be addressed are not so very different from those that should be in the mind of an experienced historian examining a primary or secondary source document. Obvious questions arise. How old is this material? When was it written? When did it come into our hands? Who wrote it and why and in what circumstances? Was he writing to please a particular audience? Is it self-exculpatory? What is known of the other reporting of this author/agent? Is this the original document or a copy? Is the copy a photocopy or at least likely to be in the same form as the original? If the latter, how long after the original was it made, and by whom? Where was it written? What does it say and is this based on direct observation or second-hand accounts? Is it likely that the author/agent had first-hand experience of what he is writing about or, if reporting the views of others, that they had direct knowledge? And so on. We can imagine many such questions about the validity of information in the archives being posed by Secret Intelligence Service (MI6) analysts as they pored over the scraps of paper smuggled out of KGB headquarters by the British agent Vassili Mitrokhin, on which he had jotted down notes on the contents of the KGB archive files. Validation of secret intelligence needs care, as we have seen in recent years with Iraq. Validation requires understanding of the past circumstances by which the information came into our hands or, as military commanders have from time to time found out to their cost, was meant to find its way into our hands. Deception in war is as old as war itself. Validation is therefore historiography by another name.

Analysis of the intelligence means placing it alongside other reports, establishing its meaning as part of a jigsaw puzzle (for which, as has often been said, the pieces are mixed up with those of other puzzles and there is a misleading picture on the box lid) very much as the historian would with newly uncovered correspondence between two historically significant figures.

Intelligence assessment, on the other hand, is more than analysis. It implies an explanation of events leading up to the present, and a judgment of their significance. Such an assessment will be put together by the analyst from all the information available from secret sources and diplomatic reporting, as well as publicly available information, to form what is termed an "all-source" assessment. Just as the historian tries to make sense of the past by imposing order on it, the analyst is trying to impose sense on the present, but in L. P. Hartley's phrase, "The past is another country. They do things differently there." Even with the best agent reporting or SIGINT intercepts the evidence will always be capable of different interpretations. Judgment, in which explanation plays a major part, will always be needed when assessments try to be predictive. The best assessments are forward-looking, informed by a sound understanding of the past.

All explanatory hypotheses are, however, provisional. When new evidence is uncovered (as it habitually is) that cannot be explained, there has to be a rethink. The intelligence analyst, like the historian, has to be scrupulously honest in acknowledging when favorite theories can no longer be sustained. Politicians hate it when they have to change their minds, and even more so, to admit it in public, given the inevitable media cries of "U-turn." But for the analyst it should be a point of honor not to cling to outdated theories, and fall into the temptation to dismiss the obstinate data points as outliers that should be discarded to allow the neat correlation to stand.

That lesson applies well beyond the analyst. Norman Dixon, in his masterly book *The Psychology of Military Incompetence*, happily still in print, captures a large number of examples where senior military commanders fail to take in fresh evidence or intelligence, and stubbornly head into disaster. So not only must there exist data points, an intelligence organization capable of capturing them, and an intelligence analyst capable of understanding them and explaining them, but also the analyst has to be part of a system that will get that intelligence in a timely and accurate manner into the hands of the military commander or other decision maker, the commander has to be receptive to the new analysis and not suffer from cognitive dissonance, and finally, the commander must be in a position to do something in terms of time, space, and capability to make use of the intelligence. It is perhaps surprising from the historical record that there are so many examples where intelligence was used to make a difference to the outcome.

There is a more fundamental point. Looking backward, we have our knowledge of where we have been to guide us. Looking forward, the possibilities are infinite. Even when we think that we can be sure of how events will unfold, we can still be surprised by the unexpected: snow that makes the mountains impassable (I recall vividly from 1982 the first report from the raid to recapture South Georgia to reach the Ministry of Defence, of a white-out and a special forces helicopter crashed on the glacier), enemy formations that turn up where they were not expected, flooding that makes the rivers unfordable, new weapons in the hands of the enemy or used in unexpected ways; there are so many side-winds that can blow the commander off course. More fundamentally, in terms of the wider security domain, we may discover that the world no longer behaves the way we thought it did. Without our fully realizing it, there may have been a paradigm shift: the rules of the international game may have changed, power has shifted within the palace, new weapons have changed the strategic balance or, as we saw in the 1990s, the Soviet Union is no longer prepared to fight to retain its Warsaw Pact empire.

In the case of intelligence assessment, the aim is to predict with a stated degree of confidence a range within which the future is likely to lie. That provides the base case for prediction. The intelligence machine has probably been more successful at prediction when circumstances suit an inductive method, taking the evidence of the recent past and simply extrapolating forward. Thus, for example, during the Battle of the Atlantic in 1942 convoys could be rerouted as a result of SIGINT on the last known position of the U-boat wolf packs. As we know from weather forecasting, you can get very reliable results most of the time using past data intelligently. But the problem with the inductive method is that it can generate spectacularly wrong results when, unknown to the analysts, the underlying conditions have changed. As Michael Goodman and others have pointed out from studies such as that of Douglas Nicoll into the Joint Intelligence Committee record of assessment, the system is much better at tracking an ongoing crisis than predicting its onset. Failures in prediction are also liable to be more obvious publicly than surmises, since the latter remain for the most part unknown.

A current example of a hard assessment task is trying to assess the strength of al-Qaida as a global jihadist movement. I sense a growing consensus among the experts that the al-Qaida organization is in strategic decline, without the capacity to sustain a global insurgency campaign. It has probably passed the high-water mark of its effectiveness under the relentless pressure of Western security operations that are becoming increasingly professional. The global jihad is therefore quite likely to break down into local struggles in the Islamic world between insurgents sharing at least for tactical reasons the al-Qaida ideology and government in which the latter are likely to prevail. Analysts would be wise, however, to be cautious in such predictive judgments. No doubt there will be some setbacks on the way, including further murderous attacks. That would be an example (one with which incidentally I would agree) of a central assessment or base case. We could assign it a probability, perhaps "highly likely," which is in the 75–85 percent bracket. For a military commander such odds on any operation would no doubt be regarded as excellent. But that still leaves a residual risk of 15–25 percent that things will turn out very differently, and thus a significant risk in political terms. What might invalidate such an assessment? Here we might start to look with a historical perspective for "wild cards" that represent low probability but high impact developments that would negate our prediction. For example, al-Qaida might acquire a new safe haven in which to build up its capability again, or might acquire a serious means of mass destruction, or a new charismatic leader might arise and take al-Qaida in a different and dangerous direction.

There are a very large number of such wild cards that can be dreamed up that would be historically plausible. Each one is unique and for that reason, individually very improbable. Mentioning such possibilities is certainly not to say that is what is expected to occur. But it is worth examining such scenarios, essentially for three reasons; first, because like history, they remind us that our base case prediction is not certain, and there will certainly be surprises of some sort to come; second, because examining the drivers that might lead to the wild cards may help us refine our understanding of our base case; and third, because they can act as cues for our research and development effort and for cuing information-harvesting systems, to help our intelligence antennae be tuned to signs of new danger. By posing such hypotheses we increase the chances that our analysts will recognize the significance of fragmentary information and join up the dots correctly. That is the process that I would describe as providing the military commander or government policymaker with "strategic warning."

Like the historian Braudel, the analyst should also be concerned with *histoire a la longue durée*. We could divide up intelligence history as far as military intelligence is concerned by the impact of the experience of 1914–18, fading but thankfully still remembered by the time of the rise of Nazism, the subsequent years of preparation for war with Germany and fighting the Axis powers, then the "Great Cold War," in the title of Gordon Barrass's new intelligence history, preparing NATO commanders on the Central Front and the Atlantic, and then of course the current upheavals of the post–Cold War world of combating terrorism. Certainly much of the organization and methods of military intelligence would be explicable within that framework. Chance also plays its part. In 1916, as US forces arrived in Europe, Field Marshall Haig's staff cultivated the young American cryptographer, William Friedman, and ensured that the nascent US army intelligence effort was based on close cooperation with the British model, not that of the French as Friedman's superiors had suggested; the same Friedman, by then the leading US cryptographer, was sent to the United Kingdom at the outset of the Second World War to assess the case for partnership with Bletchley Park, with predictable and welcome results, whose historical resonance flourishes today in the UK–USA SIGINT partnership.

From the Second World War came so many lessons, not least the effect of mobilizing intelligence on a national scale, and industrializing the process, the creation of scientific intelligence and nuclear intelligence, the use of mathematics and computing in cryptanalysis, and the development of imagery intelligence, whose first steps go back to 1936 and the cooperation between SIS and the Deuxième Bureau. The Cold War saw comparable developments, as intelligence from space and acoustic sensors on the bottom of the ocean, and from a variety of military platforms, transformed the supply of near–real time intelligence to the war fighter.

Taking such a historical approach, we can identify a paradigm shift at the end of the century from the "Secret State" of the Cold War to the "Protecting State" of the early twenty-first century. The former had to provide the support for nuclear deterrence, forward defense in NATO and civil defense, with plans kept secret from the public. In the UK, the intelligence agencies had a special secret status, with no legal existence. And international mistrust (with the Anglo-Saxon world an exception) between intelligence agencies and well-justified fears of Soviet and Warsaw Pact agency penetrations inhibited cooperation with most of the world, even some allies. Now we have avowed intelligence agencies. We have widespread overseas cooperation in countering terrorism and insurgencies. Military counter-insurgency operations now take place in cluttered environments with complex rules of engagement and a premium on preemptive intelligence for force protection and precise location of the adversary so that force can be delivered with great precision and minimum collateral damage. The challenges for the intelligence community are huge. But I will not pursue that line further here.

When you dip into intelligence history, there are many lessons to learn. One is what Braudel called the persistence of "old attitudes of thought and action, resistant frameworks dying hard, at times against all logic." There are many examples in British intelligence history. The Foreign Office (FO) refused to attend the Joint Intelligence Committee (JIC) for its first few years of existence, even as world war approached, on the grounds that only the FO could assess diplomatic intelligence. It is a hard truth, but the great successes of the Second World War, from Enigma to the network of double agents successfully used to support the Normandy landings, the Double Cross System, would not have been possible without the innovation brought by the influx of new talent into the intelligence agencies from the universities and the legal profession. After every war, the "bow is unbent." Professor R. V. Jones, founder of scientific intelligence in WWII, was called back from his professorship at Aberdeen to try to improve the 1950s Air Ministry intelligence, which had fallen into the doldrums. He resigned in frustration after a short period of failing to get the machine to behave more as it had so successfully during the war. In particular, he found that the direct and productive interaction between the scientific intelligence officer with front line pilots and navigators had ceased, was even disapproved of, and the front line and scientists only interacted via a new intelligence staff bureaucracy. Perhaps we are learning more from history when we see the British Ministry of Defence having to adopt the R. V. Jones approach in fast-tracking urgent operational requirements for our forces in Afghanistan, such as rapid countering of enemy IEDs. Given past institutional tensions, let us be glad when we see innovations such as the UK Joint Terrorism Analysis Centre (JTAC) thriving today, bringing all three agency staffs together with the Defence Intelligence Staff, police, and departmental personnel.

The last one hundred years have been called the century of intelligence. I mentioned *l'histoire a la longue durée* to explain changes during that period in terms of two world wars, a cold war, and a new age of terrorism and insurgency. Another source of explanation can be found in tracking the scientific revolutions within the one-hundred-year period as broken into three overlapping phases, with a fourth just starting.

A first phase, or first intelligence revolution, came with the radio era, just under way in 1909, initially with wireless telegraphy, and then through the application of James Clerk Maxwell's equations, electromagnetic waves. Let us take the words of the pioneer, Herz, as a warning to us: "It's of no use whatsoever . . . this is just an experiment that proves Maestro Maxwell was right—we just have these mysterious electromagnetic waves that we cannot see with the naked eye. But they are there." But the consequences for the military art, in particular naval warfare, mobile ground forces, and the direction of fighter air power, were profound, and the intelligence world was very quick to cotton on to the operational value of direction finding (DF) of radio transmitters, followed of course by *funkspiel*, as the Germans called radio deception in World War II.

The second phase, or second revolution, the electronic era, was accelerated by the intelligence effort in the Second World War with the development of valve-based computing and data processing for SIGINT and such breakthroughs as germanium diodes, initially for radar. The ramifications of electronics for the military world are too many to mention, especially in weapons systems, as well as, for example, the SIGINT world. By the late 1940s, the Bell labs had invented the transistor. Within a decade, primitive electronics were sufficiently miniaturized to allow space-based applications. After Sputnik came the race for intelligence collection from space, with optical then electro-optical radar, SIGINT, stationary orbiters, low earth orbiters, and elliptical orbiting satellites. Space dominated US intelligence spending, a hugely significant fact in intelligence, and intelligence organizational history.

The third phase, or third revolution, was the quantum era, when devices were developed such as the laser and the optical disc reader, and the theoretical understanding of quantum effects that allowed microminiaturized solid-state devices to be designed with billions of transistor equivalents on a single chip. That revolution has given us the mobile telephone, the laptop computer, the internet, the pilotless drone and stand-off missile, and the massive data storage and manipulation behind much modern intelligence analysis and battlefield intelligence fusion.

We are now in the fourth phase, the cyber era. The volumes of information now involved in intelligence work are huge. Now vast quantities of information about target groups and countries, their economies, culture, armed forces, physical geography, and so on, are available not just centrally but to any access point to the internet. Self-regulating internet tools such as an adaptation of Wikipedia have found application, at least within the US intelligence community. And intelligence targets also use the internet, as seen by the imaginative use by jihadists of websites to promote radicalization and recruitment, maintain contact within networks, and disseminate information about targets, tactics, and weapons. A whole branch of intelligence work is therefore having to be created to access (not a straightforward matter), monitor, and exploit such material and to present it in a way that provides real-time situational awareness to commanders using virtual reality visualization tools that would have been unimaginable to Montgomery or Patton.

That said, let me reassure you that I fully accept the caveat John Keegan has so clearly described in his writings on intelligence, that in the end the clash of arms is determined by factors that Clausewitz would have understood. Is there a further intelligence revolution yet to come? I cannot be sure, but let me offer two possibilities. One would be a second quantum revolution stemming from recent discoveries in basic quantum physics showing the theoretical validity of quantum computing that would make previously wholly infeasible tasks possible, since the quantum computer would work in a near infinite number of parallel universes. Basic proof of concept has been achieved, but the technical problems of scaling up are formidable, so that may be a generation or more away. And a second revolution might be that sparked by modern neuroscience, as genetic engineering becomes ubiquitous and new compounds, including cognitive enhancers, arrive, along with the development of direct person brain-machine interfaces. But those are just guesses. What is certain from history is that the military art, and the way intelligence supports it, will change again, and for the foreseeable future it would be wise to understand better the experience of the past.

PART I

The Organization and Oversight of Intelligence

CHAPTER 1

The Postwar Organization of Intelligence

The January 1945 Report to the Joint Intelligence Committee on "The Intelligence Machine"

MICHAEL HERMAN

Editors' Note:

In this chapter a distinguished former secretary of the Joint Intelligence Committee reconsiders that organization's origins. Emerging out of World War II victorious and full of confidence, the committee was dominated by one question: how to organize the intelligence structure to fight in the postwar world? Here, then, is a perceptive attempt, based on the deficiencies of the prewar intelligence system, to configure the central apparatus of intelligence at a time when it was not clear who or what the focus would be. Various factors emerge, as important in the twenty-first century as they were in 1945: the need for the right mixture of joint-service organization, committee structures, and centralized institution, of interdepartmentalism and centralization.

A report on postwar organization of intelligence was presented to the Joint Intelligence Sub-Committee of the Chiefs of Staff (the JIC, hereafter "the committee") on January 10, 1945, and was given the striking subtitle of "The Intelligence Machine," in itself a sign of the new way of thinking about intelligence that had developed during the war. The idea of intelligence as a single entity had some ancestry. Shakespeare wrote of it in the singular, as in "Where hath our Intelligence been drunk, where hath it slept?" in his *King John*, and the 1945 report followed this antique usage in referring to "our Intelligence *Service*" and "our *Secret Service*."[1] But this idea of "the intelligence" as a collective had always been a shadowy one. This report was the first serious British attempt—possibly the first attempt anywhere—to set out a plan for it as a complete, interlocking, peacetime system, perhaps the first recognition of intelligence power as part of the modern state.

The individual intelligence institutions in it were of course older. The British navy and army had acquired their intelligence directors and staffs in the last quarter of the nineteenth century, but there was no particular thought then about a collective identity or cooperation between them. A wide-ranging investigation of intelligence led to the creation of the Secret Service Bureau in 1909, but the result was to separate covert collection from the naval and army directorates, not bring all the elements together. Though the First World War produced intelligence activity on a quite unprecedented scale, it remained organized mainly in single-service bodies, not joint-service ones. Even before 1914 the offices just established for espionage and counterespionage were developing separately, and from the postwar reviews of 1919 and 1921 they emerged as the separate civilian Security Service (MI5) and Secret Intelligence Service (SIS or MI6), divided roughly between home and foreign targets. (This chapter uses these two organizational titles but otherwise uses "service" and "services" to denote armed forces.) The postwar reviews also established codebreaking in the civilian Government Code and Cypher School (GC&CS) under C, the head of SIS (the abbreviation "C" for "Chief" dates back to the first occupant of the post and is still used). The interwar period saw varied relationships between these new bodies and the older service directorates, and there was a hint of the future in the creation of the small, nondepartmental, civilian Industrial Intelligence Centre (IIC) to study the economies of potential enemies. Nevertheless, the post-1918 system was mainly one of separate institutions without formal coordinating machinery. There was still a particular gulf between the civilian collectors of secret intelligence and the military intelligence authorities who used the results. Treating it all as a whole was some way ahead.

This began in a small way with the creation of the JIC in 1936 for the coordination of Service Intelligence by the three armed forces' directors, reporting to the chiefs of staff. It acquired its Foreign Office membership and chairmanship in 1939, and the SIS, Security Service, and Ministry of Economic Warfare (MEW) became members in the following year. It received directions in the summer of 1939 for coordinating, reporting, and assessing intelligence for top government (its expert assessment role), and for managing intelligence to include consideration of "any further measures which might be necessary in order to improve the efficient working of the intelligence organisation of the country as a whole."[2] Much was subsequently made in the official intelligence history of this reference to "intelligence as a whole" as a landmark, an idea that "had been evolving for twenty years, but evolving slowly, haphazardly and only in response to events in the absence of a single coordinating authority."[3]

Ideas were certainly changing, but there is a danger of reading too much into the wording produced in that 1939 summer of preparation for war. The civilian agencies were by then well aware of the JIC: the IIC director, Desmond Morton, (with an SIS affiliation) had attended some of its meetings, and Security Service and SIS representatives had been present occasionally.[4] But the civilian-military gap remained: in 1945 Morton, who had been the director of intelligence at the

MEW in 1939–40, wrote later that even in that first year of war "the military men . . . could not bring themselves to admit that war was really the concern of men in plain clothes."[5] The JIC's purpose was still to get the military services to talk to each other, and the civilians were incidental. There is no evidence that they had been consulted about the 1939 wording that on the face of it brought them within the military's purview.

What is more important is that wartime intelligence was subsequently not quite as close-knit as has sometimes been presented. The JIC's assessments were important at the top politico-strategic level, but below it the war was run mainly through single-service command structures with single-service intelligence staffs. In its managerial role, the JIC and its subcommittees were a success in the establishment and control of new joint-service organizations, but in this the civilian agencies were less involved. Signals Intelligence (SIGINT), the most important wartime intelligence source, had its own nominal supervisory machinery, and remained outside the JIC's control. So did the disputes between SIS and the Security Service, though those between SIS and the Special Operations Executive (SOE) did come to the committee. The war certainly closed the military-civilian gaps, but by no means completely.

Nevertheless, by 1944–45 the idea of "the intelligence organisation as a whole" was catching on. The January 1945 report put it that the JIC "has developed into a forum for discussion of all matters of common 'intelligence' interest to its members, and thus into a kind of Board of Directors laying down interservice intelligence and security policy at home and abroad."[6] This was still gilding the lily, but was nevertheless not far from what was happening, and what people thought was happening. Intelligence had developed greatly since 1939, and the 1945 report's title of the "machine" captured the wartime shift from cottage industry towards mass production, speed, and interconnection, though we now prefer to call it the less mechanistic "community."[7] It needed a peacetime structure, and it got it from the 1945 report and how it was implemented. These are subjects of this chapter.

Background

Government's planning of postwar Britain began in early 1943, and in intelligence the postwar future of its effort on economic targets was raised by the MEW in the summer of that year. The JIC's chairman proposed in a minute dated October 13 that postwar planning should have some consideration, and at a committee discussion on October 26 there was agreement that "it was most desirable that the present machinery for collecting and collating intelligence" should continue after the war, and that "if possible, there should continue to be a central coordinating body."[8] In the first half of 1944 the three service directors were asked to produce papers on the future of the wartime interservice bodies for which they had taken responsibility, but these do not seem to have appeared.[9] In September the

Director of Naval Intelligence raised the future of the interservice topographical studies that he ran, but this study seems to have been held up until the JIC's report appeared in January 1945.[10]

Postwar planning was by then a growth area everywhere, and this report was by no means the only intelligence study under way. It mentioned the separate study of topographic intelligence.[11] It also referred to the "enquiries being made under other auspices" into the future of SIS and the Security Service.[12] The fate of SOE was being canvassed. A further study was also in progress that led to the creation of Government Communications Headquarters (GCHQ) as the national SIGINT center, replacing GC&CS. Bletchley had begun its own work on this in September 1944, and in the process developed its own ideas about intelligence as a whole.[13] On scientific and technical intelligence (hereafter S and T), we have the similar recollections of R. V. Jones, the Air Ministry's wartime Assistant Director (Science), who recorded Whitehall's interest in this work's postwar future from summer 1944 onwards, and his own strong belief in combining the separate single-service efforts in one organization.[14] From naval intelligence there is a similar memory of papers in 1944 that "advocated a postwar organization which would concentrate economic, scientific, and much non-secret intelligence in a department that would be, so to speak, supra-service."[15] There was a movement for change.

This was the background when work on the JIC report started. It was in progress by October 24, 1944, though its genesis is not clear.[16] The authors refer in the report's first line to the JIC's "invitation" to them to prepare it, but the JIC minutes of the period do not record any commission of this kind. It is also not clear whether the work was approved by ministers, and how the various intelligence studies were to be coordinated. The JIC was still supposed to be a military subcommittee. The civilian agencies had been nominally overseen since the First World War by the high-level Secret Service Committee, but it had rarely met. Churchill inquired in 1940 who was in charge of intelligence, but the answer was no clearer in 1944. He could have ordered a comprehensive postwar study, but there is no evidence that he did so.

Hence the paper for the JIC was only part of the postwar planning, but it was the nearest thing to a complete survey. The authors took their remit for postwar organization to allow them to discuss the whole machine, but they were careful to limit their formal recommendations to the JIC itself and the temporary wartime organizations that no one else was looking into, while also offering observations and suggestions (but not formal recommendations) about almost everything else. They presumably sought to make the report as influential as possible without being told by those looking at the civilian agencies to mind their own business.

This seems an untidy way of planning, though it was made less so by the wartime JIC's collegiality and personalities. The wartime committee had been a constant meeting point—several times a week—for the top intelligence people, military and civilian. C, as head of both SIS and GC&CS, had been a regular attendee, as was MEW's intelligence head; the Security Service less so. There was also the personal standing of those who produced the report and put their names to it: the committee's Chairman and Secretary. JIC reports were normally prepared by the drafting staff and departments, and this report by the Chairman and Secretary over their joint names was unprecedented and must have carried unusual weight. They referred archly in it to the "enquiries under other auspices" that were taking place about the civilian agencies, but this was formulaic. The Chairman was one of the group looking into the postwar SIS, with the JIC secretary as its group secretary, and it is a reasonable guess that the two had comparable fingers in the other postwar pies.[17] They were probably what kept the postwar planning together.

Their influence needs explanation. Both had been with the JIC throughout the war and were among wartime Whitehall's quintessential insiders. The Chairman was Victor (Bill) Cavendish-Bentinck of aristocratic family, career diplomat, in the chair since 1939, and longer in place than any of his colleagues.[18] At the beginning of the war he was still quite junior, and, even after promotion to counsellor in 1942, was still a nominal grade down from the service directors. But he had handled them with skill and aplomb and had a reputation for independence and impartiality. One who saw him in action recorded that he was "both astute and prescient" yet "had the gift of producing harmony among the service chiefs."[19] He had a high standing with everyone, and historians credit him with much of the JIC's wartime success.

The secretary, Colonel Denis Capel-Dunn, was a more mysterious character. A prewar civilian of obscure background, he had risen to become JIC secretary and subsequently combined this with heading the Cabinet Office's Joint Staff Secretariat. As such, he was secretary for some of Churchill's top meetings, attended the allied conferences in Moscow and Yalta, helped to plan the United Nations at Dumbarton Oaks in the autumn of 1944, and is among the six people listed as the top British delegation to the UN's inauguration in San Francisco the following year. He was killed while flying back from it in early July 1945, and Cavendish-Bentinck was then joint author of an unusually warm tribute to him in *The Times*.[20] By contrast, the few postwar recollections of him give an unattractive picture of a careerist, a schemer, trying so hard that he was almost a figure of fun; though they endorse his ability and wartime influence, and suggest that he would have had a successful postwar future. He and Cavendish-Bentinck must have been a powerful combination. One can guess that he was the "ideas man" behind the report as well as drafting it, with Cavendish-Bentinck adding authority and common sense.[21]

Concepts and Doctrine

The report's principal question was the future of the JIC itself, but its continuation was virtually taken for granted. The other pressing question was the future of the temporary wartime bodies, and on these it made detailed proposals. The rest of the machine—the prewar service intelligence directorates, Security Service, SIS, and SIGINT—was accepted more or less as it stood, but this did not stop the authors in their observations from conveying their lack of empathy for the military, and from offering to the civilian organizations "certain general points which have come to our notice and which we feel it useful to record."[22] It is a sign of their standing that they could toss these *obiter dicta* into the other postwar studies.

The declared aim of their report was not just to adapt the wartime arrangements to peacetime, but to produce something better. Hence it was a mixture of a reform agenda, postwar doctrine, and practical recommendations. For reform the immediate rationale was the need for postwar economy and the elimination of duplication: "we should strive not merely to ensure that our Intelligence Service after the war is the most efficient possible, but to ensure that it is as economical as can be without sacrifice of efficiency." The wartime arrangements had been marked by "some overlapping of responsibilities and duplication of work which should not be acceptable or permissible in peace-time, and should, if possible, be avoided in war." In their view "a more symmetrical organization could have done at least as well at less cost." Wartime intelligence had had too many masters. "There were no doubt excellent reasons for the decisions that led to this state of affairs. It may have been right under the pressure of war to avoid the dislocation that any attempt at rationalisation would have caused." Nevertheless the country "cannot afford in peace (or even perhaps in war) the kind of intelligence organization we have today." Economy was worthy in itself, but for Cavendish-Bentinck and Capel-Dunn it was linked with the greater aim of reducing the dominance of the three single-service directorates by making organization more interdepartmental and "national," less single-service. This had happened in the war, but needed consolidation and extension.[23]

The report therefore opened with a short argument that modern war needed more varied intelligence than the traditional single-service studies of enemy forces. It went on to lambaste the service directorates for their prewar state. Intelligence was as important to the military as ammunition, fuel, and food, yet "no one would be so bold as to contend that our Service Intelligence Staffs entered this war adequately equipped for the task confronting them." They had been allowed to "wither." The Admiralty had been "rather better" than the others, but the Air Ministry had been "less impressive" and in the prewar army "intelligence was a dangerous branch of the Staff for an ambitious officer to join." There had been first-class SIGINT in the war but "full value could not be got unless the machine at the centre was properly equipped to collate and assess it against cognate intelligence from other sources." Yet there was no guarantee that the postwar military would do anything about it. Those in control, like their predecessors, could not be blamed if they give preference to "ships, aircraft, guns, and warlike stores." Despite intelligence's wartime importance, "it would be rash to assume . . . that the lesson will be remembered."[24]

In a report for the military JIC this was strong stuff, but now seems consistent with the wartime record. The three big intelligence successes were SIGINT, deception, and the work of the Joint Intelligence Staff (the JIS) serving the JIC, none of them under the military directorates' immediate control. Collectively, the military in Whitehall were not the heroes of Sir Harry Hinsley's official intelligence history. Noel Annan (later Lord Annan) recalled from his time in the JIS that "our masters in the JIC were not an impressive team," and his reminiscences are of producing agreed JIS assessments and having to water them down through single-service opposition at the JIC level.[25] On the services' management of intelligence, we have recently had Sir Arthur Bonsall's judgment on the Air Ministry's attitude to Bletchley's so-called low grade SIGINT sources, that "it will probably never be known how much the allied cause could have gained, or not suffered, if there had been no delay [by the Air Ministry] in recognizing that useful intelligence could be produced from very unpromising material."[26] With some naval exceptions, intelligence's wartime stars were not the military regulars who got drawn into it.

The report's criticism of the single-service directorates also fitted the mood of the day. There was anger about prewar inadequacies everywhere and little sympathy for military hierarchy. There were already intimations that intelligence might be a key to postwar survival, and there was a mood for radical thinking about it. There was also a generational factor: the intelligence war had been a young man's war, and the young men now had influence. Neither Cavendish-Bentinck nor Capel-Dunn was a young radical—their ages were at the two ends of the 40s—but they would be receptive to the radical view.[27] Neither had any stake in the prewar military or intelligence establishments.

So single-departmentalism was the problem, and their solution was in the JIC's joint-service organizations, or "jointery," as this became known in military jargon.[28] Reducing single-service duplication to economize was bound to get Whitehall's support, but the report also set it out as intelligence doctrine. Single-service approaches were not only wasteful but also liable to be incomplete, blinkered by service self-interest, and wrong. Handling intelligence should not depend on the color of uniforms: the organization best fitted for a particular kind of intelligence should do it. Material should be collated and evaluated so that all relevant information was brought together, including all nonintelligence data. Analysis should include some "quite objective check" that stopped policymakers from interpreting reports in the light of their preconceptions. "One who is concerned in devising and recommending policy and assisting in its execution is likely, however objective he may try to be, to interpret the intelligence he receives in the light of the policy he is pursuing." Hence "no Department . . . has anything to lose by bringing the intelligence directly available to it to the anvil of discussion and appreciation among other workers in the same field." The results should be made available to all needing them. To these ends the system "should be controlled at the top by a strong interservice and interdepartmental body representing the needs of producers and consumers." It was an impressive articulation of what had emerged in war, as good a summary of the JIC philosophy for assessment as has ever been produced, and still just as relevant.[29]

But this was only half the philosophy. The wartime system had also depended on the temporary joint service, nondepartmental organizations that had been created for the tasks that would otherwise have been left in separate single-service packets. Single departmentalism had been countered not only by the JIC, but equally by the creating the single, integrated organizations for topographical intelligence, photographic interpretation, strategic interrogation, and intelligence support for political warfare. The intelligence department of the wartime MEW was in the same category, though with different origins; so too was the emergence of Bletchley as the controlling and coordinating center for all the service and civilian SIGINT effort. Britain had been successful as an intelligence builder as well as an intelligence assessor. The wartime success was in the combination of committees and centralization, with the second as important as the first.

Not everyone had seen the force of the combination. The young men did not like committees. R. V. Jones was explicit in his criticism of the JIC—which had been particularly weak in handling the German V–1 and V–2 threat in the later years of the war[30]—and wanted a single S and T organization. (He did not get it and went back to academe.)[31] Cavendish-Bentinck and Capel-Dunn were wedded to the JIC, but sought equally to build on the wartime joint-service organizations. What shines through their report is a surprising enthusiasm for what they had seen in them of the squeezing of valuable intelligence from apparently unrewarding evidence, including publicaly available material. Someone—presumably Capel-Dunn or one of his minions—had been bitten by the excitement of applying large-scale scanning, indexing, and collation to produce gold dust from low-grade ore, a striking prevision of intelligence as it evolved in the computer age.

Thus the report's philosophy was two-pronged: coordination by committees combined with moving towards centralized institutions. The conclusions and recommendations in which it can be traced can now be discussed.

Recommendations: The JIC Itself

The committee was to have "as far as possible all intelligence producing and using agencies" represented on it.[32] It was to be the "principal interservice *and interdepartmental* body," to make sure the civilians' organizations were included.[33] The official membership would follow the wartime one (except for the wartime MEW): the Foreign Office, the three service directors, and C. The position of the Security Service was left open. The Board of Trade might be represented, though surprisingly the wartime MEW intelligence effort, by then being administered by the Foreign Office in its Economic Intelligence Organization, was said not to be needed.

The chairmanship was not mentioned, but when the report was considered by JIC members the Foreign Office occupancy of it was "generally agreed" to be "preferable in principle." Cavendish-Bentinck's biographer reports that only his success in the job made the appointment of another civilian acceptable to the military.[34] Capel-Dunn privately argued at the time that the Foreign Office should keep the post, as otherwise it would lose interest altogether.[35]

Despite civilian involvement, the committee was to remain responsible to the chiefs of staff, as it did until its transfer to the Cabinet Office in 1957. As a chiefs of staff body, it remained a committee of equals, proceeding by consensus, and this was reinforced at first by continuing to have a civilian chairman junior to his uniformed colleagues. When Air Chief Marshal Sir Douglas Evill reviewed it two years later, he got its chairmanship upgraded, but that did not affect its consensus character.[36]

So what was this high-powered body to do? The report said very little about its assessment role. There was a marker that it should not be limited to military needs: "the practice that has grown up, of the committee giving advice on request to other Departments and authorities, should be preserved."[37] The JIS would continue to prepare the committee's reports. Otherwise, the service to top government was taken for granted.

There was more attention to the management role, which may have been seen as the committee's main postwar function. The report's language about it was robust: "We think it essential that all the intelligence authorities should be brought under the J.I.C. umbrella." The postwar machine was described as an organization with the JIC as its head, "directing its general policy."[38]

The committee would have its standing subcommittees "dealing with the various aspects of intelligence," including a general requirements subcommittee "to lay down the priorities to be accorded to the nation's 'intelligence effort' [original quotation marks], to coordinate the work of the different collection agencies, and to allocate responsibilities between them." It would also "exercise general supervision over the Central Intelligence Bureau [a new body, see below]."[39] It reads as if the JIC and its subcommittees would be involved in everything, with "policy" and "direction" as the themes, but what these meant was not expanded.

The report also dealt with S and T matters but did not move much beyond the wartime single-service situation that R. V. Jones coordinated where he could. We have seen that Jones wanted a single postwar organization: "a single Head of Intelligence is far better than a Committee."[40] Critics thought he wanted the job, and there was strong service opposition.[41] The report pointed out that "while the Joint Intelligence Staff is well equipped to prepare for the J.I.C. papers on enemy intentions generally, there exists no similar interservice body to draft papers for the J.I.C. on enemy technical developments." It wanted technical intelligence to be "integrated," and recommended a committee from the three services' technical sections, but stopped there. Despite further investigation the situation was not properly sorted out for another decade. It was a political hot potato, subsequently made hotter by the complex sensitivities of atomic intelligence, and Cavendish-Bentinck and Capel-Dunn presumably judged that they could not shift the single services over it. But it was a weak part of their report. [42]

Imagery and the Central Intelligence Bureau

Some of the wartime organizations would not be needed in peacetime, and the report conscientiously made recommendations for the disposal of their records or the maintenance of their expertise.[43] Of those that were to continue there were important but straightforward recommendations for the Central Interpretation Unit, the interservice photo-interpretation establishment that had operated under a JIC subcommittee's direction and RAF administration. The report discussed the potential of imagery and speculated on its worldwide civilian applications, and argued that "the interest of the consumers is so considerable that we do not believe that any one Ministry should be burdened with the exclusive responsibility for the general control and direction of this branch of intelligence."[44] It suggested that a variety of RAF and army photo-interpreter training and equipment provision might be taken over centrally, implying that imagery was too important to be left entirely to the RAF.[45]

Nevertheless, the recommendations essentially continued the wartime arrangements, with the joint-service unit under RAF command, and a Photographic Reconnaissance Committee reporting to the JIC for policy direction and "the production, interpretation and distribution of aerial photographs."[46] The air force subordination of what became the Joint Air Reconnaissance Intelligence Centre made good sense, since the RAF was the main collector and interpreter of photography as well as a principal customer. The JIC's postwar oversight eventually withered in favor of exclusive Ministry of Defence control, in contrast to what later evolved in the United States for the development of imagery, including satellite imagery, as a major national source with agency status.

Much more innovative was the report's proposal for the new Central Intelligence Bureau. It was to be formed around the wartime Interservice Topographical Department (ISTD), which had been established in 1940 under JIC direction and Admiralty administration, and had made topographical intelligence an important wartime subject, for example on European transport facilities and the targeting of them in the assault on Western Europe. It was also to take over the records and expertise of the Political Warfare Executive (PWE), whose intelligence effort had supported its black propaganda and had become a leading authority on the non-military aspects of the enemy, *inter alia* through the exploitation of foreign press and broadcasting sources.[47] The same would apply to a nucleus of the wartime Postal and Telegraphic Censorship Department.

The Bureau was evidently created to be the center for handling the low-grade evidence *en masse*, about which the report was so enthusiastic. ISTD's publications, files, and registries "seem to provide the best possible basis for the Central Bureau we have in mind."[48] The report rejoices over the "some 7,000 files and records of some 190,000 personalities"[49] that could also accrue from the PWE. It also had two long appendices on the organization and methods of the Censorship Department, which were said to reflect the "efficiency of its administration and the wisdom with which it has been directed," and were recommended for the Bureau's information-handling methods.[50]

So the Bureau was to be an analysis center, but on what, apart from the ISTD's topographic remit? Here the report was expansive but unclear. It spotted the significance of publicly available ("open") sources such as newspapers, fifty years before they became a fashionable intelligence topic. Apart from government's needs, the Bureau might meet those of private interests in trade and industry for this material and some official sources such as overseas trade reports, and hence might be divided into classified and unclassified sections.[51] Both sections would serve government. "We have in mind that information required as a basis of high policy should be collected and collated in the first instance in the non-secret branch of the bureau. It should then be tested in the light of any secret information that is available,"[52] and then, if necessary, put to the JIS and the JIC itself. For 1944–45 this was indeed visionary, and it anticipated the concern in the 1960s and 1970s for economic intelligence, as well as our current enthusiasm for the information society.

This was a response to the young men's urge for a central body of some kind. Yet it needed more teeth to be convincing. Cavendish-Bentinck and Capel-Dunn must have had economic intelligence in mind; and their warm words about the wartime ISTD, PWE, and censorship could have been applied even more to MEW Enemy Branch, for example, for the value of its work on the German economy as the basis for the allied strategic bombing campaign. Its representative was a powerful member of the wartime JIC. [53] Yet economic intelligence is barely mentioned in the report. One can only guess that its postwar future was another political hot potato, connected with its transfer to Foreign Office control in April 1944 as part of its Economic Intelligence Organisation.[54] In the event the omission was rectified when the report was first discussed by JIC members.

Central analysis was not all. The Bureau was also to have a role derived from another wartime creation, Intelligence Section (Operations), or IS(O), which had been created in early 1942 to cope with the increased demand for the detailed intelligence needed to plan the invasions of North Africa, Italy, and France. Multiple and often duplicative requests were being addressed to different producers, creating overload and confusion. IS(O) was established under JIC control and War Office administration, and became what the official historians later described as "more of a clearing house than an agency to collate intelligence," in order to "regulate and rationalise" the many demands for this kind of information.[55]

This body was to be in the Bureau, but much expanded. It was to receive information from all intelligence sources, and "within the Bureau, this information should be brought together and reproduced in the form required by the different customers of the intelligence machine."[56] Each intelligence-producing organization would collect intelligence from its own sources, but "should not normally receive intelligence from other Departments and organisations save through the medium of the Central Bureau."[57] It reads like a mixture of collation, clearing-house, intelligence warehouse, a summarizing center, and the provision of what the Americans now call "tailored intelligence" to meet individual customers' requirements.

It would go even further, and would have liaison sections from departments that needed intelligence to state their requirements, and decide what agency was best fitted to meet them. It would support the JIS by providing "in the shape of memoranda or reference books such factual information as was required," and the report also suggests that the information required "as a basis for high policy" could be collected and collated in it. The intention was clear: "we believe that if our recommendation is accepted, the central machinery will sufficiently justify itself to encourage Departments to refrain from duplicating its work." Hence the Central Bureau in its varied ways would be the heart of what Cavendish-Bentinck and Capel-Dunn summarized as "an uncertain amalgamation" of existing interservice and interdepartmental bodies so as to provide a central intelligence agency and to leave it to departments to work out the alterations in their own organization that would be possible and desirable were that proposal accepted."[58]

It would have suitably heavyweight management. It was asserted that ideally C would direct it, but he could not be the public figure. A deputy would be needed for "the public side of his activities." He would be the Bureau's director-general, an ex officio member of the JIC and all its subcommittees, and would run a common secretariat for the JIC and the Bureau.[59] These would be responsible, under him, for "ensuring the coordination of the different branches of the national intelligence machine."[60] The vision of the strong center was therefore of a powerful JIC and its subcommittees, plus the Bureau and its director-general, all at the expense of single-service approaches.

The Prewar Institutions

The observations—not recommendations—about the rest of the intelligence effort can be summarized briefly. On the civilian agencies, the report criticized the division of counterespionage between the Security Service and SIS, and opined that "we doubt whether any case can be made for the retention of the present system, under which the responsibility for counterespionage is divided between two authorities with no better basis for division than that of geography."[61] This was a sore spot then, and perhaps still is. Otherwise the authors steered clear of the Security Service.[62] On SIS, the report argued that it should incorporate the postwar rump of the wartime SOE and keep it; it was on the winning side in that Whitehall battle.[63] Nothing was said about the military directorates explicitly, but there was a passing kick at them over the quality of their attachments to SIS and Security Service, since "in the early days of the war there existed an impression that . . . certain of . . . [them] were officers for whom it was not easy to find employment elsewhere."[64]

For SIGINT, despite the wartime successes, "some pulling together of the strings appears to us to be desirable." GC&CS should remain under C's direction. (It did not, and became GCHQ, and nothing happened to this and the other proposals about C's responsibilities.)[65] The SIGINT board should no longer be independent of the JIC (this never happened). SIGINT funding should no longer be shown on the Foreign Office budget (this remained a complicated issue for many years). The three services' intercept organizations should continue, but the idea of a central intercept organization should be studied. (A consolidated civilian one was created over the next two decades.) The Radio Security Service should be brought under the SIGINT board, and its independence reviewed. (Its integration into the main interception force followed soon afterwards.) SIGINT reporters should not be banned from including "appreciations" in their reports. (A sensible point, but Bletchley had already won most of this wartime battle, even though some of it had to be fought again later.)[66] It is not clear what effect these observations had on the other postwar studies, but the remarks about SIGINT give an impression of rather gratuitous observations from the sideline. It was as well that the advice was not all followed.

The Outcome

The report's issue on January 10, 1945, was followed by a delay, perhaps as a result of JIC members' absences at the Yalta conference. They then had a "preliminary discussion" of it (not recorded as a formal meeting) on Sunday, March 11. As noted above, they agreed that "an outline of the history and achievement of the economic intelligence organization" should be included, and favored the continued Foreign Office chairmanship. The Central Bureau was welcomed in principle, and a subcommittee was to go into the details. Another subcommittee would be established for the S and T issues. There were conflicting views about the JIC's proposed oversight of SIGINT, but otherwise the report had a smooth passage.[67]

The report was then rewritten as a normal, much shorter, one, minus most of the discussion, approved by the committee on May 29, and submitted to the chiefs of staff as "the broad lines on which we are thinking," plus specific proposals for the new Bureau as an appendix. The main paper repeated the criticism of the prewar single-service arrangements and the ad hoc expansion of wartime, and also promoted the use of open sources as a major objective. The rest of the first version was omitted and with slight changes the kernel of the report became the January recommendations.[68]

The appendix about the new Central Bureau was more detailed, and very different from the original scheme. It was now to be the Joint Intelligence Bureau (JIB), with analysis restricted to defense subjects, and without the managerial functions envisaged for it. It would take over the ISTD's topographic work. It would also have the economic intelligence that originally had been omitted, but all this was to be only in respect of military needs, so that it became "collating and appraising" the "economic intelligence required by the Service Departments."[69]

This still produced quite a wide remit. "In the field of defence" it was to "collect, assess and, where appropriate, appreciate, intelligence material of interdepartmental significance," including overt material.[70] It was to "cover subjects concerning more than one Service, which in the interests of efficiency and economy can best be studied on an inter-Service basis."[71] The specified subjects were quite broad and ranged from obviously military ones such as static defenses and armaments production to the study of more diffuse economic, industrial, and other targets. But these were all "in relation to any probable war condition," and on anti-aircraft defenses and shipbuilding there were caveats about further demarcation discussions with the RAF and navy; some S and T subjects were included with similar provisos.[72]

We do not know how this trimming happened between the discussion of the original report on March 11 and the JIC meeting on May 29. Individual absences may have played a part, notably Capel-Dunn's, which may well have prevented him from explaining and defending the original proposals.[73] Departments may have weighed in with their own interests: the Foreign Office will have wanted to keep its nondefense economic portfolio, and the service directors will have wanted something to meet their needs and not those of the Board of Trade. Whatever the motives, the revision to the defense-oriented JIB had the merit of coherence. It was not the central organization the young men wanted, but they were still busy with the war and perhaps were persuaded (though R. V. Jones never was) that the JIB was a big step towards it. It has to be added that the job description for the proposed director-general of the Central Bureau and JIC Secretariat now seems so close to Capel-Dunn's wartime position of power that it may have been thought he was thinking of a job for himself.

A further report on the JIB was sent to the chiefs in late July.[74] The organization would be mainly civilian, but with a strong service and ex-service flavor. Some demarcation lines with the single services still had to be established. The separate S and T studies had recommended that the single-service staffs should have common accommodation with the JIB, but without integration. The plan for the JIB was approved and it came into existence the following year.

As for the rest of the postwar proposals, a final version of the JIC report was considered by the chiefs on September 11 for submission to the prime minister as a defense requirement.[75] There were some shifts in emphasis. There was an explicit statement of the need for "a first-class system in peacetime." As before, intelligence should be centrally directed, but the emphasis was now on interdepartmental assessment: thus "the *collating* staffs should work as far as possible on an interservice basis [my emphasis]." The JIS teams were reduced from two to one, and the members were now permanent members of departments, more clearly limiting their nondepartmental independence. On S and T arrangements there were now to be separate scientific and technical subcommittees, but still without any joint-service element. In addition to other tasks, the JIB would collect and collate open source material to avoid duplication elsewhere, but this never came to much. For the first time a world view was set out of the London JIC's position at the hub of a postwar system of JICs overseas and complementary committees in the Dominions.[76]

The postwar arrangements were completed the following year. They were reviewed by Evill in 1947 but no major changes ensued. There have been some since,[77] but the main feature of the system—a community operating by consensus in and through the JIC—has been unchanged. A JIC member transposed from 1945 would not be much surprised by what he would now find. The Cavendish-Bentinck and Capel-Dunn report and the 1945 decisions that followed it settled the form of the British system. How well was it all done?

Lessons Learned?

The postwar organization was not preceded by any comprehensive study of intelligence requirements or institutions. The civilian agencies had separate investigations of them, and we have seen how Cavendish-Bentinck's and Capel-Dunn's report established the postwar JIC's role and the community structure under it, but made only detached comments on some of the components. It was produced at some speed, amid wartime pressure, and we have seen that it was not fully implemented. Some of its exposition was brilliant and of lasting importance. It was a vision of a postwar system written from the center of wartime action, but it was stronger on vision than on reflection, or indeed some of the detail. It might have considered the nature of its postwar machine rather more deeply.

This includes what the JIC was actually to do. The authors assumed that the committee's dual role of intelligence management and assessment would continue, and did not discuss whether it was sensible for it to combine the two. The joining of the two functions had happened almost by accident in 1939, and was never questioned until 2009 when some separation of them took place.[78] In a similar way the committee's chairmanship was not covered, and in the event it was accepted as a Foreign Office commitment without apparent examination of alternatives. Evill two years later posed the option of filling the post from the (new) Ministry of Defence,[79] but without result.

Indeed, a weakness of the report was that it did not consider the Foreign Office's special position as the nonintelligence body among intelligence specialists, *inter alia* for the effect this had on the nature of the JIC's peacetime product for government: did its assessments present an intelligence view, or a consensus of intelligence and policymakers' judgments? The report sought to reduce the single-departmental influences of the three military directorates, but apparently regarded the Foreign Office's departmental position as off limits. There was also the report's omission of the Foreign Office's economic intelligence effort (the omission rectified later on others' insistence), and of its wartime research and political intelligence departments. The omissions presumably reflected the Foreign Office view that it did not "do" intelligence—one that still applies to the present (nonintelligence) Research and Analysis Department that succeeded these wartime bodies.[80]

Yet it is understandable that Cavendish-Bentinck and Capel-Dunn did not delve so deeply. Their aim in 1945 was not to produce a new system from scratch,

but to build quickly on the wartime successes that commanded widespread support. Making the JIC the peacetime center, and sorting out the wartime organizations, was pushing at an open door, but they did it in style, with their positive
message of developing the committee approach while moving from single-service
institutions towards national or joint-service ones. But what effect did their message have? It was intended to influence intelligence's management as well as its
production, and the effects on the two can best be discussed separately.

For postwar management, their enthusiasm for the JIC's central role was
clear from their tone. The SIGINT Board was to come under it; had it happened,
it would have been a considerable increase in the JIC's responsibilities. The JIC
would have been strengthened by the management role proposed for the Central
Intelligence Bureau and its director-general, but this never happened, and other
specifics were lacking. No draft terms of reference were produced at the time. So
we do not really know how far what became the JIC's style of peacetime management reflected the hopes of Cavendish-Bentinck and Capel-Dunn and those who
supported their ideas in 1945. But the indications are that they "intended that
coming under the JIC's umbrella" would signify a higher management profile for
the committee than it actually developed.

This may have been because JIC did not have the best of peacetime starts in
the high summer and autumn of 1945. By then Capel-Dunn was dead. Cavendish-Bentinck had been away in the United States in April and was again absent,
presumably on leave, for some weeks before a valedictory JIC appearance in mid-
August. His Foreign Office successor then took a long time to appear, and longer
to take the chair, so the committee was leaderless for much of the transition to
peace. Evill two years later was still critical that the committee was not providing the postwar leadership that intelligence needed.[81] The Foreign Office subsequently filled the chairman's post at a more senior level, but by then the postwar
mold would have been established and difficult to change.

It is equally possible that Cavendish-Bentinck and Capel-Dunn had expected
too much of management by consensus in peacetime. They may have allowed too
little for the special circumstances of war that had made it effective (and indeed
underestimated their own personal contributions), and for the renewed importance in peacetime of proper lines of command and budgets. It has been suggested
that Britain as a nation was at that time too enthusiastic about committees, and
did not consider how authority and responsibility fitted into them as carefully as
we would now.[82] The report used the analogy of the JIC with a board of directors
and did not consider the place of a chief executive. Attlee's submission to Churchill
in the autumn of 1940 that "there should be one directing mind at the head of the
Intelligence Service" remained in limbo.[83] The report writes of the JIC's "policy"
and "direction," but does not explore the responsibilities for finding resources and
ensuring effectiveness.

Whatever the causes, the reality has been that the postwar community has
always needed some central authority that the JIC could not provide, and has met
the need by a gradual growth of Cabinet Office power and influence. The JIC's

position as a forum for managerial issues has remained a key part of the system, and its collegial style has promoted more interagency cooperation than can be found in other countries. The result has been a system that has combined authority and collegiality within a relatively loose federation. In some respects this has been a national asset, and in others it has been a feature once characterized by the Committee of Parliamentarians as its "weakness in the centre."[84] It has had a high reputation and has served the United Kingdom reasonably well, but it is difficult not to feel that in following the wartime committee model it has failed to incorporate something of the authority, and leadership, which Churchill had radiated from the center.

On the community's assessment role the effects of the report's message have also been mixed. The JIC's system of assessment by committee under Foreign Office chairmanship has been highly regarded. It has done well in producing relevant and useful product for top government: the close linkage of intelligence and policy has been a world success. There has always been some inherent tension between the merits of assessment by consensus compared with the advantages of having a single chief intelligence officer figure, not tied to being a committee spokesman; and the balances between the two have varied considerably. Yet the needs of the day have been met reasonably well, and recent years have seen a more consistent recognition of the chairman's personal standing within what is still much prized as a consensus system.[85]

Yet it has had its assessment failures. A disinterested observer might conclude that in getting things right it has done no worse than the comparable American and Commonwealth systems, but not much better. The main lesson drawn from its performance on Iraqi weapons of mass destruction before the war of 2003 has been to improve the quality of the professional analysis that underlies the committee's judgments.[86] Cultivating this quality was implicit in Cavendish-Bentinck's and Capel-Dunn's vision of better analysis through the Central Intelligence Bureau and the reduction of single-service approaches, but it was not recognized. In 1945 the wartime successes in single-source collection and exploitation (especially SIGINT) and in JIC assessment had obscured for most people the importance of the unglamorous analytic work that linked the two.

That said, we should still recognize that despite the rejection of Cavendish-Bentinck's and Capel-Dunn's Central Bureau the decision to go as far as the JIB was a brave move in the right direction. As approved by the chiefs of staff it was to have an establishment of 212 people plus clerks, as well as outposts overseas.[87] The peacetime total for the three service directorates in Whitehall was then being planned as 249 officers and civilians, so the Bureau would be almost the same size as those it was created to support.[88]

It was also a success as far as it went. It became a strong player in the West's work on Soviet defense production, and despite the early problems over S and T organization it became particularly valuable in assessing the rate of Soviet missile production in the late 1950s and early 1960s when the missile threat was the hottest Western topic. It recruited the young civilians who later became the backbone of the defense intelligence staff. It was a genuine move away from single-department analysis towards a new model.

But the glass was half empty as well as half full. Major-General Sir Kenneth Strong, the JIB's first and only director, wrote later that "the Bureau had a considerable battle for existence. The armed forces never really liked it and many of their senior men regarded it as a threat to the traditional forms of service intelligence.[89] In his old age Cavendish-Bentinck said the same.[90] Though some of its Cold War analysis was important, a substantial part of its work served military contingency planning and war planning, for example through its inventory of world airfields and their characteristics. It periodically broke out from the yoke of military requirements, notably stepping into the breach in the 1960s on the effect of sanctions on Rhodesia's economy after its government had declared its independence of United Kingdom authority. But it was always restricted by its defense remit and was never able to become a proper national center. Most important, it was too small to offer analysis as a career to compete with intelligence's other specialties. Its image came to be of retired officers studying obscure subjects that might be useful sometime—in fact just what the military directorates had wanted in 1945. It was never staffed to be intelligence's research center on Soviet policies and intentions, and no other intelligence body ever was.

Those opting for it in 1945 can hardly be criticized. The case put for the Central Bureau was too vague, and where it was more precise it was a mixture of good ideas and bad. It did not have enough critical scrutiny. Yet inside it was something that deserved a better fate. The January 1945 report was full of foresight—on the place of economic, scientific, and technical intelligence, the need to exploit open sources as well as low-grade intelligence ones, the potential of imagery, the future of nonmilitary subjects as well as defense ones—and the same was true of its enthusiasm for central analysis. But the case for it was not well made, and it was left to the United States to lead it in the decade that followed.

In Britain the idea was not completely forgotten. The JIB managed *de facto* to meet Whitehall needs on some nondefense subjects, mainly on matters of foreign economics and technology. Field Marshal Sir Gerald Templar in his report on service intelligence in 1960 proposed that the Bureau should become part of the Cabinet Office. The JIC chairman proposed separately in 1963 that the integrated tri-service and JIB organization that was to become the Defence Intelligence Staff (the DIS) should be a "Combined Intelligence Bureau" in the Cabinet Office, perhaps harking back to the proposal of twenty years earlier. The idea of a central economic intelligence body still rumbled around Whitehall until the end of the 1960s, but died.[91]

There must be some regret that the United Kingdom did not go further towards the Central Bureau in 1945. Yet the British situation was always stacked against it. Like Cavendish-Bentinck's and Capel-Dunn's hopes for powerful JIC management, their idea of central analysis was ahead of its time. Intelligence's value was still thought in 1945 to be rooted in war and military power, and British military power was still single service, with the chiefs of staffs' committee of equals at the top. The postwar machine was bound to stick with the system. It was another twenty years before the JIB could be amalgamated with the military intelligence directorates, and by then Britain had become comfortable with its own mixture of departmental organization and intelligence by committee. The new, amalgamated organization became the DIS, part of the Ministry of Defence, and still a departmental body. Probably it would now need a national disaster for the idea of central analysis to be revived.

NOTES

I am grateful for information and advice from Gill Bennett, Pete Davies, Michael Goodman, Huw Dylan, Keith Jeffery, John Steele, Tony Comer, and Patrick Salmon. The archive reference TNA denotes the British National Archive, Kew. The report discussed in this chapter is available there as reference 1. Unless otherwise indicated, the paragraph numbers in these notes are from that report, and those at the end of a paragraph refer to all the quotations in it from that report. References at the end of a paragraph in the text apply to all quotations in it unless otherwise indicated.

1. "The Intelligence Machine. Report to the Joint Intelligence Committee." Unreferenced, January 10, 1945, paras. 11 and 49. The National Archives, Kew, London (hereafter TNA): CAB 163/6. Emphasis added.
2. F. H. Hinsley with E. E. Thomas, C. F. G. Ransom, and R. C. Knight, *British Intelligence in the Second World War: Vol. I* (London: HMSO, 1979), 43.
3. Hinsley, *British Intelligence: Vol.1*, 43.
4. I am indebted to Gill Bennett for this information.
5. Gill Bennett, *Churchill's Man of Mystery: Desmond Morton and the World of Intelligence* (Abingdon Oxon: Routledge, 2009), 207.
6. Para. 16. Quotation marks of "intelligence" in original.
7. First used in the United States in 1952, according to Christopher Andrew, *For the President's Eyes Only* (London: Harper Collins, 1995), 197. The source is not quoted.
8. JIC(43)53rd Meeting(O), item 1. TNA: CAB 81/91. Earlier correspondence is also in this file.
9. JIC(44)4th and 18th Meetings, items 6 and 3. TNA: CAB 81/91.
10. JIC(44)50th Meeting(O), item 1. TNA: CAB 81/92.
11. Para. 24.
12. Para. 11.
13. GCHQ's own postwar planning committee of Welchman, Hinsley, and Crankshaw is said to have called for "a more centralised Foreign Intelligence Office." Richard J. Aldrich, "GCHQ and SIGINT in the Early Cold War," in Matthew M. Aid and Cees Wiebes (eds.), *Secrets of Signals Intelligence during the Cold War and Beyond* (London: Frank Cass, 2001), 69. It is not clear whether this was to be a centralized SIGINT organization (as GCHQ became) or something more

comprehensive, but I remember being told around 1959–60 by William Millward at GCHQ that Hinsley had wanted a unified all-source intelligence organization of some kind, something that did not happen.

14. Jones, "Scientific Intelligence," 364. His criticisms of single-service organization are set out at more length in his *Reflections on Intelligence* (London: Heinemann, 1989), 7–34.

15. Donald McLachlan, *Room 39: Naval Intelligence in Action 1939–45* (London, Weidenfeld and Nicolson, 1968), 369.

16. On that date Capel-Dunn visited the Security Service to discuss its future as part of his JIC investigation and was sent packing. Cavendish-Bentinck then had to smooth feathers by confirming to the Security Service's director-general that the study was in progress at the JIC's invitation, but would not significantly involve his Service (JIC/1494/44, Cavendish-Bentinck to Petrie, October 27, 1944. TNA: CAB 163/6). The note of the contretemps that occasioned this letter is Nigel West (ed.), *The Guy Liddell Diaries: Vol. II* (Abingdon, Oxon: Routledge, 2005), 237. If the report had been commissioned in the normal JIC way Petrie would surely have been well aware of it.

17. Patrick Howarth, *Intelligence Chief Extraordinary: The Life of the Ninth Duke of Portland* (London: Bodley Head, 1968), 199.

18. Victor Frederick William Cavendish-Bentinck (1897–1990): Entered the postwar diplomatic service in 1919; JIC Chairman 1939–45; then ambassador to Poland; resigned 1947; had a successful business career. Became ninth Duke of Portland, 1979. See Howarth, *Intelligence Chief Extraordinary*.

19. Noel Annan, *Changing Enemies: The Defeat and Regeneration of Germany* (London: HarperCollins, 1996), 61–62.

20. Letter signed VFWC-B and EICJ ([Sir] Ian Jacob), *The Times*, July 25, 1945, 7. I am grateful to Michael Goodman for the reference.

21. Denis Capel-Dunn (1903–45): Said to have been the son of a Leipzig consular clerk; undergraduate at Trinity College, Cambridge, 1922–24 and 1930. Described by a member of the JIS as an "elusive, secretive barrister" (Annan, *Changing Enemies*, 17). A man of mystery, drawn on for an unsympathetic character in Anthony Powell's postwar novel *A Dance to the Music of Time* (confirmed in Powell's *Journals 1990–92* [London: Heinemann, c.1998], 151, 161–62). The few other personal recollections of him are equally uncomplimentary, completely at variance with the tribute in the Cavendish-Bentinck/Jacob letter. Biographical details obtained from Trinity College, Cambridge.

22. Para. 49.

23. Quotations in this paragraph are from para. 8, except the final one from para. 9.

24. Quotations from para. 2, except the final two from para. 4.

25. Annan, *Changing Enemies*, 63; also 59–68. He had previously served in the Military Intelligence Directorate and was subsequently a distinguished academic. For Cavendish-Bentinck's own criticisms of his service colleagues, see Howarth, *Intelligence Chief Extraordinary*, 165–66.

26. Sir Arthur Bonsall, "Bletchley Park and the RAF Y Service: Some Recollections," *Intelligence and National Security*, 23:6 (December 2008). See also the criticisms of the estimates of German aircraft production in mid–1943 to mid–1944: "These miscalculations arose generally from lapses in organization within the Air Intelligence Branch." (Hinsley, *British Intelligence*, vol. 3, no. 1, 62–63).

27. Cavendish-Bentinck was born in 1897; Capel-Dunn was born in 1903. Capel-Dunn was already arguing for a central postwar organization in the spring of 1943. I am grateful to Huw Dylan for this reference, "Defence Organisation after the War," April 29, 1943. TNA: TNA CAB 163/6.

28. The noun "jointery" did not itself appear until after the Joint Services Staff College's opening in 1947, described in M. D. Thornton, *Latimer Remembered* (Latimer, Bucks: National Defence College, 1983), 43–53.

29. Paras. 12 and 13. See also the description of the JIS's methods in McLachlan, *Room 39*, particularly 251–52.

30. Described in Reginald V. Jones, *Most Secret War: British Scientific Intelligence 1939–1945* (London: Hamish Hamilton, 1978), chapters 44–46. For confirmation see Hinsley, *British Intelligence*, vol. 3-1, section V, particularly 411, 444, 455.

31. Jones, *Most Secret War*, chapters 50–52.

32. Para. 17.

33. Para. 17. Emphasis added. Compare the inclusion of "interdepartmental" for the postwar role with the narrower "interservice" (armed service), used to describe the wartime role in para 16.

34. His successor was the future Lord Caccia (Howarth, *Intelligence Chief Extraordinary*, 203).

35. J.S./72/45, Capel-Dunn to Cavendish-Bentinck, February 20, 1945. TNA: CAB 163/6.

36. Misc/P 4781, Review of Intelligence Organization 1947 by Air Chief Marshal Sir Douglas Evill, November 6, 1947. TNA: CAB 163/7.

37. Para. 59.

38. Quotations up to this point in the paragraph are from para. 59.

39. Para. 70.

40. Jones, *Most Secret War*, 517. The same view is set out in his 1947 lecture "Scientific Intelligence," *RUSI Journal* 92.567 (August 1947), 364.

41. A recollection of a contemporary view that Jones "felt he had won the war single-handedly" is recorded in Michael S. Goodman, *Spying on the Nuclear Bear* (Stanford, CA: Stanford University Press, 2007), 135.

42. Para. 19.

43. These were the wartime Combined Service Detailed Interrogation Centre, the Secret Communications Organisation, and the Inter-Service Security Board. On this last subject, the JIC had established important wartime subcommittees for radio and cipher security. The 1945 report and the decisions of that year gave the JIC a postwar security role, which was significant but subsidiary to the committee's intelligence activities, and is not discussed here.

44. Para. 37.
45. Para. 39.
46. Para. 68.
47. Note, however, the rather different explanation of the official history, that PWE was a user rather a supplier of intelligence, except for its valuable studies of enemy propaganda that had a bearing on studies of enemy morale (Hinsley, *British Intelligence*, vol. 2, note 7. The Foreign Office's Political Intelligence Department (see note 80) was located with PWE at Woburn Park. It is not clear whether it was part of it or used as a cover term for it all.
48. Para. 25.
49. Para. 44.
50. Para. 46.
51. Para. 60.
52. Para. 71.
53. Charles Geoffrey Vickers, VC (1894–1982): Lawyer, administrator, writer, and pioneering systems scientist; recommissioned in the Second World War as colonel, knighted 1946; junior in wartime rank to the military JIC members, but his ability (and the Victoria Cross) must have made him an influential member.
54. Hinsley, *Official History*, vol. 3-1, 54 fn.
55. Hinsley, *Official History*, vol. 2, 11, 15.
56. Para. 59.
57. Para. 59.
58. All quotations from para. 71 except the last, which is from para. 10.
59. Para. 63.
60. Para. 62.
61. Para. 49.
62. The scanty treatment of the Security Service may have stemmed from Capel-Dunn's unhappy visit to it. See note 16.
63. Para. 56.
64. Para. 51.
65. If all the suggestions in the report had been followed, C would have remained responsible for GC&CS and become chairman of the SIGINT board, and would have become responsible via a deputy for the new Central Bureau. His job as head of SIS would have expanded to take on a large proportion of Security Service's effort if the suggested rationalization of counterespionage had ended in SIS's favor. At the JIC's meeting to discuss the report, it was suggested that he should also be responsible for exploiting open sources. Had this all happened he would have become the most important intelligence person, the absolute *eminence grise*. But the recommendations for his responsibilities outside SIS all fell by the wayside.
66. SIGINT discussion in paras. 52–55, 58, 64.
67. J.S./108/45, The Intelligence Machine, March 21, 1945. TNA: CAB 163/6.
68. JIC(45)181(0)(Final), June 1, 1945. TNA: CAB 81/129.
69. Ibid., outline in para. 5(c) of report and expansion in Annex. Quotations are from para. 4(j) of report and para. 8 of Annex.

70. Ibid., para. 5(c)(i) and Annex para. 19.

71. Ibid., para. 5(c).

72. Ibid., details in Appendix to the Annex, quotation in its first item.

73. The working party to consider the original proposal for the Central Bureau was due to meet on April 18 under Cavendish-Bentinck's chairmanship (JIC(45)27th Meeting item 13, April 17, 1945. TNA: CAB 81/93). The record did not survive. Cavendish-Bentinck then went to Washington for the rest of the month (Howarth, *Intelligence Chief Extraordinary*, 197). The April 18 meeting may well have been a decisive one, with staff left to work out the details of what had been agreed and to prepare the report that was eventually considered by the JIC in late May. JIC minutes show that, after JIC directors had considered the original report proposing the Central Intelligence Bureau on March 11, Capel-Dunn was absent from all the committee's meetings from March 13 onwards, except for one attendance on April 27, not on this subject. The San Francisco conference that he attended began on April 25, but it went on until early July and presumably he traveled out by air and skipped the beginning.

74. JIC(45)226(Final), July 24, 1945. TNA: CAB 81/130.

75. COS(45)220th meeting item 2, September 11, 1945, taking the paper at note 76. TNA: CAB 79/39.

76. JIC(45)265(O)(FINAL) Post-War Organisation of Intelligence, September 7, 1945. TNA: CAB 81/130. Quotations are from paras. 1 and 3, and Annex part I para. 6.

77. The peacetime machine was the JIC itself, its JIS support, and its members the Foreign Office, the three single-service directorates, and the Security Service, SIS and JIB. GCHQ became a member some years later. Subsequently the committee became part of the Cabinet Office; the service directorates and JIB were rolled into the Defence Intelligence Staff; the JIS became the Assessments Staff. Another change has been for more civilians from policy departments to become committee members since 1983.

78. Cabinet Office paper of July 2009 (released October 8 that year), *Improving the Central Intelligence Machinery* (www.cabinetoffice.gov.uk/sites/default/files/nim-november2010.pdf). This emphasized the JIC's responsibilities for assessment, with the transfer of managerial functions to the Cabinet Office. For revised terms of reference and explanation see www.cabinetoffice.gov.uk/security_and_intelligence/community/central_intelligence_machine (accessed October-November 2009).

79. Misc/P 4781, Review of Intelligence Organization 1947 by Air Chief Marshal Sir Douglas Evill, November 6, 1947. TNA: CAB 163/7.

80. Brief references to wartime arrangements are in Foreign Policy Document (Special issue) No. 263, Robert A. Longmore and Kenneth C. Walker, *Herald of a Noisy World—Interpreting the News of All Nations: The Research and Analysis Department of the Foreign and Commonwealth Office* (London: Foreign and Commonwealth Office, 1995). I am indebted to Patrick Salmon for drawing this history to my attention.

81. Misc/P 4781, Review of Intelligence Organization 1947 by Air Chief Marshal Sir Douglas Evill, November 6, 1947. TNA: CAB 163/7.
82. I am indebted to Pete Davies for this suggestion.
83. Bennett, *Churchill's Man of Mystery*, 267.
84. Intelligence and Security Committee, *Annual Report 1999–2000* (London: Stationery Office, 2000), para. 23. The same section also has "the Agencies need stronger coordination." The weakness appears as a "void" at para. 41 of that report.
85. The most important recent influence has been the conclusion of the Butler Committee that "We see a strong case for the post of Chairman of the JIC being held by someone with experience of dealing with Ministers in a very senior role, and who is demonstrably beyond influence, and thus probably in his last post." (Report of a Committee of Privy Counsellors, *Review of Intelligence on Weapons of Mass Destruction HC 898* [London: Stationery Office, 2004], para. 63).
86. Ibid., chapters 5–8.
87. JIC(45)293(Final), 13 October 1945. TNA: CAB 81/131.
88. Ibid.
89. Major-General Sir Kenneth Strong, *Intelligence at the Top: The Recollections of an Intelligence Officer* (London: Cassell, 1968), 224.
90. Howarth, *Intelligence Chief Extraordinary*, 199.
91. I am indebted for the contents of this paragraph to Pete Davies and his draft on British defense intelligence for the forthcoming special issue of *Intelligence and National Security* on intelligence in the Cold War.

DOCUMENT 1.1:   The Intelligence Machine: Report to the Joint Intelligence Sub-Committee, January 10, 1945

k 1 45.

THIS DOCUMENT IS THE PROPERTY OF HIS BRITANNIC MAJESTY'S GOVERNMENT

The circulation of this paper has been strictly limited.   It is issued

for the personal use of .... *Col. King Salter*

TOP SECRET

Copy No. *10*

10 January 1945

THE INTELLIGENCE MACHINE

Report to the

Joint Intelligence Sub-Committee

[28984]

B

DOCUMENT 1.1:   The Intelligence Machine: Report to the Joint Intelligence Sub-Committee, January 10, 1945 *(Continued)*

I.—Introduction.

THE Joint Intelligence Sub-Committee invited us to prepare a report on the post-war organisation of intelligence. " Intelligence," in the military sense, covers all kinds of information required for the conduct of war. By natural extension, it has come to cover also security—preventing an enemy or a potential enemy from obtaining information which might help him or harm us. With the coming of total war, the meaning of warfare has been extended to cover a wide area, embracing such fields as those of economic warfare, political and psychological warfare and deception. Those responsible for these latter forms of warfare, no less than those directing our main operations at sea, on land and in the air, require intelligence. Intelligence covers also the means by which information is conveyed, *i.e.,* communications.

2.   Before the present war, the Intelligence Branches were not much favoured parts of the Staff in any of the three fighting Services. Indeed, it would be foolish to pretend that even now, in the sixth year of the war, intelligence has not many critics. Intelligence is, however, of high importance as a servant of those conducting military operations. It is no more. It cannot win battles, but if it is absent or faulty, battles may easily be lost. It is important, therefore, that the Intelligence Branch, no less than the branches responsible for the supply of ammunition, fuel and food, and the branches responsible for reinforcement of the forces in the field, should be as efficient as we can make it. Yet no one would be so bold as to contend that our Service Intelligence Staffs entered this war adequately equipped for the task confronting them. There existed no sufficient trained cadre of intelligence officers. Our topographical information was woefully lacking. Fortunately, there existed in the product of the Government Code and Cypher School one certain channel of first-class information, but its full value could not be got unless the machine at the centre was properly equipped to collate and assess it against cognate intelligence from other sources. In the War Office in peace time there was no separate Directorate of Intelligence, and in the Air Ministry the peace-time intelligence organisation was, frankly, not impressive. In the Admiralty, the position was rather better. There existed a system of naval reporting centres in ports all over the world. Moreover, the Naval Intelligence Division, even in peace, was a senior division of the Naval Staff under the direction of a senior officer and, accordingly, carried more weight within the Navy than did the parallel organisations in the other two services. In no Service was there a school of intelligence. There was a tendency to employ officers in intelligence, not because they were particularly suited to the work, but because they possessed a language qualification. In the Army, at any rate, intelligence was a dangerous branch of the Staff for an ambitious officer to join.

3.   It is sometimes forgotten that the Directors of Intelligence in the Service Departments are in a different position from that of any of the other heads of divisions. The Directors of Intelligence are responsible to their Chiefs of Staff and, as members of the J.I.C., to the Chiefs of Staff Committee, for advice in war as to the probable intentions of the enemy, and in peace as to the development of warlike actions or policies on the part of foreign countries. In addition to this responsibility the Directors of Intelligence are the heads of great organisations with world-wide ramifications. This combination of advisory and administrative function places upon them a heavy burden.

4.   While we believe that it is right to record the situation described above, so that it may not be reflected in the conditions obtaining in the future, we recognise that the decision to allow the Intelligence Branches, which had achieved much in the last war, to wither in the period between the wars, was a natural decision. The fighting Services had terribly scanty financial provision out of which to ensure the security of the country and the Empire. Those in control could not be blamed if they decided that as there was not enough to go round, ships, aircraft, guns and warlike stores must be brought before intelligence. We all hope the country will have learned its lesson and that, in future, it will be publicly recognised that it is poor economy to save on the armed forces to such an extent as to encourage potential enemies to become actual enemies, and then to pay at shortage rates in life and treasure for our unreadiness. It would, however, be rash to assume that the lesson will be remembered. Therefore, " taking the worst case " as we are taught to do in our appreciations for the Chiefs of Staff, it is clear that we should strive not merely to ensure that

DOCUMENT 1.1:   The Intelligence Machine: Report to the Joint Intelligence Sub-
Committee, January 10, 1945 *(Continued)*

3

our Intelligence Service after the war is the most efficient possible, but to ensure
that it is as economical as can be without sacrifice of efficiency.

5.   One of the most vivid of the impressions we have gained in the course of
our association with the Joint Intelligence Sub-Committee, and, particularly,
during our recent enquiry, has been of the great volume of the available material
and of the number and variety of the Departments and organisations interested
in it as producers or consumers of intelligence, or both.

6.   Intelligence reaches this country in war-time through many channels, of
which the following are the principal :—

(a) The reports reaching the Foreign Office from our Diplomatic and
Consular officers abroad.

(b) The reports reaching the Service Ministries from Naval, Military and
Air Attachés, Naval Reporting Stations, the interrogation of
prisoners of war, captured documents and equipment, &c.

(c) The product of the " Y " Services.

(d) The product of the Government Code and Cypher School.

(e) The reports from agents of S.I.S.

(f) The reports received through the channels of the Security Service,
including the interrogations of persons entering the United Kingdom.

(g) The product of Postal and Telegraph Censorship.

(h) The product of aerial photographic reconnaissance received in the Air
Ministry.

(i) The reports reaching the Dominions Office from our High Commissioners
in the Dominions.

(j) The reports reaching the Colonial Office from our Governments in
Colonial and Mandated Territories.

(k) Reports to S.O.E. from their agents.

(l) The foreign press-reading organisation of P.W.E.

7.   In addition to these official channels, a deal of information reaches this
country both in peace and war through private channels. There is correspondence
between the representatives of British commercial and financial organisations
abroad, and their head offices in this country.   There is the information obtained
from the correspondence of individual scientists and academic figures as well as
that of learned societies.   Learning knows no boundaries.   There is the information collected by newspaper correspondents abroad and by private travellers.   In
war-time, much valuable information is drawn from this mine of unofficial
intelligence.   In peace-time, however, much of it is wasted as far as the Government machine is concerned.   Even the information reaching this country through
official channels, as outlined in the last paragraph, has rarely, till recently, found
its way to all those who could put it to the best use.

8.   War-time relaxation of financial control and the urgent need of the
different organisations engaged directly in military operations to be sure of
getting quickly the intelligence they require, have resulted in some overlapping
of responsibilities and duplication of work which should not be acceptable or
permissible in peace-time, and should, if possible, be avoided in war.   The
remarkable diversity of controls during most of the war both in intelligence
producing and intelligence consuming organisations, has fostered the tendency
to duplication.   The three principal fighting Services, though they have their own
Ministries as in peace, are operationally directed by the Chiefs of Staff Committee
under the ultimate control of the Minister of Defence.   S.O.E. (which developed
into an intelligence producing agency) has, however, been under the ministerial
direction of the Minister of Economic Warfare; the Political Warfare Executive
under that of the Foreign Secretary and the Minister of Information; the S.I.S.
under that of the Foreign Secretary; the Security Service, until recently, under
the Chancellor of the .Duchy of Lancaster, though now under the Foreign
Secretary; and the Postal and Telegraph Censorship Department, under the
Minister of Information.   There were, no doubt, excellent reasons for the decisions
that led to this state of affairs.   It may well have been right under the pressure
of war to avoid the dislocation that any attempt at rationalisation would have
caused.   Goodwill, and the national genius for making the best of anomalies,
has produced remarkably good results from this strange machine.   None the less,
we believe that a more symmetrical organisation could have done at least
as well at less cost.   Certainly, if we are to plan an organisation for peace capable
of ready adaptation to the needs of a future war, something simpler and more
economical must be devised.

[28984]   B 2

DOCUMENT 1.1: The Intelligence Machine: Report to the Joint Intelligence Sub-Committee, January 10, 1945 *(Continued)*

4

9. In the international field it is now generally recognised that the price of peace and security in the modern world is some surrender of national sovereignty. Hence such experiments as the League of Nations and the Dumbarton Oaks concept. The pressure of war has led to the remarkable innovation of the Combined Chiefs of Staff and the various integrated Allied Headquarters. It is, however, noteworthy that this country, which has taken the lead in these directions, pays perhaps more regard to departmental sovereignties than any other. This is explained by the responsibility of Ministers to Parliament for the conduct of their Departments. Yet, in defence matters, the war has brought about a considerable degree of inter-departmental co-operation through the machinery of the Chiefs of Staff organisation. We believe that few now would contend that this development had been anything but advantageous. If, therefore, in this report we recommend its extension, involving the surrender of some departmental sovereignties, we do so in the firm belief that it is essential. We recognise that each Department affected could make a convincing case for the retention unimpaired of its own sole authority, but we are confident that whatever disagreement there may be with our individual recommendations, any objective study of the problem confronting us would have led to the same general conclusion, namely, that we cannot afford to start another war unprovided with the necessary intelligence; and that we cannot afford in peace (or even perhaps in war) the kind of intelligence organisation we have to-day.

10. We have not, in this report, dealt in detail with the internal organisation of the intelligence directorates in the three Service Departments. To have done so would have destroyed the balance of the report and laid us open to the charge of making proposals on insufficient evidence and superficial enquiry. We have preferred instead to propose a certain amalgamation of existing inter-service and inter-departmental bodies so as to provide a central intelligence agency and to leave it to Departments to work out the alterations in their own organisation that would be possible and desirable were that proposal accepted.

11. Enquiries under other auspices have been or are being made into the two principal branches of our Secret Service, and we do not, therefore, propose in this report to deal in detail with this aspect of the problem, save in so far as it is necessary for our purpose. We believe, however, that there will be general acceptance of the contention that the secret vote should be relieved of as much as possible of the expenditure on intelligence. A great part of the expenditure now, in war-time, borne on the secret vote for, for example, P.W.E. and S.O.E., represents acknowledgeable activities. The more that expenditure on intelligence can be placed on the public vote, the less temptation there will be in future to raid the secret vote in times of financial stringency. It is because we are convinced of the need for the strongest possible Secret Service in peace-time in preparation for our war needs, that we urge that everything possible should be done to protect the Secret Service from having to bear responsibility for activities that need not of themselves be regarded as secret.

12. As regards the other peace-time intelligence producing Departments, there is one general observation that we desire to make. Whereas in the Service Departments intelligence is the sole responsibility of certain officers specially selected for dealing with it, in the Political Departments, *e.g.* the Foreign Office and the Colonial Office, the officials who receive, collate and assess information are also responsible for formulating policy. This is not necessarily a bad thing, but the system does possess a serious weakness. One who is concerned in devising and recommending policy, and in assisting in its execution is likely, however objective he may try to be, to interpret the intelligence he receives in the light of the policy he is pursuing. To correct this possible weakness, it is clearly desirable that some quite objective check be placed on all intelligence received. So far as intelligence affecting the conduct of the war is concerned, the problem has been to some extent solved in the Foreign Office by the establishment of the Services Liaison Department, whose function it is to take part at all levels in the deliberations of the J.I.C. in the preparation of intelligence appreciations, and to interpret to the Planning Staffs the foreign policy of His Majesty's Government. This departure has justified itself in war, and we hope that it will be decided to continue it in peace. We believe that no Department, however experienced and well staffed, has anything to lose by bringing the intelligence directly available to it to the anvil of discussion and appreciation among other workers in the same field.

13. To sum up, the machine that it is our task to devise should, we suggest, have the following characteristics. It should ensure that the agency best fitted

DOCUMENT 1.1: The Intelligence Machine: Report to the Joint Intelligence Sub-Committee, January 10, 1945 *(Continued)*

5

for the collection of a particular type of intelligence continues to collect it. It should ensure that, as far as possible, no other agency should collect the same material from the same source. It should ensure that the material collected is collated with other material bearing on the same subject, so that the best possible evaluation may be made. It should ensure that the information, when received and collated, is made available to all those with a legitimate interest in it and whose work will profit from its receipt. It should be controlled at the top by a strong inter-service and inter-departmental body, representing the needs of producers and consumers of intelligence.

V.—The Post-War Intelligence Organisation.

59. In paragraph 13 above, we gave an outline of the characteristics which our post-war intelligence organisation should, in our opinion, display. The proposal which we now put forward is designed to create an organisation

DOCUMENT 1.1:　The Intelligence Machine: Report to the Joint Intelligence Sub-Committee, January 10, 1945 *(Continued)*

17

possessed of those characteristics. At the head of the organisation and directing its general policy we propose should be the Joint Intelligence Sub-Committee. The J.I.C. should remain directly responsible to the Chiefs of Staff, though we think that the practice that has grown up, of the Committee giving advice on request to other Departments and authorities, should be preserved. Under the J.I.C. we propose that there should be a system of standing sub-committees dealing with all the various aspects of intelligence. We think it essential that all the intelligence authorities should be brought under the J.I.C. umbrella. In addition to these sub-committees, we propose the establishment of a Central Intelligence Bureau. Into this bureau this information should be fed information from all existing intelligence sources. Within the bureau, this information should be brought together and reproduced in the form required by the different customers of the intelligence machine. We have in mind that each intelligence-producing organisation should continue to collect intelligence from its own sources, but should not normally receive intelligence from other Departments or organisations save through the medium of the Central Bureau.

60. In peace-time, a certain limited amount of officially acquired intelligence is made available to the general public either in the form of official publications, such as the commercial reports issued by the Department of Overseas Trade, or in answer to direct enquiries generally addressed to that Department by particular commercial firms. We believe that there is scope for a considerable extension of this practice. It is evident that the revival of our export trade after the war will be as difficult as it is important. It is no part of our responsibility to make recommendations to this end, but we believe that we can serve both the interests of defence and the wider economic interests of this country in peace-time by providing a comprehensive intelligence agency. Even in war, much of the information which is of value to the Foreign Office and the Defence Services is in no way secret. We propose, therefore, that the Central Intelligence Bureau should be available, not only to Government Departments and agencies, but also to the general public. While its services, like those of any other Government agency, would be provided free of cost to official customers, there is no reason why members of the public making use of it should not pay for its services. His Majesty's Stationery Office make a charge for their publications, as does the Ordnance Survey for those of its maps that are made publicly available. This proposal would have a twofold advantage. In the first place, as has been said, it should provide trade and industry with much information which should assist them in their normal business. Secondly, it should provide a revenue which should assist the Defence organisation in meeting its expenditure on intelligence.

61. We fully recognise that no Department or Service can absolve itself from direct responsibility for the technical assessment of the intelligence relating directly to its own constitutional responsibilities. We are satisfied, however, that there is a wide field of common interest where it should be possible to avoid duplication of effort. This field covers some highly secret matters as well as a large area of matters which are hardly, if at all, secret.

62. If the J.I.C. is to take over the responsibility for the direction of the kind of organisation that we have outlined above, it may be that its constitution should be to some extent modified. In particular, the Board of Trade should, we think, at any rate in peace be represented. In any case, the Foreign Office, "C" and the Directors of Intelligence must clearly continue to be members. Separate representation on the J.I.C. of the Economic Intelligence Organisation within the Foreign Office should not, in our opinion, be necessary. Representation of the Security Service must evidently be a matter to be decided in the light of the decisions taken on the future of that body.

63. A committee as large as the J.I.C., while competent to lay down policy, is evidently unsuited to the day-to-day administration of a large organisation. This task requires the whole time services of a single individual aided by a competent departmental staff. Here a special difficulty confronts us. We have little doubt but that the best arrangement would be for "C," who is the head of S.I.S. and G.C. and C.S., the Chairman of the S.I.G.I.N.T. Board and the ultimate head of the Special Communications Organisation, to accept responsibility for the direction of the new Central Intelligence machine. Since the Central Bureau will, if our recommendations are accepted, be the principal clearing house for the product of "C's" organisations, it would, in our opinion, be both administratively convenient and correct from the point of view of

DOCUMENT 1.1: The Intelligence Machine: Report to the Joint Intelligence Sub-Committee, January 10, 1945 *(Continued)*

18

security for " C " to be in charge. At the same time, " C " for obvious reasons may not be a public figure, known to the world at large. Perhaps it would be possible to arrange for a deputy to be appointed to " C," who would be responsible to him for the public side of his activities, but would bear a title which would not disclose to the outside world that he was a subordinate. In the following paragraphs we refer to the head of the organisation as the " Director-General."

We propose that the Director-General and, in his absence, his deputy, should be *ex-officio* members not only of the J.I.C., but of all its various sub-committees, though it should not be necessary for them to attend all sub-committee meetings. The Director-General would have the services of a permanent secretariat common to the J.I.C. and its sub-committees. The secretariat should be responsible, under the Director-General, for ensuring the co-ordination of the activities of the different branches of the national intelligence machine. The sub-committees we have in mind are the following, but the list is not intended to be exclusive. Moreover, there should be power to establish *ad hoc* sub-committees when need arises.

The S.I.G.I.N.T. Board.

64. This Board should be composed as at present, but its responsibility should cover not only G.C. and C.S., but also Special Communications and R.S.S., and ensure co-ordination between them. Should it, in future, be found possible to bring about some further integration of the " Y " Services, it would be proper that it should be under the Board.

Joint Intelligence Staff.

65. We have in mind that a Joint Intelligence Staff should exist as at present to draft strategic intelligence appreciations for the J.I.C. and to advise the Planning Staffs. Its members would take their instructions, as at present, from their own Ministries.

Joint Technical Intelligence Committee.

66. We propose that there should, in future, be established a permanent committee representative of the technical sections of the three Service Departments, which should be responsible for giving joint advice on foreign technical developments in the defence field to the Planning Staffs and the research and development organisations working under the Chiefs of Staff. [In the light of experience it could be decided whether this committee should itself be served by a whole-time inter-service staff on the lines of the Joint Intelligence Staff.]

Security Committee.

67. This Committee as its name implies, would advise the J.I.C. on all questions of military security in peace, and form the nucleus for the war-time Inter-Service Security Board. We propose that it should have sufficient contacts with the remainder of the Government machine for it to be unnecessary at any future date to re-establish anything on the lines of the Security Executive.

Photographic Reconnaissance Committee.

68. This Committee should, under the J.I.C., be responsible for the policy direction of aerial photographic reconnaissance and for the production, interpretation and distribution of aerial photographs. If it is agreed that a special air communications service can properly be run by the Intelligence Organisation, its policy direction should be in the hands of this sub-committee.

War Planning Committee.

69. We contemplate that a sub-committee with a small staff should be charged with planning and making all preparations for the expansion and modification of the intelligence machine that would be required for war. Such war-time needs as censorship and political warfare intelligence should be catered for by this sub-committee.

General Intelligence Requirements Committee.

70. This sub-committee's task would be to lay down the priorities to be accorded to the nation's " intelligence effort," to co-ordinate the work of the

DOCUMENT 1.1:   The Intelligence Machine: Report to the Joint Intelligence Sub-Committee, January 10, 1945 *(Continued)*

19

different collecting agencies, to allot responsibilities between those agencies and to exercise general supervision over the Central Intelligence Bureau described below.

The Central Intelligence Bureau.

71. We propose that the inter-service, inter-departmental intelligence organisations, such as the Postal and Telegraph Censorship, I.S.T.D. and the intelligence side of P.W.E., should find their home in peace-time in the Central Bureau, which should be so constituted as to permit of their expansion in time of war to fulfil their full functions. It would be wrong to attempt to produce a detailed blue-print at this stage, of the bureau, but there may be advantage in providing a rough outline. We have in mind that the bureau should be organised on the lines of the Information and Records Branch of the Postal and Telegraph Censorship Department. That is to say that it should provide machinery, through liaison sections staffed by the consumer Departments, for conveying the needs of the consumers to the bureau, who would be responsible for ensuring that the information was collected by the agency best fitted to collect it. The bureau would also be responsible for ensuring that the material it produced was distributed to all those with a legitimate interest in it. The bureau should be divided into two parts, one of which would deal with secret information, and the other with information that is not secret. It is suggested that in both its secret and its non-secret parts the bureau should be organised both by geographical areas and by subjects. We have in mind that information required as a basis of high policy by, for example, the Foreign Office or the Chiefs of Staff should be collected and collated in the first instance in the non-secret branch of the bureau. It should then be tested in the light of any secret information that is available. The next stage, if appropriate for inter-service or inter-departmental assessment, would be for the material to be dealt with by the Joint Intelligence Staff, and the final assessment would be made by the Joint Intelligence Sub-Committee itself. The bureau would be responsible for providing in the shape of memoranda or reference books such factual information as was required. It will be for Departments to determine how far they will wish to maintain their own collating and appreciating machinery once the Central Bureau has been established. We believe that if our recommendation is accepted, the central machine will sufficiently justify itself to encourage Departments to refrain from duplicating its work.

72. Our proposals are illustrated in the Chart attached to this report (Annex B).

Ministerial Responsibility.

73. The centralised intelligence machine described in the preceding paragraphs will be a fairly large organisation, and it will be necessary for its expenses to be carried on the vote of some Department, though we believe that some of its expenses may be met from revenues produced by itself and that, in any case, its creation should result in some saving. Much will depend on the organisation of which the Joint Intelligence Sub-Committee itself forms a part. If we revert to a system similar to that which existed before the present war, with no central defence organisation other than the Committee of Imperial Defence and its sub-committees and secretariat, it would perhaps be most convenient for the Treasury vote to carry the unified intelligence organisation. The Treasury carries the vote for His Majesty's Stationery Office, which is an existing semi-autonomous Government agency. On the other hand, if a Defence Ministry were created, it would be logical for the intelligence organisation to form part of that Ministry.

                (Signed)   V. CAVENDISH-BENTINCK.

                                 DENIS CAPEL-DUNN.

Offices of the War Cabinet,
    10th January, 1945.

[28984]

                                                           E

CHAPTER 2

"A Formidable Power to Cause Trouble for the Government"?

Intelligence Oversight and the Creation of the UK Intelligence and Security Committee

PETER GILL

Editors' Note:

Peter Gill explores the oversight of British intelligence through the parliamentary debates that led to the establishment of the Intelligence and Security Committee (ISC) of Parliament. Gill explores oversight as a concept, juxtaposing it with notions of control, but ultimately focuses on the very practical concerns and experiences of the ISC in operation and the extent to which it has called upon official documentation and held the government and agencies to account. This chapter provides an interesting and instructive example to all those who think about the oversight of intelligence activities.

T his chapter examines the passage of the Intelligence Services Act 1994, with particular reference to the establishment of the Intelligence and Security Committee (ISC) to examine the expenditure, administration, and policy of the three United Kingdom intelligence agencies. My objective is to set out the main debates at the time, which were about how intelligence oversight by members of Parliament might be conducted, and to evaluate the success or otherwise of those arrangements in the light of our experience with the ISC since it began its work. As with the study of any other specific documents, the detailed examination of a parliamentary debate will not give the full context on any issue; depending on when the debate occurs, members have a variety of concerns that they bring into the debate even if they are tangential to the central issue. But the advantage of the study is that it does give the flavor of the times when the measure was introduced and helps to answer the question "why now?"

The history of intelligence oversight is relatively brief, even in democratic states, certainly in comparison with the history of intelligence. To the extent that oversight of intelligence includes at least some element of the scrutiny of intelligence by people *outside* the agencies who have no management role in them, then the history starts after the Second World War. The Netherlands and what was then West Germany established forms of external oversight in the 1950s, but it did not develop elsewhere until the 1970–80s, since when it has spread rapidly. In the old democracies of Europe this occurred because of a mixture of political scandals and the growing impact of the European Court of Human Rights' (ECHR) decisions, while increasing the democratic control and oversight of intelligence is a central feature of reform in the new postauthoritarian democracies in Europe, Latin America, and elsewhere.

The Intelligence Services Bill

In the United Kingdom specifically, a central aspect of the process was a series of actual or anticipated decisions by the ECHR, which, broadly, required that intelligence agencies' special powers for covert surveillance be authorized in law (rather than just by executive decree) and that there be procedures by which citizens could challenge their use.[1] There was no such statutory basis for intelligence governance in the United Kingdom, and through the 1980s this was rapidly assembled, first by legislation governing the interception of communications (1985), and then by providing the Security Service (MI5) with a legal mandate (1989). In both cases, procedures were instituted for ministers to authorize interception of communications (then telephone tapping and mail opening) and "interference with property" (covering burglary, theft of documents, etc.). Judicial commissioners were to be appointed to review the lawfulness of the *procedures* by which warrants were granted (but not to second-guess the reasons) and to report annually on their findings. Tribunals, also staffed by lawyers, were established to receive and investigate complaints from the public who believed that their rights had been transgressed. But opposition moves to establish parliamentary oversight were resisted. Yet, just four years after the Security Service Act, the government introduced the Intelligence Services Bill (ISB) that, logically, provided equivalent statutory mandates for the Secret Intelligence Service (SIS or MI6) and Government Communications Headquarters (GCHQ) but also, surprisingly, to establish a committee in Parliament. In fact, planning for this had started after John Major's election win in 1992.[2] The ISB was first introduced in the House of Lords and Lord McKay, the Lord Chancellor, explained this *volte face*:

> Why, some of your Lordships may ask, are the Government introducing now something which less than five years ago we deemed inappropriate. I myself, your Lordships may recall, felt during the debate on the Security Service bill that the time was not right for such a step. What has changed? In deciding that in 1989 that the Security Service should continue to be accountable

to parliament through Ministers, the Government argued that to give Parliament a greater oversight role would be unsatisfactory since, in order to preserve the effectiveness of the service and the safety of those working for it, Parliament would have to respect the secrecy of certain information. An oversight body with no access to secrets would have access to little of interest or importance to the service's work and be of scarce interest to Parliament. On the other hand, a body with broad access to secrets would be unable to report in full to Parliament and therefore would also be unsatisfactory . . . The Government have continued to look for ways to allow greater access and to disclose more information when this has been deemed compatible with national security. Back in 1989, for example, the Secret Intelligence Service had not even been avowed. Given the close cooperation between the Security Service and SIS in certain areas, oversight of the Security Service alone would clearly have led to problems. Since 1989, however, the Government have named both the director general of the Security Service and the chief of SIS; announced the moves of the respective agencies into Thames House and Vauxhall Cross; released a number of previously withheld government records; and this year . . . published information booklets on both the Security Service and the central intelligence machinery. And most recently, the Government have disclosed the size of the aggregate budget for the agencies, and undertaken to bring all this expenditure into a single Vote. The Bill has been prepared with the benefit of more than four years experience since the Security Service Act. Things have moved on. The climate has changed. Greater openness has gained momentum. We believe that it is now right to take this further important step.[3]

Clearly there were other reasons. Some have been alluded to above: The end of the Cold War had made some space within which greater openness could be contemplated, and the agencies themselves felt that oversight would be helpful to them in resisting yet larger budget cuts as a result of the "peace dividend." There was also the advantage from their point of view that limited reform under the Conservatives would be preferable to the more radical step of a select committee as envisaged in the Labour Party's (1983) publication and the amendments proposed during the Security Service Bill debate in 1989. These inclinations were reinforced by continuing revelations as to the agencies' ambiguous role in controversies such as surveillance of the National Union of Mineworkers during the 1984–85 miners' strike.[4]

The key to understanding the limited role of the ISC is that it was only ever intended to supplement the existing "ministerial oversight" of the intelligence services and yet to do so in such a way that would be compatible with the ECHR.[5] It is important to distinguish "control" from "oversight"; for example, Peter Mandelson shared "the views of . . . colleagues who do not believe that oversight means involvement or dabbling in the day-to-day details and activities of the security services. But operational supervision is very important indeed. Day-to-day control of the security services is not, and should not be, a function of any parliamentary committee; it is a function of Ministers, and Ministers alone."[6]

Thus, control refers to the management and direction of organizations and is essentially the job of political executives, whether elected or appointed.[7] Oversight can be defined as "the scrutiny of agencies' actions, whether contemporaneously or after the event, in order to ensure their effectiveness, legality and propriety on behalf of the public."[8] To be effective, this oversight needs to take place both within and outside agencies, but here we are concentrating on external and specifically parliamentary oversight.[9] Note that we need to distinguish parliamentary oversight in general from that of specific intelligence oversight committees such as ISC; such oversight, as we shall see, is not strictly parliamentary. The former includes the role of individual MPs, other committees, and special bodies such as the National Audit Office.

Although the proposal for the ISC may have surprised many, by the 1990s there was a move towards some form of oversight by Parliaments (or, as in Canada, an extraparliamentary body) in many countries. So we now have quite a wide body of experience on which to draw in evaluating the impact of these innovations and some suggestions as to what constitutes principles and "best practice" for parliamentarians who would undertake this challenging role.[10] We can identify the following main variables:[11]

- form of committee
- membership
- resources, including expertise and staff
- mandate
- access to information
- reporting
- "political will"

Section 10 of the Intelligence Services Bill dealt with the proposal for the Committee:

10. The Intelligence and Security Committee
   (1) There shall be a Committee, to be known as the Intelligence and Security Committee and in this section referred to as "the Committee," to examine the expenditure, administration and policy of—
      (a) the Security Service;
      (b) the Intelligence Service; and
      (c) GCHQ.
   (2) The Committee shall consist of six members—
      (a) who shall be drawn both from the members of the House of Commons and from the members of the House of Lords; and
      (b) none of whom shall be a Minister of the Crown.

(3) The members of the Committee shall be appointed by the Prime Minister after consultation with the Leader of the Opposition, within the meaning of the [1975 c. 27.] Ministerial and other Salaries Act 1975; and one of those members shall be so appointed as Chairman of the Committee.

(4) Schedule 3 to this Act shall have effect with respect to the tenure of office of members of, the procedure of and other matters relating to, the Committee; and in that Schedule "the Committee" has the same meaning as in this section.

(5) The Committee shall make an annual report on the discharge of their functions to the Prime Minister and may at any time report to him on any matter relating to the discharge of those functions.

(6) The Prime Minister shall lay before each House of Parliament a copy of each annual report made by the Committee under subsection (5) above together with a statement as to whether any matter has been excluded from that copy in pursuance of subsection (7) below.

(7) If it appears to the Prime Minister, after consultation with the Committee, that the publication of any matter in a report would be prejudicial to the continued discharge of the functions of either of the Services or, as the case may be, GCHQ, the Prime Minister may exclude that matter from the copy of the report as laid before each House of Parliament.[12]

Form of committee This was probably the central issue regarding the ISC on which the parties were divided; as we have seen, the Labour Party had been proposing for ten years that a select committee would be the appropriate mechanism and the Home Affairs Select Committee (1992) had endorsed this course of action for the Security Service. Instead, the Conservative government proposed a "committee of parliamentarians" from both houses who would have the same mandate as a select committee—"expenditure, administration and policy"—but who would be appointed by the Prime Minister and to whom they would report. Their annual reports would be laid before Parliament once any "prejudicial" security material had been removed (ISA s.10(7)). For the opposition, Jack Cunningham stated: "It is proposed that the committee should not report to Parliament but to the Prime Minister. I do not regard that as parliamentary scrutiny or oversight, because the Prime Minister has the right to veto sections of its report—I call it prime ministerial oversight and scrutiny. If we are to have an effective parliamentary watchdog to oversee such matters and to probe and scrutinise, it should report to parliament. It cannot legitimately be called a parliamentary committee unless it does so."[13] And, at the report stage, David Winnick said: "I do not think the Bill gives the impression that there will be genuine parliamentary scrutiny. The Committee will report to the Prime Minister; I assume that it will be serviced by the Cabinet

Office. The Parliamentary Secretary nods. Such a committee would appear to
be virtually a subcommittee of the Cabinet Office, although it would include
parliamentarians."[14]

This remains an issue on which opinions are split: in academic reviews of
the first ten years or so of the ISC, Anthony Glees and others concluded that the
present status was the "least bad" while Mark Phythian argued that making the
ISC a select committee was necessary if the committee were to retain public confidence.[15] Similarly, two parliamentary inquiries reporting in August 2009 on the
continuing allegations that the UK agencies were at least "complicit" in the rendition and torture of some people detained after 9/11 have recommended that the
ISC be strengthened in this way:

> A good first step would be for the Government to propose to establish the
> ISC as a proper parliamentary committee, with an independent secretariat
> (including independent legal advice), which would establish ministerial
> accountability to parliament in this area at a stroke. The recent allegations
> about complicity in torture should be a wake up call to Ministers that the
> current arrangements are not satisfactory.[16]
>
> We conclude that, notwithstanding the recent changes to House of
> Commons standing orders, the (ISC) remains a creature of the Government,
> not a committee of Parliament, and that consequently there continues to be a
> deficit in the parliamentary scrutiny of intelligence and security matters. We
> reiterate our previous recommendation that the ISC should be reconstituted
> as a select committee of the House of Commons.[17]

One of the problems for both these committees is that their attempts to question
the heads of the agencies would be rebuffed for the reason that those heads were
responsible to the ISC. The problem seemed to be not just that the ISC itself had
failed on this issue but that its existence was preventing fuller enquiry by others.

Membership A recurring theme throughout the debate was whether or not members of the ISC should be privy councillors; since they swear specific oaths of allegiance and secrecy, it is assumed that secrets will be safe in their hands. Opinions
were divided; for example, David Steele, for the Liberal Democrats, argued: "I
believe that there is a case for the committee's being composed of Privy Councillors. I do not say that because I believe that they have any particular wisdom, and
I do not share the view that they belong to a cosy, conspiratorial club, but, unless
the members are Privy Councillors, we might find that the fact that there are non-
Privy Councillors on the committee is used as an excuse for failing to provide the
committee with the information it needs."[18] The government had not proposed
that members would be privy councillors and there is no evidence that Steele's
fears were borne out.

The related issue of leaks arose. Archie Hamilton commented: "It will obviously be of great benefit to keep the committee relatively small. The more members

the committee has, the more likely it is that leaks or mistakes will be made by Members of Parliament—who, let us face it, are not renowned for their discretion. Briefing the press seems to occupy most of the daylight hours of many of my colleagues. It will be quite a cultural change for them to become involved in any part of the Government's activities, in which people are not briefing the press day or night."[19]

The likelihood of leaks was downplayed in a later intervention by Michael Mates, citing his experience on the Defence Select Committee when Ministry officials became alarmed at the imminent appointment of two members of the Campaign for Nuclear Disarmament (CND). But secret information continued to be provided to the committee and no leaks occurred.[20] There have been no leaks from the ISC, although the BBC obtained a copy of their first report on the July 7, 2005, London bombings the day before publication. It is not known whether this was from the Committee or from Downing Street.

The actual size of the ISC was the one issue on which the government did accept an amendment: the bill envisaged six members, the Act provides for nine. Since 1994 just one member at any one time has come from the House of Lords. The only marginal change made to the process of appointments in 2008 was that the list of members, from whom appointments would be made by the prime minister after consultation with the leader of the opposition, would be provided by the committee of selection, as for select committees. But the issue of the chair remains more contentious in that the government continues to appoint the chair from the governing party. Given the proximity of intelligence to political power, arguably the legitimacy of any oversight committee will be enhanced if it is chaired by a member of the opposition.[21] Tom King, the initial Conservative chair, was reappointed by Labour in 1997, perhaps to reassure the agencies, but from his retirement in 2001 until 2008, the ISC has been chaired by Labour members. Some concern has been expressed that the ISC seems to have become a temporary parking place for people between ministerial appointments—successively, Ann Taylor, Paul Murphy, and Margaret Beckett spent some time as chair before resuming ministerial office. Kim Howells, the current chair, is also an ex-minister. In the annual debate on the 2007–08 ISC report, Andrew Mackinlay described this process as "Cabinet cryonics."[22]

Resources It is one thing to establish a committee with powers to oversee intelligence agencies but quite another to ensure that it has the resources to enable it to do the job in other than a purely symbolic fashion. Chris Mullin observed:

> Reference has been made to the staff who will work for the committee. That is an important point which has not been touched on so far. Who will be the staff? Will persons be sent down from Millbank or Vauxhall to service the committee? Will it be people who are employed by parliament, and who share Parliament's desire for scrutiny? Will they come from the Cabinet Office in Whitehall?

> That is rather important because hon. Members who serve on Select
> Committees know the extent to which we are dependent upon those who
> staff those Committees. Obviously hon. members could be easily led astray,
> or the committee could be led into complacency, if the staff were not of a suit-
> ably rigorous frame of mind.[23]

This has been an issue that has dogged the ISC. The members seem to have been
very energetic, meeting weekly, and with a higher attendance rate than normal for
select committees, but their staff have been from the Cabinet Office. By 2008 there
were six of them, but they were acknowledged to be overworked in preparing for
evidence sessions and drafting reports and did not conduct any research.[24] This
means that the information obtained by the ISC would normally be just written
or oral responses from the agencies to questions posed, because the ISC lacked
the resources to do the digging necessary to establish the accuracy or otherwise
of those answers. The significance of this can be illustrated by comparing their
modus operandi for the two inquiries into the July 7, 2005, bombings in London:[25]
the inadequacy of the first one, when they just "listened to" what they were told,
was acknowledged compared with the second report, when they studied the relevant surveillance tapes, videos, and notes.[26]

Between 1998 and 2004 the ISC had the services of a part-time investigator, John Morrison, a former deputy chief of defense intelligence, who carried
out several studies each year, but who was sacked after losing the confidence
of the agencies when he criticized publicly (though not with his ISC hat on)
the Government's 2002 Iraq weapons of mass destruction dossier.[27] ISC said it
had no immediate plans to replace him and the shortage of research capacity
was not to be alleviated until 2008, when the Home Secretary announced that
staffing was to be increased to eight and a new general investigator was to be
appointed.[28]

Mandate In general, committee mandates may be broader or narrower, and that
proposed for the ISC, being the same as for a select committee, was not controversial. The mandate of the ISC extended to the three intelligence agencies, but, of
course, they are not the only players in the UK intelligence community. Early in its
life, the ISC realized this and actually extended its own oversight to the Defence
Intelligence staff and to police intelligence with respect to organized crime,[29]
but the more general role of military intelligence seems to be in limbo. The ISC
did report on the handling of detainees in Iraq and Afghanistan by intelligence
personnel but did not consider the key question of the extent to which military
personnel might have been involved in the preparation of detainees for interrogation.[30] Nor has this been considered by the Defence Select Committee.[31] The issue
of oversight on military intelligence did not come up in the Commons debate on
the IS Bill but was raised by Merlyn Rees in the Lords, undoubtedly because of his
experience as Northern Ireland Secretary:

With regard to Northern Ireland, I discovered that the "dirty tricks" campaign in Northern Ireland—I possess the papers now though I did not have them at the time—included a list of politicians in all parties. They are listed under the headings of sex, politics, and finance. It is the most illiterate rubbish that I have ever read, even worse than that found in some of our national newspapers. It was quite extraordinary. A psych-ops operation was run against politicians in the south and politicians in Northern Ireland.

The Army were involved in that. I know that it has now stopped—I was told that it was stopped many years ago. But it was out of control and is another reason—I should have mentioned it earlier—why the Army, the defence security forces and intelligence bodies should come under this legislation.[32]

Access The Intelligence Services Bill, Schedule 3, read:

Access to information

3. (1) If the Director-General of the Security Service, the Chief of the Intelligence Service or the Director of GCHQ is asked by the Committee to disclose any information, then, as to the whole or any part of the information which is sought, he shall either—
    (a) arrange for it to be made available to the Committee subject to and in accordance with arrangements approved by the Secretary of State; or
    (b) inform the Committee that it cannot be disclosed either—
        (i) because it is sensitive information (as defined in paragraph 4 below) which, in his opinion, should not be made available under paragraph (a) above; or
        (ii) because the Secretary of State has determined that it should not be disclosed.
    (2) The fact that any particular information is sensitive information shall not prevent its disclosure under sub-paragraph (1)(a) above if the Director-General, the Chief or the Director (as the case may require) considers it safe to disclose it.
    (3) Information which has not been disclosed to the Committee on the ground specified in sub-paragraph (1)(b)(i) above shall be disclosed to them if the Secretary of State considers it desirable in the public interest.
    (4) The Secretary of State shall not make a determination under sub-paragraph (1)(b)(ii) above with respect to any information on the grounds of national security alone and, subject to that, he shall not make such a determination unless the information appears to him to be of such a nature that, if he were requested to produce it before

a Departmental Select Committee of the House of Commons, he
would think it proper not to do so.

(5) The disclosure of information to the Committee in accordance with
the preceding provisions of this paragraph shall be regarded for the
purposes of the 1989 Act or, as the case may be, this Act as necessary
for the proper discharge of the functions of the Security Service, the
Intelligence Service or, as the case may require, GCHQ.[33]

Sensitive information

4.   The following information is sensitive information for the purposes of
paragraph 3 above—

(a) information which might lead to the identification of, or provide
details of, sources of information, other assistance or operational
methods available to the Security Service, the Intelligence Service
or GCHQ;

(b) information about particular operations which have been, are being
or are proposed to be undertaken in pursuance of any of the functions of those bodies; and

(c) information provided by, or by an agency of, the Government of a
territory outside the United Kingdom where that Government does
not consent to the disclosure of the information.

In essence, the government proposed that the agencies could make any information available to the ISC unless either they determined it to be "sensitive" or if a
minister decided it should not be disclosed. Sensitive information was that concerning sources, methods, operations, and third party information from other
countries (Schedule 3). This prescription was challenged throughout by arguments that the ISC should have the same power as a select committee "to send for
persons and papers"; for example, David Steele, for the Liberal Democrats, stated:
"If it does not yet have the power to send for persons and papers, such a power
should be written into the Bill in (Standing) Committee because the committee
will not be able to operate effectively without it."[34]

Similarly, Peter Mandelson, for Labour, said: "I question whether the powers
of intelligence chiefs and Ministers to block information and restrict access are
too great. . . . Paragraph 4 of schedule 3 refers to 'sensitive information,' which is
by any measure extremely embracing, not to say draconian, in its sweep. I wonder
whether there should be some override mechanism or some means of arbitration
between the individuals and bodies proposed in the Bill."[35] And even the Conservative Michael Mates, subsequently to become the longest-serving member
of the ISC, agreed: "The powers to send for persons and papers and to summon
witnesses have been excluded from the Bill because they would make it look too
much like a Select Committee. The Government had better give the committee
the right to make such requests, or there is little point in setting it up. It will lose
its credibility before it has begun its work. If members of the committee have the

power to make such requests, it will cause some chagrin in official circles, but the Government always have the power not to respond. The Government and ministers may refuse to answer questions."[36]

On the specific issue of access to information on operations Dale Campbell-Savours, appointed to the ISC in 1997, asked: "If the committee is neither parliamentary nor a select committee, but almost a quasi-departmental committee with Members of Parliament nominated to it by the Prime Minister, and if its members are subject to the Official Secrets Act—as was said in the House—why, in principle, should it not be able to ask questions about operational matters?"[37]

But even some members of his own party did not support him; Jack Cunningham argued, "As always, I give my hon. friend full marks for persistence. Whatever the status of the committee, it should not be able to interfere in operational matters."[38] Intentionally or otherwise, Cunningham seemed to miss the point: "interfering" does smack of a control function whereas "asking questions about" is a legitimate oversight function.

But the government was not to be moved: Douglas Hogg emphasized that:

> in the end there is a difference between our concepts and those of Opposition Members. In effect, Opposition Members are trying to create a Select Committee. We are against that. They are seeking to cloak the committee that we are establishing with all the powers of a Select Committee. I am against that. I believe that the committee we have created has been given adequate powers to perform its oversight functions. Opposition Members want to give it an unfettered right to call for persons and papers. . . . In the generality of cases, the information or the personnel will come before the committee subject to the authority of the head of the agency and the terms of schedule 3.[39]

Has access to information been a problem for the ISC? Not in the sense that members have been routinely denied that for which they asked; indeed they report just one case in which the Government has failed to make documents available.[40] Just because information could be defined as sensitive does not mean that it has been refused to the ISC; for example, Stephen Lander, while MI5 Director General (2001), declared that he would be a rich man if he had received a pound for every time he had discussed operations with members of the Committee. Certainly, in some cases the ISC has been given unprecedented access, including to ministerial papers of previous governments, which is almost unheard of. But this has occurred when it suited the government itself to have the ISC carry out an inquiry into a controversial matter, as, for example, the Mitrokhin papers.[41] This archive of KGB files had been brought out of the USSR by a British agent in 1992 and were subsequently published in 1999. They revealed the identities of British citizens who had spied for the KGB but had not been prosecuted.[42] There is something to be said for the argument that, by building trust with the agencies and the government and ensuring that its own information handling was secure, the ISC has developed a relationship in which the agencies feel comfortable sharing information that they could, if they wished, keep hidden, because the ISC simply does not have the resources to ferret it out. But there is a more subtle dimension to obtaining information. As any academic or journalist will testify, if you are interviewing intelligence officers you have to know what questions to ask because they will respond (or not) *only* to what they are asked. In its first report the ISC said "we hope and expect to be kept informed of information that is relevant to our remit,"[43] but some years later Tom King observed more realistically, "If you don't ask for it, you don't get it."[44]

Reporting This issue provoked arguments similar to those regarding access: how independent of ministers would ISC be? The bill proposed that the ISC would make its annual report to the prime minister, who would lay it before Parliament after the exclusion of any material prejudicial to the functions of the agencies (s.10 (5)-(7)). The opposition argued throughout that ISC should report direct to Parliament; for example, their amendment at report stage proposed this subject to the committee excluding any material "prejudicial to national security." Any disputes between the ISC and the agencies would be resolved by the prime minister. Though the effect would have been much the same, the symbolism would have been quite different—government anxious to retain the PM's position as ultimately responsible for national security, the opposition more concerned that the committee be seen to be independent of government. Peter Mandelson proposed the amendment:

> Our justification in making the change is threefold. First, we think that it is important to make clear that the authority for the committee's oversight responsibility is derived from parliament and that that is borne out by its reporting directly back to its parent, which is parliament. The committee is an important extension of the scrutiny role of parliament, and not simply an instrument of the executive role of Government. It is the voice of parliament, not an extension of the Prime Minister's office. That would be made all the clearer by making the committee submit its annual report to parliament, rather than via the Prime Minister.
>
> Secondly, we think that it is important that everything possible is done to engage the sincere interest of the House of Commons in the important oversight function of the committee . . . and the change we are proposing would have some considerable symbolic value in achieving that.
>
> Thirdly, although we acknowledge that the committee's powers are circumscribed, it is nonetheless important for the committee to exercise some control over the timing of its report, even though the Prime Minister's veto remains in some form over the contents of the report. As presently drafted, the Intelligence and Security Committee does not have the right to publish its own report, let alone any power to determine the timing of the publication of the report. The Opposition think that is surely wrong.[45]

Again, the government rejected the argument, Douglas Hogg stated: "(The ISC's) members are appointed by the Prime Minister—it is not a select Committee—who is responsible to the House for intelligence and security. It is logical that the committee should report to him, for he appointed it and is accountable for the policies in respect of which it exercises oversight for the House."[46]

Clearly, what does happen prior to the publication of the report is the same process of negotiation between members and officials over what should be excluded—John Gilbert described during a Commons debate the process that had been going on for years in the Defence Select Committee[47] which, according to members interviewed by this author in 2008, characterizes the ISC also.[48] The ISC reports proudly that no material has ever been excluded from the report going to Parliament without their consent but that is not necessarily the best way to judge an *oversight* committee.[49] Some observers have suggested that the ISC has been too ready to accommodate agency requests for deletions.[50]

Political will   Whatever final decisions were made as to the mandate of the ISC and the rules relating to access and reporting, the effectiveness of the committee would depend much on the energy of the members. In social science terminology: the *structures* would provide the context for the committee, but the energy and skills of the members as agents would be important factors in determining its impact. The required qualities of members came up several times in debate; for example, one suggestion was that members should have some knowledge of intelligence work.[51] This was not taken up but does make the point that those with such experience would certainly have the advantage of understanding aspects of the world of intelligence while possibly raising questions as to whether their former loyalties might lead to too much "understanding" of the difficulties faced. But a more frequent comment was of the need for independence in members, for example; in the Lords debate, Roy Jenkins, the former deputy leader of the Labour Party, having criticized the fact that the prime minister had complete freedom to fire as well as hire members, said:

> In my view a more important point in relation to the committee is that people of questioning, sceptical and even iconoclastic turn of mind should be appointed to it. Those qualities are in no way incompatible with full loyalty to the state and nation, but it is a field in which soft obfuscating answers are rather part of the tradition. If the committee is to be effective, as I hope it will be, and if the bill is to be worthwhile, as I hope it will be, we need members of the committee who will not accept such soft or obfuscating answers.[52]

Nobody has carried out an analysis of those appointed to the ISC over the years in terms of any "index of independence:" looked at superficially, it seems as though the committee has the same mixture of talents as any other, but there is certainly no evidence that only sycophants have been appointed. For example, after his 1997 election victory, Blair may have retained Tom King as chair but he also appointed Kevin Barron, the former miner; Dale Campbell-Savours, one of Jenkins's icono-clasts; and the young, up-and-coming Yvette Cooper, who was a strong critic of the ISC's lack of powers in key areas during her short membership.

"Formidable power" or *"pretence"*? As is the nature of things in the adversarial parliamentary system in the United Kingdom, the conclusion of the debate sharp-ened rather than resolved differences. For the government, William Waldegrave concluded the second reading debate.

> The committee will be fully trusted, and fully inside the secret wall. I believe that the result . . . will be to spread the reassurance that senior, trusted people on both sides of the House share the secrets of the services, and have a formi-dable power to cause trouble for the Government.
>
> Somebody asked earlier where the teeth were. The teeth consist of the fact that the committee, staffed by very senior members of the House, will have the right not to publish stuff that would damage national security—which it would not want to do—but to write a report saying, 'We believe that things are not being handled properly, and that Ministers are not responding properly.' No Government in their senses would want to risk such criticism. That is why the committee will be powerful, and that is why I commend the Bill to the House.[53]

But Allan Rogers, to be appointed to the first ISC, concluded the opposition's case at report stage:

> Unfortunately, clause 10, which sets up the Intelligence and Security Com-mittee, does not also set up a process of accountability. There is no breaking of the ring of secrecy. There is no way of operating outside the ring of the Secretary of State and the Joint Intelligence Committee tasking the security services, of the Secretary of State issuing a warrant so that they can operate outside the law where they feel that is necessary, of the services reporting back to the Secretary of State, the Secretary of State filtering information before it comes to the Intelligence and Security Committee and the Prime Minister and the head *sic* of the agencies using their right to sideline infor-mation. The circle is too tight and too complete.
>
> The committee will be a charade, a pretence at accountability.[54]

Lessons Learned?

These last comments might have led one to expect that when Labour came into power in 1997, they would have radically strengthened the ISC, but that would mis-understand the extent to which parliamentary debates are set pieces of opposition to government proposals rather than deeply held convictions. It was not until 2008 that any changes were made in the ISC and these were only marginal, such as could be achieved without requiring new legislation. Thus, the key issues of prime ministerial appointment, access to information, and reporting remain unchanged. This might support the cynical view that opposition in Parliament is synthetic and not to be taken seriously, but the points raised in the debate are important; it is rather that perspectives on security matters change significantly when people become part of government.

However, it cannot be said that there has been any great outcry as to the short-comings of the committee. Those academics who have studied the ISC, including this author, have broadly agreed that the ISC succeeded in developing oversight from its beginnings, introduced financial accountability of the agencies, produced informative reports, and established itself as a serious critic of the agencies. Less positively, it has been criticized for failing to investigate serious allegations relating to, for example, Libya and Northern Ireland, and for soft-pedaling on occasions. The main criticism concerns the ISC's poor performance on the intelligence aspects of the controversial invasion of Iraq, including suggestions that it needed to revisit the issue.[55] This possibility would appear to have been superseded now by the June 2009 announcement of the privy council inquiry to be led by John Chilcot, which has produced, at the time of writing, some interesting revelations by former intelligence officials about the conduct of the British government in the approach to the Iraq war.

Although, as noted above, the ISC's second report on the 7/7 bombings provided a much more detailed examination of the possibility that they could have been prevented, and will be much studied by students of counterterrorist intelligence, it has still failed to satisfy some observers.[56] Most importantly, the families of the victims renewed their calls for an independent inquiry because of what one of them described as a "catalogue of excuses for MI5's narrow focus and failure of intelligence caused by failure of imagination and failure of cooperation" between MI5 and special branch at a critical time.[57] It remains to be seen whether the verdicts and recommendations of the inquest to be published in May 2011 satisfy them or whether a further inquiry is ordered. The continuing resource problem at ISC can be gauged by looking at the workload since the 2005 election. The committee was formed a few days after the July 7 London bombings with only three members remaining from the previous one, none of them on the government side. It sent its report of the 7/7 investigation to the prime minister in March 2006 and its annual report for 2005–6 in June. About this time ISC started its investigation into rendition, on which it reported a year later in June 2007. A month earlier, the conclusion of the CREVICE trial, in which five British men, arrested in 2004, were convicted for their planning of bombing attacks. The publication suggested that MI5 had known more about the 7/7 plotters before the bombings than had been revealed in their first 7/7 report. This led the ISC to reinvestigate and it sent its second report to the prime minister in July 2008. In the meantime, it sent its annual report for 2006–7 in December 2007 and then that for 2007–8 in December 2008.

The actual publication of the second 7/7 report was held up by ongoing court proceedings; when these were completed in April 2009, the ISC updated its report with a brief appendix and the whole report was published in May 2009. It is the relative thoroughness of this second 7/7 report, from a committee with no research staff, that probably explains why the 2007–8 annual report is one of the weakest. Careful reading shows the extent to which it is based on documentary evidence from the agencies and other departments rather than on actual investigation. Another reason is possibly the disruption of personnel during 2008: Paul Murphy left the chair in January to become minister for Wales, his replacement, Margaret Beckett, lasted nine months before going to the Ministry of Housing, and one of the two original members, Alan Beith, left in November.

But behind these disruptions caused by shifting personnel, there is a deeper structural issue relating to the ISC that must be considered. Whereas both Labour and Liberal parties made broadly similar proposals in the 1980s for systematic reform and oversight of the security intelligence agencies, the only legislation emanating from the Thatcher government was defensive and minimal, in response to an adverse ECHR decision on interception of communications, or in anticipation of another one on security surveillance. The Interception of Communications Act 1985 (IOCA) established a commissioner to provide an annual review of ministerial authorizations for interception and a tribunal to receive and investigate public complaints, both of which passed the ECHR test for minimal protection of rights but neither of which could be considered adequate oversight. By 1992, the government was prepared to move forward with the establishment of the ISC but, rather than instituting a more coherent overall oversight structure, chose merely to attach it to the commissioner and tribunal. The home secretary said:

> "The three bits of machinery have different functions. . . . The commissioner is responsible for the exercise by the Secretary of State of the authority given to the Secretary of State under the Bill. The tribunal is responsible for investigating complaints and may ask the commissioner to follow up the investigation of such complaints. The oversight committee . . . is responsible for overseeing policy, administration and expenditure.
>
> It is an issue that hon. members will want to debate in detail in Committee, but I do not see why there should be an overlap between the three separate functions allocated under the Bill to the three separate mechanisms, individuals, or groups which the Bill proposes.[58]

Overlap would, indeed, be wasteful, given that resources for oversight are scarce, but the government actually sought to prevent positive interaction between the commissioner and the ISC, refusing the committee's request to have sight of the confidential appendices in the reports made to the prime minister.[59] But it is precisely because oversight resources are few that an effective structure *requires* cooperation between those involved, albeit from different perspectives. For example, while it is not appropriate for members of Parliament to adjudicate personal complaints about security matters, it can only help their education in intelligence matters to know of complaints and how they were disposed of. Labour did propose this in an amendment at report stage but it was rejected by the government because the superior access to information enjoyed by commissioners and tribunal—to whom members of the agencies had a legal duty to disclose—would give them access to sensitive material unobtainable by the ISC.[60] In recent years, the ISC has itself sought to reduce the compartmentalization by holding "informal discussions" with the intelligence services and Interception of Communications commissioners but the formal "compartmentalization" of oversight remains.[61]

The story of intelligence oversight in the United Kingdom so far has been concerned with the accountability of state intelligence agencies in this country. Broadly, despite the inadequacies of the structure discussed above, it is a story of success, certainly when compared with the absurdities of secrecy about intelligence perpetrated in the 1980s, as illustrated by the doomed attempt to ban *Spycatcher*. These memoirs of a former MI5 officer alleged that a previous director general had been a Soviet spy.[62] Yet, the nature of the challenge has shifted significantly in recent years, specifically with the growth of intelligence *networks* across both state and corporate sectors and transnationally. The issue that has brought this into sharp relief is the policy of extraordinary rendition after 9/11 and the question of the alleged involvement, or at least complicity, of the UK agencies. There is inadequate space here to do justice to the unfolding complexities of this issue, which has, in fact, already been visited by the ISC.[63] In 2005 it reported on the handling of detainees in Afghanistan, Guantánamo, and Iraq, and in 2007 on rendition.[64] These reports identify some shortcomings in terms of training for intelligence officers in human rights issues and other procedural matters, and that on rendition makes some unusually robust criticism of US practice in ignoring caveats as to the use of UK intelligence passed to them.[65] But the fact that the ISC just did not have the resources or the will necessary for a proper inquiry was repeatedly indicated as further substantial allegations of UK complicity in mistreatment surfaced through a variety of mechanisms, including the reports of the Council of Europe, journalists, and court cases in which detainees sought disclosure of documents and/or redress.[66]

The High Court was especially critical of the Security Service in an August 2008 judgment in the case of Binyam Mohamed, and this prompted a reinvestigation by the ISC which led to the "rediscovery" of thirteen MI5 and MI6 documents that should have been disclosed to the court. In a somewhat unusual step, the ISC issued a press release in March 2009, to the effect that it had sent a report and recommendations to the prime minister on its further investigations. While ISA s.10(6) required the prime minister to lay a copy of each annual report before parliament, there is no such obligation with other reports, so it will be interesting to see whether this one sees the light of day. Gordon Brown has said that new guidance to intelligence officers regarding interrogations would be published once reviewed by the intelligence services.[67] The new government did so in July 2010 at the same time as announcing a judicial inquiry into the torture allegations.[68] However, it seems that the advice promulgated in 2004 will not be published, although the ISC saw the advice and referred to it in their 2005 report on detainees.[69]

Clearly, there are aspects of legal accountability, such as complaints and civil or criminal actions, which must be kept separate from a political body such as the ISC. Nevertheless, the committee does need to build on its informal contacts with other oversight institutions, including lawyers, journalists, and NGOs, so that it leverages its own limited research resources. This includes avoiding turf battles with other parliamentary committees such as Foreign and Home Affairs and the Joint Committee on Human Rights (JCHR). When ministers and agency heads use the existence of the ISC to avoid appearing before these other committees—for example, Jonathan Evans used his accountability to ISC as a reason for not appearing before the JCHR, though he offered them a "confidential briefing"—the ISC should make sure that those committees' questions inform their own interviews.[70]

An early observer of the ISC commented that its development should be understood less in terms of an incoming tide of democratic oversight than as a form of risk management in the new post-Cold War era. As the agencies moved into the more public arenas of combating terrorism and organized crime, and in the context of ECHR requirements, they would be unable to rely on the old nostrum of complete secrecy. Therefore, the ISC was envisaged as part of a package, providing increased but carefully controlled openness. It would also provide a further forum within which Whitehall struggles for budgets and powers could be continued: "if you can manage to convince the (ISC) that your proposals are the right ones, they will do the advocacy for you!".[71] Certainly, the language of ISC reports is the language of Whitehall and Westminster, intelligible in all its subtlety to citizens of that peculiar village but far less enlightening to the rest of us, even allowing for the extensive redactions. Whether the scandalous intelligence abuses of human rights in recent years have much impact on the ISC in the longer run depends on the extent to which complicity of the UK agencies is demonstrated and, if so, whether this was the result of policy or individual aberration. If the former, then it will be critical for the legitimacy of the ISC that it demonstrates greater political will to locate responsibility on ministers than it managed in its report on the intelligence shortcomings prior to the invasion of Iraq.

NOTES

1. Laurence Lustgarten and Ian Leigh, *In from the Cold: National Security and Parliamentary Democracy* (Clarendon Press: Oxford, 1994), 344–46.
2. Richard Norton-Taylor, "Major Asks MI6 Chief to Stay on to Advise on Key Changes," *Guardian*, July 20, 1992, 5.
3. House of Lords, December 9, 1993, *Hansard*, cols. 1027–28.
4. Mark Phythian, "The British Experience with Intelligence Accountability," *Intelligence and National Security*, 22 (2007): 75–99.

5. House of Lords, December 9 1993, op.cit., col. 1028.

6. House of Commons, February 22, 1994, *Hansard*, col. 229.

7. It is worth noting that in some presidential systems, such as in the United States, the legislature may retain "control" powers, for example, over budgets, and be notified of covert actions in advance. Congressional committees have no power to veto proposed covert actions but may deny the necessary funds.

8. Peter Gill, "The Intelligence and Security Committee and the Challenge of Security Networks," *Review of International Studies*, 35 (2009): 929–41 at 929.

9. Peter Gill and Mark Phythian, *Intelligence in an Insecure World* (Cambridge: Polity 2006), 156–61.

10. Hans Born and Ian Leigh, *Making Intelligence Accountable: Legal Standards and Best Practice for Oversight of Intelligence Agencies* (Oslo: Publishing House of the Parliament of Norway, 2005).

11. Peter Gill, "Evaluating Intelligence Oversight Committees: the UK Intelligence and Security Committee and the 'War on Terror,'" *Intelligence and National Security* 22 (2007): 16–18.

12. www.legislation.gov.uk/ukpga/1994/13/contents.

13. House of Commons, February 22, 1994, *Hansard*, col. 171.

14. House of Commons, April 27, 1994, *Hansard*, col. 328.

15. Anthony Glees et al., *The Open Side of Secrecy: Britain's Intelligence and Security Committee* (London: Social Affairs Unit, 2006), 177–78; Mark Phythian, "The British Experience with Intelligence Accountability," (2007), op.cit. 98.

16. Joint Committee on Human Rights, *Allegations of UK Complicity in Torture*, Twenty-Third Report of Session 2008–09, HL152/HC230, August 2009, para. 66.

17. Foreign Affairs Committee, *Human Rights Annual Report 2008*, Seventh Report of Session 2008–09, HC557, August 2009, para. 63.

18. House of Commons, February 22, 1994, *Hansard*, cols. 186–87.

19. Ibid., col. 183.

20. Ibid., cols. 205–6.

21. Hans Born and Iain Leigh, *Making Intelligence Accountable* (2005), op.cit., 85; Glees et al., *The Open Side of Secrecy*, op.cit., 181–82.

22. House of Commons, May 7, 2009, *Hansard*, col. 424.

23. House of Commons, February 22, 1994, *Hansard*, cols. 195–96.

24. Peter Gill, "The Intelligence and Security Committee and the Challenge of Security Networks," *Review of International Studies*, op.cit., 936.

25. ISC, *London Terrorist Attacks on 7 July 2005*, Cm6785, May, 2006; ISC, *Could 7/7 Have Been Prevented?*, Cm7617, May, 2009.

26. Peter Gill, "The Intelligence and Security Committee and the Challenge of Security Networks," *Review of International Studies* (2009), op.cit., 936.

27. Peter Gill, "Evaluative Intelligence Oversight," op.cit., 29.

28. House of Commons, May 7, 2009, col. 435.

29. ISC, *Interim Report*, Cm2873, May 1995.

30. ISC, *Handling of Detainees by UK Intelligence Personnel in Afghanistan, Guantánamo Bay and Iraq*, Cm6469, March 2005.

31. House of Lords, December 9, 1993, *Hansard*, col. 1055.
32. Ibid., col. 186.
33. www.legislation.gov.uk/ukpga/1994/13/contents.
34. House of Commons, February 22, 1994, *Hansard*, col. 186.
35. Ibid., col. 228.
36. Ibid., col. 206.
37. Ibid., col. 171.
38. Ibid.
39. House of Commons, April 27, 1991, *Hansard*, col. 333.
40. ISC, *Annual Report*, 2006–7, Cm7299, January 2008, 38.
41. ISC, *Agencies Handling of the Information Provided by Mr. Mitrokhin*, Cm4764, June 2000.
42. See Christopher Andrew and Vasiliy Mitrokhin, *The Mitrokhin Archive* (London: Allen Lane).
43. ISC, *Interim Report*, Cm2873, May 1995, para. 8.
44. Cited in Glees et al., op.cit., 101.
45. House of Commons, April 27, 1994, *Hansard*, col. 322.
46. Ibid.
47. House of Commons, February 22, 1994, *Hansard*, cols. 181–82.
48. Peter Gill, "The Intelligence and Security Committee and the Challenge of Security Networks," op.cit., 936.
49. ISC, *Annual Report for 2007–08*, Cm7542, March 2009, iv.
50. Glees et al., *The Open Side of Secrecy*, op.cit., 186.
51. House of Lords, December 9, 1993, *Hansard*, col. 1051.
52. Ibid., col. 1036.
53. House of Commons, February 22, 1994, *Hansard*, col. 240.
54. House of Commons, April 27, 1994, *Hansard*, col. 351.
55. Peter Gill, "The Intelligence and Security Committee and the Challenge of Security Networks," op.cit., 931–32.
56. ISC, *Could 7/7 Have Been Prevented?*, Cm7617, May 2009.
57. Rachel Williams and Richard Norton-Taylor, "Police and MI5 Cleared of Blame despite Failure to Follow Up Terror Links of Bombers' Leader," *Guardian*, May 20, 2009, 7.
58. House of Commons, February 22, 1994, *Hansard*, col. 161.
59. HMG, *Government Response to ISC Annual Report for 1999–2000*, Cm5013, December 2000, para. 15.
60. House of Commons, April 27, 1994, *Hansard*, cols. 338–41.
61. ISC, *Annual Report for 2007–08*, Cm7542, March 2009, 158.
62. Peter Wright, *Spycatcher* (London: Viking, 1987).
63. See fuller discussions in Richard Aldrich, "Global Intelligence Cooperation versus Accountability: New Facets to an Old Problem," *Intelligence and National Security*, 24 (2009): 26–56; Peter Gill, "Security Intelligence and Human Rights: Illuminating the 'Heart of Darkness'?" *Intelligence and National Security*, 24 (2009): 78–102.

64. ISC, *Handling of Detainees by UK Intelligence Personnel in Afghanistan, Guantánamo Bay and Iraq*, Cm6469, March, 2005; ISC, *Rendition*, Cm7171, July 2007.

65. ISC, *Rendition*, Cm7171, July 2007, para. 137.

66. Dick Marty, *Secret Detentions and Unlawful Transfers of Detainees involving Council of Europe Member States: Second Report*, Doc.11302 rev., Council of Europe, June 11, 2007; Grey, *Ghost Plane: The True Story of the CIA Rendition and Torture Program* (New York: St, Martin's Press, 2006); Ian Cobain, "The Truth about Torture: Britain's Catalogue of Shame," *Guardian*, July 8, 2009.

67. House of Commons, March 18, 2009, *Hansard*, col. 55WS.

68. Ian Cobain, "Pressure from Courts and Victims Forced Torture Inquiry," *Guardian*, July 7, 2010.

69. ISC, *Handling of Detainees by UK Intelligence Personnel in Afghanistan, Guantánamo Bay and Iraq*, Cm6469, March 2005, paras. 101 and 123.

70. Joint Committee on Human Rights, *Allegations of UK Complicity in Torture*, Twenty-Third Report of Session 2008–09, HL152/HC230, August 2009, para. 55.

71. Kenneth Robertson, "Recent Reform of Intelligence in the United Kingdom: Democratization or Risk Management?," *Intelligence and National Security* 13 (1998): 144–58.

DOCUMENT 2.1:   Intelligence Services Bill

Intelligence Services Bill [H.L.]

HL Deb 09 December 1993 vol 550 cc1023-79 1023

§ 3.31 p.m.

§ *The Lord Chancellor (Lord Mackay of Clashfern)*

My Lords, I beg to move that this Bill be now read a second time.

A little over five years ago I presented to your Lordships' House the Security Service Bill. I described it at the time as a most important and appropriate legislative response to the desirability of putting the Security Service on a statutory basis. That step, which I believe has proved a most successful one, marked the start of this Government's policy to be as open as possible about security and intelligence matters without prejudicing national security, the effectiveness of the security and intelligence services or the safety of their staff. Since making that positive and carefully measured move, this Government have avowed the continuing existence of the Secret Intelligence Service and published booklets on the Security Service and the central intelligence machinery. The first of those booklets touched on the excellent work, some of it on new tasks, being done by the Security Service. The second described the central mechanisms for tasking, co-ordinating and resourcing the United Kingdom's intelligence services and for overseeing and reporting on the intelligence they produce.

As a further step forward in this process, I now welcome the opportunity to present the Intelligence Services Bill. . . .

col. 1027 . . . As for the intelligence and security committee which I mentioned earlier, that is provided for under Clause 10 and Schedule 3. It will comprise six members drawn from both Houses, who will be appointed by the Prime Minister after consultation with the Leader of the Opposition. The committee's role will be to examine the expenditure, administration and policy of all three services: SIS, GCHQ and the Security Service.

Like the commissioner, the committee will be required to make an annual report to the Prime Minister which will be laid before Parliament, subject to security excisions. It will be able to submit *ad hoc* reports to the Prime Minister on matters relevant to its functions. Provision is made of course to ensure the secrecy of the committee's proceedings and to enable the heads of the three services to disclose information, subject to only limited restrictions, to the committee.

DOCUMENT 2.1: Intelligence Services Bill *(Continued)*

Why, some of your Lordships may ask, are the Government introducing now something which less than five years ago we deemed inappropriate. I myself, your Lordships may recall, felt during the debate on the Security Service Bill that the time was not right for such a step. What has changed? In deciding in 1989 that the Security Service should continue to be accountable to Parliament through Ministers, the Government argued that to give Parliament a greater oversight role would be unsatisfactory since, in order to preserve the effectiveness of the service and the safety of those working for it, Parliament would have to respect the secrecy of certain information. An oversight body with no access to secrets would have access to little of interest or importance to the service's work and be of scarce interest to Parliament. On the other hand, a body with broad access to secrets would be unable to report in full to Parliament and therefore would also be unsatisfactory. Nonetheless, in other ways the Security Service Act was a far-reaching step in terms of greater openness and accountability, putting the service on a statutory basis and establishing a commissioner and a tribunal to deal with grievances.

But a good deal of water has passed under the bridge since then, and, as your Lordships will know, the Government have continued to look for ways to allow greater access and to disclose more information when this has been deemed compatible with national security. Back in 1989, for example, the Secret Intelligence Service had not even been avowed. Given the close co-operation between the Security Service and SIS in certain areas, oversight of the Security Service alone would clearly have led to problems. Since 1989, however, the Government have named both the director general of the Security Service and the chief of SIS; announced the moves of the respective agencies into Thames House and Vauxhall Cross; released a number of previously withheld government records; and this year, as I have already mentioned, published information booklets on both the Security Service and the central intelligence machinery. And most recently, the Government have disclosed the size of the aggregate 1028 budget for the agencies, and undertaken to bring all this expenditure onto a single Vote. The Bill has been prepared with the benefit of more than four years' experience since the Security Service Act. Things have moved on. The climate has changed. Greater openness has gained momentum. We believe that it is now right to take this further important step.

. . . .

col. 1034 Lord Jenkins of Hillhead . . . I shall deal first with MI5's political surveillance role. That involves above all a fine judgment between what is subversion and what is legitimate dissent, which in my experience is unlikely

DOCUMENT 2.1:   Intelligence Services Bill *(Continued)*

to be found in those who live in the distorting and *Alice-through-the-Looking-Glass* world in which falsehood becomes truth, fact becomes fiction and fantasy becomes reality. I would therefore pull MI5 totally out of its political surveillance role.

I am almost equally doubtful about the associated internal political intelligence role. Presumably the object of that is to help Ministers with useful information. However, in my experience the organisation concerned consumed far more of my time as a Minister with its own internal squabbles than any useful information which it ever provided. The balance was distinctly negative.

That leaves the other two main activities; anti-terrorism and counter-espionage. Clearly, both are still necessary, although the latter perhaps a little less urgently so than at times in the past. I do not doubt that we need some of the continuing activities of the security services. However, at a time when some of their roles have shrunk and some ought to be shrunk we should heed the wise words of the noble and learned Lord, Lord Howe of Aberavon, who in last month's television programme on MI6, said: <u>1035</u> We don't want to be inventing or appearing to invent new targets to keep people busy when their old targets have disappeared". People like to be kept busy in their jobs. They certainly like to have their budgets kept intact and those involved here are considerable. I am not convinced that the international crime rings are a suitable new target for the security services. I believe that the police are much more skilled and expert in dealing with crime than are the security services. It is a different range of operation from anything that they have done previously. We should be cautious about putting them into that area to provide, as it were, a substitute for other activities, some of which have become less necessary as a result of changes in the international situation . . . .

. . . . The mechanism provided in the Bill is for the committee to be made up of six Members of both Houses of Parliament who can come, in varying proportions, from both Houses of Parliament. It is not specified, which is rather unusual in regard to these <u>1036</u> arcane matters, that they should be Privy Counsellors. I do not object to that in the least. I believe that it is probably wise not to include that provision. Apart from anything else, the number of Privy Counsellors who are not members of the Conservative Party are running rather thin. Therefore, that widens the field as regards choice.

I understand that it is proposed that three members should be from the government side of the House, two should be from the Official Opposition and I understand that it is intended that one should be from my own party.

DOCUMENT 2.1: Intelligence Services Bill *(Continued)*

The mechanism of appointment, as laid down, is that it should be made by the Prime Minister after consultation with the Leader of the Opposition. I assume that there will be equal consultation with the leader of any other party from which a member is to be appointed.

It seems to me that Schedule 3(2) (d) is a rather curious provision. It appears to give the Prime Minister the right to replace a member at any time. Can that really be intended? I cannot imagine that working out in practice, but it seems to be an odd infringement of the independence of a member of the committee. Of course, if he ceases to be a Member of either House, which is also provided for, he would go automatically, but it seems to me rather odd that it should be done, even in theory, at the whim of the Prime Minister.

In my view a more important point in relation to the committee is that people of a questioning, sceptical and even iconoclastic turn of mind should be appointed to it. Those qualities are in no way incompatible with full loyalty to the state and nation, but it is a field in which soft, obfuscating answers are rather part of the tradition. If the committee is to be effective, as I hope it will be, and if the Bill is to be worthwhile, as I hope it will be, we need members of the committee who will not accept such soft or obfuscating answers. . . .

col. 1051 Lord Campbell of Croy: . . . In addition to the points made by the noble Lord, Lord Hunt of Tanworth, I should like tentatively to make the following suggestion. Members of the new committee should have some knowledge and experience of secret intelligence or security work. As I said, they do not need to be Privy Counsellors, although those who have been selected in the past have all been in that position. In particular, they should have a familiarity with that boundary beyond which subjects are secret and should not be mentioned or touched upon, even in the most tangential way, usually because they are connected with operations. Any lapses of that kind in security are likely to happen when such familiarity is absent . . . .

col. 1054 Lord Merlyn-Rees: . . . Perhaps I can raise one other issue before turning to Northern Ireland; that is, the issue of the special branch. Like others, I had close contact with the special branch over several years and lived cheek by jowl with its members. I know the excellent work that they do. Most police forces have a special branch and the biggest is in the Met. They have a national responsibility for anti-terrorist work. I looked at the report yesterday of the HM Chief Inspector of Constabulary, which refers to the work of special branches in different police forces. The Met Commissioner of Police refers to his.

DOCUMENT 2.1: Intelligence Services Bill *(Continued)*

MI5 and special branch have always worked together and now MI5 takes the lead. I ask the noble and learned Lord the Lord Chancellor to pass on to the Government that if special branch in this respect—not in crime—is involved in the work that is covered by the Bill, then in that respect also its work should be covered by the Bill. 1055 Where does the distinction lie? One distinction is that special branch makes the arrest. MI5 has no constable powers, but that matter should at least be considered.

With regard to Northern Ireland, I discovered that the "dirty tricks" campaign in Northern Ireland—I possess the papers now though I did not have them at the time—included a list of politicians in all parties. They are listed under the headings of sex, politics and finance. It is the most illiterate rubbish that I have ever read, even worse than that found in some of our national newspapers. It was quite extraordinary. A psych-ops operation was run against politicians in the south and politicians in Northern Ireland. It is no way to win the battle of Northern Ireland, let alone to get involved in politics here.

The Army were involved in that. I know that it has now stopped—I was told that it was stopped many years ago. But it was out of control and is another reason—I should have mentioned it earlier—why the Army, the defence security forces and intelligence bodies should come under this legislation.

House of Commons: February 22, 1994, Second Reading Debate

col. 161 Mr. Hurd: . . . The three bits of machinery have different functions, which I am trying to describe to the House. The commissioner is responsible for the exercise by the Secretary of State of the authority given to the Secretary of State under the Bill. The tribunal is responsible for investigating complaints and may ask the commissioner to follow up the investigation of such complaints. The oversight committee, with which I shall deal later, is responsible for overseeing policy administration and expenditure.

It is an issue that hon. Members will want to debate in detail in Committee, but I do not see why there should be an overlap between the three separate functions allocated under the Bill to the three separate mechanisms, individuals or groups which the Bill proposes. I was about to deal with the second, the tribunal.

Clause 9 establishes the tribunal to deal with complaints against the intelligence service or GCHQ. It is closely modelled on the security service tribunal, which has been working effectively since its establishment under the 1989 Act. The tribunal will, for the first time, give those complaining about the activities of SIS or GCHQ the assurance of an independent review and

DOCUMENT 2.1: Intelligence Services Bill *(Continued)*

redress in matters that could particularly affect their privacy and prospects. The arrangements for the tribunal--now for the two agencies with which the Bill mainly deals and, formerly, for the Security Service--have regard to the European Convention on Human Rights and, we believe, fully comply with it.

Clause 10 provides something new, about which hon. Members have already asked me. It proposes an entirely new form of oversight of all three security and intelligence agencies--a committee of parliamentarians. As several hon. Members will remember, that idea was discussed in 1989, when there was considerable concern, especially among my hon. Friends, that further widening the circle of secrecy to an oversight committee might put national security at risk.

Five years ago, I shared that concern. It seemed to me that either one put such a parliamentary group inside the ring of secrecy, in which case what its members could say to the world outside, including the House, would be strictly limited, or one kept them outside the ring of secrecy, in which case they would have nothing especially important to communicate--although they would be free to communicate it. In 1989, that seemed to me a dilemma which we had not resolved. I believe that the House will judge that, with the hindsight derived from four years' experience of the Security Service Act, and since the avowal of SIS, we have now found a way of overcoming the difficulty and reconciling those considerations. I believe that the committee proposed in the Bill will provide welcome additional and effective monitoring of the agencies, without putting national security at risk. . . .

col. 171 Mr. Campbell-Savours: May I take my right hon. Friend back to my intervention during the Foreign Secretary's speech. If the committee is neither parliamentary nor a Select Committee, but almost a quasi-departmental committee with Members of Parliament nominated to it by the Prime Minister, and if its members are subject to the Official Secrets Act--as was said in the House--why, in principle, should it not be able to ask questions about operational matters ? I could understand my right hon. Friend's reservations if the committee were to be a Select Committee, but as it will be a quasi-departmental committee with Members of Parliament on it, why can it not ask questions on issues about which those Members are concerned? They will not be reporting back to Parliament.

Dr. Cunningham: As always, I give my hon. Friend full marks for persistence. Whatever the status of the committee, it should not be able to interfere in operational matters. I made that clear at the outset and I am not persuaded to change my mind.

DOCUMENT 2.1:   Intelligence Services Bill *(Continued)*

I am also concerned that the committee will apparently not have the power to call witnesses and commission papers to be brought before it. That is another weakness for a committee that is seriously expected to deal with scrutiny or oversight. Those are all serious matters and they dramatically weaken the proposal at the heart of this legislation.

Furthermore, it is proposed that the committee should not report to Parliament but to the Prime Minister. I do not regard that as parliamentary scrutiny or oversight, because the Prime Minister has the right to veto sections of its report--I call it prime ministerial oversight and scrutiny.

If we are to have an effective parliamentary watchdog to oversee such matters and to probe and scrutinise, it should report to Parliament. It cannot legitimately be called a parliamentary committee unless it does so. That is another major difference of opinion between the Opposition and the Government over the details of the legislation. . . .

col. 183 Sir Archibald Hamilton . . . . I come now to the question of the committee of parliamentarians and the great debate as to whether its members should be Privy Councillors. It will obviously be of great benefit to keep the committee relatively small. The more members the committee has, the more likely it is that leaks or mistakes will be made by Members of Parliament--who, let us face it, are not renowned for their discretion. Briefing the press seems to occupy most of the daylight hours of many of my colleagues. It will be quite a cultural change for them to become involved in any part of the Government's activities in which people are not briefing the press day and night. The smaller the committee is, therefore, the more likely it is to be secure. There seems to be an almost direct relationship between the size of a committee and the likelihood that it will operate in a reasonably secure way. . . .

col. 186 Sir David Steel: . . . I agree with the right hon. Member for Dudley, East (Dr. Gilbert) that if the committee is not covered by privilege--I do not understand why it should not be--it must be. If it does not yet have the power to send for persons and papers, such a power should be written into the Bill in Committee because the committee will not be able to operate effectively without it.

I suspect that I shall be in a minority, and I disagree with the right hon. Gentleman in this case, but I believe that there is a case for the committee's being composed of Privy Councillors. I do not say that because I believe that

DOCUMENT 2.1: Intelligence Services Bill *(Continued)*

they have any particular wisdom, and I do not share the view that they belong to a cosy, conspiratorial club, but,

[Column 187]

unless the members are Privy Councillors, we might find that the fact that there are non-Privy Councillors on the committee is used as an excuse for failing to provide the committee with the information that it needs. I think I am right in saying that one of the members of the Franks inquiry was made a Privy Councillor after his appointment so that that very danger could be avoided. The House should consider the matter very carefully. . . .

col. 195 Mr. Mullin: . . . The committee should be accountable to Parliament and, as my right hon. Friend the Member for Dudley, East (Dr. Gilbert) has said, it should have powers to send for persons and papers and should be covered by privilege. Reference has been made to the staff who will work for the committee. That is an important point which has not been touched on in the debate so far. Who will be the staff? Will

[Column 196]

persons be sent down from Millbank or Vauxhall to service the committee? Will it be people who are employed by Parliament, and who share Parliament's desire for scrutiny? Will they come from the Cabinet Office in Whitehall?

That is rather important, because hon. Members who serve on Select Committees know the extent to which we are dependent upon those who staff those Committees. Obviously, hon. Members could be easily led astray, or the committee could be led into complacency, if the staff were not of a suitably rigorous frame of mind.

Dr. Gilbert: There is another point on the question of staff to which my hon. Friend has not alluded. Will not it be necessary for the committee to have at least one member of staff from this place to advise it on procedure?

Mr. Mullin: That is right. Who staffs the committee is nearly as important as who sits on it.

As the committee will not be a Select Committee, it will not be accountable to Parliament, will not have powers to send for persons and papers that are not covered by privilege and may not have the power to select its staff, we will be dependent entirely on those lucky people who are appointed to sit on the committee.

DOCUMENT 2.1:   Intelligence Services Bill *(Continued)*

If the Government are serious in their desire to make the intelligence services accountable to the people whose interests they are supposed to serve, I hope that those who are appointed to the committee will be of a sufficiently rigorous and inquiring frame of mind. I hope that they will not be tame pussycats who will roll over to have their tummies tickled at the first sound of the magic words "national security" being whispered in their ears. . . .

col. 205 Mr. Mates: . . . My right hon. Friend the Member for Honiton (Sir P. Emery) talked about leaks. That is not something that the House or Government need to fear. There have been leaks from Select Committees, but they have never involved security. I shall tell the House an anecdote. In my 12 years on the Select Committee on Defence, nothing of a sensitive nature was ever leaked. I was present when the Committee system began in 1979. Initially, the Ministry of Defence was a little suspicious about letting us see things here and there, but we worked our way through that and by 1987 there was nothing that we did not see. On a cross-party basis, we were shown information of the most highly sensitive nature because we had shown ourselves to be trustworthy. The Labour party, in its wisdom, then decided to submit for appointment two members of the Campaign for Nuclear Disarmament. An enormous frisson went through the MOD as if things could never be the same again, and its good working relationship with the Committee was going to stop.

A very senior person in the organisation, who had better remain nameless, asked me what we should do. I said, "You must carry on as before until the trust is broken. That is the only way in which we can proceed, and if we do not a number of members of the Committee will explain vociferously." We went on sharing the most sensitive and highly secret information and there was never any form of leak. Some of my hon. Friends may have been nervous about the information that was passed over, and it was not always done with the best grace, but it was passed over and nobody was let down. *[Laughter.]* I am glad that the jovial reaction of my right hon. Friend the Member for Epsom and Ewell (Sir A. Hamilton) confirms that. The

[Column 206]

Government might be being unnecessarily fearful about the nature of the information that they will have to share with the members of the committee. I hope that they will put those fears behind them. The powers to send for persons and papers and to summon witnesses have been excluded from the Bill because they would make it look too like a Select Committee. The Government had better give the committee the right to make such requests, or

DOCUMENT 2.1: Intelligence Services Bill *(Continued)*

there is little point in setting it up. It will lose its credibility before it has began its work. If members of the committee have the power to make such requests, it will cause some chagrin in official circles, but the Government always have the power not to respond. The Government and Ministers may refuse to answer questions.

There have been celebrated occasions in the Select Committee on Defence when distinguished hon. Members have come before it and refused to answer questions. Whether that did the individual more harm than the Committee is another matter, but it happened and it is everybody's right so to act. The powers of the committee are not something that anybody needs to fear, particularly as I cannot imagine that the committee will very often sit in public. Its public session would probably be confined to once a year when it announced its report and published details of its work. For the rest of the time, it would sit in private, as the Select Committee on Defence did for much of the time. It would ask questions in private, its proceedings would be private and its report to the Prime Minister would be private. There will follow a process with which those who have served on the Defence Committee will be familiar. It will ask how the exclusion of particular information can be considered when it is published elsewhere. The argument will go backwards and forwards before a solution is reached, with the Government always having the final say. . . .

col. 228 Mr. Peter Mandelson: . . . Reference has been made to clause 7 of the Bill, which enables the Secretary of State to authorise illegal activities outside Britain. I question, as others have done before me, whether the powers outlined in clause 7 are too sweeping. I ask the Minister specifically whether the terms of clause 7 refer to illegal activities authorised by the Secretary of State himself or to activities authorised in his name but not necessarily by him directly or personally. That makes an enormous difference to our attitude to that authorisation. I hope that the Minister will refer to what level of decision-making might be envisaged in the authorisation.

Thirdly, I question whether the powers of intelligence chiefs and Ministers to block information and restrict access are too great. My right hon. Friend the Member for Dudley, East (Dr. Gilbert) referred to schedule 3. Paragraph 4 of schedule 3 refers to "sensitive information", which is by any measure extremely embracing, not to say draconian, in its sweep. I wonder whether there should be some override mechanism or some means of arbitration between the individuals and bodies proposed in the Bill. I should like to know the Minister's views on that. . . .

DOCUMENT 2.1:   Intelligence Services Bill *(Continued)*

---

col. 229 . . . For me, the heart of the issue is not simply the external oversight of the security services, but the operational supervision--a term which I use advisedly. I share the views of my colleagues who do not believe that oversight means involvement or dabbling in the day-to-day details and activities of the security services. But operational supervision is very important indeed. Day-to-day control of the security services is not, and should not be, a function of any parliamentary committee ; it is a function of Ministers, and Ministers alone. . . .

col. 240 The Chancellor of the Duchy of Lancaster (Mr. William Waldegrave): . . . The committee will be involved in very secret areas that have never before been shared with others outside the Secretary of State's responsibilities--for example, matters to do with the tasking of the services. The committee will not only deal with high-level policy in a broad-brush way ; it will be able to examine the actual tasking, the money and the organisational structures.

The committee will be fully trusted, and fully inside the secret wall. I believe that the result, while it will not establish within the House the parliamentary accountability that, for reasons that I have not had time to do more than sketch out tonight, we believe would be extremely difficult to organise, will be to spread the reassurance that senior, trusted people on both sides of the House share the secrets of the services, and have a formidable power to cause trouble for the Government.

Somebody asked earlier where the teeth were. The teeth consist of the fact that the committee, staffed by very senior Members of the House, will have the right not to publish stuff that would damage national security--which it would not want to do--but to write a report saying, "We believe that things are not being handled properly, and that Ministers are not responding properly." No Government in their senses would want to risk such criticism. That is why the committee will be powerful, and that is why I commend the Bill to the House. Question put and agreed to.

Bill accordingly read a Second time.

House of Commons, Third Reading, April 27, 1994 cols. 249-352.

Col. 322 Mr. Mandelson . . . Amendment No. 20, however, involves a slightly more serious test of the Government's true attitude to the important committee which is being established by the Bill, and of the good faith with which the Government are approaching the committee's role and status--a matter to which we attach considerable importance. The effect of the amendment would be to oblige the committee to lay its annual report on the

DOCUMENT 2.1: Intelligence Services Bill *(Continued)*

discharge of its functions before Parliament, rather than simply submitting its report directly to the Prime Minister as the Bill provides for at the moment.

Our justification for making the change is threefold. First, we think that it is important to make clear that the authority for the committee's oversight responsibility is derived from Parliament and that that is borne out by its reporting directly back to its parent, which is Parliament. The committee is an important extension of the scrutiny role of Parliament, and not simply an instrument of the executive role of Government. It is the voice of Parliament, not an extension of the Prime Minister's office. That would be made all the clearer by making the committee submit its annual report to Parliament, rather than via the Prime Minister.

Secondly, we think that it is important that everything possible is done to engage the sincere interest of the House of Commons in the important oversight function of the committee. It is important to gain a commitment to the work of the committee from the House of Commons, and the change that we are proposing would have some considerable symbolic value in achieving that.

Thirdly, although we acknowledge that the committee's powers are circumscribed, it is nonetheless important for the committee to exercise some control over the timing of its report, even though the Prime Minister's veto remains in some form over the contents of the report. As presently drafted, the Intelligence and Security Committee does not have the right to publish its own report, let alone any power to determine the timing of the publication of the report. The Opposition think that that is surely wrong.

It certainly looks absurd that a committee of parliamentarians--with all the authority and importance of the role that is being invested in that committee by the Bill--should not even have the power to publish its annual report and to determine the timing of it. One need only imagine the circumstances in which an annual report is made containing certain matters and references which are politically unattractive to the Prime Minister. They may be uncongenial or unpalatable at the time of elections, whether local elections, by-elections, European elections or even leadership elections.

One can imagine all sorts of elections that the Prime Minister might face in which he did not care to have a potentially controversial report by the committee published. It would be up to him under the terms of the Bill as it is currently drafted to put off the

DOCUMENT 2.1: Intelligence Services Bill *(Continued)*

[Column 323]

publication of the committee's report until a time that was more acceptable and satisfactory from his point of view rather than the point of view of the committee or, indeed, the needs of Parliament. In our view, that is wrong.

The amendment deals with an important point of principle. It is the principle of ownership of the committee, which we believe should be located, and seen to be located, clearly among Members of Parliament. . . .

col. 328 Mr. Winnick . . . The amendments deal with the crux of the Bill. My hon. Friend the Member for Hartlepool (Mr. Mandelson) rightly said that, to a large extent, the credibility of the committee is at stake. Those of us who have campaigned for genuine parliamentary scrutiny over the years have always taken the view that at some stage we will succeed : in 1986, I said in a speech that the time would come when the Government of the day accepted the necessity for some scrutiny of the intelligence services. So far, the Government's response has always been that such scrutiny is unnecessary. When the issue has been raised in Adjournment debates and on other occasions, Ministers have always told me that, because of ministerial control, there is no need for concern or for the establishment of any such committee. I do not think that the Bill gives the impression that there will be genuine parliamentary scrutiny. The committee will report to the Prime Minister ; I assume that it will be serviced by the Cabinet Office. The Parliamentary Secretary nods. Such a committee would appear to be virtually a sub-committee of the Cabinet Office, although it would include parliamentarians. That may not be the Government's wish, and it may not happen in practice. However, it would be important because it would not only give the impression of genuine parliamentary scrutiny but to ensure that it takes place.

[Column 329]

That is why I think that a Select Committee should be set up, although I accept that the Government are not going to establish one at this stage . . .

col. 333 Mr. Hogg: . . . I move on to persons and papers. There is a case to be made but in the end there is a difference between our concepts and those of Opposition Members. In effect, Opposition Members are trying to create a Select Committee. We are against that. They are seeking to cloak the committee that we are establishing with all the powers of a Select Committee. I am against that. I believe that the committee that we have created has been given adequate powers to perform its oversight functions. Opposition Members want to give it an unfettered right to call for persons and papers. In

DOCUMENT 2.1: Intelligence Services Bill *(Continued)*

Committee, I described the obligations of the heads of agencies and, for that matter, the officers of the services. We need not go over that ground again. In the generality of cases, the information or the personnel will come before the committee subject to the authority of the head of the agency and the terms of schedule 3 . . . .

col. 351 Mr. Rogers: . . . Our main concern has always been the control aspect--the process of accountability that is enshrined within the Bill. We regret the Government's minimalist approach. It does not fulfil the Bill's original intention, which was to create a more open society and more open government. I agree with my right hon. Friend the Member for Dudley, East that the Government have missed an opportunity to bring about an openness in an aspect of society that has been secret for too long. We are probably the most secretive society of all the western democracies.

Unfortunately, clause 10, which sets up the Intelligence and Security Committee, does not also set up a process of accountability. There is no breaking of the ring of secrecy. There is no way of operating outside the ring of the Secretary of State and the Joint Intelligence Committee tasking the security services, of the Secretary of State issuing a warrant so that they can operate outside the law where they feel that that is necessary, of the services reporting back to the Secretary of State, the Secretary of State filtering information before it comes to the Intelligence and Security Committee and the Prime Minister and the head of the agencies using their right to sideline information. The circle is too tight and too complete.

The committee will be a charade, a pretence at accountability. The Minister responsible for open government may shake his head, but the proof is in the pudding. I hope that the committee has a better record than the tribunal that was set up under the Security Service Act 1989. That tribunal has been what I feel this committee will be--a pretence at accountability.

We will not force a Division because the Opposition accept that we need secret services, and that they need to be secret. We commend the Government for going as far as they have, but we wish that they had taken this opportunity to go a little bit further, accepted many of our constructive amendments and ended up with a better Act. Question put, That the Bill be now read the Third time : The House divided : Ayes 216, Noes 10.

PART II

Political Interference
in Intelligence

CHAPTER 3

The Scott Report: Intelligence
and the Arms Trade

ROBERT DOVER

Editors' Note:
Robert Dover, an expert on the arms trade, tackles the thorny issue of what intelligence can reveal about the less savory areas of government licensing of military equipment for sale to other governments, as revealed in the Scott Report. Two overarching lessons emerge: one for the intelligence and policy community, and the other for the remit and conduct of official inquiries. For the former, it is clear that the relationships between the two, their proximity and terms of reference, are crucial in ensuring that the right information is conveyed to the right people; similarly, without a level of interconnectedness, deliberate and unintentional mistakes will be allowed to grow. For inquiries the lessons are equally obvious: The way that sources are used and the way that officials are interviewed can shape the entire contours of an inquiry.

The 1996 Scott Report (officially, the *Report of the Inquiry into the Export of Defence Equipment and Dual-Use Goods to Iraq and Related Prosecutions)* was a seismic event in British politics. The Conservative government, on the rack after five years of a wafer-thin parliamentary majority, a multitude of sex scandals, and internecine fighting over the issue of European integration, had commissioned the senior appeal court judge, Sir Richard Scott, to investigate the collapsed trial of three directors of a medium-sized manufacturing company in the West Midlands known as Matrix Churchill, and a failed export of dual-use technologies (machine tools and the long-range artillery piece known as the "super-gun") to Iraq in 1988. Scott's inquiry focused on the circumstances surrounding the prosecutions brought against the three company directors, and the decisions made by the British government to relax their own strict controls on exports to Iraq (known as the Howe guidelines and established in 1984) without informing Parliament or the relevant prosecuting authorities. The inquiry also considered the use of government intelligence in the case, and the evidence it called upon goes to the heart of questions about the coordination of intelligence in government, and the role of the intelligence agencies in lobbying government about the importance of their sources and in shaping the debate about these exports. As a brief window into the workings of the British government, it stands as an almost unsurpassed achievement, with lessons that still resonate today and that are explored in this chapter.

Scott produced a two-thousand-page report, which had called on 130,000 submitted documents, and 268 witnesses drawn from all the relevant government departments and intelligence agencies. It heavily criticized the government of the day and specific ministers within the government, and yet for such a weighty and sustained critique of government, it did not cause the government to fall, nor did it result in the resignation of a single minister, not even those heavily criticized in the report. Despite its analytical traction and its mammoth empirical base, it is disappointingly underexplored in the extant literature. Davina Miller's book *Export or Die* is the best account of the circumstances surrounding the Scott Report and the export of dual-use equipment to Iraq, and was published around the same time, but this chapter explores the lessons we, as those interested in the study of intelligence, can learn from this moment in history and the report it inspired.[1]

This chapter is framed by a short contextual history of the "arms to Iraq scandal," and then the lessons we can learn from the Scott Report about the role of intelligence in the arms trade, the way that intelligence product is used by government, the sanctity of the historical record, and what we can learn from official inquiries (a series of "how we know what we know" questions). The chapter is based on a document titled "DTI/44.2.2709: Matrix Churchill Ltd: Export Licence Applications for Iraq," dated September 25, 1989, which was issued within the Department for Trade and Industry (DTI) as ministerial advice to rebut the arguments advanced by the Foreign Office to reject one of the export license applications made by Matrix Churchill. It provides an excellent account of the debates that took place among the DTI, the Ministry of Defence, and the Foreign Office over these exports, with the appropriately hidden element of the intelligence agencies lurking as the elephants in the room (see the transcript following this chapter).

The wider history and political analysis made in this chapter draws on the evidence and analysis provided in the Scott Report and these are cited, in brackets, without "Scott" or the 1996 date of the report accompanying them. So, for example, a citation will look like (D2.279), which is the reference to the section, subsection, and paragraph number within the main report. I have done this to avoid breaking up the flow of the analysis with unwieldy notations that I had to draw on, given the nature of the report.

The Context: Intelligence Product and Government

The Scott Report represented a key moment in contemporary understanding of British government (what it is and how it works) partly because of the sheer number of documents it examined, the officials and ministers it interviewed, and, of course, because of the critical attention it generated in the British media, opposition parties, and activists to the activities and mechanisms of the inner workings of government. It also brought into critical focus what ministerial responsibility meant, which is an important aspect of the mostly unwritten conventions of British parliamentary democracy.[2] The report is also important to our understanding of how intelligence product is generated and used within government, and highlights the absence of what we would now call joined-up government—the timely and appropriate sharing of information, in this instance important intelligence product, or the sorts of investigations (often with judicial weight) each department was carrying out. The overemphasis on secrecy and isolation from other departments was, to a great extent, one of the reasons the government mired itself in this scandal, and great strides have been made (in the counterterrorism sphere) to overcome these institutional walls, with the establishment, for example, of the Joint Terrorism Analysis Centre (JTAC).

At the absolute heart of the Scott inquiry was the intersection between high diplomacy and statecraft (the government's decision to try and balance Iran and Iraq as warring parties in the Middle East and to effectively facilitate the continuation of conflict), with intelligence (what the intelligence community and ministers knew about the dual-use equipment to be exported, and what it would be used for). Given that the trial of the Matrix Churchill directors (technically referred to as *R. v Henderson and others 1992*) took place on the basis of breaching export license laws, some dating from 1939, the intelligence within Whitehall about the relationships among SIS, MI5, and Matrix Churchill and what their exports would be used for was absolutely crucial. The same was true in the case of other British firms exporting material to Iraq, but the *Henderson* case collapsed first, in 1992, and therefore became the focus of the Scott inquiry.

The company in question, Matrix Churchill, was an engineering firm based in Coventry in the West Midlands, and 70 percent owned by Iraqi interests. It applied for three licenses to export machine tools to Hutteen in Iraq in August 1987. These machine tools were for "general engineering products" (D2.279), and did not, as would be routine today, provide any further detail about the sorts of things that would be produced by the tools, nor the likelihood of the products being used for militarized purposes. In November 1987, the SIS prepared a report on the facility at Hutteen, which noted that "Iraq intends to use the machinery purchased to manufacture its own munitions" (D2.265–66). As these were the days before post-9/11 cooperation, MI5 were operating on their own distinctive track and had garnered more specific intelligence—in the form of a written note from Mark Gutteridge, the exports manager at Matrix Churchill in May 1987, and then from meetings that the MI5 officer, known to the inquiry as Mr. P, had held with Gutteridge—that the Iraqis were buying machine tools for military purposes. Gutteridge's position as an asset of the British intelligence community then became used as a reason for the Ministry of Defence (MoD) and Department of Trade and Industry (DTI) to argue for allowing the export of the 141 Matrix Churchill machine tools. Their argument was that to stop the export because of his intelligence would put him and any future intelligence he might provide at risk; an indication perhaps of how highly prized intelligence assets are within the community (D2.304 & D.2311). The Defence Intelligence Staff (DIS), within the MoD, had also noted that Hutteen was a munitions factory, but had chosen not to pass this on to the Foreign and Commonwealth Office (FCO), MoD Main Building, nor the DTI—in other words, all of the licensing agencies (D2.267). In evidence to the inquiry the three licensing departments said that "export licenses would not have been granted" had they known the intelligence about the machine tools being for military purposes (D2.282), although once they had received the intelligence about the Iraqis' intended use for the machines they then did not discuss revoking the licenses until early 1988, when only a tenth of the total machines to be exported had actually been transferred, which casts some doubts over the veracity of the statements they made to the inquiry.

The precise export license that the directors of Matrix Churchill were prosecuted on was ELA 53234, which contained a request to export two precision lathes and twelve "vertical spindle machining centres," which were not to be sent to Hutteen, as above, but to Nassr, which was another militarized site in Iraq (D6.73). Nassr had also been assessed (by October 1988) to be a weapons production facility, but no further detail or information was requested by the DTI to assess the export application, which certainly would not be the case today (D6.75). While the MoD initially concluded that the application should be refused, SIS and MI5 became interested in how this application was being handled, mostly as a result of how it would impact their human and institutional sources—source protection, in their words—to keep this export game going long enough to glean more information about what the Iraqi government aimed to do with advanced military equipment, coupled with concerns over whether the loss of this contract would mean the end of Matrix Churchill as a viable business concern and a profitable source of information (D6.78, D6.82 & D6.87). The Defence Intelligence Staff (DIS) were resolutely opposed to the granting of this license, which they stated would be a breach of the Howe guidelines, as it was clear to them that this equipment would substantially improve Iraqi military capabilities, to the tune of half a million artillery shells a year, but the DIS, just like Parliament, had not been told that the Cabinet had decided to relax these rules.[3] While it is true that not all of the equipment was exported to Iraq, that was only the case because the Iraqi invasion of Kuwait brought about such tough and universal export sanctions on Iraq that the transit of any additional machines was next to impossible. Consequently, shells made with British machine tools were not used against British troops during the first Gulf War. Scott is very critical of the failure of the DIS to pass on their intelligence-driven assessments to the licensing departments (a failure of coordination and joined-up government) (D2.287), and also of their failure to pass on their strong concerns to the Foreign Office (D6.103). It is important to note that, since the Scott Report, intelligence product is now passed on and used as a matter of routine in the decisions to grant or refuse export licenses.[4] There is, however, a degree of

suspicion within the report about the extent to which the British government pur-
posefully ignored the important intelligence coming to it, intelligence that should
have caused it to immediately revoke the licenses granted to Matrix Churchill. For
example, an anonymous employee at Matrix Churchill wrote to Geoffrey Howe,
the foreign secretary, to tell him that the machine tools were for military purposes, something we would now call whistle blowing, which is protected by law
(D2.318). SIS and the MoD also received this information, but chose to ignore it,
raising the important question of whether this was a failure to put all the intelligence together, or whether this was a concerted attempt to ignore awkward facts.
Alan Clark (who was then at the DTI), following his famous "economical with the
actualité" testimony in the Henderson trial, followed it with further illuminating
testimony at the inquiry, saying that he felt it was paradoxical that the intelligence
agencies were telling government that the machine tools would be used for military ends, but concluding that it was imprudent to stop the export as it jeopardized
important intelligence assets; as he put it, "a total circularity." As an aside, the DTI
and its successor departments (which are mainly just changes in name) now also
employ former arms industry insiders to help them prepare the assessments on
pieces of military and dual-use equipment that have an application for a license.[5]
While there is a culture and an emphasis among the licensers to grant permission
for export, there are now greater efforts made to check the technical possibilities
of each piece of equipment, using military and engineering experts.

The final applications for export licenses made by Matrix Churchill helped
generate the most criticism of the politicians involved in making the decisions
about what technology to export, and their use of the intelligence, both raw and
synthesized, that was given to them. These final six applications again involved
state-of-the-art lathes and machining centers, and were destined for Nassr (D6.58).
The Ministry of Defence recommended that the applications be refused, on very
similar grounds as its previous recommendations, and the Foreign Office also
opposed export, which was a change in its view from earlier applications. However, there was a significant change of political leadership in the process (albeit
with the same personnel) when the maverick politician Alan Clark moved from
the DTI to the MoD in the role of minister for defense procurement (but retained
a very pro-trade outlook, contrary to the institutional wisdom of the MoD at the
time), while Lord Trefgarne moved from the MoD to the DTI, and immediately
took up its more pro-trade line. The effect of this double move was to change the
mood in which applications for exports were discussed, leaving the Foreign Office,
in the person of Minister William Waldegrave, outnumbered by the MoD and
DTI, who had been briefed by their officials in a manner that Sir Richard Scott
later disapproved of. Scott's criticism focused on these briefings having excluded
the important intelligence assessments made about the activities going on at Nassr
(e.g., D5.25).

The officials who had prepared the respective ministerial briefings were
interviewed as part of the Scott inquiry, and their evidence showed clearly that
there was too much emphasis on an individual case officer handling and using the

intelligence and no systematic approach to the use of this material in reports. In the case of the DTI brief, Scott said it was "positively misleading" (D6.133), in the MoD it had been carelessly "forgotten," and in the case of the FCO, the SIS officer liaising with the official writing the brief did not realize that he was being asked to provide SIS sanction to the brief and so thought he had only been informally consulted (D6.149–154). I suppose it is no surprise then, given the absence of relevant intelligence product, that Clark, Trefgarne, and Waldegrave concluded that they should grant the export licenses in this context. It seems from the Scott Report that the primary failure in coordinating the intelligence picture and flow in this case lay with SIS, who it appears had a long-term misunderstanding with the government over what intelligence product was due, where it should be sent, and the priorities it should be following. For example, the JIC provided SIS with an emphasis on countering the proliferation of weapons of mass destruction, not artillery pieces. Furthermore, neither the Scott Report nor the later 2004 Butler Report make clear the extent of civilian control of the intelligence agencies or the extent to which the agencies maintain an autonomy or semi-autonomy from government.[6] This is also manifest in the primary legislation, which gives MI5 what appears to be a largely autonomous role: the director general has to report to the home secretary but is not controlled by him or her. That MI5 engaged in lobbying to persuade the government to grant the export licenses so that their intelligence assets would remain in play (while other agencies withheld intelligence on the basis of having judged it too sensitive or immaterial) is suggestive of a system where the agencies hold a controlling hand. But this is not a clear position that holds for all time or for all subjects; it was alleged in the summer of 2009 that MI5 intelligence was passed to the airports operator BAA by the Department for Transport about the protest group Plane Stupid, who oppose the expansion of Heathrow Airport by direct action, implying an acutely political use of government intelligence, which is contrary to the Scott Report example.[7] We know that that the systematic use of government intelligence has improved from the 1980s in both its creation and its application, but to what extent this is true in the licensing process is reasonably difficult to glean.

The question of oversight is of course a difficult one in intelligence terms. The "ring of secrecy" that one naturally expects in and around the intelligence community is open to greater risk of abuse and breach the wider the ring goes. The Intelligence Services Act (1994) not only publicly and legally acknowledged SIS and GCHQ but also provided for some parliamentary scrutiny of the intelligence agencies via a committee of Parliament (as distinct from a parliamentary select committee). The strength of this system is more in terms of insider advocacy than a formal ability to censure the agencies. Similarly, the Quadripartite Committee (now the Committees on Arms Export Controls), established in 1999, brings all the export licensing departments together in one forum to discuss the operation of the licensing process in the previous twelve months and the success of the control measures. It is crucial to note that the committee cannot prevent licenses being granted, nor exports going ahead; its function is exclusively retrospective, and so one could once again argue that these are symbolic checks and balances, providing only the most notional sense of accountability.

The main use of intelligence in the export arms trade is to provide crucial contextual information about the situation in which the materials will be provided, the dual-use potential of any particular piece of equipment, and the end uses for the equipment. A document released by Paul Henderson, one of the Matrix Churchill defendants, to Davina Miller (from the director of the export licensing unit to HM Customs and Excise) states: "we have to accept what is said as the only evidence we have of the end user. In state-run economies there is a recognition that the end user could be switched but since we do not exercise territorial control, we cannot prevent that happening."[8] So the intelligence over a particular country and a particular end user is conditional and often contested. This allows those trying to use military equipment to assist diplomatic relations a particular kind of flexibility in which to operate; and this is perhaps one of the key wider lessons of the Scott Report.

Sanctity of the Historical Record

One of the most interesting aspects of the Scott Report is that it was conducted using a large number of documents and witnesses from the Cabinet Office, MoD, FCO, DTI, and the British intelligence agencies (B.1.2–5). This means that any reader of the Scott Report and its appendices gets a bird's-eye view of the inner workings of the British state. Such a view is of course fragmentary, given the onus on the individual departments to respond to the requests of the inquiry team (and therefore the completeness of the record depends partially on the success of the inquiry team in knowing what to ask for), the redaction of documents, and the censoring of documents that were perceived to present a threat to national security. Scott lists a large number of incidences where documents were delivered late or merely by chance to the inquiry (for example, B.1.11), including documents being "found in a cupboard." Scott comments critically on the number of requests that were not met by departments and felt that the departments had almost no idea what other departments were doing.

Commenting on the delivery and sequencing of documents in the inquiry, often an underexplored element of the research process, Scott said:

> The impact of a steady drip-feed of documents submitted in a piecemeal fashion cannot be understated. Whenever new documents were submitted, they had to be considered whether or not they turned out to be relevant. It must be said, however, that the problem was recognized within departments and that steps were taken to try to meet it. Thus, for example, on 21 October 1993, the FCO submitted what they described as "a large number of additional papers" not previously sent to the Inquiry; on 4 November 1993 a further three volumes of papers were sent under cover of a letter from Sir Timothy Daunt.[9] Sir

Timothy explained the circumstances of the FCO's second oversight, which the Inquiry accepted; but he also went on to record that, at the then Permanent Under Secretary's express request, all FCO Departments and Heads of Division were to be instructed to conduct a further search for relevant papers and to certify that they had done so (B.1.12).

One often thinks of the construction of a narrative as a linear process—as the evidence is presented the story grows and so on—but of course it is common within scholarly and official circles to have the narrative line in mind and to fit the available evidence to it. What is not often discussed, and yet will be common to everyone with a PhD, is the challenge of obtaining information that fundamentally changes the character of a piece of work, but also leads to the researcher investigating different lines of inquiry and being nudged off the course he was pursuing. A PhD or postgraduate dissertation is a relatively limited forum for this to happen; an official inquiry containing 130,000 documents is of an altogether different magnitude. So, the Scott Report challenges us to grasp the difficulty of understanding a unified narrative about the export of dual-use technologies to Iraq, and of how intelligence product was used by the British government when documents were continually presented that spurred further investigation and challenged the team's existing understandings. What is also clear from the Scott Report is that the team understood that their report was entirely the sum of its constituent parts; it was as if they had started with an entirely blank sheet of paper and each piece of evidence was carefully slotted into the whole. To this degree, therefore, the narrative drive of the report (which, after all, had very important political ramifications for a Conservative administration already looking certain to lose the next election) could be shaped and molded by the release of documents and the testimony provided to the inquiry.

The use of witness evidence is a standard practice across most official inquiries in the United Kingdom. The official inquiry into the war in Iraq was met with a great deal of criticism by the political opposition and antiwar activists who wanted those giving evidence to the inquiry to swear an oath prior to appearing before the panel of experts.[10] The decision not to take witness statements under oath was made to prevent a recurrence of one of the perceived problems during the Scott inquiry of junior officials bringing legal representatives with them (raising the cost of the inquiry to the taxpayer and also limiting the range and scope of answers given).[11] The Scott inquiry faced a multilevel barrage of lawyers, from those representing officials to those representing the interests of government departments. The "Bloody Sunday" inquiry into the deaths in Derry in January 1972, which was reported in June 2010, is a good example of how official inquiries can become mired by legal argument, both in terms of the time taken to report findings but also in the escalating costs associated with running it.[12]

The question of whether witnesses give their statements under oath relates closely to the question of how it is possible to know whether someone we are interviewing is telling us the truth. In the case of the inquiry into the war in Iraq, the focus on witnesses being under oath has centered on the two sessions of testimony of the former prime minister, Tony Blair. In the case of the Scott Report, the challenge was to persuade officials and ministers, who were still part of the government, to speak openly about a period of British foreign policy that was at variance with their own publicly declared policy and with international expectations. Compounding this were statements by, for example, Alan Clark, MP, in the *Henderson* trial, that he had been "economical with actualité"; what to believe then becomes an acute challenge. While Clark's testimony that he had lied throws open how we judge truth from oral evidence, we are left to employ the time-honored traditions of judgment, and also triangulation (with the documentary record) to correctly weigh the evidence. Scott is explicit about the criteria used to invite witnesses to the inquiry:

(a) to obtain oral confirmation of some important point or points that had emerged from the written evidence or the documents; (b) to fill in evidential gaps that seemed not to be covered by the written evidence or the documents; (c) to enable individuals to explain documents, or passages in documents, from which, in the absence of explanation, certain inferences might be drawn; (d) to enable witnesses to meet criticisms of their conduct that might otherwise be made; (e) to explain or expand upon written evidence that they had submitted or to comment on written evidence submitted by others (B.1.21).

Only ten of the witnesses who attended the inquiry were explicitly intelligence officers, although some of the other witnesses came from departments that also have responsibilities for intelligence product; most came from the Ministry of Defence, with seventy-four officials providing oral testimony. It is important to note from these that witnesses did not have to present their case fresh, so not like a classic courtroom cross-examination; they were essentially there to provide context to the documentary evidence gathered by the inquiry, and this process of clarification, and in some cases rebuttal, took the inquiry a full year to conduct (B.2.23). The prepublished report was also sent to those named in it, to allow them a further opportunity to clarify their positions and their evidence prior to publication. The final report is, therefore, an accurate representation of how those who participated in it wished to be seen (B.2.24).

As people coming to this report and inquiry thirteen years after it was published, we must also accept and understand that if two witnesses provide evidence at variance with each other it does not necessarily follow that one is not telling the truth; we also have to put into the equation the structural positioning of the officials, their access to documents and individuals, the passing of time, and crucially what the totality of the report and its appendices may have done to witnesses' recollections. The more complete record may have filled in crucial gaps for participants caught up in the minutiae of their departmental lives at the time. What the Scott Report shows us, therefore, is that the acquisition of facts about the specifics of the case and the machinery of government is very difficult, coming down to success of the inquiry team in knowing what to ask for, the range of documents and witnesses available or made available, and ultimately down to the fine judgment of Sir Richard Scott and his advisers to make sense of it. It is an excellent tutorial into that classic researcher's question of: how do I know what I know?

The Document: Scott Inquiry Reference: DTI/44.2.2709, Matrix Churchill Ltd: Export Licence Applications for Iraq, September 25, 1989

The document selected was written by the official Tony Steadman (who was head of the Export Licensing Unit, but whose exact position within the DTI has been redacted on the document) to Mr. Beston, his superior. It is a document that appears in the middle of the tensest period of this episode; Matrix Churchill had made an application for a temporary export license to take some high-precision machine tools to Baghdad for the large annual arms fair, and while they were there they secured contracts to sell this equipment to the Iraqi military, which was not terribly surprising given the 70 percent ownership of Matrix Churchill by Iraqi shell companies. After signing these contracts Matrix Churchill consequently made a further application to have full licenses granted to them. The equipment itself remained in Iraq after the arms fair, apparently in a secure location pending the granting of the full licenses.

The document shows the very clear personal and political tension among the three departments involved in this process (the Ministry of Defence, the Foreign and Commonwealth Office, and the Department for Trade and Industry), particularly based on William Waldegrave's assertion that the MoD and DTI were happy to grant licenses based on their desire to protect the intelligence sources within Matrix Churchill. The two other departments refuted this but offered a more nuanced account that amounted to the same: a desire to preserve the intelligence that came from Matrix Churchill, a desire to see Matrix Churchill continue to be a viable business, and a pragmatic position that even though the head of the facility at Nassr (where the Matrix Churchill machine tools had been destined to go to) had been trying to acquire nuclear technologies, this did not prevent the granting of this license, because he was likely to acquire this technology from another supplier regardless of Matrix Churchill's viability. Finally, it was not beyond comprehension that since the Iran-Iraq war was in ceasefire the Howe doctrine could be lapsed or relaxed; it had been created, after all, to deal with Iran and Iraq at war. In many respects this view forms one of the pillars of criticism that the government faced on this issue: this pragmatism seemed to stretch and stretch, from the logic of the drug dealer that if we did not supply it, someone else would, to the protection of a set of intelligence sources in direct contravention of a publicly stated British government policy.

It is perhaps here that we can see the utility and value of this particular document, written in haste and distilling the issues into a short form. The British government was determined to keep this particular intelligence line open into Iraq, and thus we can see the potential power of the intelligence imperative in government. The extent to which the intelligence gleaned from Matrix Churchill was particularly useful is not clear, or whether MI5 and SIS were just keen to maintain an established link.[13] The lack of clarity over this question and the clear absence of joined-up government (that eventually saw this situation explode) raise long-lasting questions about the role of intelligence in government.

The key to the changed dynamic between the government's licensing departments was the swap of Lord Trefgarne and Alan Clark to and from the MoD and DTI, which had the effect of changing the emphasis among the interested licensing parties. Prior to their swap the emphasis on applications had been a cautious, almost precautionary, principle. But now both Clark and Trefgarne were resolutely in favor of granting licenses while only the Foreign Office minister, William Waldegrave, was against. This document appears in the context of Waldegrave's letter of September 6, 1989, recommending that the latest Matrix Churchill license application be rejected, and this is the internal DTI response to that letter.

The document provides a series of arguments to rebut the Foreign Office view. These are presented under a subheading "argument" and stretch from paragraph 10 to paragraph 15. Steadman's view is that the Foreign Office are pursuing a somewhat simplistic and, he implies, a somewhat rule-based approach to this question. We can glean from the document that the Foreign Office had invoked the Howe guidelines in their recommendation to refuse, and this document is stark in its revelation that the guidelines were watered down and modified by ministers in December 1988. Steadman describes this as a "flexible interpretation," and therefore machine tools that could be used to produce munitions were no longer to be automatically barred from export. This particular line was highly criticized by both the Scott Report and by the opposition in Parliament on its publication; the decision to effectively change the Howe guidelines without notifying Parliament had undermined parliamentary sovereignty, notions of accountability, and had led to the prosecution of the Matrix Churchill directors.

The approach taken towards nuclear nonproliferation, as set out in this document, sits very uneasily with the position as it would be observed today within the British government. Steadman states that there is "no firm evidence" that Matrix Churchill's machine tools had been used in the Iraqi nuclear program, and so, in the advice he provides, he suggests that this is not a reason to bar export. This is a historically contingent view; the Soviet Union had yet to collapse entirely, and nuclear nonproliferation had yet to reach the top of many countries' security agendas. The view presented here is confined to the period when the document was written, but it gives us a good insight into the sort of analysis that was being done within the British government at the time. That classic dilemma of all intelligence analysts—looking into the crystal ball to see what the future might hold—is amply brought out by the complacency shown here about nuclear proliferation. There is also a nice vignette about the relative unfairness (in paragraph 13) of treating Iraq and South Africa differently regarding their nuclear weapons programs. The British government's treatment of South Africa was a large political issue in the 1980s, as the prime minister, Margaret Thatcher, was one of the last of the world leaders to condemn and take diplomatic measures against the apartheid regime. Steadman's argument seems to fit into that debate, questioning why a tougher line was being taken against South Africa than Iraq, a sentiment that would have been clearly understood within government.

The trade implications of a refusal to grant licenses are also brought up by Steadman's document. Anti-arms trade campaigners, like the Campaign Against Arms Trade, have often accused the government of allowing "immoral" exports to prop up British defense manufacturing. Paragraph 15 of this document brings this tension to the fore; Steadman argues that the machine tools industry would be seriously compromised by a refusal, as it would open up Iraq to British competitors and would also have a consequent effect of undermining wider British trade with Iraq. There is a good amount of evidence available in the wider arms trade literature to suggest that the economic and balance of payments imperatives drive the decisions made in the licensing process, and this document provides further evidence for this. Often the balance between export receipts and a moral dimension is a matter of personal choice, with agency for the end use being removed from the exporter and on to those receiving the goods. It is important to note, however, that since the Scott Report, arms export licensing has changed markedly. There is a formalized use of intelligence in the prelicensing stage, and former industry insiders are utilized to provide scientific and technical expertise to the process in a codified way. The presence of a parliamentary select committee to review arms export licensing has also imposed a greater level of accountability over a process that had conspicuously lacked accountability before; in these ways the Scott Report resulted in a large reform of the British arms export trade. The final argument presented by Steadman focuses on the media attention given to exports to Iraq; he simply notes that to refuse the license now might appear to be giving in to adverse media attention, a pre–New Labour example of wanting to manage the media message.

This document neatly highlights the elements within this episode that we can learn from. It is a concise account of the major arguments and threads within the British government's decision to grant export licenses to Matrix Churchill. But this document is also valuable because it illuminates what we often miss in political science, which is the role and interplay among individuals (in this case officials, ministers, and intelligence officers), the impact of time on decision making, and the realities of the "real world": decisions have to be taken because the bureaucratic process rolls on. Although such considerations might seem banal and beneath the lofty ambitions of scholarship, vital issues of international statecraft and nonproliferation have rested on such things. It is a chastening thought.

Lessons Learned?

The Scott Report was unique in its time for a government taking the decision to invite criticism upon itself for decisions it had made in complicated domestic and international arenas; other inquiries like Franks (into the Falklands War) do not seem so obviously geared to self–flagellation. It did so in an inquiry that had Sir Richard Scott as the judge, jury, and prosecuting barrister, who could ban defense lawyers from the side of witnesses. That this sort of inquiry should spring from the collapse of a trial of three directors of a manufacturing firm that was strongly supported by the British government and British intelligence, and that the trial collapsed on the admission of a British government minister that he had lied is somewhat surprising, but these were exceptional circumstances. Having changed the export guidance rules without telling Parliament or the relevant authorities, the government, via Attorney General Sir Nicholas Lyell, then prevented the defendants from revealing in the court that they had been acting with government approval and, in one case, working as an intelligence asset, details that would have secured their acquittals. While some of the material covered by the Public Interest Immunity certificates was secret government intelligence, much of it was not, and it was widely perceived that the government wished to hide the internal processes by which various decisions had been made, hide the responsibility of the ministers involved, and the advice they had received from named civil servants. As Scott himself pointed out, all this suggested a government system obsessed by secrecy and with a disposition to retain information in almost every given circumstance.

The disposition to secrecy—which is hardly a surprise in modern government—was compounded in this case by a similar acceptance of misleading Parliament as a matter of course, and even further compounded by the lack of ministerial accountability for these actions. Although the Labour opposition in Parliament demanded the resignations of Sir Nicholas Lyell (for his handling of the Public Interest Immunity certificates) and of William Waldegrave (for having misled Parliament on over twenty separate occasions), neither were asked to resign by the prime minister, and neither offered their resignation. Sir Richard Scott did not make any recommendation that they should resign (he did say that Waldegrave had breached the ministerial code), but he was scathing about the decision to change the export guidance policy and not tell Parliament, in his view the very apex of constitutionality in the United Kingdom.

Ultimately, the Scott Report provides us with a multitude of lessons. It provides a rich empirical picture about a particular moment in British foreign and security policy when the government engaged in high politics over the balance of power in the Middle East, and failed in their constitutional obligations to inform Parliament of a change of policy that resulted in the prosecution of three company directors. The report also illuminates the use of intelligence within government, as well as the problems of coordinating intelligence throughout the government machine, and the peculiar constitutional issue of the intelligence agencies occupying a semi-autonomous role within government. The evidence provided to the inquiry really showed that in this case the principal intelligence agencies had the capacity to steer policy and policymakers' perceptions through the tactical revelation or suppression of information, and also, in the case of MI5, in lobbying ministers about the importance of a particular human source. In short, it was not clear where the lines of responsibility, or indeed control, lay. And while the Butler Report (2004) shows us a completely different snapshot of the government controlling and moving SIS in line with its own preferences, the example of Scott demonstrates the government being moved by its intelligence agencies into policy failure. It is illuminating, but raises more questions than answers about this important relationship at the heart of government.

The relationship between the political and intelligence communities is so diverse and so fluid that drawing firm conclusions from either Scott or Butler would be a mistake. It is clear, however, that this relationship (from the Scott Report and its appendices) is one where the key politicians did not fully grasp the (often partial) intelligence they were being fed (and one should acknowledge the difficulty for those outside of the community to make sense of some intelligence product); that there was a double bind of intelligence officers and civil servants making tactical judgments about what intelligence to show their civil service counterparts and ministers; and that the agencies held a semi-autonomous position akin to a state alongside the state, that saw them being part of the British government and yet also strangely detached from it.

Finally, the Scott Report provides scholars and students with an excellent case study in the business of research, in the "how we know what we know" questions that dominate social inquiry. The report provides a comprehensive account of how it went about selecting documents and witnesses, and provides a sensible account of how it can be said to have reached its conclusions on information that the agencies and government departments were willing to give it. So, Scott provides an excellent and salutary tale about the nonlinearity of research projects; of how it is possible to disappear down investigative rabbit holes; and on one level how the honesty and transparency of witnesses can affect and undermine the production of knowledge. On a second level we can see that even on agreed facts the difference of interpretation and recollection of witnesses can be stark.

It might be easy to conclude that the difficulties posed by this kind of investigation, for someone as well-resourced as Sir Richard and his team, are too great. But to conclude this would be to deny parliamentarians, the public, academics, and the media a greater understanding of the machinery of government and how government intelligence fits within it.

NOTES

1. Davina Miller, *Export or Die: Britain's Defence Trade with Iran and Iraq* (Cassell: London, 1996).
2. And it seemed to overturn the traditional notion that a minister took responsibility (code, often, for resigning) when his or her department notably failed.
3. The Howe guidelines drawn up by Foreign Secretary Geoffrey Howe and Prime Minister Margaret Thatcher were: (1) We should maintain our consistent refusal to supply any lethal equipment to either side; (2) subject to that overriding consideration, we should attempt to fulfill existing contracts and obligations; (3) we should not, in future, approve orders for defence equipment which, in our view, would significantly enhance the capability of each side to prolong or exacerbate the conflict; (4) in line with this policy, we should continue to scrutinize rigorously all applications for export licenses for the supply of defence equipment to Iran and Iraq (*Hansard*, October 25, 1985, vol. 84, col. 454).
4. Robert Dover, "For Queen and Company: The Role of Intelligence in the Arms Trade," *Political Studies* 55:4 (2007), 690.
5. Ibid., 693.
6. One should note that Robin Butler was interviewed as part of the Scott inquiry, and his definition of ministerial accountability has been considerably criticized. It is perhaps a nice twist of British political and constitutional life that he was then given charge of the review of the intelligence on weapons of mass destruction in 2004.
7. Although the stronger evidence is the police coordination unit, the National Extremism Tactical Coordination Unit had been collecting intelligence on the group and had tried to run an infiltrator within it (Lewis, April 24, 2009).
8. Miller, *Export or Die*, 56.
9. Sir Timothy was ambassador to Turkey between 1986 and 1992.
10. The Iraq Inquiry, www.iraqinquiry.org.uk (accessed October 30, 2009).
11. See www.iraqinquiry.org.uk/background/protocols/witnesses.aspx (accessed October 30, 2009).
12. See "The Bloody Sunday Inquiry," www.bloody-sunday-inquiry.org.uk (accessed October 30, 2009).
13. Certainly MI5 were more keen than the SIS.

DOCUMENT 3.1   Matrix Churchill Ltd: Export Licence Applications for Iraq, September 25, 1989

SECRET

SCOTT INQ REF:
DTI/44.2.2709

To:

		cc	PS/S of S
1.	Mr Beston ᶜᴬ⁾·ᵘ/₇		PS/MFT
2.	PS/MFT		PS/Sir P Gregson

From:

Tony Steadman
OT2/3 ELU
██████

⊃5 September 1989

cc
PS/S of S
PS/MFT
PS/Sir P Gregson
Mr Dell
Mr Meadway   OT2
Mr Muir   OT4
Mr Petter   OT4/1
Mr Gallaher   OT4/1
Mr Morgan   EM2
Mr Nunn   OT2/3

MATRIX CHURCHILL LTD: EXPORT LICENCE APPLICATIONS FOR IRAQ

ISSUE

1.   How to repond to Mr Waldegrave's letter of 6 September recommending refusal of 4 licences for the export by Matrix Churchill of machine tools to Iraq.

RECOMMENDATION

2.   The FCO recommendation for refusal is not so clear cut as Mr Waldegrave suggests. Before reaching a decision it is suggested that MFT should seek a meeting with Mr Waldegrave and Mr. Clark to explore in greater detail the arguments for and against the exports. A draft letter inviting Mr Waldegrave to such a meeting is attached.

TIMING

3.   Urgent.

BACKGROUND

Historical Licensing Position

4.   In 1987 export licences were issued to 3 UK machine tool firms including Matrix Churchill (then TI Machine Tools Ltd), for exports to Iraq for a total licensable value of £37m. The stated end use was the manufacture of general engineering products. Subsequent to the issue of the licences and after some shipments had been made, intelligence sources reported that the factories in which the machines were to be used, namely the Nassr Establishment for Mechanical Industries and the Huteen Establishment for Technical Industries, were engaged in a munitions manufacturing programme as well as general engineering activities. Even so there was no evidence that the machine tools would be used other than for the purpose originally stated. In addition the intelligence services were anxious that their source should not be put at risk by the publicity which the revocation of licences would have provoked. In the circumstances DTI, FCO and MOD Ministers agreed in January 1988 that the licences should stand.

CCC2709

DOCUMENT 3.1   Matrix Churchill Ltd: Export Licence Applications for Iraq, September 25, 1989   *(Continued)*

---

5.   Since that time, apart from a temporary licence issued to
      600 Services Group for the Autumn 88 Baghadad Fair only
      Matrix Churchill has continued to apply for export licenc
      for Iraq.

6.   In both May and September 1988 temporary export licences
      were granted to the company for exhibitions in Baghadad.
      The equipment was used again for exhibition in May 1989 a
      is said to be still held in bonded store in Iraq awaiting
      licence approval to allow its sale for general engineerin
      use.

7.   During 1988 a further 3 applications were submitted all f
      Nassr as end user. FCO Ministers' recommendation for
      approval in February 1989 was based upon the fact that
      though the lathes could be used for munitions manufacture
      in the circumstances of the ceasefire this was not
      sufficient reason to withhold licences. In addition,
      though Matrix Churchill was majority owned by Iraqis and
      though the equipment was destined for an organisation, the
      head of which was known to be acquiring nuclear technology
      this did not appear to involve Matrix Churchill. Finally,
      it was considered that withholding the licenceswould not
      stop Iraq developing a nuclear weapon, but could force the
      closure of Matrix Churchill and the loss of an important
      intelligence source.

      <u>Current Licence Applications from Matrix Churchill</u>

8.   There are currently 10 applications for Iraq under
      consideration (total value £9m) 4 of which are the subject
      of the FCO letter. These are listed in the attached
      schedule of licence applications.

<u>Company Background</u>

9.   Matrix Churchill is one of the leading UK manufacturers of
      CNC lathes. It employs 810 people based in Coventry and in
      addition relies on UK sub contractors. The company was
      bought from the TI Group in 1987 by a holding company, TMG
      Engineering, largely owned by the Iraqi Technology and
      Development Group of London thought to be linked to Iraqi's
      attempts to procure nuclear missile technology. Matrix
      Churchill has a turnover of £40 million and it sold about
      £8 million of equipment to Iraq in 1988. The company has
      claimed and continues to do so that the Iraqi orders are
      essential to its cash flow.

ARGUMENT

10.   Mr Waldegrave's letter recommends refusal on the grounds
      that we have firm evidence that equipment has previously
      been shipped to Iraqi munitions factories and because of
      broader concerns about Iraqi procurement activities in the
      UK about which the PM expressed concern in April. In
      addition he states that the only reason for approval in the
      past was the need to protect intelligence sources which is
      now no longer a factor. This was not our understanding
      (see para 7 above). The issues are not as clear cut as the

CCC 271C

DOCUMENT 3.1   Matrix Churchill Ltd: Export Licence Applications for Iraq, September
25, 1989   *(Continued)*

SECRET

recommendation implies. There are weaknesses in the FCO'
argument and there are grounds for exploring with FCO and
MOD Ministers whether these applications, including those
still in pipeline, should be approved. The relevant
factors are as follows:

Iran/Iraq Guidelines

11.   The ceasefire has been in place for over a year. In
December 1988 Ministers agreed on a more flexible
interpretation of the guidelines to reflect a more relaxed
approach to the less sensitive items such as civil aircraf
spares and machine tools. Though the need to protect
intelligence sources was a factor in approving the
company's licences last February, the fact that the lathes
could be used for munitions manufacture was regarded as
less of a concern in the light of the cease fire, in that
the machines would not, under the more relaxed
interpretation of the Guidelines, be of direct and
significant assistance in the conduct of offensive
operations in breach of the cease fire.

Nuclear Missile Development

12.   No firm evidence has been offered that Matrix Churchill
machines have been used to further Iraqi's nuclear
programme. The February approvals took account of the fact
that a, refusal of the licences would not prevent Iraq
developing a nuclear weapon. Though the company is largely
Iraqi owned and Mr Safa al-Habobi, a director, is Head of
Nassr and known to have an interest in acquiring nuclear
technology, this is not in self evidence of Matrix
Churchill's involvement in that programme. Nassr is said
to undertake a range of general engineering work. The
present licences cover the same type of equipment as that
already shipped under previous licences. We are not
therefore giving the Iraqis a capability they do not already
have.

13.   There would appear to be some inconsistency in the FCO
attitude to Iraq as distinct from other nuclear sensitive
destinations eg South Africa, where end use undertakings
for non nuclear, non military use are acceptable. This
begs the question why these exports to Iraq should be
treated differently.

Implications for Matrix Churchill

14.   The Iraqi business is claimed to be significant in terms of
the company's cash flow. Given the level of shipments
already made and the value of licences outstanding
this must be so. We cannot rule out the possibility of
redundancies and if, as FCO argue, the company is less
dependent on the Iraqi market, to close that market to the
company would result in a weakening of its financial
position.

CCO2711

DOCUMENT 3.1 Matrix Churchill Ltd: Export Licence Applications for Iraq, September 25, 1989 *(Continued)*

SECRET

Trade Implications

15. A refusal of general purpose CNC machine tools also has wider implications for our trade with Iraq and the machine tool sector specifically. Coming hard on the heels of the decision on the Hawk Trainer Project, a refusal will be regarded by Iraq as provocative and this could affect our export effort generally to that market. This has been impressive in recent years. In 1988 there was a 51% increase over 1987 to £412m and the first seven months of 1989 indicates a further 30 per cent increase. General industrial machinery (including machine tools) is the second most important import into Iraq and is our 3rd best market in machine tools. To close this market to CNC machine tools for UK companies would be a serious loss to the industry (£31m last year). Equivalent products could easily be sourced from other competitor countries, such as Switzerland, Germany, Italy and Japan.

CONCLUSION

16. When balanced against these arguments the FCO line is unconvincing. We would have difficulty defending a refusal under the guidelines and, as previously accepted by FCO, the supply of Matrix Churchill machine tools is not critical to Iraqi's nuclear development programme. A refusal would be seen as presentational in the face of recent press publicity about the Iraqi procurement network and the fact that Matrix Churchill is largely Iraqi owned. However this could be turned against us, the implication being that we were wrong to approve the previous applications and are now only reacting to press reports.

17. A refusal of general purpose equipment to Iraq would have serious implications for UK machine tool sales into an important market and is likely to have repercussions generally for our expanding trade with Iraq.

A D STEADMAN

0002712

CHAPTER 4

Political Interference in the Intelligence Process

The Case of Iraqi WMD

MARK PHYTHIAN

Editors' Note:

This chapter explores the pernicious intelligence problem of politicization. Using Gregory Treverton's comprehensive taxonomy, Phythian details the complex and fluid incidences of politicization within British intelligence in the approach to the 2003 war against Iraq. He traces this politicization in the agencies, the domestic political level, and the international sphere, through the influential 2004 Butler Report.

"Convictions are more dangerous enemies of truth than lies."
Friedrich Nietzsche, *Human, All Too Human* (1878)

"All lies and jest
Still a man hears what he wants to hear
And disregards the rest"
Paul Simon, *The Boxer* (1969)

In September 2002, the Labour government led by Tony Blair published a dossier highlighting the threat posed by Iraq's weapons of mass destruction (WMD). In his foreword to the dossier, Blair explained that it was "based, in large part, on the work of the Joint Intelligence Committee [JIC]," that there were limits regarding how much information based on intelligence sources could be made public, which meant that "we cannot publish everything we know," but that he "and other Ministers have been briefed in detail on the intelligence and are satisfied as to its authority."[1] On this basis, Blair informed the public that Iraqi WMD represented a "current and serious threat to the UK national interest," and one that had "become more not less worrying" over recent months. Presenting the dossier to the specially recalled House of Commons on September 24, 2002, Blair further explained that he was aware "that people will have to take elements of this on the good faith of our intelligence services, but this is what they are telling me, the British prime minister, and my senior colleagues. The intelligence picture that they paint is one accumulated over the last four years. It is extensive, detailed and authoritative." This picture showed that "Iraq has chemical and biological weapons, that Saddam has continued to produce them, that he has existing and active military plans for the use of chemical and biological weapons, which could be activated within 45 minutes, including against his own Shia population, and that he is actively trying to acquire nuclear weapons capability."[2]

None of this turned out to be true. In the aftermath of the March 2003 US-led war, it was discovered that Iraq had no chemical or biological weapons, and so they could not have been activated within 45 minutes. Neither was the regime at that point attempting to acquire nuclear weapons. Moreover, far from being "extensive, detailed and authoritative," the evidentiary basis on which these claims had rested was found by Lord Butler of Brockwell, who chaired a postwar inquiry into British intelligence on WMD, to be "very thin."[3] The present study seeks to explain how this situation arose, how intelligence regarded as "very thin" by Lord Butler could be presented to Parliament and the public as "extensive, detailed and authoritative" by the prime minister. In doing so it focuses on the question of political interference in the intelligence process—in other words, politicization.

Politicization

Before I discuss the significance of the document on which this case is based, it will be useful to define the term "politicization," which has come to be used as a shorthand for forms of political interference in the intelligence process. Gregory Treverton has outlined five different forms that politicization of intelligence can take, ranging from what may be considered "hard" to "soft" forms.[4] At the hard end of the scale lies *direct pressure* from senior figures in government to arrive at a desired conclusion in line with an existing policy preference. A second form suggested by Treverton is the *house line,* whereby over a period of time a dominant assumption regarding an issue has emerged and any challenge to it is regarded as heresy. While this variant shifts the focus from policymakers to the intelligence community, and particularly its managers, it is implicit that any analytical shift here would be in line with policymaker preference. A third form is *cherry-picking,* whereby senior policymakers select the intelligence that best supports their policy preference from a wider picture presented by overall assessments. Treverton also notes that with regard to US intelligence on Iraq's WMD, policymakers were not content simply to engage in cherry-picking, but went so far as to "grow their own" through the stove piping of intelligence via the Department of Defense's Office of Special Plans.[5] A fourth form is *question asking,* wherein the form in which a question is asked suggests the desired answer or wherein analysis that is not consistent with a policy preference is subjected to repeated questioning in a bid to shift it more in line with that policy preference. Finally, at the softer end of the scale comes *shared mindset*, wherein strong presumptions are shared by both policymakers and the intelligence community and where, to the extent that this is a form of politicization, it is a self-imposed one.

This is a useful typology that gives clearer meaning to what is something of an umbrella term. However, it does not necessarily capture every dimension of politicization, which can be an almost intangible process. As Paul Pillar, the former US national intelligence officer for the Near East and South Asia from 2000 to 2005, remarked with regard to US inquiries into intelligence on Iraq's WMD:

> Unfortunately, this issue [i.e. politicization] has been reduced in some post mortem inquiries to a question of whether policymakers twisted analysts' arms. That question is insufficient. Such blatant attempts at politicization are relatively rare, and when they do occur are almost never successful. It is more important to ask about the overall *environment* in which intelligence analysts worked. It is one thing to work in an environment in which policymakers are known to want the most objective analysis, wherever the evidence may lead. It is quite another thing to work in an environment in which the policymaker has already set his course, is using intelligence to publicly justify the course, will welcome analysis that supports the policy, and will spurn analysis that does not support it. The latter environment was what prevailed on Iraq in the year before the war.[6]

The structure of what follows is designed so that readers can, with reference to Treverton's typology, assess for themselves which form(s) of politicization may have been present in this case.

The Significance of the Document

It is useful to outline the significance of the Butler inquiry into intelligence on WMD, and so of the document around which this study is based, annex B of the Butler report. The postwar failure to find any WMD inside Iraq raised questions about the veracity of the claims underpinning the invasion. These were posed more frequently as time passed and the failure to locate WMD became more evident. In particular, those members of Parliament who had opposed the war demanded answers, and it was in this context that the Foreign Affairs Committee (FAC) decided to investigate the accuracy of governmental claims.[7] One unforeseen outcome of its hearings was the series of events that culminated in the suicide of Ministry of Defence biological weapons expert David Kelly.

By the time a second inquiry into the intelligence basis for the war decision, by the Intelligence and Security Committee (ISC), reported in September 2003, Blair had been obliged to set up a further judicial inquiry under a former Lord

Chief Justice of Northern Ireland, Lord Hutton, "urgently to conduct an investigation into the circumstances surrounding the death of Dr Kelly."[8] The public hearings conducted by the Hutton inquiry and evidence available to it, notably internal Downing Street e-mail traffic concerning the production of the September 2002 dossier, suggested a critical outcome. However, the report exonerated the government of any bad faith in relation to its creation, although any governmental relief at this outcome was short-lived, because on the same day that the Hutton inquiry was published, January 28, 2004, in Washington, DC, arms expert David Kay testified that Saddam had destroyed all WMD, possibly even as early as 1991. The intelligence that Tony Blair had consistently cited as demonstrating the threat posed by Iraq was again called into question. Hence, Blair felt obliged to announce a fourth inquiry, to be conducted by a team of privy councillors, led by former Cabinet secretary Lord Butler.

In conducting its inquiry, the Butler team had an advantage denied to both the FAC investigation and the Hutton inquiry—access to the JIC assessments on Iraqi WMD. The FAC had been allowed to interview the foreign secretary in closed session, but had been denied access to the heads of the intelligence agencies and the chairman of the JIC, John Scarlett. It had also been denied access to JIC assessments, although extracts were read to the committee in private. Although the Hutton inquiry had access to intelligence officials and key political figures, it too operated without access to JIC assessments. This gave those who had made the case for war with Iraq an information advantage and meant that key assertions could not be challenged.

For instance, in giving evidence to the Hutton inquiry, Tony Blair explained his advocacy of military intervention in Iraq and decision to publish the September 2002 dossier thus: "What changed was really two things which came together. First of all, there was a *tremendous amount of information and evidence* coming across my desk as to the weapons of mass destruction and the programs associated with it that Saddam had. . . . There was also a renewed sense of urgency, again, in the way that this was being publicly debated. . . . *Why did we say it was a big problem? Because of the intelligence.* And the people were naturally saying: produce that intelligence then." (My emphasis—this evidence should be read in conjunction with the three JIC assessment excerpts contained in the document.) This was a point he reinforced later, telling Lord Hutton: "So, in a sense, the September 24 dossier was an unusual—the whole business was unusual, but it was in response to an unusual set of circumstances. We were saying this issue had to be returned to by the international community and dealt with. Why were we saying this? Because of the intelligence."[9] Without access to the JIC assessments, the judge was in no position to do anything but accept Blair's account, one which the Butler Report, with access to the JIC assessments, challenged.

Hence, access to the JIC assessments was the crucial difference between the Butler inquiry and the earlier FAC and Hutton inquiries. The ISC had also had access to JIC assessments. While it assumed that it had seen all relevant assessments, in fact eight had been withheld. Moreover, it reported in a "pre-Kay" climate and, possibly as a consequence of its proximity to the agencies, seemed to assume that Iraq had possessed WMD but had concealed them via a sophisticated denial and deception strategy.[10] The post-Kay environment, the greater distance between the Butler inquiry process and the intelligence agencies, and a greater willingness to comment on the underlying political context, distinguished the Butler inquiry from that of the ISC.

The document on which this study is based presents substantial extracts from JIC assessments from March, August, and September 2002, which fed into the September 2002 government dossier, *Iraq's Weapons of Mass Destruction: The Assessment of the British Government,* and contrasts these assessments with the presentation of the Iraqi WMD threat in the main body of that document and Tony Blair's foreword to it.

This format allows us to see three important things. First, intelligence on Iraq's WMD by March 2002 was wide of the mark in some key respects.[11] Second, the thin base of the intelligence underpinning conclusions on Iraqi WMD, which created the possibility that the intelligence could be wrong, was made clear at several points in the March 2002 JIC assessment. However, this was not flagged in the key judgments, which would have given this fact added prominence. Nevertheless, the fact of the thin intelligence base should have alerted an experienced user of intelligence to the potential for inaccuracy. In the terms used by the US intelligence community, the logic of this thin base was that the agencies and users could not have *high* confidence in the judgments, but something falling short of this, only *moderate* or *low* confidence. Third, caveats as to the limits of the intelligence base were excluded from the government's presentation of its case in the dossier, in Parliament, and beyond. This created an alternative reality. The certainty with which the government spoke of the threat posed by Iraqi WMD had a reflexive quality and created a threat that did not exist. Notwithstanding the overall conclusion of the March 2002 JIC assessment that the containment regime to which Iraq had been subject since the 1991 Gulf War had been largely effective (see document), by excluding the caveats Tony Blair's foreword to the September 2002 dossier presented a threat of sufficient seriousness for him to be able to claim that containment had, in effect, failed. The reality was rather different. Carne Ross, who served as first secretary to the UK mission to the UN from December 1997 until June 2002, where he was responsible for Iraq policy, told the Butler inquiry:

> I read the available UK and US intelligence on Iraq every working day for the four and a half years of my posting. This daily briefing would often comprise a thick folder of material, both humint and sigint. . . . During my posting, at no time did HMG assess that Iraq's WMD (or any other capability) posed a threat to the UK or its interests. On the contrary, it was the commonly-held view among the officials dealing with Iraq that any threat had been effectively contained. . . . There was moreover no intelligence or assessment during my time in the job that Iraq had any intention to launch an attack against its neighbours or the UK or US. I had many conversations with diplomats

representing Iraq's neighbours. With the exception of the Israelis, none expressed any concern that they might be attacked. Instead, their concern was that sanctions, which they and we viewed as an effective means to contain Iraq, were being delegitimised by evidence of their damaging humanitarian effect.

I quizzed my colleagues in the FCO and MoD working on Iraq on several occasions about the threat assessment in the run-up to the war. None told me that any new evidence had emerged to change our assessment; what had changed was the government's determination to present available evidence in a different light. I discussed this at some length with David Kelly in late 2002, who agreed that the Number 10 WMD dossier was overstated.[12]

The Political Context

An appreciation of the political context in which the Blair government took the decision to produce and publish a dossier highlighting the threat posed by Iraq is essential to assessing the question of politicization. In the wake of the 9/11 terrorist attacks on New York and Washington, DC, Tony Blair visited the United States, and was made aware of the current within the Bush administration in favor of extending the "war on terror" to Iraq once operations in Afghanistan were complete.[13] This US commitment to removing Saddam was signaled publicly in President Bush's January 29, 2002, State of the Union address, in which he announced the existence of an "axis of evil" involving Iraq, Iran, and North Korea. "What we have found in Afghanistan," Bush explained, "confirms that, far from ending there, our war against terror is only beginning. . . . I will not wait on events, while dangers gather. I will not stand by as peril draws closer. The United States of America will not permit the world's most dangerous regimes to threaten us with the world's most destructive weapons."

The Blair government's early support for the Bush approach to Iraq and its parallel understanding of the threat posed by Iraq's WMD are revealed in a series of leaked memos and minutes (collectively referred to as the "Downing Street memos"). These show that, in early March 2002, Blair dispatched foreign policy adviser David Manning to Washington, in advance of a visit Blair himself was to make to meet with President Bush in Crawford, Texas. By mid-March 2002, Manning's report on a dinner with US National Security Adviser Condoleezza Rice suggests that Blair may well have already offered his government's support over Iraq:

> We spent a long time at dinner on Iraq. It is clear that Bush is grateful for your support and has registered that you are getting flak. I said that you would not budge in your support for regime change but you had to manage a press, a Parliament and a public opinion that was very different than anything

in the States. And you would not budge on your insistence that, if we pursued regime change, it must be very carefully done and produce the right result. Failure was not an option. Condi's enthusiasm for regime change is undimmed. But there were some signs, since we last spoke, of greater awareness of the practical difficulties and political risks.[14]

Three days later, on March 17, Paul Wolfowitz, US Defense Secretary Donald Rumsfeld's deputy, lunched with British Ambassador Christopher Meyer, providing an opportunity for Meyer to reinforce Blair's support for regime change in advance of the Texas visit. "I opened by sticking very closely to the script that you used with Condi Rice," Meyer reported. "We backed regime change, but the plan had to be clever and failure was not an option. It would be a tough sell for us domestically and probably tougher elsewhere in Europe."[15]

Outside Downing Street and the British Embassy, however, concerns over the manner in which Blair was aligning Britain so closely to the Bush administration over Iraq policy were being voiced from within the Labour Party, Blair's own cabinet, and the Foreign Office. From there, on March 2, Foreign Secretary Jack Straw's policy director, Peter Ricketts, summarized his concerns. "The truth," explained Ricketts, "is that what has changed is not the pace of Saddam Hussein's WMD programmes, but our tolerance of them post-11 September."[16] Already the government was working on what would emerge, in an attempt to convince British public opinion of the necessity of war, as the September 2002 Downing Street dossier, but Ricketts warned Straw that more work was needed on it, and that, "even the best survey of Iraq's WMD programmes will not show much advance in recent years on the nuclear, missile, or CW/BW fronts."[17] Getting public opinion to accept the imminence of the threat from Iraq would be problematic, especially given that other proliferators, such as Iran, were thought to be closer to achieving a nuclear capability.

Straw summarized these concerns in a memo to Blair, sent less than two weeks before his US visit:

> The rewards from your visit to Crawford will be few. The risks are high, both for you and for the Government. . . . Colleagues know that Saddam and the Iraqi regime are bad. Making that case is easy. But we have a long way to go to convince them as to:
> (a) the scale of the threat from Iraq and why this has got worse recently;
> (b) what distinguishes the Iraqi threat from that of e.g. Iran and North Korea so as to justify military action;
> (c) the justification for any military action in terms of international law; and
> (d) whether the consequence of military action really would be a compliant, law abiding replacement government.[18]

Straw confirmed that, from intelligence to date, it was, "hard to glean whether the threat from Iraq is so significantly different from that of Iran and North Korea as to justify military action," and pointed to the Foreign Office view that if the 9/11 attacks had not occurred it was doubtful whether the United States would be considering an attack on Iraq. After all, the threat from Iraq had not worsened as a result of 9/11, and there was no link between Osama bin Laden and Iraq, although members of the Bush administration continued to allude to one.

This was the background to Blair's April 2002 visit to Crawford, Texas. While there he delivered a major foreign policy speech at the George Bush Senior Presidential Library, intended as an updating of his 1999 "Doctrine of the International Community" speech delivered in Chicago. Blair ended this by making a public commitment:

> We don't shirk our responsibility. It means that when America is fighting for those values, then, however tough, we fight with her. No grandstanding, no offering implausible but impractical advice from the comfort of the touchline, no wishing away the hard not the easy choices on terrorism and WMD, or making peace in the Middle East, but working together, side by side. That is the only route I know to a stable world based on prosperity and justice for all, where freedom liberates the lives of every citizen in every corner of the globe. If the world makes the right choices now - at this time of destiny - we will get there. And Britain will be at America's side in doing it.[19]

Hence, by mid-April 2002, Blair had committed his government to support the Bush administration over Iraq. The weakness of the case against Iraq was no barrier, but it was something of which Blair should have been aware. Both Ricketts and Straw were reflecting the thinness of the case for war as reflected in a March 15, 2002 JIC assessment, "The Status of Iraqi WMD Programmes" (see document, column one). However, in his public statements suggesting the immediacy of the threat posed by Iraq, Blair discarded the caveats contained in this assessment and exaggerated its (tentative) judgments. For example, compare the March 15 JIC assessment that, "Iraq *may retain some* stocks of chemical weapons" (my emphasis) and "has available . . . a number of biological agents" with Blair's April 3, 2002, assertion in an NBC News interview that: "We know he [Saddam Hussein] has stockpiles of *major amounts of* chemical and biological weapons" (my emphasis).

This March–April 2002 period marked a turning point during which Blair began to present the threat posed by Iraq in ever starker terms, a process that had its parallel in the United States. This is significant in terms of our thinking about forms of politicization. These prime ministerial interventions affected the environment in which intelligence assessments were being made and in which intelligence was being collected. It is also important to note that some of these interventions were not actually based on intelligence assessments at all, but simply reflected the prime minister's own convictions. However, Parliament and public could not be sure for themselves of the line at which comment based (however loosely) on intelligence and comment based on conviction was being crossed.

For example, on April 10, 2002, Blair told Parliament; "there is no doubt at all that the development of weapons of mass destruction by Saddam Hussein poses a severe threat not just to the region, but to the wider world." Blair would return to this theme more frequently in the run-up to the publication of the Downing Street dossier in September 2002, for example telling a September 3 press conference that "Iraq poses a real and a unique threat to the security of the region and the rest of the world." The point would be reiterated in Blair's foreword to the dossier (see document). However, the excerpts from the March 2002 JIC assessment do not refer to this threat. It is referred to in the August 21, 2002 JIC assessment (see document, column two) that was produced in response to a request to "consider what diplomatic options Saddam has to deter, avert or limit the scope and effectiveness of a US-led attack [and] . . . his military options for facing a US-led attack," but characterized rather differently. Even in the September 9, 2002, JIC assessment—produced in the context of increasingly alarmist public statements being made by senior policymakers on both sides of the Atlantic and offering the most worrying assessment of the threat posed by Iraq's WMD to date (see document, column three)—it was assessed that it was "unlikely" that Iraq would deploy chemical and biological weapons unless it was itself under attack, in which case, as the August 21 assessment had outlined, it was anticipated that these could then be used as part of a "Samson option."

On July 23, 2002, Blair met with a select group of cabinet colleagues and officials to discuss Iraq. Here, Sir Richard Dearlove, head of MI6, reported on his recent discussions in Washington, DC, where "there was a perceptible shift in attitude. Military action was now seen as inevitable. Bush wanted to remove Saddam, through military action, justified by the conjunction of terrorism and WMD. But the intelligence and facts were being fixed around the policy. The NSC [National Security Council] had no patience with the UN route, and no enthusiasm for publishing material on the Iraqi regime's record. There was little discussion in Washington of the aftermath after military action."[20] Foreign Secretary Jack Straw agreed that it "seemed clear that Bush had made up his mind to take military action," but again warned that "the case was thin. Saddam was not threatening his neighbours, and his WMD capability was less than that of Libya, North Korea, or Iran."[21] Straw also conveyed his department's advice that it would be prudent to insist that Iraq allow weapons inspectors to reenter the country, not so as to eliminate any WMD uncovered or enable them to declare that Iraq possessed none (post-9/11, any solution that left Saddam in power was clearly unacceptable—as Blair would tell the meeting, "regime change and WMD were linked in the sense that it was the regime that was producing the WMD"), but because insistence on weapons inspections "would also help with the legal justification for the use of force."[22]

This was especially important because, as the attorney-general, Lord Goldsmith, told the meeting, "the desire for regime change was not a legal base for military action." There were only three possible legal bases for an attack on Iraq: self-defense, humanitarian intervention, or United Nations Security Council (UNSC) authorization based on Iraqi noncompliance with UNSC resolutions. The first two could not apply, so the only route that could confer legality on an attack involved Iraq's continued breach of UNSC resolutions.

This, then, was the political environment and state of government knowledge against which the decision was taken to publish a dossier that would convince Parliament and public of the threat posed by Iraq. The assessments that fed into the dossier seem to have been affected by the shifting political climate concerning Iraq (compare the key judgments from the March 15 and September 19, 2002, JIC assessments in the document). However, the dossier drafting process itself further exacerbated this tendency by generating a climate in which intelligence professionals were confronted by strong political preferences, and in which a number of them, possibly extending to the chairman of the JIC, John Scarlett, succumbed to the pressures of politicization.

The decision to publish summaries of intelligence material in a dossier designed to generate support for the government's policy is one that the Butler Report criticizes. It echoed the ISC's criticism that the Downing Street dossier gave no indication of existing gaps or uncertainties in intelligence, or of the thin base of some judgments, thereby creating the impression of a more solid intelligence base than actually existed. Moreover, it found that the dossier simply omitted reference to JIC judgments that were unhelpful in advancing the government's case, but that were nevertheless essential to a balanced understanding of the full picture. The structure of the dossier and the language used within it seemed to have one purpose, to persuade the reader of the imminence of the Iraqi threat and so increase support for the government's still undeclared policy of regime change. The Butler Report concluded that:

> The dossier did include a first chapter on the role of intelligence, as an introduction for the lay reader. But, rather than illuminating the limitations of intelligence either in the case of Iraq or more generally, the language in that chapter may have had the opposite effect on readers. Readers may, for example, have read language in the dossier about the impossibility for security reasons of putting all the detail of the intelligence into the public domain as implying that there was fuller and firmer intelligence behind the judgements than was the case: our view, having reviewed all of the material, is that judgements in the dossier went to (although not beyond) the outer limits of the intelligence available.[23]

One thing that emerges clearly from the Butler inquiry is that human intelligence sources proved highly unreliable in this case. MI6 had just five main sources of human intelligence inside Iraq, but the majority of these were subsequently deemed to be unreliable, leading to the postwar withdrawal of intelligence that had underpinned the most eye-catching claims contained in the Downing Street dossier. The length of reporting chains was a further problem. Because there were so few human sources within Iraq, they came to be asked to gather intelligence on areas outside their usual expertise. This resulted in their moving beyond firsthand knowledge or experience and drawing on subsources (and even sub-subsources), heightening the risk of unreliable reporting.

However, these were problems that were, in large part, generated by the dossier decision and the looming deadline for its publication, as contemporaneous internal Downing Street e-mails released to the Hutton inquiry demonstrate. These show that in the early stages of drafting the dossier the then-available intelligence was recognized as constituting a problem. A September 11 e-mail from Downing Street advisor Philip Bassett to Daniel Pruce and Alastair Campbell (i.e., just 13 days before the dossier's publication) makes this clear: "Very long way to go I think. Think we're in a lot of trouble with this as it stands."[24] The same day an e-mail sent out to the intelligence community appealed for additional intelligence: "No. 10 through the Chairman want the document to be as strong as possible within the bounds of available intelligence. This is therefore a last (!) call for any items of intelligence that agencies think can and should be included. Responses needed by 12.00 tomorrow."

That the intelligence services owned the text of the dossier was, of course, crucial to its credibility. However, a trail of e-mails and memos to and from Downing Street staffers show that they were unhappy with what they called the "Scarlett version" of the dossier—that is, the one initially approved by JIC Chairman John Scarlett—and were discussing amendments designed to heighten the sense of threat. The Hutton inquiry revealed a rich seam of e-mail traffic as the drafting process neared its end. In a September 10 e-mail from Daniel Pruce to Mark Matthews, Pruce advises "we make a number of statements about Saddam's intentions/attitudes. Can we insert a few quotes from speeches he has made which, even if they are not specific, demonstrate that he is a bad man with a general hostility towards his neighbours and the West? . . . Much of the evidence we have is largely circumstantial so we need to convey to our readers that the cumulation of these facts demonstrates an intent on Saddam's part - the more they can be led to this conclusion themselves rather than have to accept judgments from us, the better." These coexisted with more despairing e-mails such as this sent to Alastair Campbell by Philip Bassett a day earlier: "Needs much more weight, writing, detail, and we need to find a way to get over this a) by having *better* intelligence material, b) by having *more* material (and better flagged-up), and c) more *convincing* material." The Butler Report notes the possibility that this pressure led to more credence being given to untried sources than would usually be the case.[25]

The common thread running through these exchanges is the need to demonstrate Saddam's malign intent, ideally towards the United Kingdom. Hence, on September 11, Daniel Pruce e-mailed Alastair Campbell: "I think we need to personalise the dossier onto Saddam as much as possible - for example by replacing references to Iraq with references to Saddam. In a similar vein I think we need a device to convey that he is a bad and unstable man . . . a few quotes from Saddam to demonstrate his aggressive intent and hatred of his neighbours and the West would help too." The same day Tom Kelly e-mailed Alastair Campbell, commenting on the current draft and again emphasizing the importance of demonstrating intent: "This does have some new elements to play with, but there is one central weakness—we do not differentiate enough between capacity and intent. We know that he is a bad man and has done bad things in the past. We know he is trying to get WMD—and this shows those attempts are intensifying. But can we show why we think he intends to use them aggressively, rather than in self-defence. We need that to counter the argument that Saddam is bad, but not mad. . . . The key must be to show that Saddam has the capacity, and is intent on using it in ways that threaten world stability, and that our ability to stop him is increasingly threatened."

However, this was a far cry from the intelligence picture contained in the JIC assessments of March 15, August 21, and September 9, 2002. These did not discuss any Iraqi plans to use these weapons aggressively; as noted above, this idea was rooted in Blair's conviction rather than intelligence community evaluation. In short, the bid to demonstrate intent, and hence imply imminence, involved moving beyond a position supported by the assessments produced by the JIC. War was being treated as simply another policy that had to be sold to the electorate.

Within the dossier the "45-minutes claim," that Iraqi chemical and biological weapons could be deployed within 45 minutes of an order being given, represented the headline threat. It was a claim that appeared in three separate parts of the dossier, in the main body, the executive summary, and Blair's foreword. Its appearance in Blair's foreword could reasonably have been interpreted as reflecting both intelligence and governmental confidence in the reliability of this evidence. However, this jewel in the dossier's crown had arrived and been uncritically and gratefully accepted at the eleventh hour of the dossier's preparation. The dossier had been about threat creation. Through the 45-minutes claim it had succeeded. In July 2004 the Butler Report criticized both its inclusion in this form and its repetition. Moreover, it revealed that "the validity of the intelligence report on which the 45-minute claim was based has come into question."[26] In fact it was false, and in October 2004 Jack Straw announced that it had been formally withdrawn.[27]

The Butler Report noted that the process of assessing the validity of a source and the intelligence emanating from it must be "informed by an understanding of policymakers' requirements for information, but must avoid being so captured by policy objectives that it reports the world as policymakers would wish it to be rather than as it is."[28] Although the report avoided diagnosing politicization (indeed, the word does not appear once in the 216-page report), it is not insignificant that Butler identified "a strong case for the post of Chairman of the JIC being held by someone with experience of dealing with Ministers in a very senior role, and who is demonstrably beyond influence, and thus probably in his last post."[29] Perceptions of political pressure could also help explain why there was no JIC reassessment of Iraq's WMD programs once Hans Blix's UNMOVIC weapons inspection team was admitted to the country and failed to locate the previously reported programs, an omission the Butler Report termed "odd."[30]

Lessons Learned?

In his foreword to the September 2002 Downing Street dossier and in his presentation of this to the House of Commons—recalling Parliament a day early in order to heighten the sense of threat—Tony Blair emphasized that Iraq's "WMD programme is active, detailed and growing. The policy of containment is not working. The WMD programme is not shut down. It is up and running."[31] In his foreword to the dossier, Blair claimed that the "picture presented to me by the JIC in recent months has become more not less worrying," and wrote of Iraq's WMD programs constituting "a current and serious threat to the UK national interest" (see document). In contrast, the Butler Report concluded that "the Government's conclusion in the spring of 2002 that stronger action (although not necessarily military action) needed to be taken to enforce Iraqi disarmament was not based on any new development in the current intelligence picture on Iraq."[32] Moreover, in his evidence to the inquiry Blair was obliged to agree with "the view expressed at the time that what had changed was not the pace of Iraq's prohibited weapons programmes, which had not been dramatically stepped up, but tolerance of them following the attacks of 11 September 2001." Damningly, and contradicting the picture presented by Blair in Parliament, in the dossier, and to the Hutton inquiry, the Butler Report concluded that "there was no recent intelligence that would have given rise to a conclusion that Iraq was of more immediate concern than the activities of some other countries."[33]

However, as former Foreign Secretary Robin Cook, who resigned from the government on the eve of war with Iraq, argued, "Downing Street did not worry that the intelligence was thin and inferential or that the sources were secondhand and unreliable, because intelligence did not play a big part in the real reason why we went to war."[34] Robin Butler agreed. Appearing before the Public Administration Select Committee and asked about the high proportion of human intelligence sources in Iraq who proved unreliable, but had supplied what might be considered the more alarming intelligence to emerge from the country, he was quick to remind MPs "that what we discovered was that the government did not go to war on the basis of those intelligence reports. It went to war on wider grounds and the intelligence reports were not the basis for the decision."[35] Ironically, then, while intelligence was central to Downing Street's strategy for selling the war, it was not central to the actual war decision.

What other lessons can be learned from this case? First, that the term that has come to be used as a shorthand for political interference in the intelligence process, politicization, is a complex term that covers a number of variants. How many of those, as identified by Gregory Treverton and discussed in the early part of this study, were present in this case? Were there any additional variants not covered by Treverton's typology? We need a more informed understanding of just what we mean by politicization, and Treverton has provided an important framework for taking this thinking forward. There is a danger that, otherwise, the charge will be regarded as no more than a form of political abuse. In reality it is a multifaceted phenomenon. There is a tendency, encouraged by the concept of the intelligence cycle, to see intelligence failure as having one cause, to identify one stage of the intelligence cycle and locate failure there. Failure, however, is a much more complex phenomenon than this and tends to be multicausal in nature. Thinking about just what we mean by politicization can help in appreciating this. Politicization can occur at every stage of the intelligence cycle and, where it is a factor, is usually aided and abetted by supporting failures (as, in this case, in the intelligence management-policymaker interface—see below).

It is significant that the Butler Report—the result of the most detailed official inquiry into the Iraq intelligence failure to date—catalogues a number of instances of political interference and/or intelligence management acquiescence in the face of it and yet nowhere does the report diagnose politicization. Nor is this a trait unique to Butler: the Silberman-Robb inquiry (the US equivalent of the Butler inquiry) similarly avoids the diagnosis, instead highlighting the extent to which "groupthink" was a contributory factor, a diagnosis that raises more questions than it resolves. This leads to a further lesson: that inquiries into intelligence and security scandals or failures are likely to be highly political and keenly contested processes. In a US context, Kenneth Kitts has suggested that the executive branch regards these more as devices through which they can exert damage control than as truth-seeking missions.[36] The public needs to be alert to this fact. To take the Butler Report as an example, did the fact that it did not conclude that politicization was to blame, at least in part, for the failure have anything to do with the fact that chair of the ISC and former member of the Blair Cabinet Ann Taylor was a member? Did the fact that two members of the ISC that had already concluded that the content of the September 2002 dossier was consistent with the intelligence available by September 2002 influence the Butler inquiry's conclusion that "judgments in the dossier went to (although not beyond) the outer limits of the intelligence available"?[37] How do we reconcile this judgment with the observation some 130 paragraphs further into the report that "in the particular circumstances, the publication of such a document in the name and with the authority of the JIC had the result that more weight was placed on the intelligence than it could bear"?[38] Is this evidence of internal disagreement over the conclusions to be reached? To reiterate, the key point here is that inquiries are highly political processes and their conclusions and the ordering of their evidence and conclusions are all political acts that are the product of debate and bargaining.

Additional lessons were highlighted by both the Butler Report and the US Silberman-Robb report. The importance of flagging gaps and uncertainties in intelligence assessments so as to allow readers to appreciate the full intelligence picture has been reinforced. The importance of some form of competitive analysis to challenge the dominant assumption (what Treverton, in his typology of politicization, calls the "house line") has been reemphasized, although the barriers to finding an effective way of doing this do not seem any lower than previously. The fact that Iraq represented a "hard target" has taken on the status of a mantra since 2003. Yet this should not conceal the fact that Western intelligence agencies fell into the trap of assessing Iraqi intentions and the world view of its leadership via analysis of its weapons programs rather than vice versa. Collecting intelligence on the former was accorded a lower priority than on the latter. Where was the intelligence community (or, for that matter, academic community) analysis that anticipated the findings of the Iraq Survey Group with regard to Saddam's worldview and strategic motivation? In practice there was something of a vacuum, which (in a UK context) Blair's conviction about the threat posed by Saddam occupied almost without challenge (where challenges did emerge they were easily dismissed as coming from the usual suspects on the old left of the Labour Party).[39]

There are also lessons to be drawn from the question of the distance that should be maintained between intelligence managers and policymakers. The intelligence-policymaker interface has long been viewed as the most frequent location of intelligence failure.[40] In this context, the case of Iraqi WMD has also revived the longstanding debate about the correct distance between analysts and customers, and whether the two should be separated by a wall. Famously, in giving evidence to the Hutton inquiry, Alastair Campbell referred to JIC Chairman John Scarlett, the man who formally steered the dossier process so as to ensure JIC ownership of its contents, as a "mate." Did this mean that he was too close to government to draw necessary lines?

On one side of the debate stand those who emphasize that the purpose of intelligence organizations is to serve the policymaker and that the relationship should be close,[41] on the other stand those who see proximity as potentially compromising objectivity, thereby heightening the risk of politicization.[42] One way of reducing the risk of politicization might be for analysts to consciously seek to "know the customer," the background, areas of interest, and areas where they believe they have special expertise. If, as Richard Neustadt and Ernest May have argued, policymakers base their decisions on formative experiences and decisions they took that served them well in these contexts, awareness of this in the presentation of analysis could prove useful.[43]

For example, formative experiences in Tony Blair's premiership included joining the Clinton administration in the 1998 Operation Desert Fox air strikes on Iraq, and the military interventions in Kosovo and Sierra Leone in 1999. These clearly were a factor in his judgments over Iraq during 2002–3. Had they been asked to assess the likelihood of a successful and relatively bloodless occupation of Iraq (a key qualifier, given that none was requested), intelligence analysts could have framed their analysis so as to emphasize the differences between Iraq and the cases of Kosovo and Sierra Leone.

In an increasingly complex world, it makes little sense to erect false walls between policymakers and analysts, but equally for analysts to pull back from the water's edge of what might, in an earlier era, have looked like policy advice. At the same time, truth must resist the temptation to be supine in the face of power. Intelligence managers have a professional responsibility to convey their "best truth" to policymakers and resist any attempts to mold it into a preferred but different shape.

Nevertheless, the risk of politicization is omnipresent.[44] To reemphasize an earlier point, in recognition of this risk, analysts and intelligence community managers must ensure that the degree of uncertainty that underpins any judgment is clearly understood by policymakers, and that they are as fully educated as their time and interest allow into the limitations of intelligence and proper role of estimative analysis. For their part, oversight bodies need to appreciate the omnipresent risk of politicization and rise above party political ties in identifying, naming, and thereby deterring it. In this context the record to date in the United Kingdom is hardly reassuring and overseers will need to up their game.

NOTES

1. Tony Blair's foreword to the dossier can be found in column five of the document (fig. 4.1) on which this study is based, "Intelligence Assessment and Presentation: From March to September 2002," which was originally published as Annex B to Lord Butler, *Review of Intelligence on Weapons of Mass Destruction* (London: The Stationery Office, July 2004, HC 898) [henceforward, Butler Report]. The dossier itself, *Iraq's Weapons of Mass Destruction: The Assessment of the British Government*, is available at www.fco.gov.uk/resources/en/pdf/pdf3/fco_iraqdossier.

2. Hansard, September 24, 2002, col. 3. Blair's speech can be found in the fifth column of the document on which this study is based.

3. Hansard, House of Lords, September 7, 2004, col. 463.

4. See Gregory F. Treverton, "Intelligence Analysis: Between 'Politicization' and Irrelevance," in Roger Z. George and James B. Bruce (eds.), *Analyzing Intelligence: Origins, Obstacles, and Innovations* (Washington, DC: Georgetown University Press, 2008), 91–104, at 93–96.

5. Ibid., 95. Stove piping is the term used to describe the process of pairing raw information directly from an intelligence source to a policymaker, thereby bypassing the analytic filter of the intelligence process.

6. Paul R. Pillar, "Democratic Policy Committee Hearing. An Oversight Hearing on Prewar Intelligence Relating to Iraq," 109th Congress, Second Session, June 26, 2006, 183–84, www.democrats.senate.gov/dpc/hearings/hearing33/pillar.pdf.

7. Foreign Affairs Committee, *The Decision to Go to War in Iraq* (London: The Stationery Office, HC 813–1), July 7, 2003, para. 3.

8. Intelligence and Security Committee, *Iraqi Weapons of Mass Destruction—Intelligence and Assessments* (Cm 5972, London, HMSO, 2003).

9. Hutton Inquiry, Evidence of Tony Blair, August 28, 2003. www.the-hutton-inquiry.org.uk/content/transcripts/hearing-trans22.htm. Last accessed March 26, 2007.

10. See, for example, ISC, *Iraqi Weapons of Mass Destruction*, paras. 65–66.

11. An analysis of the reasons for this is beyond the scope of this study, which focuses on the question of political interference. For an analysis, see Mark Phythian, "Flawed Intelligence, Limited Oversight: Official Inquiries into Prewar UK Intelligence on Iraq," in James P. Pfiffner and Mark Phythian (eds.), *Intelligence and*

National Security Policymaking on Iraq: British and American Perspectives (Manchester: Manchester University Press, 2008), 191–210.

12. Carne Ross, "Supplementary Evidence Submitted to the Foreign Affairs Committee December 2006" (originally drafted for the Butler inquiry), June 9, 2004. www.publications.parliament.uk/pa/cm200607/cmselect/cmfaff/167/6110810.htm.

13. See, Christopher Meyer, *DC Confidential* (London: Weidenfeld and Nicolson, 2005); Bryan Burrough, Evgenia Peretz, David Rose and David Wise, "The Path to War," *Vanity Fair*, May 2004.

14. "Your Trip to the US." Memo from David Manning to Tony Blair, March 14, 2002. www.downingstreetmemo.com/docs/manning.pdf.

15. Memo from Christopher Meyer to Sir David Manning, March 18, 2002. www.downingstreetmemo.com/docs/meyermemo.pdf.

16. "IRAQ: Advice for the Prime Minister." Memo from P. F. Ricketts to Jack Straw, March 22, 2002. www.downingstreetmemo.com/docs/ricketts.pdf.

17. Ibid.

18. "Crawford/Iraq." Memo from Jack Straw to Tony Blair, March 25, 2002. www.downingstreetmemo.com/docs/straw.pdf.

19. Prime Minister's speech at the George Bush Senior Presidential Library, April 7, 2002. www.pm.gov.uk/output/Page1712.asp.

20. "Iraq: Prime Minister's Meeting, July 23." Memo from Matthew Rycroft to David Manning, July 23, 2002.www.downingstreetmemo.com/memos.html#originalmemo.

21. Ibid.

22. Ibid.

23. Butler Report, para. 331.

24. The e-mails quoted from here are either reproduced on the Hutton Inquiry website, or discussed in evidence given there. www.the-hutton-inquiry.org.uk/content/evidence.htm#full. On the role of Alastair Campbell generally, and more specifically in the creation of the dossier, see Peter Oborne and Simon Walters, *Alastair Campbell* (London: Aurum Press, 2004), esp. ch. 15.

25. Butler Report, paras. 438–42.

26. Ibid., para. 512.

27. Marie Woolf, "The 45-Minute Claim Was False," *Independent*, 10.13.04.

28. Butler Report, para. 58.

29. Ibid., para. 597.

30. Ibid., para. 364.

31. Hansard, September 24, 2002, col. 3.

32. Butler Report, para. 427.

33. Ibid.

34. Robin Cook, "The Die Was Cast: The Dossiers Were Irrelevant," *Independent on Sunday*, July 18, 2004.

35. Public Administration Select Committee, Minutes of Evidence, October 21, 2004. www.publications.parliament.uk/pa/cm200304/cmselect/cmpubadm/606/4102106.htm.

36. Kenneth Kitts, *Presidential Commissions and National Security: The Politics of Damage Control* (Boulder, CO: Lynne Reinner, 2006).
37. Butler Report, para. 331.
38. Ibid., para. 466.
39. For a discussion of the evolution of the Labour Party's approach to the question of committing British troops to war situations and the divisions within it, see Mark Phythian, *The Labour Party, War and International Relations, 1945–2006* (London: Routledge, 2007).
40. See Richard K. Betts, "Analysis, War, and Decision: Why Intelligence Failures Are Inevitable," *World Politics*, no. 31 (1978): 61–89.
41. For example, Michael Herman, *Intelligence Power in Peace and War* (Cambridge: Cambridge University Press, 1996).
42. For example, Sherman Kent, *Strategic Intelligence for American World Policy* (Princeton: Princeton University Press, 1949), 195–201.
43. Richard E. Neustadt and Ernest R. May, *Thinking in Time: The Uses of History for Decision Makers* (New York: Free Press, 1988).
44. See the discussion in Peter Gill and Mark Phythian, *Intelligence in an Insecure World* (Cambridge: Polity Press, 2006), esp. ch. 6.

DOCUMENT 4.1   The Butler Report: Annex B: Intelligence Assessment and Presentation: From March to September 2002

ANNEX B

INTELLIGENCE ASSESSMENT AND PRESENTATION: FROM MARCH TO SEPTEMBER 2002

15 March 2002	21 August 2002	9 September 2002	24 September 2002	24 September 2002
JIC(02)069: THE STATUS OF IRAQI WMD PROGRAMMES (15 March 2002) (substantial extracts) Key Judgements i. Iraq **retains up to 20 Al Hussein ballistic missiles**, produced prior to the Gulf War, with a range of 650km and capable of hitting Israel. The location and condition of these is unknown, but there is sufficient engineering expertise to make them operational. ii. Iraq has begun development of **medium range ballistic missiles over 1000km** that could target countries throughout the Middle East and Gulf Region, **but will not be able to produce such a missile** before 2007 provided sanctions remain effective. iii. **Iraq is pursuing a nuclear weapons programme. But it will not be able to indigenously produce a nuclear weapon while sanctions remain in place, unless** suitable fissile material is purchased from abroad. iv. Iraq **may retain some stocks of chemical agents.** Following a decision to do so, Iraq could produce: • significant quantities of **mustard within weeks;** • significant quantities of **sarin and VX within months,** and in the case of VX may have already done so. v. Iraq currently **has available,** either from pre Gulf War stocks or more recent production, a number of **biological agents.** Iraq could	JIC(02)181: IRAQ: SADDAM'S DIPLOMATIC AND MILITARY OPTIONS (21 August 2002) (relevant extracts) Key Judgements v. Early on in any conflict Saddam would order missile attacks on Israel, coalition forces and regional States providing the US with bases. vi. Saddam would order the use of CBW against coalition forces at some point, probably after a coalition attack had begun. Once Saddam was convinced that his fate was sealed, he would order the unrestrained use of CBW against coalition forces, supporting regional states and Israel. ... Secondary goals will be to preserve and enhance his WMD capability. ... As we have	JIC(02)202: IRAQI USE OF CHEMICAL AND BIOLOGICAL WEAPONS – POSSIBLE SCENARIOS (9 September 2002) (substantial extracts) Key Judgements I. Iraq has a chemical and biological weapons capability and Saddam is prepared to use it. II. Faced with the likelihood of military defeat and being removed from power, Saddam is unlikely to be deterred from using chemical and biological weapons by any diplomatic or military means. III. The use of chemical and biological weapons prior to any military attack would boost support for US-led action and is unlikely. IV. Saddam is prepared to order missile strikes against Israel, with chemical or biological warheads, in order to widen the war once hostilities begin. V. Saddam could order the use of CBW weapons in order to deny space and territory to Coalition forces, or to cause casualties, slow any advance, and sap US morale. VI. If not previously employed, Saddam will order the indiscriminate use of whatever CBW weapons remain available late in a ground campaign	EXTRACTS FROM THE GOVERNMENT DOSSIER (24 September 2002) Executive Summary 1. Under Saddam Hussein Iraq developed chemical and biological weapons, acquired missiles allowing it to attack neighbouring countries with these weapons and persistently tried to develop a nuclear bomb. Saddam has used chemical weapons, both against Iran and against his own people. Following the Gulf War, Iraq had to admit to all this. And in the ceasefire of 1991 Saddam agreed unconditionally to give up his weapons of mass destruction. 2. Much information about Iraq's weapons of mass destruction is already in the public domain from UN reports and from Iraqi defectors. This points clearly to Iraq's continuing possession, after 1991, of chemical and biological agents and weapons produced before the Gulf War. It shows that Iraq has refurbished sites formerly associated with the production of chemical and biological agents. And it indicates that Iraq remains able to manufacture these agents, and to use bombs, shells, artillery rockets and ballistic missiles to deliver them. 3. An independent and well-researched overview of this public evidence was provided by the International Institute for Strategic Studies (IISS) on 9 September. The IISS report also suggested that Iraq could assemble nuclear weapons within months of obtaining fissile material from foreign sources. 4. As well as the public evidence, however, significant additional information is available to the Government from secret intelligence sources, described in more detail in this paper. This intelligence cannot tell us about everything. However, it provides a fuller picture of Iraqi plans and capabilities. It shows that Saddam Hussein attaches great importance to possessing weapons of mass destruction which he regards as the basis for Iraq's regional power. It shows that he does not regard them only as weapons of last resort. He is ready to use them, including against his own population, and is determined to retain them, in breach of United Nations Security Council Resolutions (UNSCR). 5. Intelligence also shows that Iraq is preparing plans to conceal evidence of these weapons, including incriminating documents, from renewed inspections. And it confirms that despite sanctions and the policy of containment, Saddam has continued to make progress with his illicit weapons programmes. 6. As a result of the intelligence we judge that Iraq has: • Continued to produce chemical and biological agents;	FOREWORD TO THE GOVERNMENT DOSSIER (signed by the Prime Minister) The document published today is based, in large part, on the work of the Joint Intelligence Committee (JIC). The JIC is at the heart of the British intelligence machinery. It is chaired by the Cabinet Office and made up of the heads of the UK's three Intelligence and Security Agencies, the Chief of Defence Intelligence, and senior officials from key government departments. For over 60 years the JIC has provided regular assessments to successive Prime Ministers and senior colleagues on a wide range of foreign policy and international security issues. Its work, like the material it analyses, is largely secret. It is unprecedented for the Government to publish this kind of document. But in light of the debate about Iraq and Weapons of Mass Destruction (WMD), I wanted to share with the British public the reasons why I believe this issue to be a current and serious threat to the UK national interest. In recent months, I have been increasingly alarmed by the evidence from inside Iraq that despite sanctions, despite the damage done to his capability in the past, despite the UN Security Council Resolutions expressly outlawing it, and despite his denials, Saddam Hussein is continuing to develop WMD, and with them the ability to inflict real damage upon the region, and the stability of the world. Gathering intelligence inside Iraq is

NOTE: Redactions are not indicated

DOCUMENT 4.1   The Butler Report: Annex B: Intelligence Assessment and Presentation: From March to September 2002 *(Continued)*

ANNEX B

15 March 2002	21 August 2002	9 September 2002	24 September 2002	24 September 2002
produce more of these biological agents within days. vi. A decision to begin CBW production would probably go undetected. vii. Iraq can deliver CBW weapons by a variety of means including ballistic missiles. **Iraq's CBW production capability is designed to survive a military attack and UN inspections.** Intelligence on Iraq's weapons of mass destruction (WMD) and ballistic missile programmes is sporadic and patchy. Iraq is also well practised in the art of deception, such as concealment and exaggeration. A complete picture of the various programmes is therefore difficult. But it is clear that Iraq continues to pursue a policy of acquiring WMD and their delivery means. Intelligence indicates that planning to reconstitute some of its programmes began in 1995. WMD programmes were then given a further boost in 1998 with the withdrawal of UNSCOM inspectors. **Ballistic Missiles** Iraq has rebuilt much of the military production infrastructure associated with the missile programme damaged in the Gulf War and the few high profile sites targeted in Operation Desert Fox in 1998. New infrastructure is being built, with a particular focus on improving the support to the solid propellant missile programme. Since the Gulf War, Iraq has been openly developing **short-range ballistic missiles (SRBM)** up to a range of 150km, which are permitted under UN Security Council Resolution 687. Intelligence indicates that:	previously judged, even if inspectors were allowed to return, Iraq would embark on a renewed policy of frustration, involving denial, deception, obstruction and delay. ... Saddam could: • Threaten the use of WMD against regional states. **Missiles and WMD** We judge that Saddam would probably order missile attacks on Israel and the coalition early on in a conflict in an attempt to attract Israeli retaliation and thus widen the war, split the coalition and arouse popular opinion in the Arab States. Such missiles could be armed with chemical or biological warfare (CBW) agents. Saddam might be deterred, at least initially, by the threat of Israeli nuclear retaliation. Other factors would be the limited number of long range missiles Iraq would have available (we	or as a final act of vengeance. But such an order would depend on the availability of delivery means and the willingness of commanders to obey. Recent intelligence casts light on Iraq's holdings of weapons of mass destruction and on its doctrine for using them. Intelligence remains limited and Saddam's own unpredictability complicates judgements about Iraq use of these weapons. Much of this paper is necessarily based on judgement and assessment. Iraq used chemical weapons on a large scale during the Iran/Iraq War. Use on the same scale now would require large quantities of chemical weapons and survivable delivery means in the face of overwhelming US air superiority. Iraq did not use chemical weapons during the Gulf War. Intelligence suggests that Iraq may have used the biological agent, aflatoxin, against the Shia population in 1991. We do not believe that Iraq possesses nuclear weapons and there is no intelligence that Iraq is currently interested in radiological dispersal devices. **Chemical and biological capabilities** Based on intelligence on the nature of Iraqi CBW weapons, known delivery means, continuing procurement activity, and experience from previous	• Military plans for the use of chemical and biological weapons, including against its own Shia population. Some of these weapons are deployable within 45 minutes of an order to use them; • Command and control arrangements in place to use chemical and biological weapons. Authority ultimately resides with Saddam Hussein. (There is intelligence that he may have delegated this authority to his son Qusai); • Developed mobile laboratories for military use, corroborating earlier reports about the mobile production of biological warfare agents; • Pursued illegal programmes to procure controlled materials of potential use in the production of chemical and biological weapons programmes; • Tried covertly to acquire technology and materials which could be used in the production of nuclear weapons; • Sought significant quantities of uranium from Africa, despite having no active civil nuclear power programme that could require it; • Recalled specialists to work on its nuclear programme; • Illegally retained up to 20 al-Hussein missiles, with a range of 650km, capable of carrying chemical or biological warheads; • Started deploying its al-Samoud liquid propellant missile, and has used the absence of weapons inspectors to work on extending its range to at least 200km, which is beyond the limit of 150km imposed by the United Nations; • Started procuring the solid-propellant Ababil-100, and is making efforts to extend its range to al least 200km, which is beyond the limit of 150km imposed by the United Nations; • Constructed a new engine test stand for the development of missiles capable of reaching the UK Sovereign Base Areas in Cyprus and NATO members (Greece and Turkey), as well as all Iraq's Gulf neighbours and Israel; • Pursued illegal programmes to procure materials for use in its illegal development of long range missiles; • Learnt lessons from previous UN weapons inspections and has already begun to conceal sensitive equipment and documentation in advance of the return of inspectors.	not easy. Saddam is one of the most secretive and dictatorial regimes in the world. So I believe people will understand why the Agencies cannot be specific about the sources, which have formed the judgements in this document, and why we cannot publish everything we know. We cannot, of course, publish the detailed raw intelligence. I and other Ministers have been briefed in detail on the intelligence and are satisfied as to its authority. I also want to pay tribute to our Intelligence and Security Services for the often extraordinary work, that they do. What I believe the assessed intelligence has established beyond doubt is that Saddam has continued to produce chemical and biological weapons, that he continues in his efforts to develop nuclear weapons, and that he has been able to extend the range of his ballistic missile programme. I also believe that, as stated in the document, Saddam will now do his utmost to try to conceal his weapons from UN inspectors. The picture presented to me by the JIC in recent months has become more not less worrying. It is clear that, despite sanctions, the policy of containment has not worked sufficiently well to prevent Saddam from developing these weapons. I am in no doubt that the threat is serious and current, that he has made progress on WMD, and that he sees the building up of his WMD capability, and the belief that it has to be stopped. Saddam has used chemical weapons, not only against an enemy state, but against his own people. Intelligence reports make clear that he sees the building up of his WMD capability, and the belief overseas

NOTE: Redactions are not indicated

DOCUMENT 4.1 The Butler Report: Annex B: Intelligence Assessment and Presentation: From March to September 2002 *(Continued)*

ANNEX B

15 March 2002	21 August 2002	9 September 2002	24 September 2002	24 September 2002
• the 150km range liquid propellant Al Samoud missile has been extensively flight-tested. Intelligence indicates that Iraq has produced at least 50 Al Samouds, including those test fired, and preparations are underway to military deploy some of these to military units. Iraq has reportedly succeeded in developing a number of 200km range variants of Al Samoud, although it is unclear if these are for operational use or longer-range systems. A small number of transporter-erector-launchers (TELs) have been seen, although others may exist; • the solid propellant Ababil-100 has also been tested, and has reached ranges up to 150km. We judge that this system is likely to become operational as an SRBM within 2 years. It might enter service earlier as an artillery rocket. Intelligence indicates that Iraq has plans to extend the range of the Ababil-100 to 250km. *Immediate missile capability* *We judge that Iraq has the following missiles available for immediate use:* *Some Al Samoud (up to 150km)* *Up to 20 Al Hussein (650km)* *There are a limited number of launchers available.* *Both missiles could deliver basic chemical and biological warheads.* We judge Iraq has also retained some 20 Al Hussein missiles (650km range stretched SCUD), the type fired at Israel and Saudi Arabia during the Gulf War. We do not know the location of these missiles or their state of readiness, but judge that the engineering expertise available would	assess he has retained 12-20 650km-range Al Hussein missiles) and the need, in the case of attacking coalition forces in Kuwait, to deploy short-range missiles (we assessed in March that at least 50 150km range al-Samoud missiles had been produced; more will have been produced since then) into the 'no drive zone'. Although a pre-emptive missile attack on Israel would offer many of the same advantages, we judge this would be less likely because it would show Iraq had been lying about its retention of long range missiles prohibited by the UN, providing a justification for US action. Although we have little intelligence on Iraq's CBW doctrine, and know little about Iraq's CBW work since late 1998, we judge it likely that Saddam would order the use of CBW against	conflicts, we judge that: • Iraq currently has available, either from pre Gulf War stocks or more recent production, a number of biological warfare (BW) and chemical warfare (CW) agents and weapons; • following a decision to do so, Iraq could produce significant quantities of mustard agent within weeks; significant quantities of the nerve agents sarin and VX within months (and in the case of VX Iraq may have already done so). Production of sarin and VX would be heavily dependent on hidden stocks of precursors, the size of which are unknown; • Iraq could produce more biological agents within days. At the time of the Gulf War Iraq had developed the lethal BW agents anthrax, botulinum toxin and aflatoxin. Iraq was also researching a number of other agents including some non-lethal (incapacitating) agents; even if stocks of chemical and biological weapons are limited, they would allow for focused strikes against key military targets or for strategic purposes (such as a strike against Israel or Kuwait); • Iraq could deliver CW and BW agents by a variety of means including free fall bombs, airborne sprays, artillery shells, mortar	7. These judgements reflect the views of the Joint Intelligence Committee (JIC). More details on the judgements and on the development of the JIC's assessments since 1999 are set out in Part 1 of this paper. **PART 1** **IRAQ'S CHEMICAL, BIOLOGICAL, NUCLEAR AND BALLISTIC MISSILE PROGRAMMES** **CHAPTER 1: The Role of Intelligence (extract)** 1. Since UN inspectors were withdrawn from Iraq in 1998, there has been little overt information on Iraq's chemical, biological, nuclear and ballistic missile programmes. Much of the publicly available information about Iraq capabilities and intentions is dated. But we also have available a range of secret intelligence about these programmes and Saddam Hussein's intentions. This comes principally from the United Kingdom's intelligence and analysis agencies – the Secret Intelligence Service (SIS), the Government Communications Headquarters (GCHQ), the Security Service, and the Defence Intelligence Staff (DIS). We also have access to intelligence from close allies. 2. Intelligence rarely offers a complete account of activities which are designed to remain concealed. The nature of Saddam's regime makes Iraq a difficult target for the intelligence services. Intelligence, however, has provided important insights into Iraqi programmes and Iraqi military thinking. Taken together with what is already known from other sources, this intelligence builds our understanding of Iraq's capabilities and adds significantly to the analysis already in the public domain. But intelligence sources need to be protected, and this limits the detail that can be made available. 3. Iraq's capabilities have been regularly reviewed by the Joint Intelligence Committee (JIC), which has provided advice to the Prime Minister and his senior colleagues on the developing assessment, drawing on all available sources. Part 1 of this paper includes some of the most significant views reached by the JIC between 1999 and 2002. **CHAPTER 2: Iraq's Programmes, 1971–1998 (extract)** [This historical chapter covers past Iraqi research into chemical and biological warfare; what quantities of agent Iraq had produced by the early 1990s; its use of chemical weapons during the Iran/Iraq war,	that he would use these weapons, as vital to his strategic interests, and in particular his goal of regional domination. And the document discloses that his military planning allows for some of the WMD to be ready within 45 minutes of an order to use them. I am quite clear that Saddam will go to extreme lengths, indeed has already done so, to hide these weapons and avoid giving them up. In today's inter-dependent world, a major regional conflict does not stay confined to the region in question. Faced with someone who has shown himself capable of using WMD, I believe the international community has to stand up for itself and ensure its authority is upheld. The threat posed to international peace and security, when WMD are in the hands of a brutal and aggressive regime like Saddam's, is real. Unless we face up to the threat, not only do we risk undermining the authority of the UN, whose resolutions he defies, but more importantly and in the longer term, we place at risk the lives and prosperity of our own people. The case I make is that the UN Resolutions demanding he stops his WMD programme are being flouted; that since the inspectors left four years ago he has continued with this programme; that the inspectors must be allowed back in to do their job properly; and that if he refuses, or if he makes it impossible for them to do their job, as he has done in the past, the international community will have to act. I believe that faced with the

NOTE: Redactions are not indicated

DOCUMENT 4.1   The Butler Report: Annex B: Intelligence Assessment and Presentation: From March to September 2002 *(Continued)*

ANNEX B

15 March 2002	21 August 2002	9 September 2002	24 September 2002	24 September 2002
allow these missiles to be effectively maintained. Iraq is seeking to develop new, larger **liquid and solid propellant missiles**, contrary to UN limits. Recent intelligence indicates personnel associated with the Al Samoud programme have now been tasked to concentrate on designing liquid propellant systems with ranges of 2000–3000km. New intelligence indicates the main focus may be on the development of a SCUD derivative, which we judge has an intended range of around 1200km. Work on an engine for this system began in 1998, involving personnel who had been reviewing the details of previous Al Hussein production since 1995, although by the end of the year 2000 they were still experiencing technical problems. Additional personnel were probably assigned to other parts of the programme during 2000. A large static test stand capable of testing liquid propellant engines bigger than the SCUD engine has been under construction since mid-2000, probably in support of this programme. Work on large motor cases for longer-range solid propellant systems has been noted over the last 2–3 years. Providing sanctions remain effective, Iraq is **unlikely to be able to produce a longer-range missile before 2007.** Despite retaining engineers with expertise in missile design and production, **UN sanctions and the work of the inspectors have caused** significant problems for Iraq's missile industry in acquiring components and production technology, in particular for improving guidance and control systems and therefore missile accuracy. Iraq is actively seeking to procure materials for its missile programme.	coalition forces at some point, probably after coalition attacks had begun, Iraqi CBW use would become increasingly likely the closer coalition forces came to Baghdad. Military targets might include troop concentrations or important fixed targets in rear areas such as ports and airfields. **Alternative scenarios and at the death** It is also possible that Saddam might pursue an extreme course of action at an earlier stage than we have envisaged . . . In particular, unorthodox options might include: • The early or pre-emptive use of **CBW. Because** of the time lag between infection and incapacitation, there is some incentive to use biological weapons early. Coalition forces would also be most geographically concentrated	bombs and battlefield rockets; • Iraq told UNSCOM in the 1990s that it filled 25 warheads with anthrax, botulinum toxin and aflatoxin for its Al Hussein ballistic missile (range 650km). Iraq also admitted it had developed 50 chemical warheads for Al Hussein. We judge Iraq retains up to 20 Al Husseins and a limited number of launchers; • Iraq is also developing short-range systems Al Samoud/Ababil 100 ballistic missiles (range 150km plus). – One intelligence report suggests that Iraq has "lost" the capability to develop warheads capable of effectively disseminating chemical and biological agent and that it would take six months to overcome the "technical difficulties". However, both these missile systems are currently being deployed with military units and an emergency operational capability with conventional warheads is probably available; • Iraq may have other toxins, chemical and biological agents that we do not know about; the effectiveness of any CBW attack would depend on the method of delivery, concentration of the target, dissemination efficiency, meteorological conditions and the	including against its own (Kurdist) citizens; the progress of its nuclear programme by 1991; its ballistic missile programmes; its use of such missiles during the first Gulf war; and Iraq's admission to UNSCOM of having had chemical and biological warheads available for its ballistic missiles.] 13. Based on the UNSCOM report to the UN Security Council in January 1999 and earlier UNSCOM reports, we assess that when the UN inspectors left Iraq they were unable to account for: • up to 360 tonnes of bulk chemical warfare agent, including 1.5 tonnes of VX nerve agent; • up to 3,000 tonnes of precursor chemicals, including approximately 300 tonnes which, in the Iraqi chemical warfare programme, were unique to the production of VX; • growth media procured for biological agent production (enough to produce over three times the 8,500 litres of anthrax spores Iraq admits to having manufactured); • over 30,000 special munitions for delivery of chemical and biological agents. 14. The departure of UNSCOM meant that the international community was unable to establish the truth behind these large discrepancies and greatly diminished its ability to monitor and assess Iraq's continuing attempts to reconstitute its programmes. **CHAPTER 3: The Current Position: 1998–2002 (extract)** 1. This chapter sets out what we know of Saddam Hussein's chemical, biological, nuclear and ballistic missile programmes, drawing on all the available evidence. While it takes account of the results from UN inspections and other publicly available information, it also draws heavily on the latest intelligence about Iraqi efforts to develop their programmes and capabilities since 1998. The **main conclusions** are that: • Iraq has a useable chemical and biological weapons capability, in breach of UNSCR 687, which has included recent production of chemical and biological agents; • Saddam continues to attach great importance to the possession of weapons of mass destruction and ballistic missiles which he regards as being the basis for Iraq's regional power. **He is determined to** retain these capabilities; • Iraq can deliver chemical and biological agents using an extensive range of artillery shells, free-fall bombs, sprayers and ballistic missiles;	information available to me, the UK Government has been right to support the demands that this issue be confronted and dealt with. We must ensure that he does not get to use the weapons he has, or get hold of the weapons he wants. **HOUSE OF COMMONS, TUESDAY 24 SEPTEMBER 2002** The Prime Minister, Mr Speaker, thank you for recalling Parliament to debate the best way to deal with the issue of the present leadership of Iraq and weapons of mass destruction. Today we published a 50-page dossier, detailing the history of Iraq's weapons of mass destruction programme, its breach of United Nations resolutions, and its attempts to rebuild that illegal programme. I have placed a copy in the Library. At the end of the Gulf war, the full extent of Saddam's chemical, biological and nuclear weapons programmes became clear. As a result, the United Nations passed a series of resolutions, demanding that Iraq disarm itself of such weapons and establishing a regime of weapons inspections and monitoring to do the task. The inspectors were to be given unconditional and unrestricted access to all and any Iraqi sites. All this is accepted fact. In addition, it is fact, documented by UN inspectors, that Iraq almost immediately began to obstruct the inspections. Visits were delayed; on occasions, inspectors threatened; material was moved; special sites, shut to the inspectors, were unilaterally designated by Iraq. The work of the inspectors continued, but against a background of increasing obstruction and non-compliance.

NOTE: Redactions are not indicated

DOCUMENT 4.1 The Butler Report: Annex B: Intelligence Assessment and Presentation: From March to September 2002 *(Continued)*

ANNEX B

15 March 2002	21 August 2002	9 September 2002	24 September 2002	24 September 2002
Chemical and Biological Warfare (CBW) We continue to judge that Iraq has an offensive chemical warfare (CW) programme, although there is very little intelligence relating to it. From the evidence available to us, we believe Iraq retains some production equipment, and some small stocks of CW agent precursors, and may have hidden small quantities of agents and weapons. Anomalies in Iraqi declarations to UNSCOM suggest stocks could be much larger. Given the size and scope of Iraq's pre Gulf War programme, little or no research and development work would need to be carried out. Intelligence on production facilities is scarce; the reconstructed former precursor production facility near Habbaniyah in itself is insufficient to support large-scale CW agent production. Other industrial chemical facilities could be used in support of a chemical weapons programme, but we have no intelligence to suggest that they are currently being used in that role. Intelligence has indicated an Iraqi interest in transportable production facilities for chemical weapons, but these could produce only small amounts of agent and we judge it more likely that the mobile units are for filling munitions rather than producing agent. We assess that following a decision to do so, Iraq could produce: • **Significant quantities of mustard within weeks**, using hidden stocks of precursors and with support from Iraq's chemical industry; • **Significant quantities of nerve agent within months**, mainly sarin and VX. This would be heavily dependent on hidden stocks of precursors. There has been one uncorroborated report that Iraq made some artillery rocket munitions with VX in the period 1996-1998, and	directly before or at the onset of a military campaign. He might also consider: • **CBW terrorism**: although Saddam probably lacks the capability to using CBW, is committed to using CBW if he can and is aware of the implications of doing so. Saddam wants it to dominate his neighbours and deter his enemies who he considers are unimpressed by his weakened conventional military capability. Should he feel his fate is sealed, Saddam's judgement might change to bring the temple down on his enemies no matter what the cost to the country as a whole. We judge that at this stage, Saddam would order the unrestrained use of CBW against coalition forces, supporting regional states and Israel, although he would face practical problems of command and control, the loyalty of his commanders, logistics problems and the availability of chemical or biological agents in sufficient quantities to be	availability of suitable defensive counter measures. **Other recent intelligence indicates that:** • production of chemical and biological weapons is taking place; • Saddam attaches great importance to having CBW, is committed to having the capability to deploy a sophisticated device, he could cause widespread panic. • Iraq has learned from the Gulf War the importance of mobile systems that are much harder to hit than large static sites. Consequently Iraq has developed for the military, fermentation systems which are capable of being mounted on road-trailers or rail cars. These could produce BW agent; • Iraq has probably dispersed its special weapons, including its CBW weapons. Intelligence also indicates that chemical and biological munitions could be with military units and ready for firing within 20-45 minutes. **Intentions for use** Intelligence indicates that Saddam has already taken the decision that all	• Iraq continues to work on developing nuclear weapons, in breach of its obligations under the Non-Proliferation Treaty and in breach of UNSCR 687. Uranium has been sought from Africa that has no civil nuclear application in Iraq; • Iraq possesses extended-range versions of the SCUD ballistic missile in breach of UNSCR 687 which are capable of reaching Cyprus, Eastern Turkey, Tehran and Israel. It is also developing longer-range ballistic missiles; • Iraq's current military planning specifically envisages the use of chemical and biological weapons; • Iraq's military forces are able to use chemical and biological weapons, with command, control and logistical arrangements in place. The Iraqi military are able to deploy these weapons within 45 minutes of a decision to do so; • Iraq has learnt lessons from previous UN weapons inspections and is already taking steps to conceal and disperse sensitive equipment and documentation in advance of the return of inspectors; • Iraq's chemical, biological, nuclear and ballistic missiles programmes are well-funded. **CHEMICAL AND BIOLOGICAL WEAPONS** 4. In the last six months the JIC has confirmed its earlier judgements on Iraqi chemical and biological warfare capabilities and assessed that Iraq has the means to deliver chemical and biological weapons. **Recent intelligence** 5. Subsequently, intelligence has become available from reliable sources which complements and adds to previous intelligence and confirms the JIC assessment that Iraq has chemical and biological weapons. The intelligence also shows that the Iraqi leadership has been discussing a number of issues related to these weapons. This intelligence covers: • **Confirmation that chemical and biological weapons play an important role in Iraqi military thinking**: intelligence shows that Saddam attaches great importance to the possession of chemical and biological weapons which he regards as being the basis for Iraqi regional power. He believes that respect for Iraq rests on its possession of these weapons and the missiles capable of delivering them. Intelligence indicates that Saddam is determined to retain this capability and recognises that Iraqi political weight would be diminished if Iraq's military power rested solely on its conventional military forces.	Indeed, Iraq denied that its biological weapons programme existed until forced to acknowledge it after high-ranking defectors disclosed its existence in 1995. Eventually, in 1997, the UN inspectors declared that they were unable to fulfil their task. A year of negotiation and further obstruction occurred until finally, in late 1998, the UN team was forced to withdraw. As the dossier sets out, we estimate on the basis of the UN's work that there were up to 360 tonnes of bulk chemical warfare agents, including 1.5 tonnes of VX nerve agent; up to 3,000 tonnes of precursor chemicals; growth media sufficient to produce 26,000 litres of anthrax spores; and over 30,000 special munitions for delivery of chemical and biological agents. All of this was missing and unaccounted for. Military action by the United States and United Kingdom followed and a certain amount of infrastructure for Iraq's weapons of mass destruction and missile capability was destroyed, setting the Iraqi programme back, but not ending it. From late 1998 onwards, therefore, the sole inhibition on Saddam's WMD programme was the sanctions regime. Iraq was forbidden to use the revenue from its oil except for certain specified non-military purposes. The sanctions regime, however, was also subject to illegal trading and abuse. Because of concerns about its inadequacy—and the impact on the Iraqi people—we made several attempts to refine it, culminating in a new UN resolution in May of this year. But it was only partially effective. Around $3 billion of money is illegally taken by Saddam every

NOTE: Redactions are not indicated

DOCUMENT 4.1   The Butler Report: Annex B: Intelligence Assessment and Presentation: From March to September 2002 *(Continued)*

ANNEX B

15 March 2002	21 August 2002	9 September 2002	24 September 2002	24 September 2002
another that a team of chemists was formed in 1998 to produce 5 tons of VX. The source was told this had been completed by the end of 1998; • Incapacitants including the mental incapacitant Agent 15. Iraq's military forces used chemical weapons during the Iran-Iraq War. Intelligence indicates command, control and logistical arrangements are in place. *Immediate CBW capability* *The following chemical agents could be produced within weeks, if not already:* Mustard, sarin and VX; *The following biological agents could be produced within days, if not already:* Anthrax spores, botulinum toxin, aflatoxin and possibly plague *These could be delivered by a variety of means, including ballistic missiles and special forces.* Iraq was forced by UNSCOM discoveries and the detection of Hussein Kamil to admit to having had a **biological warfare (BW) programme** at the time of the Gulf War. BW work continued throughout the period of UNSCOM inspections and intelligence indicates that this programme continues. Key figures from the pre-Gulf War programme are reported to be involved. Research and development is assessed to continue under cover of a number of legitimate institutes and possibly in a number of covert facilities. We judge that Iraq could produce significant quantities of BW agents within days of a decision to do so. There is no intelligence on any BW agent production facilities, but one source indicates that Iraq may have	effective and the means to deliver them.	resources, including CBW, be used to defend the regime from attack. One report states that Saddam would not use CBW during the initial air phase of any military campaign but would use CBW once a ground invasion of Iraq has begun. Faced with the likelihood of military defeat and being removed from power, we judge that it is unlikely there would be any way to deter Saddam from using CBW. We judge that several factors could influence the timing of a decision by Saddam to authorise the use of CBW weapons: • the availability of stocks of CW and BW agents; • the survivability of his delivery means. Many are vulnerable. Once a military campaign is underway the pressure will increase to use certain assets before they are destroyed; • the survivability of command and control mechanisms. The method and timing of such decision making is unknown. Intelligence indicates that Saddam's son Qusai may already have been given authority to order the use of CBW. Authorising front line units to use chemical and biological weapons could become more difficult once fighting begins. Saddam may therefore specify in advance of a	• **Iraq attempts to retain its existing banned weapons systems:** Iraq is already taking steps to prevent UN weapons inspectors finding evidence of its chemical and biological weapons programme. Intelligence indicates that Saddam has learnt lessons from previous weapons inspections, has identified possible weak points in the inspections process and knows how to exploit them. Sensitive equipment and papers can easily be concealed and in some cases this is already happening. The possession of mobile biological agent production facilities will also aid concealment efforts. Saddam is determined not to lose the capabilities that he has been able to develop further in the four years since inspectors left. • **Saddam's willingness to use chemical and biological weapons:** intelligence indicates that as part of Iraq's military planning Saddam is willing to use chemical and biological weapons, including against his own Shia population. Intelligence indicates that the Iraqi military are able to deploy chemical or biological weapons within 45 minutes of an order to do so. **Chemical and biological agents: surviving stocks** 6. When confronted with questions about the unaccounted stocks, Iraq has claimed repeatedly that if it had retained any chemical agents from before the Gulf War they would have deteriorated sufficiently to render them harmless. But Iraq has admitted to UNSCOM to having the knowledge and capability to add stabiliser to nerve agent and other chemical warfare agents which would prevent such decomposition. In 1997 UNSCOM also examined some munitions which had been filled with mustard gas prior to 1991 and found that they remained very toxic and showed little sign of deterioration. 7. Iraq has claimed that all its biological agents and weapons have been destroyed. No convincing proof of any kind has been produced to support this claim. In particular, Iraq could not explain large discrepancies between the amount of growth media (nutrients required for the specialised growth of agent) it procured before 1991 and the amounts of agent it admits to having manufactured. The discrepancy is enough to produce more than three times the amount of anthrax allegedly manufactured. **Chemical agent: production capabilities** 8. Intelligence shows that Iraq has continued to produce chemical agent. 9. Other dual-use facilities, which are capable of being used to support the production of chemical agent and precursors, have been rebuilt and re-equipped. New chemical facilities have been built, some with illegal	year now, double the figure for the year 2000. Self-evidently, there is no proper accounting for this money. Because of concerns that a containment policy based on sanctions alone would not sufficiently inhibit Saddam's weapons programme, negotiations continued, even after 1998, to gain readmission for the UN inspectors. In 1999, a new UN resolution demanding their re-entry was passed and ignored. Further negotiations continued. Finally, after several months of discussion with Saddam's regime, in July this year, Kofi Annan, the UN Secretary-General, concluded that Saddam was not serious about readmitting the inspectors and ended the negotiations. All this is an established fact. I set out the history in some detail because occasionally debate on this issue seems to treat it almost as if it had suddenly arisen, coming out of nowhere on a whim in the last few months of 2002. It is actually an 11-year history: a history of UN will flouted, of lies told by Saddam about the existence of his chemical, biological and nuclear weapons programmes, and of obstruction, defiance and denial. There is one common, consistent theme, however: the total determination of Saddam to maintain that programme; to risk war, international ostracism, sanctions and the isolation of the Iraqi economy to keep it. At any time, he could have let the inspectors back in and put the world to proof. At any time, he could have co-operated with the United Nations. Ten days ago, he made the offer unconditionally under threat of war. He could have done it at any

NOTE: Redactions are not indicated

DOCUMENT 4.1   The Butler Report: Annex B: Intelligence Assessment and Presentation: From March to September 2002 *(Continued)*

ANNEX B

15 March 2002	21 August 2002	9 September 2002	24 September 2002	24 September 2002
developed **mobile production facilities**. A liaison source reports that: • the transportable production programme began in 1995; • 6 road based facilities, on trailers, and 1 rail based facility, on railway carriages, were constructed and by March 1999; three were operational; • the facilities were capable of making 5 different (unspecified/unknown) biological agents. Between November 1998 and March 1999 20-30 tons of BW agent was produced. Though not corroborated, we judge the reporting is technically credible. We do not know which types of agents are produced by these facilities, but judge that **Iraq currently has available, either from pre Gulf War stocks or more recent production, anthrax spores, botulinum toxin, aflatoxin and possibly plague.** The continued operation of the castor oil extraction plant at the former Habbaniyah chemical weapons site may provide the base for producing ricin, although there is no evidence that Iraq is currently doing so. Iraq's declarations to UNSCOM acknowledged that it worked on a number of other BW agents including agents which would incapacitate, rather than kill, humans and on anti-crop and anti-livestock agents. Iraq almost certainly retains the capability to produce such agents. **Iraq is judged to be self-sufficient in the production of biological weapons.** Iraq has a variety of **delivery means** available for both chemical and biological weapons, some of which are available for Iraq's civil industry.		war the specific conditions in which unit commanders should use these weapons e.g. once coalition forces have crossed a particular geographical line; • the reliability of the units in question. Late in any military campaign commanders may not be prepared to use CBW weapons if they judge that Saddam is about to fall. **Possible scenarios: pre-emptive use before a conflict begins** The aim of a pre-emptive strike would be to incapacitate or kill Coalition troops in their concentration areas. Intelligence indicates that Saddam has identified Bahrain, Jordan, Qatar, Israel and Kuwait as targets. Turkey could also be at risk. Both chemical and biological weapons could be used; biological agents could be particularly effective against such force concentrations. But the use of CBW weapons carries serious risks and Saddam will weigh up their military utility against the political costs. Use of CBW weapons would expose the lies and deception about Iraq's WMD capabilities, undermining Iraqi diplomatic efforts and helping build support for rapid and effective US action. Saddam might also consider using non-lethal agents in a deniable manner, whilst it would be difficult to quickly establish a clear attribution of responsibility,	foreign assistance, and are probably fully operational or ready for production. These include the Ibn Sina Company at Tarmiyah, which is a chemical research centre. It undertakes research, development and production of chemicals previously imported but not now available and which are needed for Iraq's civil industry. The Director General of the research centre is Hikmat Na'im al-Jaiu who prior to the Gulf War worked in Iraq's nuclear weapons programme and after the war was responsible for preserving Iraq's chemical expertise. 10. Parts of the al-Qa'qa' chemical complex, damaged in the Gulf War have also been repaired and are operational. Of particular concern are elements of the phosgene production plant at al-Qa'qa'. These were severely damaged during the Gulf War, and dismantled under UNSCOM supervision, but have since been rebuilt. While phosgene does have industrial uses it can also be used by itself as a chemical agent or as a precursor for nerve agent. 11. Iraq has retained the expertise for chemical warfare research, agent production and weaponisation. Most of the personnel previously involved in the programme remain in country. While UNSCOM have a number of technical manuals (so called 'cook books') for the production of chemical agents and critical precursors, Iraq's claim to have unilaterally destroyed the bulk of the documentation cannot be confirmed and is almost certainly untrue. Recent intelligence indicates that Iraq is still discussing methods of concealing such documentation in order to ensure that it is not discovered by any future UN inspections. **The Problem of Dual-Use Facilities** Almost all components and supplies used in weapons of mass destruction and ballistic missile programmes are dual-use. For example, any major petrochemical or biotech industry, as well as public health organisations, will have legitimate need for most materials and equipment required to manufacture chemical and biological weapons. Without UN weapons inspectors it is very difficult therefore to be sure about the true nature of many of Iraq's facilities. For example, Iraq has built a large new chemical complex, Project Baiji, in the desert in north west Iraq at al-Sharquat. This site is a former uranium enrichment facility which was damaged during the Gulf War and rendered harmless under supervision of the IAEA. Part of the site has been rebuilt, with work starting in 1992, as a chemical production complex. Despite the site being far away from populated areas it is surrounded by a high wall with watch towers and guarded by armed guards. Intelligence reports indicate that it will produce nitric acid which can be used in explosives, missile fuel and in the purification of uranium.	time in the last 11 years, but he did not. Why? The dossier that we publish gives the answer. The reason is that his chemical, biological and nuclear weapons programme is not an historic left-over from 1998. The inspectors are not needed to clean up the old remains. His weapons of mass destruction programme is active, detailed and growing. The policy of containment is not working. The weapons of mass destruction programme is not shut down; it is up and running now. The dossier is based on the work of the British Joint Intelligence Committee. For over 60 years, beginning just before world war two, the JIC has provided intelligence assessments to British Prime Ministers. Normally, its work is obviously secret. Unusually, because it is important that we explain our concerns about Saddam to the British people, we have decided to disclose its assessments. I am aware, of course, that people will have to take elements of this with the good faith of our intelligence services, but this is what they are telling me, the British Prime Minister, and my senior colleagues. The intelligence picture that they paint is one It is extensive, detailed and authoritative. It concludes that Iraq has chemical and biological weapons, that Saddam has continued to produce them, that he has existing and active military plans for the use of chemical and biological weapons, which could be activated within 45 minutes, including against his own Shia population, and that he is actively trying to acquire nuclear

NOTE: Redactions are not indicated

DOCUMENT 4.1   The Butler Report: Annex B: Intelligence Assessment and Presentation: From March to September 2002 *(Continued)*

ANNEX B

15 March 2002	21 August 2002	9 September 2002	24 September 2002
very basic. These include, free fall bombs, artillery shells, helicopter and aircraft borne sprayers and ballistic missile warheads, although the exact numbers are unknown. Iraq is also continuing with the L-29 remotely piloted vehicle programme, which could have chemical and biological weapons delivery applications. Covert delivery also remains an option. Because of the shortage of some platforms, such as aircraft and helicopters, we judge that Iraq would not be able to conduct a sustained CBW campaign in the manner of the Iran-Iraq War, even if Iraq could produce enough CBW agents to do so. But a single major attack or a number of small attacks would be feasible. **Nuclear Weapons Programme** We judge that Iraq **does not possess** a nuclear weapons capability. We previously assessed that Iraq was within three years of producing a nuclear weapon when the Gulf War intervened. Its programme was effectively dismantled by the IAEA and subject to the monitoring process subsequently installed. Although there is very little intelligence we continue to judge that Iraq is pursuing a nuclear weapons programme. We assess the programme to be based on gas centrifuge uranium enrichment, which was the route Iraq was following for producing fissile material prior to the Gulf War. Recent intelligence indicates that nuclear scientists were recalled to work on a nuclear programme in the autumn of 1998, but we do not know if large scale development work has yet recommenced. Procurement of dual-use items over the last few years could be used in a uranium enrichment programme. There have been determined efforts to purchase high strength aluminium alloy, prohibited under the Nuclear Suppliers Group		Saddam could not be sure of the US reaction to an outbreak of a non-lethal disease. The early, widespread use of CBW or non-lethal agents would affect Coalition military planning; disruption of the build-up of personnel and material could delay operations. On balance however we judge that the political cost of using CBW weapons would outweigh the military advantages and that Saddam would probably not use CBW weapons pre-emptively. **Possible scenarios: use during the ground phase of a conflict** There is no intelligence on specific Iraqi plans for how CBW would be used in a conflict. Large numbers of chemical munitions would need to be used to make a major battlefield impact. BW could also be used although it is less effective as a tactical weapon against Coalition units than CW. But the use of even small quantities of chemical weapons would cause significant degradation in Coalition progress and might contribute to redressing Coalition conventional superiority on the battlefield. Iraq could make effective use of persistent chemical agents to shape the battlefield to Iraq's advantage by denying space and territory to Coalition forces. Booby-traps and improvised explosive devices could be used as	**Biological agent: production capabilities** 12. We know from intelligence that Iraq has continued to produce biological warfare agents. As with chemical equipment, UNSCOM only destroyed equipment that could be directly linked to biological weapons production. Iraq also has its own engineering capability to design and construct biological agent associated fermenters, centrifuges, sprayer dryers and other equipment and is judged to be self-sufficient in the technology required to produce biological weapons. The experienced personnel who were active in the programme have largely remained in the country. Some dual-use equipment has also been purchased, but without monitoring by UN inspectors Iraq could have diverted it to their biological weapons programme. This newly purchased equipment and other equipment previously subject to monitoring could be used in a resurgent biological warfare programme. Facilities of concern include: • the Castor Oil Production Plant at Fallujah: this was damaged in UK/US air attacks in 1998 (Operation Desert Fox) but has been rebuilt. The residue from the castor bean pulp can be used in the production of the biological agent ricin; • the al-Dawrah Foot and Mouth Disease Vaccine Institute: which was involved in biological agent production and research before the Gulf War; • the Amariyah Serra and Vaccine Plant at Abu Ghraib: UNSCOM established that this facility was used to store biological agents, seed stocks and conduct biological warfare associated genetic research prior to the Gulf War. It has now expanded its storage capacity. 13. UNSCOM established that Iraq considered the use of mobile biological agent production facilities. In the past two years evidence from defectors has indicated the existence of such facilities. Recent intelligence confirms that the Iraqi military have developed mobile facilities. These would help Iraq conceal and protect biological agent production from military attack or UN inspection. **Chemical and biological agents: delivery means** 14. Iraq has a variety of delivery means available to UNSCOM for both chemical and biological agents. These include: • free-fall bombs: Iraq acknowledged to UNSCOM the deployment to two sites of free-fall bombs filled with biological agent during 1990–91. These bombs were filled with anthrax, botulinum toxin and aflatoxin. Iraq also acknowledged possession of four types of aerial bomb with various chemical agent fills including sulphur mustard, tabun, sarin and cyclosarin;	weapons capability. On chemical weapons, the dossier shows that Iraq has continued to produce chemical agents for chemical weapons; has rebuilt previously destroyed production plants across Iraq; has bought dual-use chemical facilities; has retained the key personnel formerly engaged in the chemical weapons programme; and has a serious ongoing research programme into weapons production, all of it well funded. In respect of biological weapons, again, production of biological agents has continued; facilities formerly used for biological weapons have been rebuilt; equipment has been purchased for such a programme; and again, Saddam has retained the personnel who worked on it prior to 1991. In particular, the UN inspection regime discovered that Iraq was trying to acquire mobile biological weapons facilities, which of course are easier to conceal. Present intelligence confirms that it has now got such facilities. The biological agents that we believe Iraq can produce include anthrax, botulinum toxin, aflatoxin and ricin—all eventually result in excruciatingly painful death. As for nuclear weapons, Saddam's previous nuclear weapons programme was shut down by the inspectors, following disclosure by defectors of the full, but hidden, nature of it. The programme was based on gas centrifuge uranium enrichment. The known remaining stocks of uranium are now held under supervision by the International Atomic Energy Agency. But we now know the following: since

NOTE: Redactions are not indicated

DOCUMENT 4.1 The Butler Report: Annex B: Intelligence Assessment and Presentation: From March to September 2002 *(Continued)*

ANNEX B

171

15 March 2002	21 August 2002	9 September 2002	24 September 2002	24 September 2002
because of its application in uranium enrichment. A shipment stopped in Jordan was inspected by the IAEA, who accepted that, with some modifications, **the aluminium would be suitable for use in centrifuges. But we have no definitive intelligence that the aluminium was destined for a nuclear programme**. We continue to judge that: • while sanctions remain effective, Iraq cannot indigenously develop and produce nuclear weapons; • **if sanctions were removed or became ineffective, it would take at least five years to produce a nuclear weapon**. This timescale would shorten if fissile material was acquired from abroad. Iraq is capable of producing an **improvised nuclear device, but it lacks suitable fissile material**. **Dispersal of key equipment** Following 11 September 2001 Iraq temporarily dispersed key equipment from its missile production facilities, and is likely to do so again if it believes an attack is imminent. Recent intelligence indicates that Qusai Saddam Hussain has directed the Military Industrialisation Commission to ensure that all sensitive weapons and chemical technology was well hidden in case of further UN inspections. Dispersal makes the targeting of production equipment very difficult, but it also prevents any surge in production while dispersed.		chemical and biological weapons to inflict local losses in urban areas. It is also possible that Saddam would seek to use chemical and biological munitions against any internal uprising; intelligence indicates that he is prepared to deliberately target the Shia population. One report indicates that he would be more likely to use CBW against Western forces than on Arab countries. **Drawing Israel into the conflict** Launching a CBW attack against Israel could allow Saddam to present Iraq as the champion of the Palestinian cause and to undermine Arab support for the Coalition by sowing a wider Middle East conflict. One intelligence report suggests that if Saddam were to use CBW, his first target would be Israel. Another intelligence report suggests that Iraq believes Israel will respond with nuclear weapons if attacked with CBW or conventional warheads. It is not clear if Saddam is deterred by this threat or judges it to be unlikely. **Unconventional use of CBW** Although there is no intelligence to indicate that Iraq has considered using chemical and biological agents in terrorist attacks, we cannot rule out the possibility. Saddam could also remove his existing constraints on	• artillery shells and rockets: Iraq made extensive use of artillery munitions filled with chemical agents during the Iran-Iraq War. Mortars can also be used for chemical agent delivery. Iraq is known to have tested the use of shells and rockets filled with biological agents. Over 20,000 artillery munitions remain unaccounted for by UNSCOM; • helicopter and aircraft borne sprayers: Iraq carried out studies into aerosol dissemination of biological agent using these platforms prior to 1991. UNSCOM was unable to account for many of these devices. It is probable that Iraq retains a capability for aerosol dispersal of both chemical and biological agent over a large area; al-Hussein ballistic missiles (range 650km): Iraq told UNSCOM that it filled 25 warheads with anthrax, botulinum toxin and aflatoxin. Iraq also developed chemical agent warheads for al-Hussein. Iraq admitted to producing 50 chemical warheads for al-Hussein which were intended for the delivery of a mixture of sarin and cyclosarin. However, technical analysis of warhead remnants has shown traces of VX degradation product which indicate that some additional warheads were made and filled with VX; • al-Samoud/Ababil-100 ballistic missiles (range 150km plus): it is unclear if chemical and biological warheads have been developed for these systems, but given that Iraq has the technical expertise for doing so; we judge that Iraq has the technical expertise for doing so; • L-29 remotely piloted vehicle programme (see figure 3): we know from intelligence that Iraq has attempted to modify the L-29 jet trainer to allow it to be used as an Unmanned Aerial Vehicle (UAV) which is potentially capable of delivering chemical and biological agents over a large area. **Chemical and biological warfare: command and control** 15. The authority to use chemical and biological weapons ultimately resides with Saddam but intelligence indicates that he may have also delegated this authority to his son Qusai. Special Security Organisation (SSO) and Special Republican Guard (SRG) units would be involved in the movement of any chemical and biological weapons to military units. The Iraqi military holds artillery and missile systems at Corps level throughout the Armed Forces and conducts regular training with them. The Directorate of Rocket Forces has operational control of strategic missile systems and some Multiple Launcher Rocket Systems. **Chemical and biological weapons: summary** 16. Intelligence shows that Iraq has covert chemical and biological weapons programmes, in breach of UN Security Council Resolution 687	the departure of the inspectors in 1998, Saddam has bought or attempted to buy specialised vacuum pumps of the design needed for the gas centrifuge cascade to enrich uranium; an entire magnet production line of the specification for use in the motors and top bearings of gas centrifuges; dual-use products, such as anhydrous hydrogen fluoride and fluoride gas, which can be used both in petrochemicals but also in gas centrifuge cascades; a filament winding machine, which can be used to manufacture carbon fibre gas centrifuge rolors; and he has attempted, covertly, to acquire 60,000 or more specialised aluminium tubes, which are subject to strict controls owing to their potential use in the construction of gas centrifuges. In addition, we know that Saddam has been trying to buy significant quantities of uranium from Africa, although we do not know whether he has been successful. Again, key personnel who used to work on the nuclear weapons programme are back in harness. Iraq may claim that this is for a civil nuclear power programme, but I would point out that it has no nuclear power plants. So that is the position in respect of the weapons — but of course, the weapons require ballistic missile capability. That, again, is subject to UN resolutions. Iraq is supposed only to have missile capability up to 150 km for conventional weaponry. Pages 27 to 31 of the dossier detail the evidence on that issue. It is clear that a significant number of longer-range missiles were effectively concealed from the previous inspectors and remain, including up to 20 extended-range Scud missiles; that in mid-2001 there was a step change in the

NOTE: Redactions are not indicated

DOCUMENT 4.1 The Butler Report: Annex B: Intelligence Assessment and Presentation: From March to September 2002 *(Continued)*

ANNEX B

15 March 2002	21 August 2002	9 September 2002	24 September 2002	24 September 2002
		dealing with Al Qaida (extremists are conducting low-level work on toxins in an area of northern Iraq outside Saddam's control). Al Qaida could carry out proxy attacks and would require little encouragement to do so. Saddam's intelligence agencies have some experience in the use of poisons and even small-scale attacks could have a significant psychological impact. Intelligence indicates that Saddam has specifically commissioned a team of scientists to devise novel means of deploying CBW.

Possible scenarios: at the death
In the last resort Saddam is likely to order the indiscriminate use of whatever chemical and biological weapons remain available to him, in a last attempt to dling on to power or to cause as much damage as possible in a final act of vengeance. If he has not already done so by this stage Saddam will launch CBW attacks on Israel. Implementation of such orders would depend on the delivery means still remaining, the survivability of the command chain and the willingness of commanders to obey. | and has continued to produce chemical and biological agents. Iraq has:

- chemical and biological agents and weapons available, both from pre-Gulf War stocks and more recent production;
- the capability to produce the chemical agents mustard gas, tabun, sarin, cyclosarin, and VX capable of producing mass casualties;
- a biological agent production capability and can produce at least anthrax, botulinum toxin, aflatoxin and ricin. Iraq has also developed mobile facilities to produce biological agents;
- a variety of delivery means available;
- military forces, which maintain the capability to use these weapons with command, control and logistical arrangements in place.

NUCLEAR WEAPONS

Joint Intelligence Committee (JIC) Assessments: 1999–2001

17. Since 1999 the JIC has monitored Iraq's attempts to reconstitute its nuclear weapons programme. In mid-2001 the JIC assessed that Iraq had continued its nuclear research after 1998. The JIC drew attention to intelligence that Iraq had recalled its nuclear scientists to the programme in 1998. Since 1998 Iraq had been trying to procure items that could be for use in the construction of centrifuges for the enrichment of uranium.

Iraqi nuclear weapons expertise

18. The IAEA dismantled the physical infrastructure of the Iraqi nuclear weapons programme, including the dedicated facilities and equipment for uranium separation and enrichment, and for weapon development and production, and removed the remaining highly enriched uranium. But Iraq retained, and retains, many of its experienced nuclear scientists and technicians who are specialised in the production of fissile material and weapons design. Intelligence indicates that Iraq also retains the accompanying programme documentation and data.

19. Intelligence shows that the present Iraqi programme is almost certainly seeking an indigenous ability to enrich uranium to the level needed for a nuclear weapon. It indicates that the approach is based on gas centrifuge uranium enrichment, one of the routes Iraq was following for producing fissile material before the Gulf War. But Iraq needs certain key equipment, including gas centrifuge components and components for the production of fissile material before a nuclear bomb could be developed.

20. Following the departure of weapons inspectors in 1998 there has | programme and, by this year, Iraq's development of weapons with a range of more than 1,000 km was well under way; and that hundreds of people are employed in that programme, facilities are being built and equipment procured—usually clandestinely. Sanctions and import controls have hindered the programme, but only slowed its progress. The capability being developed, incidentally, is for multi-purpose use, including with WMD warheads.

That is the assessment, given to me, of the Joint Intelligence Committee. In addition, we have well founded intelligence to tell us that Saddam sees his WMD programme as vital to his survival and as a demonstration of his power and influence in the region.

There will be some who will dismiss all this. Intelligence is not always right. For some of the material, there might be innocent explanations. There will be others who say rightly that, for example, on present going, it could be several years before Saddam acquires a usable nuclear weapon—though if he were able to purchase fissile material illegally, it would be only a year or two. But let me put it at its simplest: on this 11-year history, with this man Saddam; with this accumulated, detailed intelligence available, with what we know and what we can reasonably speculate, would the world be wise to leave the present situation undisturbed—to say that, despite 14 separate UN demands on the issue, all of which Saddam is in breach of, we should do nothing, and to conclude that we should trust, not to the good faith of the UN weapons inspectors, but to the good faith of the current Iraqi regime? I do not believe |

NOTE: Redactions are not indicated

DOCUMENT 4.1   The Butler Report: Annex B: Intelligence Assessment and Presentation: From March to September 2002 *(Continued)*

ANNEX B

15 March 2002	21 August 2002	9 September 2002	24 September 2002	24 September 2002
			been an accumulation of intelligence indicating that Iraq is making concerted covert efforts to acquire dual-use technology and materials with nuclear applications. Iraq's known holdings of processed uranium are under IAEA supervision. But there is intelligence that Iraq has sought the supply of significant quantities of uranium from Africa. Iraq has no active civil nuclear power programme or nuclear power plants and therefore has no legitimate reason to acquire uranium. 21. Intelligence shows that other important procurement activity since 1998 has included attempts to purchase: • vacuum pumps which could be used to create and maintain pressures in a gas centrifuge cascade needed to enrich uranium; • an entire magnet production line of the correct specification for use in the motors and top bearings of gas centrifuges. It appears that Iraq is attempting to acquire a capability to produce them on its own rather than rely on foreign procurement; • Anhydrous Hydrogen Fluoride (AHF) and fluorine gas. AHF is commonly used in the petrochemical industry and Iraq frequently imports significant amounts, but it is also used in the process of converting uranium into uranium hexafluoride for use in gas centrifuge cascades; • one large filament winding machine which could be used to manufacture carbon fibre gas centrifuge rotors; • a large balancing machine which could be used in initial centrifuge balancing work. 22. Iraq has also made repeated attempts covertly to acquire a very large quantity (60,000 or more) of specialised aluminium tubes. The specialised aluminium in question is subject to international export controls because of its potential application in the construction of gas centrifuges used to enrich uranium, although there is no definitive intelligence that it is destined for a nuclear programme. **Nuclear weapons: timelines** 23. In early 2002, the JIC assessed that UN sanctions on Iraq were hindering the import of crucial goods for the production of fissile material. The JIC judged that while sanctions remain effective Iraq would not be able to produce a nuclear weapon. If they were removed or prove ineffective, it would take Iraq at least five years to produce sufficient fissile material for a weapon indigenously. However, we know that Iraq retains expertise and design data relating to nuclear weapons. We therefore judge that if Iraq obtained fissile material and other essential components from foreign sources the timeline for production of a nuclear	that that would be a responsible course to follow. Our case is simply this: not that we take military action come what may, but that the case for ensuring Iraqi disarmament, as the UN itself has stipulated, is overwhelming. I defy anyone, on the basis of this evidence, to say that that is an unreasonable demand for the international community to make when, after all, it is only the same demand that we have made for 11 years and that Saddam has rejected. People say, "But why Saddam?" I do not in the least dispute that there are other causes of concern on weapons of mass destruction. I said as much in this House on 14 September last year. However, two things about Saddam stand out. He has used these weapons in Iraq itself—thousands dying in those chemical weapons attacks—and in the Iran-Iraq war, started by him, in which 1 million people died; and his is a regime with no moderate elements to appeal to. Read the chapter on Saddam and human rights in this dossier. Read not just about the 1 million dead in the war with Iran, not just about the 100,000 Kurds brutally murdered in northern Iraq, not just about the 200,000 Shia Muslims driven from the marshlands in southern Iraq, and not just about the attempt to subjugate and brutalise the Kuwaitis in 1990 that led to the Gulf war. I say, "Read also about the routine butchering of political opponents, the prison 'cleansing' regimes in which thousands die, the torture chambers and the hideous penalties supervised by him and his family and detailed by Amnesty International.' Read it all

173

NOTE: Redactions are not indicated

DOCUMENT 4.1   The Butler Report: Annex B: Intelligence Assessment and Presentation: From March to September 2002 *(Continued)*

ANNEX B

15 March 2002	21 August 2002	9 September 2002	24 September 2002	24 September 2002
			weapon would be shortened and Iraq could produce a nuclear weapon in between one and two years. **BALLISTIC MISSILES** **Joint Intelligence Committee (JIC) Assessment: 1999–2002** 24. In mid-2001 the JIC drew attention to what it described as a "step-change" in progress on the Iraqi missile programme over the previous two years. It was clear from intelligence that the range of Iraqi missiles which was permitted by the UN and supposedly limited to 150kms was being extended and that work was under way on larger engines for longer-range missiles. 25. In early 2002 the JIC concluded that Iraq had begun to develop missiles with a range of over 1,000kms. The JIC assessed that if sanctions remained effective the Iraqis would not be able to produce such a missile before 2007. Sanctions and the earlier work of the inspectors had caused significant problems for Iraqi missile development. In the previous six months Iraqi foreign procurement efforts for the missile programme had been bolder. The JIC also assessed that Iraq retained up to 20 al-Hussein missiles from before the Gulf War. **The Iraqi ballistic missile programme since 1998** 26. Since the Gulf War, Iraq has been openly developing two short-range missiles up to a range of 150km, which are permitted under UN Security Council Resolution 687. The al-Samoud liquid propellant missile has been extensively tested and is being deployed to military units. Intelligence indicates that at least 50 have been produced. Intelligence also indicates that Iraq has worked on extending its range to at least 200km in breach of UN Security Resolution 687. Production of the solid propellant Ababil-100 is also underway, probably as an unguided rocket at this stage. There are also plans to extend its range to at least 200km. Compared to liquid propellant missiles, those powered by solid propellant offer greater ease of storage, handling and mobility. They are also quicker to take into and out of action and can stay at a high state of readiness for longer periods. 27. According to intelligence, Iraq has retained up to 20 al-Hussein missiles, in breach of UN Security Council Resolution 687. These missiles were either hidden from the UN as complete systems, or re-assembled using illegally retained engines and other components. We judge that the engineering expertise available would allow these missiles to be maintained effectively, although the fact that at least some require re-assembly makes it difficult to judge exactly how many could be available for use. They could be used with conventional, chemical or biological warheads and, with a range of up to 650km, are capable of	and, again, I defy anyone to say that this cruel and sadistic dictator should be allowed any possibility of getting his hands on chemical, biological and nuclear weapons of mass destruction. "Why now?" people ask. I agree that I cannot say that this month or next, even this year or next, Saddam will use his weapons. But I can say that if the international community, having made the call for disarmament, now, at this moment, at the point of decision, shrugs its shoulders and walks away, he will draw the conclusion that dictators faced with a weakening will always draw: that the international community will talk but not act, will use diplomacy but not force. We know, again from our history, that diplomacy not backed by the threat of force has never worked with dictators and never will. If we take this course and if we refuse to implement the will of the international community, Saddam will carry on, his efforts will intensify, his confidence will grow and, at some point in a future not too distant, the threat will turn into reality. The threat is not imagined. The history of mass destruction is not American or British propaganda. The history and the present threat are real. If people say, "Why should Britain care?", I answer, "Because there is no way this man, in this region above all regions, could begin a conflict using such weapons and the consequences not engulf the whole world, including this country." That, after all, is the reason the UN passed its resolutions. That is why it is right that the UN Security Council again makes its will and its unity clear and lays down a strong new UN resolution

NOTE: Redactions are not indicated

174

DOCUMENT 4.1   The Butler Report: Annex B: Intelligence Assessment and Presentation: From March to September 2002 *(Continued)*

ANNEX B

15 March 2002	21 August 2002	9 September 2002	24 September 2002	24 September 2002
			reaching a number of countries in the region including Cyprus, Turkey, Saudi Arabia, Iran and Israel. 28. Intelligence has confirmed that Iraq wants to extend the range of its missile systems to over 1000km, enabling it to threaten other regional neighbours. This work began in 1998, although efforts to regenerate the long-range ballistic missile programme probably began in 1995. Iraq's missile programmes employ hundreds of people. Satellite imagery has shown a new engine test stand being constructed, which is larger than the current one used for al-Samoud, and that formerly used for testing SCUD engines which was dismantled under UNSCOM supervision. This new stand will be capable of testing engines for medium range ballistic missiles (MRBMs) with ranges over 1000km, which are not permitted under UN Security Council Resolution 687. Such a facility would not be needed for systems that fall within the UN permitted range of 150km. The Iraqis have recently taken measures to conceal activities at this site. Iraq is also working to obtain improved guidance technology to increase missile accuracy. 29. The success of UN restrictions means the development of new longer-range missiles is likely to be a slow process. These restrictions impact particularly on the: • availability of foreign expertise; • conduct of test flights to ranges above 150km; • acquisition of guidance and control technology. 30. Saddam remains committed to developing longer-range missiles. Even if sanctions remain effective, Iraq might achieve a missile capability of over 1000km within 5 years. 31. Iraq has managed to rebuild much of the missile production infrastructure destroyed in the Gulf War and in Operation Desert Fox in 1998. New missile-related infrastructure is also under construction. Some aspects of this, including rocket propellant mixing and casting facilities at the al-Mamoun Plant, appear to replicate those linked to the prohibited Badr-2000 programme (with a planned range of 700–1000km) which were destroyed in the Gulf War or dismantled by UNSCOM. A new plant at al-Mamoun for indigenously producing ammonium perchlorate, which is a key ingredient in the production of solid propellant rocket motors, has also been constructed. This has been provided illicitly by NEC Engineers Private Limited, an Indian chemical engineering firm with extensive links in Iraq, including to other suspect facilities such as the Fallujah 2 chlorine plant. After an extensive investigation, the Indian authorities have recently suspended its export licence, although other individuals and companies are still illicitly procuring for Iraq.	and mandate. Then Saddam will have the choice: comply willingly or be forced to comply. That is why, alongside the diplomacy, there must be genuine preparedness and planning to take action if diplomacy fails. Let me be plain about our purpose. Of course there is no doubt that Iraq, the region and the whole world would be better off without Saddam. Iraq deserves to be led by someone who can abide by international law, not a murderous dictator; by someone who can bring Iraq back into the international community where it belongs, not leave it languishing as a pariah; by someone who can make the country rich and successful, not impoverished by Saddam's personal greed; and by someone who can lead a Government more representative of the country as a whole while maintaining absolutely Iraq's territorial integrity. We have no quarrel with the Iraqi people. Indeed, liberated from Saddam, they could make Iraq prosperous and a force for good in the middle east. So the ending of this regime would be the cause of regret for no one other than Saddam. But our purpose is disarmament. No one wants military conflict. The whole purpose of putting this before the UN is to demonstrate the united determination of the international community to resolve this in the way it should have been resolved years ago: through a proper process of disarmament under the UN. Disarmament of all weapons of mass destruction is the demand. One way or another, it must be acceded to.

175

NOTE: Redactions are not indicated

DOCUMENT 4.1   The Butler Report: Annex B: Intelligence Assessment and Presentation: From March to September 2002 *(Continued)*

ANNEX B

15 March 2002	21 August 2002	9 September 2002	24 September 2002	24 September 2002
			32. Despite a UN embargo, Iraq has also made concerted efforts to acquire additional production technology, including machine tools and raw materials, in breach of UN Security Council Resolution 1051. The embargo has succeeded in blocking many of these attempts, such as requests to buy magnesium powder and ammonium chloride. But we know from intelligence that some items have found their way to the Iraqi ballistic missile programme. More will inevitably continue to do so. Intelligence makes it clear that Iraqi procurement agents and front companies in third countries are seeking illicitly to acquire propellant chemicals for Iraq's ballistic missiles. This includes production level quantities of near complete sets of solid propellant rocket motor ingredients such as aluminium powder, ammonium perchlorate and hydroxyl terminated polybutadiene. There have also been attempts to acquire large quantities of liquid propellant chemicals such as Unsymmetrical Dimethylhydrazine (UDMH) and diethylenetriamene. We judge these are intended to support production and deployment of the al-Samoud and development of longer-range systems.	

NOTE: Redactions are not indicated

PART III

Counterinsurgency and Counterterrorism

CHAPTER 5

Intelligence and Counterinsurgency

The Malayan Experience

MATTHEW JONES

Editors' Note:

The British response to the Malayan Emergency is often heralded as a shining example of how to deal with a counterinsurgency. In this perceptive chapter Matthew Jones, an expert on foreign policy and the history of Asia, examines the role of intelligence in quashing the uprising. Intelligence has been seen as critical in the success of the British campaign, and the question is why?, particularly when the later achievements are compared with the earlier failings. Jones finds that tactical intelligence was just as important as strategic intelligence, yet intelligence cannot be divorced from other covert operations in the reasons behind the success; equally, without good governance, intelligence cannot solve an insurgency campaign in isolation.

The Malayan Emergency, which began in June 1948 and was only finally declared over in 1960, is often held up as the classic postwar example of a successful counterinsurgency campaign. Faced with a tough and dedicated force of Communist guerrillas, the British colonial authorities and the security forces they controlled managed to quell a widespread insurrection, comprehensively defeat the armed wing of the Malayan Communist Party (MCP), and restore sufficient order to Malayan society so that independence could be granted in August 1957, and power transferred to a new elected, pro-Western, and indigenous government.[1] The campaign is often portrayed as illustrating the effective application of the techniques of "hearts and minds" warfare, where, through a careful blend of military, police, and civil measures, the local population was won over to support for the security forces, and popular following for the MCP gradually dissipated. In this analysis of the counterinsurgency effort, the Communist guerrillas of the Malayan National Liberation Army found their customary sources of recruits, money, supplies, and information among the Chinese communities in Malaya curtailed, and their remaining cadres forced deeper and deeper into the jungle interior of the country, so that survival became their sole preoccupation. This hearts and minds approach is also commonly linked with the arrival in Malaya of General Sir Gerald Templer in early 1952, who took over the roles of both director of operations on the military side, and high commissioner on the political, where he was able to introduce new drive into the civil administration and press forward with political and constitutional change. This interpretation is contested by some, however, who instead see straightforward coercion of the Malayan Chinese, through forced resettlement and harsh measures of population control (originating before Templer's arrival), as being the key to breaking support for the MCP rather than any more enlightened form of counterinsurgency doctrine.[2]

Far less controversial in the history of the Emergency have been treatments of the role of intelligence. Here, early setbacks for the British authorities, along with considerable organizational confusion and muddle, were eventually reversed, and impressive intelligence coverage of the MCP, as well as extensive penetration of Communist guerrilla units, was achieved. Above all else, it was the police intelligence service, or Special Branch, that was responsible for the superior intelligence product that resulted. Indeed, it seems incontrovertible that this intelligence success story was a crucial factor in the outcome of the counterinsurgency as a whole, with guerrilla forces killed or captured as their location and movements were discovered by the authorities, and MCP strength and morale collapsing as a result.[3] To show how this came about, this chapter offers some background on the development of the Emergency, examines the failings of the intelligence services in its early stages, and then explores the reforms to intelligence and policing that led to such a dramatic turnaround in the Malayan scene.

The Malayan Setting and the Outbreak of the Emergency

The British had first arrived on the Malayan peninsula in the late eighteenth century, establishing a trading post on the island of Penang on the northwest coast. In 1819, through the work of Stamford Raffles, Singapore was acquired and became the commercial hub of the British presence thereafter. Influence and control gradually extended throughout the whole of Malaya in the remainder of the nineteenth century, a process that was accelerated from the 1880s onwards as its tropical climate was found ideal for lucrative rubber cultivation. By the early 1900s, the Malay states were coming to be recognized as an important and valuable source of raw materials for the empire; the figure of the expatriate rubber plantation owner was already becoming the ubiquitous symbol of British imperial domination and exploitation, and immortalized in the colonial imagination by the fiction of Somerset Maugham. Under British influence a multiethnic Malayan society emerged, indentured labor from India being brought in to work on the rubber plantations, and Chinese settlers arriving as labor for the tin-mining industry, with the Chinese communities soon coming to dominate the local worlds of banking and commerce in small-town Malaya. This influx of immigration meant that by the late 1940s, Malaya's population had expanded to just below 5 million, of whom just under 2 million were Chinese (38%), compared with 2.4 million indigenous Malays (49%), and 500,000 Indians (10%). It was this ethnic mix that was to prove crucial to the pattern and outcome of the Emergency, as the MCP came to draw the overwhelming bulk of its support from within the Chinese community.

The MCP itself had been formed in 1930 with the explicit aim of overthrowing British imperial rule, and though it gained adherents as the worldwide depression hit colonial economies in the decade that followed, it struggled to present a credible challenge to the colonial authorities and was shunned by most indigenous Malays. Nevertheless, after the Japanese invasion of China in July 1937—and though it continued to operate underground—through nationalistic appeals it was able to gain more support from Malayan Chinese concerned about conditions in a country many still regarded as their homeland. The MCP's cause was not helped, however, by the remarkable fact that its general secretary from 1939 onwards, Lai Tek, was actually in the pay of Singapore Special Branch, and so was in an ideal position to pass on information about the organization, as well as influencing its strategy and tactics. In any event, by most estimates, the prewar threat to British rule from Communism in Malaya was small. The Japanese invasion of Malaya in late 1941, and the harsh occupation that ensued, turned the whole Malayan world upside down, however, and triggered an upsurge in displacement and societal violence that was not to fully abate until the end of the 1950s. While many Malays tended to collaborate with the Japanese occupiers, the Chinese suffered unimaginable horrors at their hands. The MCP immediately offered its services to the British authorities, who made a rushed attempt to train and arm a guerrilla force before being swept out of the peninsula by the Japanese advance in early 1942. Nevertheless, with much outside assistance from the British, who sent arms and agents from Special Operations Executive (SOE) back into the peninsula, the MCP's armed wing, dubbed the Malayan People's Anti-Japanese Army (MPAJA), built up a cadre of guerrillas and a stock of weaponry. As the prime source of resistance to the Japanese, the MPAJA gained prestige during the occupation period, carrying out harassing actions and preparing for the return of the British; one of their young leaders, Chin Peng, was later even awarded an OBE for his efforts.

The sudden surrender of the Japanese caught both the MCP and the British off guard. Still aware of its weakness and vulnerability, the MCP made no attempt to seize power, and though maintaining their opposition to British colonial rule did not adopt a militant line. For the first few years after the war, the MCP, able for once to operate in the open, concentrated on expanding their organizational base, particularly among the labor unions, and agitating for economic, social, and political change. It would also appear that Lai Tek was important in guiding the party along a relatively peaceful and moderate path. When Lai Tek's treachery was finally unmasked in March 1947 (he had even been "run" as an agent by the Japanese secret police during the occupation, and betrayed many Communist leaders as a consequence), the party went through a period of introspection and reappraisal of the situation, with many local activists now keen to confront the colonial power.[4] With violence in the Malayan countryside showing a steady increase and strikes proliferating in urban areas, on June 16, 1948, three European planters were murdered at Sungei Siput in the state of Perak. Having already carried out several arrests of known MCP agitators in the weeks before this incident, the British authorities saw the killings as signaling the start of a larger armed uprising, and two days later emergency regulations were introduced across the whole country with proscription of organizations deemed to be subversive. The balance of evidence is that the central MCP leadership had little control over the Communist groups in Perak at this time, but with the declaration of the Emergency, the party moved into insurrection, and its leading elements retreated to the relative safety of the jungle interior.[5] This chaotic and confusing start to the Emergency was reflected in the conduct of the counterinsurgency campaign over the months that followed. Although large-scale detentions were carried out, many of the MCP's leading figures had time to slip away (including Chin Peng, who had taken over as secretary-general of the party in 1947), while Communist appeals were able to exploit the discontent felt by the 400,000-strong displaced Chinese squatter population, who lived on the jungle fringe, and provided a ready source of recruits, supplies, and money.

At the outbreak of the Emergency there were only 9,000 police in Malaya, and ten battalions of regular infantry; the disorganized Malayan civil administration was ill-prepared for the rebellion, and much time and effort was spent protecting the lives and property of European settlers. The deteriorating security situation was compounded by the army's tactics, where counterinsurgency doctrine was still largely derived from Boer War experience, and consisted of large-scale sweeps through Malayan villages that did more to alienate local opinion than disrupt or capture Communist guerrilla units. Moreover, the army proved reluctant to submit to the authority of the civil government in Malaya, and tensions proliferated when in October 1948 the police were assigned the lead role in restoring law and order by the high commissioner, Sir Henry Gurney. The police themselves, under their controversial commissioner, W. N. Gray, were busy undergoing a rapid expansion in numbers as they took on many more paramilitary tasks, but the new recruits, drawn almost exclusively from among the Malay community, suffered from inadequate training and poor leadership. Faced with an escalating tide of attacks and ambushes, the colonial authorities resorted to coercion and enforcement measures that were often counterproductive. For the rural Chinese community, many of whom had never been brought within the ambit of the administrative state in Malaya, it was a period full of dilemmas, where the government expected loyalty and support, yet could not provide protection.[6] Meanwhile, the Malayan National Liberation Army (MNLA), the armed wing of the MCP that had been formerly called into being in February 1949 (and which numbered about 4,000 personnel, and was 95 percent Chinese in composition), established base camps in the jungle interior, emptied the arms caches that had been carefully stored during and after the Japanese occupation, and began to engage in a classic guerrilla warfare pattern of ambushes and targeted killings, mixed with efforts to disrupt the economic fabric of the colony. In addition, the MCP also worked intently on building up the *Min Yuen* or "masses" organization among the squatter communities of dispossessed Chinese, which could channel food supplies and information on security force locations and movements to MNLA units.

The Failings of Intelligence and the Onset of the Briggs Plan

Many recriminations followed the outbreak of the Emergency over the failure of the intelligence services to predict and warn the authorities about the seriousness of the Communist threat in Malaya. One obvious problem presented to any organization charged with collecting information from the general population was that the Japanese occupation had simply destroyed the intelligence branches of the police forces, whose network of contacts, informants, and files had to be reconstituted from scratch after the end of the war. Particular criticism, however, was directed at the Malayan Security Service (MSS), which had first been formed just before the Japanese invasion in 1941, and then revived during the period of British military administration in 1946, and was widely regarded as a law unto itself. The MSS was a small, mainly urban-based organization, largely staffed at a senior level with British officers more focused on the dangers posed by the potential radicalization of Malay nationalist groups than on the MCP. Furthermore, it tended to deliver reports to the colonial authorities that were an undifferentiated mass of detail, rather than a considered assessment of the overall intelligence picture in the territory (sometimes failing, for example, to distinguish between the law and order threat presented by the criminal activities of various gangs and secret societies, and the subversive work of political organizations).[7] On June 14, 1948, two days before the Sungei Supit murders, Lieutenant Colonel John Dalley, the head of the MSS, delivered a report that asserted "at the time of writing there is no immediate threat to internal security in Malaya although the position is constantly changing and is potentially dangerous. . . . There are signs that . . . the Communist Party is losing ground in the labor field and it is unlikely that the Communist Party will attempt a full-scale trial of strength unless they feel that their recent setbacks demand a display of authority to prevent any further weakening of their influence." Despite the careful caveats, the reassuring headline from Dalley was that "internal security today presents no problem for which a solution cannot be found."[8]

Hindsight is an unforgiving luxury enjoyed by the historian, but this was to prove one of the more notably inaccurate predictions of British intelligence folklore. What was palpably evident was that the MSS had failed to appreciate the depth of support the MCP had managed to generate within the Chinese community, or to anticipate its capacity for armed insurrection; whether this was attributable to a degree of complacency having enjoyed the information supplied by Lai Tek for so long, or to a shortage of proficient staff and resources, or even to the heterogeneous nature of the MCP itself (where forecasts of intentions were inevitably hazardous), became moot points after the declaration of the Emergency. Able to furnish neither reliable intelligence assessments nor information that might help to inform operational planning in the early stages of the insurgency, the MSS was dissolved in August 1948. It was reconstituted, however, as two separate Special Branches within the Criminal Investigation Departments (CIDs) of the Malayan and Singapore police forces. This was an obvious attempt to integrate information derived from regular policing work into a common intelligence pool, but it too suffered from a number of debilitating problems. Supposedly responsible for all intelligence work, the special branches were regarded as inferior bodies within their parent CIDs, lacked sufficient status, and were very short of experienced manpower. In 1948, for example, the Malayan Special Branch had only 13 officers and 44 inspectors. Moreover, almost all these personnel were European or Malay (there were in fact only three Chinese gazetted officers in the entire Malayan police force, and 27 Chinese inspectors).[9] As well as the obvious difficulty of collecting information and developing contacts from within the Chinese community with non-Chinese personnel, the immense shortage of Chinese language skills meant that when MCP documents were captured there was no quick procedure for translating them and so providing intelligence that might be timely and tactically useful. Lack of training in police intelligence work was another glaring issue, and there was no purpose-built Special Branch training institute or school. Similarly, Special Branch held no repository of knowledge concerning Communist tactics or organization, and there was no deployment of personnel beyond the major towns. All these problems would, of course, take time to address and remedy, but this is precisely what the authorities felt they lacked as the insurgency gathered momentum in 1948–49.

Indeed, the demands on Special Branch were now not only to provide general intelligence on the political scene and the MCP's structures, strategy, and key figures, but the kind of tactical intelligence that could prove of direct use to the military as they attempted to track MNLA units. John P. Morton, the head of Security Intelligence Far East at Singapore between 1949 and 1952 (and the principal MI5 officer in the region), later reflected that the intelligence organizations of the two governments in Malaya and Singapore "were hardly worthy of the name . . . there was nothing on the ground for the collection of intelligence, no facilities for interrogation, translation, document research, agent running or any of the other processes of counterintelligence work. In short, the period [of the late 1940s] was one of considerable muddle and ineptitude." The army profited from no collaboration at all with police intelligence, and so "flogged the jungles blindly, hoping to find and kill bandits." What was needed was to produce much closer integration of the civil and military efforts in the Emergency, to provide commanders with the reliable intelligence they needed to combat Communist military forces, but also to ensure adequate liaison between the army and Special Branch.[10]

The problems of Special Branch have, however, to be seen in the context of the rapid changes that the Emergency brought to the police as a whole in Malaya.

As noted above, the expectation that the police would lead the counterinsurgency effort led to an expansion in size of the force to around 67,000 by 1950 and its adoption of many paramilitary functions and roles, though there was no commensurate increase in the headquarters staff who could direct the expanded force, and no time allowed for essential training. To make matters worse, Gray's insistence that he coordinate the counterinsurgency effort almost certainly distracted him from the essential task of overseeing his expanded police force, where morale and poor conditions of service were major causes for concern.[11] Until some of these wider police issues were tackled, notably patterns of communal recruitment, improved prospects for advancement, and provision of adequate training, Special Branch performance was always likely to be severely impaired.

With the drastic deterioration in the security situation that was experienced during the first few months of 1950, Lieutenant General Sir Harold Briggs arrived in Malaya as a new director of operations in April, where he was expected to step up coordination of the military and police effort in the counterinsurgency campaign. Briggs would achieve far more than this, in fact, and in the following month he produced a plan for the future prosecution of the campaign. By advocating the mass resettlement of the squatter Chinese community away from the jungle fringe and thereby cutting off the MNLA from their chief source of support and the *Min Yuen*, he provided the blueprint for eventual success in the Emergency.[12] He also, however, singled out the failings of the intelligence services in Malaya a week after his arrival, noting that "our Intelligence organization is our 'Achilles heel' and inadequate for present conditions, when it should be our first line of attack. Our information must come from the population or from deserters and, until we can instill confidence by successes and security among the population, our information will be worse than that of the Communists. We have not got an organization capable of sifting and distributing important information quickly."[13]

Attempts were made during this period to reform the intelligence organization and improve the system, but these would prove halting. Following a recommendation contained in a May 1950 report on policing in Malaya produced by a mission led by Sir Alexander Maxwell, a former permanent undersecretary at the Home Office, Sir William Jenkin, a retired former deputy head of the Intelligence Bureau of the Home Department in India, was appointed as special adviser on CID/Special Branch affairs. Arriving in Kuala Lumpur in June, Jenkin soon grew frustrated with his lack of executive authority and by the fact that his work was often restricted to coordinating the work of police agencies between the different Malayan states rather than bringing about change at a federal level. In August, Briggs made him his director of intelligence, a wholly new post from which Jenkin set about reforming the character and outlook of Special Branch. Wanting to free Special Branch from CID and police control, Jenkin planned to create a new fully fledged intelligence bureau, answerable to the high commissioner alone. Any such major change was unacceptable to Gray, however, and the two clashed repeatedly over the issue until Jenkin, having received no support from Gurney or Briggs on this particular initiative, finally submitted his resignation in September 1951.[14]

Although Jenkin ultimately lost his prolonged bureaucratic battle with Gray, he did manage to introduce new standards of training and recruitment that were to serve Special Branch well in the years ahead. One important change was the removal of separate "racial" desks in Special Branch headquarters (where officers had been assigned to monitor particular ethnic communities, with a resultant compartmentalization of intelligence information) and a move toward the functional organization of work. Another was active pursuit of Chinese recruitment into Special Branch. Interrogation of the many thousands of suspects being held in detention camps was also brought under Special Branch, with small teams being assigned to each holding center. With the systematic gathering of information from detainees through detailed questioning it became possible to release those who were obviously innocent of any MCP connections, develop lines of information for the future, and begin to amass a picture of Communist organization, personnel, and psychology (the latter of crucial importance in inducing defections and surrenders). In January 1951, two combined Special Branch/CID training schools were opened.[15] Commendable though these changes were, and Briggs began to acknowledge an increased flow of usable intelligence to the military in early 1951, progress in the counterinsurgency campaign was still fitful and a cause of deepening concern to the British authorities. The Briggs plan certainly pointed in the right direction in that control and protection of the population, rather than attempts to hunt down MNLA guerrillas, was now the priority, but its implementation was painfully slow. Indeed, Communist attacks were rising in number and effectiveness, the civil administration was still lethargic, and morale among the security forces was low. There were few grounds for optimism, and the biggest blow was yet to come.

The Death of Gurney, the Lyttleton Report, and the Arrival of Templer

At just after 1 pm on Saturday, October 6, 1951, a small column of vehicles, having set out from the federal capital of Kuala Lumpur, slowly snaked its way up the narrow and winding road leading toward the cool air of Fraser's Hill, a hill station up in the Cameron Highlands. At its head was an open police Land Rover, which slowed to a crawl as it approached yet another sharp bend in the ascent. Lying in wait and arrayed in the jungle for 400 yards on either side of the road at this perfect ambush spot were thirty-eight members of an independent platoon of the MNLA, equipped with rifles, a Sten gun, and two Bren light machine guns. Led by Siew Ma, an experienced guerrilla commander who had received his initial training from SOE in Singapore in late 1941 and then fought throughout the Japanese occupation, the group had arrived at their carefully chosen position early the previous day. Siew Ma's main aim was to surprise a unit from the security forces, inflict casualties, and, if possible, seize much-needed weaponry and ammunition. Having maintained their position for over a day, however, the group was running low on food and Siew Ma had resolved to move back to his base camp if no suitable targets appeared by mid-afternoon. Now seizing their chance, the guerrillas immediately unleashed a hail of fire into the lead Land Rover, wounding five of its six occupants, who then tumbled into the undergrowth. They then turned their attention to the next car following up the hill, a Rolls Royce adorned with official flags, managing to hit the Malay driver, and leaving the front seat passenger to grapple the vehicle to a halt.

One of the rear seat occupants then emerged, and according to some accounts, moved to approach the guerrilla positions, perhaps to draw fire away from the survivors in the car, and in doing so was shot and killed. The final vehicle in the column, an armored police scout car, which had been held up when the column's wireless van had broken down some miles back, now forlornly appeared, blazed into the jungle with its Bren gun and then nosed its way past the Rolls Royce and continued up to the Gap road police station, two miles further on. After about ten more minutes of sporadic shooting from the guerrillas, and with the wounded police still returning fire, Siew Ma ordered his men to fall back, annoyed that he had managed to retrieve no weapons. Twenty minutes later, the officer commanding the scout car returned with police reinforcements to collect the survivors and mount a fruitless search for the guerrillas. Siew Ma had no reason to be disappointed. The unfortunate occupant of the Rolls Royce who had been killed was none other than Sir Henry Gurney, the high commissioner and top colonial official with overall responsibility for the conduct of the Emergency.[16] This was a spectacular coup for the MCP, but was also tinged with irony, as the party had only just issued new directives that appeared to deemphasize its military activities, and called for greater efforts to win allegiance from a wider spectrum of the civil population (when the "excessive" actions of some local guerrilla commanders, including attacks on buses and trains and destruction of crops and property, were serving to drive away some grass roots support).[17]

The death of Gurney marked the nadir of British fortunes in the Malayan Emergency. During 1951, there were over 500 terrorist incidents per month on average, many involving the murder of isolated planters or farmers, in a tactic to discourage European investors, and in that same year over 500 members of the security forces were killed.[18] Gurney's death had coincided with the start of a general election campaign in Britain that returned a new Conservative government to power, with Churchill once more becoming premier. The forceful new colonial secretary, Oliver Lyttleton, placed a paper before his Cabinet colleagues in November noting that "after nearly 3½ years of warfare, we are still not within prospect of a definite break in the Communist ranks."[19] The following month, Lyttleton went to Malaya to see the situation for himself, recalling later in his memoirs: "The situation was far worse than I had imagined: it was appalling. . . . I had never seen such a tangle as that presented by the Government of Malaya. There was divided and often opposed control at the top. . . . No line could be drawn to show where politics, civil administration or police action, administration of justice and the like end, and where paramilitary or military operations begin. . . . The police itself was divided by a great schism between the Commissioner of Police and the Head of Special Branch. Intelligence was scanty and uncoordinated between the Military and the civil authorities." Morale seemed to have almost collapsed, and there was a marked lack of direction in the counterinsurgency effort.[20] Weaknesses in intelligence were singled out by Lyttleton in the long paper he presented to the Cabinet after his return to London in December: "The importance of intelligence to the Malayan campaign cannot be exaggerated. Every police operation is in large measure an intelligence task and the Malayan campaign is in essence a police operation. In a country covered with dense jungle, where evasion is easy and contact with the enemy cannot be made without secret information, it is essential that intelligence should be gained from the Communist forces without their knowing. Intelligence, therefore, to use semi-technical language, must be 'live' as well as 'blown' or 'dead.'"

In other words, the intelligence services could not rely on the mundane processes of building up a very static picture of the enemy's order of battle or pattern of operations, but needed to cultivate more immediate and effective sources, such as agents within the Communist apparatus, or networks of police contacts and informants. The police's central role in the provision of intelligence information had been hampered, however, by its rapid expansion since 1948, poor state of organization, and "the striking fact that more than 90% of the enemy are Chinese while 95% [sic] of the Police are Malay." While Lyttleton acknowledged that some changes had been made over the course of the previous year, particularly in the crucial area of police training, he also maintained that there was still a long way to go, not least as no agent penetration of the MCP had been achieved.[21]

The colonial secretary went on to recommend extra efforts to increase Chinese recruitment into the police, and said that more training in "basic police and intelligence methods must be given to all police branches irrespective of race," while the training of Special Branch agents should also be stepped up. Security measures within the government apparatus and the services, including adequate screening of personnel, would need to be tightened to prevent counterpenetration and the leakage of information that might assist the Communist enemy. Combined with these reforms to intelligence, the propaganda and information services in Malaya were, in Lyttleton's view, in need of complete and radical overhaul and should be placed under one head, while black propaganda activities should be boosted. Overall, the colonial secretary's message was that without further progress with police training and the incorporation of Chinese personnel, intelligence work would "remain patchy and haphazard. At present it is only the information got from the bodies of dead bandits or from prisoners which saves the face of our Intelligence Services. If the Malayan Communist Party decided to become clandestine and concentrate on political action, the intelligence canvas would be blank indeed." In a final recommendation, Lyttleton dwelt on the potential for deception operations to disorient the enemy, where the MCP's existing strengths in its local intelligence networks could be used against it by the feeding of false information and rumor. Such tactics could not only dissipate Communist energies, but also lead them to question genuine sources of intelligence, while reducing the morale of cadres.[22]

The most important step that Lyttleton took after his Malayan tour, however, was to appoint a single military officer to replace Gurney as high commissioner, and also to take over as director of operations since Briggs stepped down because of ill health in November 1951. Lyttleton's eventual choice for this exacting post was to be singularly auspicious. Arriving in Malaya in February 1952, General Sir Gerald Templer soon galvanized the scene, put new drive and coordination into the counterinsurgency effort, and brought together the military, police, and civil authorities. Templer was a highly energetic, nervy individual, given to barked commands. He was anything but easygoing, and though he earned respect from his subordinates, there was little affection and some fear of his displeasure. But he was indisputably the right man for the task at hand, ready to inject a note of urgency into both the military command structure and the civil bureaucracy of the colony, where complacent attitudes could still be found in abundance (one of his first orders was to ban golf on weekdays for colonial civil servants). Templer, moreover, was possessed of a focused and driving intelligence that could rapidly get to the heart of a problem and discern the steps that needed to be taken to arrive at a solution. He was also imaginative and flexible and ready to immerse himself in political issues.

Although having precious little knowledge of the intricacies of Malayan politics before his appointment, he quickly appreciated that rapid political advance was a necessary accompaniment to the improvement in the security situation that he hoped to engineer; indeed, in many respects, moves toward Malayan self-government were required to reconcile the Malay population to the continuation of Emergency regulations. Templer's time in Malaya has become synonymous with the hearts and minds approach to counterinsurgency warfare that was to become a much-admired hallmark of British postwar military doctrine. It is certainly the case that Templer had an appreciation of the importance of combining military measures with initiatives to win over the civilian population. It was not enough to side with the loyal Malay population, Templer understood, and efforts to reach out to the disaffected Chinese community had to be made. To this end, citizenship provisions were widened to include more Chinese, the Malayan Civil Service was opened up to Chinese recruitment, and the Malayan Chinese Association, predominantly representing moderate Chinese business leaders in the towns, was encouraged in its political efforts. In more general terms, Templer pushed forward moves toward local and eventual self-government for Malaya, promoting an electoral process that saw the emergence of the United Malays National Organization (UMNO) as the principal vehicle for the voice of moderate, anti-Communist Malay nationalism.[23] Building on the Briggs plan, Templer injected crucial new impetus into the resettlement policy, which had shown signs of stalling during 1951, so that by the time he left Malaya in May 1954, almost half a million Chinese had been moved into the "New Villages"; redoubled efforts were also made to ensure these were properly defended, as well as equipped with the social, medical, and educational amenities that their inhabitants could come to associate as a reward for cooperation with governmental authority.

Templer and the Reorganization of Intelligence in Malaya

The three areas of the counterinsurgency campaign that Templer identified for immediate and priority attention after his appointment were the organization and training of police, a complete revamping of information services, and the improvement of intelligence provision and organization.[24] Indeed, as a former director of military intelligence at the War Office, Templer had an overriding sense of the importance of establishing an effective intelligence organization if the counterinsurgency campaign in Malaya was to be brought to a successful conclusion.[25] Before he left for Malaya in late January 1952, Templer met the Joint Intelligence Committee in London, where he set out his ideas on how to shake up and reform the existing organization in Malaya. Although he had first wanted to see a new officer given direct executive responsibility for the intelligence services, after private discussions with Sir Percy Sillitoe, the director of MI5, Templer abandoned this idea, and as he explained to the JIC, he now wanted to see an individual appointed with the task of intelligence coordination, chairing a fully representative committee.[26] He was also keen that the new appointee should be a civilian, as enough service officers were already being introduced into the Malayan scene (in what might have been a reflection on the mixed reception that had greeted announcement of Templer's own dual civil and military role). At the JIC meeting, Sillitoe voiced strong support for Templer's proposals, feeling a full-time chairman of the local intelligence committee was the best solution, rather than a new level of executive authority.[27] The result of these deliberations was the appointment of John Morton as Templer's new director of intelligence, with responsibility for providing him with fully assessed intelligence from all sources. Arriving in Malaya in April 1952, Morton recalled that "things were very bad at the time; control at the top was divided and morale was at rock bottom. The administration at all levels was at loggerheads with itself."[28]

Morton was determined that intelligence should become the direct servant of policymakers in government, which also meant there had to be a very clear and close relationship between the director of intelligence and the high commissioner. This was to be institutionalized by making the director of intelligence a member of the high commissioner's operations committee and giving him direct channels of access to Templer. Served by a small combined intelligence staff, the director of intelligence had to coordinate all sources of intelligence, whether from the army, police, civil service, or security service, and through chairmanship of the Federal Intelligence Committee (FIC), manage their compilation into a single authoritative assessment, along with forecasts of likely developments. The director had no executive decision-making powers as such: he was expected to advise and coordinate, but to perform this task he still needed authority.[29] He could inspect and inquire into the work of the various intelligence services active in Malaya, and if his advice was not heeded he could report direct to Templer, a latent last resort that was usually sufficient to ensure that Morton could carry out his task effectively. The director was also the final arbiter when there was a potential clash between the desire of the security forces to act upon information and the potential for such a tactical operation to compromise a secret source.[30]

The cultivation of those secret sources became one of Morton's chief preoccupations during his time in Malaya, and for this he placed the onus squarely on Special Branch, which was accorded prime responsibility for intelligence gathering and agent-running. Only Special Branch penetration of the MCP's apparatus, Morton understood, held the key to allowing the security forces to break the back of the insurgency. Special Branch's task would be greatly assisted in this by some of the reforms that were brought to the police force as a whole during the course of 1952. One of Lyttleton's first steps after returning to London from his Malayan tour was to order the removal of Gray as commissioner of police. Not only was Gray essentially out of sympathy with the resettlement policy of the Briggs plan, but he had lost the confidence of the planter community, and of many of his own officers.[31] His successor was Colonel Arthur Young, who had been commissioner of police in the City of London. Young took up his post ten days after Templer in February 1952, and immediately set about overhauling the headquarters structure of the force. Some 650 British volunteers were brought over from the United Kingdom and made police lieutenants to provide training and leadership skills. Conditions of service and training levels were steadily improved, but most significant of all, Young inculcated a new ethos for the police, where it played down its paramilitary side, and emphasized its role as a servant of the community, concerned with day-to-day issues of law and order, with promotion prospects tied to this kind of performance.[32] Developing relations with the Chinese community, not least in the New Villages, would, of course, help to yield the information that could be used to identify MCP supporters, such as *Min Yuen* members.

Also of crucial importance was Young's agreement (apparently at Morton's instigation) to give Special Branch independent status within the force, under its own senior assistant commissioner, removing it from subordination to CID. Special Branch's separation allowed it to control its own funds and develop its own policies and methods. A new head of Special Branch, Guy Madoc (a very experienced police intelligence officer who had received a spell of MI5 training, spoke both Malay and Thai, and had led the Communist section at Federal Special Branch headquarters since 1950), was installed in February 1952 and began to strengthen the organization at the center.[33] Special Branch would put extra efforts into assembling an order of battle of the MCP and other subversive organizations; pass dossiers of suspects to police stations; develop interrogation procedures; provide central control for agent recruitment and running; and create holding centers and policies to exploit surrendered enemy personnel. During Madoc's tenure, Special Branch strength steadily rose, and by 1953 it fielded 123 officers and 195 inspectors, amounting to 20 percent of all officers and 18 percent of all inspectors in the police force. Chinese numbers remained low until the latter half of the

1950s (forming only perhaps 10% of Special Branch strength in 1953), but Madoc and Templer were keen to underline their belief that Asian officers represented the real spearhead of Special Branch intelligence efforts. The growing professionalization of Special Branch activity in Malaya was underlined in April 1952 when the two Special Branch/CID training schools set up in 1951 were replaced with a single Special Branch school in Kuala Lumpur under the able direction of Claude Fenner. Regular one-month courses began in August, covering subjects such as intelligence tradecraft and Communist strategy and tactics (Templer himself would often give an address at the opening of each new course); by the mid-1950s, the school had the reputation of being the leading regional center for intelligence-related training.[34]

The Document: The Special Branch Charter of April 1952

The centrality of Special Branch to the intelligence effort in the Malayan Emergency was underlined by the promulgation of a new charter for the organization, which gave it prime responsibility for intelligence collection and agent running. A draft of the charter had been compiled by Morton soon after he took up the position of director of intelligence, and it was issued on April 24, 1952, as Operations "Directive No. 21" over Templer's signature, and with his full authority behind the direct and unambiguous principles it enunciated. As the opening paragraph of the charter made clear, agent penetration of the MCP was defined as the chief goal of Special Branch. This was a task of particular urgency, as the British authorities were very concerned that the MCP might switch tactics away from armed struggle and toward less visible forms of political organization and subversion. With existing sources of information limited to SEP (Surrendered Enemy Personnel) and CEP (Captured Enemy Personnel), intelligence on the Communists could easily dry up if this kind of shift took place, hence the need to run live agents inside the MCP itself. The operation of such agents might require the short-term sacrifice of low-level intelligence gain, for the longer-term goal of acquiring more substantial and valuable information. The charter provided a categorical ranking of intelligence targets for penetration at all levels of the MCP, including the "inner ring" targets of the Central Committee/Politburo, state committees, party/MNLA headquarters commands, and the central propaganda department. An outline of a centralized system of Special Branch control of agent penetration operations was also offered, while particular attention was focused on countering possible Communist infiltration of the security forces and the organs of government in Malaya.

With a clear mandate for Special Branch supremacy in intelligence operations now established, the charter reiterated the basic contention of the Emergency authorities that the army was there to assist the civil power, not to take over the executive functions of government. Special Branch would provide the army with the tactical intelligence it needed in order to conduct operations against Communist units, but those operations would also need to be cleared with the director of operations committee so that any possible compromise of intelligence sources could be properly assessed. Recognizing that the police service might not yet be in a position to offer the kind of intelligence support the army required, the charter made provision for the attachment of military intelligence personnel to police units. However, the intelligence briefings provided to army commanders by such attached officers would have to be cleared by senior Special Branch officers, so ensuring, as the charter was keen to assert, preservation of the principle that Special Branch, representing the civil power, was to control the "collection, assessment and use of information." [35] Only Special Branch was allowed to engage agents, while it had to be provided with all available security intelligence; it was also designated as the body responsible for the administration and exploitation of all defectors and prisoners.

In fact, handling detainees was an immediate and urgent task, and Special Branch interrogation teams were sent into the holding camps to sift and classify prisoners, not least so that those picked up who were innocent of any involvement in the insurgency could be released rather than be subject to attempts at indoctrination or intimidation from fellow inmates (to give some idea of the scale of the problem, there were over ten thousand detainees being held in 1950; one estimate was that 70 percent of Chinese recruits to the MCP were joining to escape police repression). The assignment of military intelligence officers to Special Branch sections was a particular success, with between twenty and thirty seconded at any one time; using their particular skills and background they were in a position to analyze and process the tactical intelligence being brought in from the field on the MCP, and to furnish it to military commanders in a form they could understand and use. One Gurkha battalion reported in June 1951 that it had received only two items of intelligence interest to assist its operations that month, but in October 1952, when it was deployed in a state where a military intelligence officer was attached to the local Special Branch organization, this had become sixty-five.[36]

In retrospect, the Special Branch charter of April 1952 marks a significant point in the turnaround of the intelligence picture in Malaya, and the culmination of some of the personnel changes that had occurred after Lyttleton's tour. Special Branch now had a clear set of objectives and the authority to carry them out, while its new brand of leadership increasingly gave it the means and expertise to succeed. By 1954, Special Branch was running agents throughout the Communist infrastructure, spreading disinformation, and giving advance warning of Communist attacks to the security forces. In many states, the name and personal information of every single Communist figure of any significance was known to the authorities. Whole networks were being mopped up, and MCP morale correspondingly plummeted. "Secret penetration was achieved at the highest Party level," Morton later recalled, "and much disruption was caused in the Party ranks. The leaders were quite pathological in their suspicions and many loyal comrades were ruthlessly purged on the slimmest of evidence."[37] Organizational intelligence could be used to foster divisions and dissent within guerrilla groups or to exploit rivalries within their leadership structures. The authorities, for example, were quick to use information that the MCP leadership enjoyed special privileges, such as enhanced food rations, personal bodyguards, and ready access to their wives and families at their base camps, to undermine their relationship with the rank-and-file guerrillas.[38] This period also saw the beginning of large-scale surrenders, which yielded even more information. The MCP, in fact, was increasingly engaged in a mere struggle for survival, not in a campaign that in any way threatened the control or legitimacy of the colonial state; by late 1955, the party leadership was ready to seek terms, but at the Baling talks held in December with the head of UMNO and now chief minister, Tunku Abdul Rahman, Chin Peng's proposals to end the insurrection and return the MCP to constitutional politics were now rejected by the authorities, who insisted on surrender, attached conditions to the granting of amnesties, and wanted to see the MCP disbanded.[39] Though the MCP continued its campaign after Baling, the appeal of its program had meanwhile been comprehensively overtaken by a political process that was propelling Malaya toward the path to independence in August 1957 under a government that was still keen to maintain close ties to the former colonial power.

Lessons Learned?

Good intelligence is invariably regarded as an essential requirement for successful counterinsurgency operations, and the Malayan Emergency was no exception.[40] In January 1977, a long-retired Templer wrote to Major General J. M. Gow at the Ministry of Defence, acknowledging that the preparatory work done by Briggs was vitally important for his own later accomplishments as high commissioner and director of operations, but also that in Malaya, "everything – as usual – depended on intelligence."[41] Against an enemy who is determined to remain elusive rather than engage in decisive battle, tactical intelligence is vital simply to locate and identify the adversary. Indeed, finding the enemy presented exceptional problems in the Malayan context, where four-fifths of the peninsula was covered in thick jungle, impenetrable to much aerial reconnaissance. Jungle patrols conducted by the security forces could take four hours to cover one mile, and pass within five yards of the enemy without being able to see him. In 1954 it was estimated that there was one contact for every thousand hours of patrolling or three hundred hours of lying in ambush.[42] Accurate information was also vital in identifying the key sources of support that the MNLA was able to call upon from groups within the Chinese communities in Malaya's small towns and villages, and in particular from the *Min Yuen* organization. On the strategic level, intelligence could indicate the general structure and organization of the MNLA and MCP, and how they intended to prosecute their insurrection. A prime example of the latter occurred when one of the MCP's courier networks was compromised in early 1952, and the British authorities gained a copy of the previous year's October resolutions, where the politburo had ordered a major change of approach, acknowledging that armed struggle alone was unlikely to succeed and would have to play a subordinate role to political action among a wider section of Malayan society.[43]

Improvements in the quality and quantity of intelligence eventually gave the security forces a decisive advantage in the Emergency, but they came about only slowly and after early setbacks. Indeed, it would seem that the capacity to learn from previous mistakes was one of the attributes of the British system, reflected in an ability to engage in a degree of introspection and critical analysis. Even when key shortcomings were identified, however, such as the need to recruit more Chinese personnel into the police force and to improve the level of training, reforms could not be carried out overnight, and would take several years to bear fruit. This was seen perhaps above all in Special Branch itself, where Jenkin's arrival as Malaya's first director of intelligence in 1950 saw important early steps taken to upgrade its status and performance. It was this work that Morton and Madoc were able to exploit when they took over the running of the intelligence effort in 1952. The critical advantage that they enjoyed over their predecessors was support from the very top, as Templer moved to prioritize reform of the intelligence machinery. According primacy to Special Branch cut away the potential for damaging rivalries among the army, police, and security service, while the emphasis that was then placed by Special Branch on agent penetration, alongside a rigorous training regime and the exploitation of SEPs, gave a coherence and purpose to the intelligence effort that soon generated impressive results. As the Special Branch charter of April 1952 had highlighted, with penetration of the Communist organization now to be the paramount goal of the intelligence services in Malaya, security force operations that had the potential to endanger penetration lines could be vetoed, or operations harnessed to satisfy penetration requirements. For example, efforts might be made to target a particular party leader so that a vacancy would arise that could be filled by a Special Branch agent. In his review of the course of the Emergency, compiled in September 1957, the then director of operations noted with approval that Special Branch had "not only charted nearly every member of the enemy army, but has brought about the great majority of contacts resulting in eliminations."[44]

Yet a narrow focus on the intelligence services themselves can be deceptive in understanding the reasons for their eventual success. One example here is the vital role of the information and psychological warfare services in spreading news of security force achievements, which had the effect of reinforcing public confidence and eroding Communist morale. Indeed, an absolutely crucial facet of this aspect of counterinsurgency work was the close links that were formed between the intelligence and the information services. It was feedback from Special Branch interrogation of disillusioned Communist cadres who had chosen to turn themselves in, or begun to work for the authorities, that formed a major part in how work in the psychological warfare field was to be directed and refined. Some guerrilla surrenders were induced by the timely offer of amnesties, and the fidelity of a Communist supporter who now claimed he was ready to work for the British was usually tested by his willingness to lead the security forces back to the location of his base camp or to reveal the identities of others in his network. Interception of couriers gave insight into Communist strategy, but also allowed bogus messages and instructions to be inserted into their communications network, so spreading confusion and uncertainty. From the middle of 1952 onwards, Chin Peng would later attest, the presence of traitors and double agents within the midst of the MCP became a major concern of the leadership, and his memoirs give evidence of the summary execution of those believed to be in the pay or service of Special Branch, as well as the crippling damage they inflicted on his organization.[45]

Finally, the intelligence effort was not conducted in a political or military vacuum. The prime lesson of the Malayan Emergency in this regard was that the loyalty of the population, and so its willingness to provide information to the authorities, lay in its confidence that it could be provided with security and protection, and also that acceding to control by the administrative state brought with it tangible benefits, whether in the form of participation in a political process that gave a voice to local aspirations, or improvements in educational, health, and welfare services. The overriding need was to demonstrate the operation of good and impartial governance. To bring this about required a unification of purpose and effort on the part of the military, police, and civil authorities in Malaya that was easy to prescribe, but dauntingly difficult to achieve in practice; Templer's commanding achievement between 1952 and 1954, alongside the reforms to intelligence, was to put these principles into action, and so assure the eventual defeat of the insurgency.

NOTES

1. The leading and most authoritative work on the Emergency remains Anthony Short, *The Communist Insurrection in Malaya, 1948–60* (London: Muller, 1975); but see also Richard Stubbs, *Hearts and Minds in Guerrilla Warfare: The Malayan Emergency, 1948–1960* (Oxford: Eastern University Press, 1989), and John Coates, *Suppressing Insurgency: An Analysis of the Malayan Emergency, 1948–1954* (Boulder, CO: Westview Press, 1992).

2. For a summary of the argument, see Coates, *Suppressing Insurgency*, 132–36. For the coercion position, see Karl Hack, "Screwing Down the People: The Malayan Emergency, Decolonisation, and Ethnicity," in Hans Antlov and Stein Tonnesson (eds.), *Imperial Policy and South-East Asian Nationalism, 1930–1957* (Richmond, Surrey: Curzon Press, 1995), 83–109; Hack, "'Iron Claws on Malaya': The Historiography of the Malayan Emergency," *Journal of Southeast Asian Studies*, 30, 1 (1999): 99–125; and Hack, "British Intelligence and Counter-Insurgency in the Era of Decolonisation: The Example of Malaya," *Intelligence and National Security*, 14 (1999): 124–55; despite the latter's title, the article's focus is principally on population control. Hack's arguments are effectively refuted in Simon C. Smith, "General Templer and Counter-Insurgency in Malaya: Hearts and Minds, Intelligence and Propaganda," *Intelligence and National Security*, 16 (2001): 60–78.

3. See e.g., Short, *Communist Insurrection*, 502; Smith, "General Templer," 73; Brian Stewart, "Winning in Malaya: An Intelligence Success Story," in Richard J. Aldrich, Gary D. Rawnsley, and Ming-Yeh T. Rawnsley (eds.), *The Clandestine Cold War in*

Asia, 1945–65: Western Intelligence, Propaganda and Special Operations (London: Routledge, 2000), 267–83.

4. Some of this is conveyed in Chin Peng's fascinating memoir, *Alias Chin Peng: My Side of History* (Singapore, Media Masters, 2003), 181–93, as well as a dramatic account of Lai Tek's assassination in Bangkok by Communist agents.

5. See Short, *Communist Insurrection*, 53–77, 90–94; Coates, *Suppressing Insurgency*, 17–18; and in particular, A. J. Stockwell, "'A Widespread and Long-Concocted Plot to Overthrow Government in Malaya'? The Origins of the Malayan Emergency," in Robert Holland (ed.), *Emergencies and Disorder in the European Empires after 1945* (London: Frank Cass, 1994), 66–88.

6. See Stubbs, *Hearts and Minds*, 69–77.

7. See, in particular, Leon Comber, *Malaya's Secret Police, 1945–60: The Role of the Special Branch in the Malayan Emergency* (Monash: Monash Asia Institute, 2008), 25–46; and for a summary, Stubbs, *Hearts and Minds*, 67–69.

8. Quoted in Short, *Communist Insurrection*, 80–82.

9. Comber, *Malaya's Secret Police*, 60.

10. John P. Morton lecture notes, "The Co-ordination of Intelligence in the Malayan Emergency," n.d., but c. 1958, TNA: KV 4/408.

11. See, e.g., Short, *Communist Insurrection*, 140–41, 234.

12. See Coates, *Suppressing Insurgency*, 77–85.

13. Quoted in Short, *Communist Insurrection*, 236.

14. See Comber, *Malaya's Secret Police*, 116–17, 123–24; Short, *Communist Insurrection*, 275–76.

15. Comber, *Malaya's Secret Police*, 131–45.

16. This account of the Gurney ambush is assembled from inward telegram no. 951, from M. V. Del Tufo to Mr. Griffiths, October 6, 1951, TNA: FO 371/93118, reproduced in A. J. Stockwell (ed.), *British Documents on the End of Empire, Series B, Volume 3, Malaya, Part II: The Communist Insurrection, 1948-1953* (London: HMSO, 1995), 301–2; Short, *Communist Insurrection*, 303–5; Chin Peng, *My Side of History*, 287–89.

17. Ibid., 279–84.

18. Short, *Communist Insurrection*, 295.

19. Annex II to C(51)26, "The Situation in Malaya," November 20, 1951, TNA: CAB 129/48, reproduced in Stockwell, *Malaya, II*, 312.

20. Oliver Lyttleton, *The Memoirs of Lord Chandos* (London: Bodley Head, 1962), 366–67.

21. Para. 25, C(51)59, "Malaya," December 21, 1951, TNA: CAB 129/48, reproduced in Stockwell, *Malaya, II*, 322.

22. Appendix IX to C(51)59, ibid., 344–48.

23. For an excellent summary of Templer's impact in the political sphere, see Smith, "General Templer," 66–71.

24. Coates, *Suppressing Insurgency*, 123; Short, *Communist Insurrection*, 343.

25. See John Cloake, *Templer: Tiger of Malaya* (London: Harrap, 1985), 227. Soon after arriving in Malaya, Templer told Harry Miller, a trusted reporter for the *Straits Times*, that "the Emergency will be won by our intelligence service, and

there are going to be many inside stories which will never be told," quoted in Comber, *Malaya's Secret Police*, 178.

26. See S. E. V. Luke to D. P. Reilly, January 29, 1952, TNA: CO 1022/51.

27. Extract from JIC(52)15th mtg (Confidential Annex), January 31, 1952, TNA: CO 1022/51. On reactions to Templer's appointment, see Short, *Communist Insurrection*, 337.

28. John P. Morton lecture notes, "The Coordination of Intelligence in the Malayan Emergency," n.d., but c. 1958, TNA: KV 4/408.

29. As the deputy director of MI5 put it, Morton "has no executive authority, but, by virtue of his position as Chairman of the FIC and Chief-Coordinator, does in fact exercise control over all Intelligence activity," Guy M. Liddell note to Colonel E. E. G. L. Searight, Secretary, JIC, October 13, 1952, TNA: CO 1022/51.

30. John P. Morton lecture notes, "The Coordination of Intelligence in the Malayan Emergency," n.d., but c. 1958, TNA: KV 4/408; the Federal Intelligence Committee was described by one official as "essentially a coordinating body on which the representatives of the suppliers and users of intelligence decide the policies they would like to see adopted," minute by Anthony Gann, June 19, 1952, TNA: CO 1022/51.

31. Short, *Communist Insurrection*, 306.

32. Coates, *Suppressing Insurgency*, 123; Comber, *Malaya's Secret Police*, 174.

33. Ibid., 184.

34. Ibid., 200–204.

35. "Director of Operations, Malaya, Directive No 21: S. B. Intelligence Targets, April 24, 1952, TNA: CO 1022/51. See also Comber, *Malaya's Secret Police*, 205–7.

36. Coates, *Suppressing Insurgency*, 125.

37. John P. Morton lecture notes, "The Malayan Emergency," n.d., but 1960, TNA: KV 4/408.

38. See Short, *Communist Insurrection*, 309. The MCP leader affirmed later that British propaganda had made effective use of the wives and families issue, with the result that noncombatants were removed from guerrilla headquarters camps; see Chin Peng, *My Side of History*, 276–77.

39. Stubbs, *Hearts and Minds*, 226–27; Short, *Communist Insurrection*, 462–68.

40. See, in general, "The Centrality of Intelligence," in Anthony James Joes, *Resisting Rebellion: The History and Politics of Counterinsurgency* (Lexington, KY: University Press of Kentucky, 2004), 145–55.

41. Quoted in Comber, *Malaya's Secret Police*, 191, n10.

42. See "Review of the Emergency in Malaya from June 1948 to August 1957," 21, Director of Operations, Malaya, September 12, 1957, TNA: WO 106/5990.

43. See Chin Peng, *My Side of History*, 314–18.

44. "Review of the Emergency in Malaya from June 1948 to August 1957," 27, Director of Operations, Malaya, September 12, 1957, TNA: WO 106/5990.

45. See Chin Peng, *My Side of History*, 324–26, 400–401; Stewart, "Winning in Malaya, 280–82.

DOCUMENT 5.1 "The Special Branch Charter," Directive No. 21, Director of Operations, Malaya, April 24, 1952

101   **36**

' SECRET.

DIRECTOR OF OPERATIONS, MALAYA

DIRECTIVE No. 21

S.B. INTELLIGENCE TARGETS

THE MAIN TASK

1. The creation of an intelligence network which will remain "alive" whatever the M.C.P. plans to do is vital. At the moment, we rely exclusively on information supplied by captured documents and S.E.P. and C.E.P. who, after their initial operational exploitation, become "blown" or "dead" as a source of information. It follows that if the M.C.P. were to disband the M.R.L.A., conceal all but a few weapons and revert to a policy of secret selective killing and the fomentation of labour unrest, Government, deprived of its existing sources of information, would find itself impotent to cope with the situation except in its most open manifestations. Hence, the vital need for the S.B., not only to build up a network of "live" agents in, or in contact with, all levels of M.C.P. organisations, but also to ensure that the identity of these agents are not compromised either by indiscreet or premature action, particularly for low level bandit kills and quick rewards.

FACTORS WHICH HAVE AN IMPORTANT BEARING ON THE SELECTION AND GRADING OF TARGETS

The Supremacy of the Party.

2. The Party, through the Central/Politburo, shapes the broad pattern of overall Party policy and Military strategy. By widely dispersing the members of the Central Committee and maintaining a constant flow of instructional literature from the Central Propaganda Department, the Party ensures strict adherence to the Central line. Its chain of command is Central/Politburo, State, District, Branch, Cell and Sympathiser. The Party by means of its Party Representatives or Political Commissars at State/Regimental, Company and Platoon Headquarters dominates all levels of M.R.L.A. formations. Finally, the Party, through its District and Branch Committees, controls the MIN YUEN Organisation, including the Armed Work Forces detached from the M.R.L.A. for service with the MIN YUEN. The role of the M.R.L.A. is one of support to the Party in the main tasks of dominating the civil population and capturing the arms and ammunition without which the armed struggle cannot hope to survive or expand.

The Main Spheres of Armed Activity.

3. Broadly speaking there are two main rings of armed potential, an inner ring, normally deep in the jungle, which harbours the State Party/Regimental Headquarters and a protecting screen of M.R.L.A. forces, and an outer ring, normally

DOCUMENT 5.1 "The Special Branch Charter," Directive No. 21, Director of Operations, Malaya, April 24, 1952 *(Continued)*

102 37

on the fringes of the jungle bordering estates and other populate⁻¹ areas, which harbours the District and Branch Commi' controlling the Armed MIN YUEN Units, including detachmᵤ ₋ₛ from (and in some areas units of) the M.R.L.A. Communication and supply routes between the inner ring and the outer ring are the responsibility of the State/Regimental Headquarters. Party leadership within this inner circle dictates both political policy and military strategy and is therefore by far the most important target for penetration and attack. To eliminate it would be to destroy the mainspring of all Party and Military activity and morale in the area.

4. The outer ring which is the more vulnerable and therefore the easier target for penetration and attack, has suffered serious local setbacks from time to time. But successes within this ring, unless repeated and extensive, are short-lived and indecisive.

S.B. Targets for Penetration

Top Priority Targets.

5. With the exception of (d) below, top priority targets for S.B. penetration lie within the inner ring. They are—

(a) Central Committee/Politburo;

(b) State Committees, Party and M.R.L.A., H.Q. Commands;

(c) Central Propaganda Department;

(d) Any external agencies or organisations for the supply of arms, personnel, etc.

Other Targets.

6. Other lesser, albeit important, targets for S.B. penetration fall within the outer ring. These are identical with those of the existing S.B. offensive against the MIN YUEN, that is,

(a) District Committee; and

(b) Branch Committee, together with the Armed MIN YUEN Units—

(i) Defence Corps;

(ii) Self-Protection Corps;

(iii) Armed Work Force.

(c) Members and sympathisers of the MIN YUEN Organisation classified as follows—

(i) Working Committees of Executives of the Masses;

(ii) Executives of the Masses;

(iii) Cells;

(iv) Sympathisers.

These are normally planted in or concealed near the following

(i) resettled areas;

(ii) rubber estates;

(iii) tin mines;

(iv) registered Trade Unions and other lawful associations and guilds;

(v) schools and colleges;

(vi) Malay kampongs;

(vii) workers, bus companies, shopkeepers, trishaw riders, etc., in the towns.

DOCUMENT 5.1 "The Special Branch Charter," Directive No. 21, Director of Operations, Malaya, April 24, 1952 *(Continued)*

103   **38**

PENETRATION PLAN—RESPONSIBILITY

The overall plan of penetration will be laid down and thereafter controlled centrally by S.A.C., S.B., Federation Headquarters. Centralised control of penetration planning is designed, *inter alia*—

    (*a*) to promote team-work;

    (*b*) to facilitate assessment of reports and information against the wider Federation and external background;

    (*c*) to concentrate activities and energies on the most profitable and important targets and ensure a correct balance;

    (*d*) to provide a comprehensive record of our Agent resources and potentialities;

    (*e*) to ensure maximum exploitation of all opportunities offered; and

    (*f*) to prevent the employment or payment of any agent by more than one handling officer.

8. Guided by directives which will be issued separately, S.B. staff at all levels will be responsible for—

    (*a*) the procurement, handling and instruction of all agents;

    (*b*) the dissemination of information deriving from Agent sources;

    (*c*) the initiation of action at the appropriate stage.

PENETRATION PLAN—METHODS

9. (*a*) Collection of particulars of all existing agents and evaluation of their potentiality in relation to the S.B. targets listed above.

    (*b*) Creation of Research Parties to study—

        (i) available intelligence relating to selected top priority targets with a view to directing the collection of additional material to fill the gaps and ultimately discovering a link with the individual target in question;

        (ii) the question of penetrating selected registered Trade Unions and open associations.

    (*c*) Preparation by O.C.P.D. under Contingent/Circle/S.B. supervision of a plan for the supply of lower level MIN YUEN intelligence from selected areas of importance. i.e.—

        (i) resettled areas;

        (ii) labour lines;

        (iii) Malay kampongs, etc.

MEASURES TO COUNTER M.C.P. PENETRATION

10. In addition, specific measures will be taken to obtain information of Communist infiltration of:

    (*a*) the Regular Police and, in particular, the Special Constabulary;

    (*b*) the Home Guards;

    (*c*) the Railways;

    (*d*) Telecoms;

    (*e*) Power Stations;

    (*f*) L.E.P., particularly those serving with RASC and REME Units.

DOCUMENT 5.1   "The Special Branch Charter," Directive No. 21, Director of Operations, Malaya, April 24, 1952 *(Continued)*

39

104

11. In respect of (*c*) to (*e*) above, measures to control entry to premises and protect vital parts of machinery and appointment of reliable members of the staff as Security Officers are essential, not only as a means of ensuring a degree of physical protection but also of providing the Uniformed Police with a pretext for regular access and with possible sources of inside information. (*f*) above is a combined S.L.O./Army responsibility.

TACTICAL INTELLIGENCE

ROLE OF THE ARMY

12. The Army is an operational force in aid of the Civil Power. The primary task of the Army is the destruction of the armed forces of the M.C.P. which include both the M.R.L.A. and the Armed Units of the MIN YUEN organisation.

INTELLIGENCE REQUIREMENTS

13. To carry out its role the Army must have the intelligence it requires for operations planned and authorised by the responsible executive authority, i.e., D. of O's Committee or the Operation Sub-Committees of S.W.E.Cs. It also must have intelligence bearing on its own security and the security of its operations.

14. The Army intelligence requirement of the Police Special Branch in relation to the M.C.P. is mainly tactical intelligence in the following forms:

PARTY AND M.R.L.A.

H.Q. Commands—
    Politburo
    State Party/MRLA
    Company
    Platoon
    Sections,

and details of their:
    Order of Battle
    Strength
    Location

Equipment—
    Weapons
    Ammunition
    Communications
    "RE" Stores
    Maps
    Compasses

Intentions and Plans Supplies—
    Organisations
    Location of dumps and their distribution, routes and
        personnel.

Tactics and Movements.

DOCUMENT 5.1 "The Special Branch Charter," Directive No. 21, Director of Operations, Malaya, April 24, 1952 *(Continued)*

40

105

ARMED MIN YUEN UNITS

H.Q. Commands—
  District Committee
  Branch Committee
Order of Battle—
  Defence Corps
  Self-Protection Corps
  Armed Work Force
and details as for Party/MRLA above.

MAIN SOURCES OF COLLECTION

15. These are—
  (*a*) S.B., Uniformed Police, S.C. and Home Guards;
  (*b*) Police and Military Patrols;
  (*c*) Police round-ups and security checks;
  (*d*) Police Jungle Squad and Company patrols;
  (*e*) Deep patrols by Malayan Scouts;
  (*f*) Air Reconnaisance and photographs;
  (*g*) Interrogation of S.E.P. and C.E.P.;
  (*h*) S.B. information as and when it becomes ripe for action;
  (*i*) Bandit documents.

ARMY ASSISTANCE TO THE POLICE

16. It is accepted that in many places the Police lack the staff to process and present intelligence in the form required by the Army. To make up this deficiency, Military Intelligence personnel will be attached to the Police. They will be placed, wherever available and necessary, alongside A.S.Ps in Communist Terrorism Sections at Contingent and also at Circle level with a view to assisting in the collation and presentation of information in conformity with military needs. Military Intelligence Officers attached to Contingent H.Q., and Circle H.Q., will work under the supervision and direction of the Superintendent S.B. and the O.S.P.C. respectively.

CONTROL OF INFORMATION

17. The Civil Power, through the Special Branch, controls the collection, assessment and use of information. Military Commanders at the various levels will normally be briefed by the Military Intelligence Officers attached to the Police. Information thus passed must have been cleared by Superintendent S.B. or O.S.P.Cs, respectively.

24th April, 1952.
[DI/P. 17/1A.]

Director of Operations.

DOCUMENT 5.1 "The Special Branch Charter," Directive No. 21, Director of Operations, Malaya, April 24, 1952 *(Continued)*

106   41

DIRECTIVE No. 21.

DISTRIBUTION LIST.

His Excellency the High Commissioner	1
The Honourable the Deputy Director of Operations ...	1
The Honourable the Chief Secretary	1
The General Officer Commanding Malaya ... ... (Copies for distribution down to Battalion Commanders)	45
The Flag Officer Malayan Area	2
The Air Officer Commanding Malaya	2
The Honourable the Attorney-General ...	1
The Honourable the Secretary for Defence	1
The Commissioner of Police ... ... (Copies for distribution to C.P.Os and State/Settlement and Circle Special Branches)	80
Director of Intelligence	2
Security Liaison Officer	1
Chairman J.I.C. (F.E.)	1
Colonial Defence Liaison Officer, Commissioner-General's Office	1
Head S.I.F.E.	2
Director of Operations Staff	10
Spare	9
	160

Government Press, Kuala Lumpur.
3637—160—30-4-52.

CHAPTER 6

"A Skeleton in Our Cupboard"

British Interrogation Procedures in Northern Ireland

RICHARD J. ALDRICH

Editors' Note:

The issues of interrogation techniques and forms of internment have been high on the international agenda since the tragedy of 9/11 and the US government's use of extraordinary measures to secure vital intelligence. In this chapter Richard Aldrich tracks the issues and debates concerning such measures from an earlier time to provide some historical and practical lessons for us to observe and analyze. What emerges starkly is that the debates that have raged about rendition and torture are timeless, and that the lessons Aldrich has identified have yet to be properly considered by governments, including the testy problem of extraterritoriality, which unifies the aftermath of the Northern Irish case study with the modern day.

During the first decade of the twenty-first century, the handling of detainees was rarely out of the headlines. The related issues of detention status, secret prisons, interrogation techniques, and rendition constituted a cause célèbre. This underlined the way in which controversial intelligence activities, which loom large in the public imagination, can become symbolic of wider debates over the direction and character of national security strategies or even entire political administrations. The same observation might be made about Iran-Contra in the 1980s. In the United States, the matter of interrogation techniques has been center stage since April 2004, with vociferous public and academic arguments moving in parallel with official inquiries. These matters were complex, since they involved different systems run by the US military, the CIA, foreign governments, and private agencies. Some of the worst excesses occurred at Abu Ghraib prison, some twenty miles west of Baghdad, where the core element included a now infamous group of part-time National Guards.[1]

America's allies watched nervously from the sidelines until November 2005, when the Pulitzer Prize–winning journalist Dana Priest revealed the existence of

CIA "secret prisons" in Europe. Thereafter, twin investigations by the Council of Europe and the European Parliament ensured that interrogation centers became a major issue in transatlantic relations. By 2007, it was clear that one of the key figures in the planning of the 9/11 attacks, Khalid Sheikh Mohammed, had been held by the CIA in Poland and had been water-boarded some 183 times.[2] In 2007, the United Kingdom's Intelligence and Security Committee examined how Britain had responded to the process of rendition and to the issue that intelligence shared by the United States might have been obtained under duress. The director-general of MI5, Eliza Manningham-Buller, confirmed that the United Kingdom had received useful intelligence specifically from the interrogation of Khalid Sheik Mohammed. This, she argued, identified six individuals working in or against the United Kingdom and "offered an illustration of the huge amount of significant information that came from one man in detention in an unknown place."[3]

The subject of interrogation has spawned a vast outpouring of both journalistic and academic literature.[4] One of the questions that academic commentators have found particularly baffling is why torture and maltreatment persists, despite the fact that repeated episodes demonstrate that it is both ineffective and politically toxic.[5] One plausible answer is the argument of exceptional circumstances, and certainly the supercharged discussion of the phenomena of "new terrorism" provides an example. Since 9/11, politicians and policymakers have been inclined to talk about new and unprecedented threats, often in the context of justifying emergency legislation.[6] While some aspects of current terrorism are innovative, an obsession with newness can lead us to ignore important and inconvenient lessons from the recent past. Few are aware that the treatment of detainees, deemed variously "suspects," "prisoners of war," or "surrendered enemy personnel," has been a contentious issue in the United Kingdom for at least a century. Episodes from the First and Second World Wars, from the Korean War, together with many postcolonial insurgencies, have bequeathed a litany of fascinating examples and lessons. Perhaps the most important lesson of all is how poor the British have been at learning these lessons. Knowledge of history is no panacea or easy guarantee of success. However, where corporate memory is weak, intelligence and security agencies may repeat past mistakes that were easily foreseen.[7] There are plenty of lessons to learn, and even a brief inspection of the UK archives reveals what some have called "the weight of the shadow of the past."[8]

With specific regard to interrogation, the most obvious lesson that the United Kingdom failed to learn was its essential lack of secrecy. Some intelligence activities, such as the running of a discreet agent, can be confidently kept clandestine for many years, even decades, since few people are involved and the activities are relatively passive. Covert actions or special operations often reveal their trail quickly and the possibility of plausible deniability is at best uncertain. Interrogation, especially in the context of insurgency or terrorism, is yet more visible and almost always results in the processing of individuals who are later released to tell their tale to the media and to human rights organizations. Former detainees have little incentive to understate any abuses they have suffered. Yet because interrogation is regarded as an intelligence activity, often conducted in secret locations, governments somehow presume that its mechanics can be kept hidden and its inner processes denied.

The United Kingdom was certainly slow to climb the learning curve in the postwar period. As early as the late 1950s, the media, lawyers, and international organizations were already sensitized to issues of detainee handling by the maltreatment of POWs held by Communist North Korea, accompanied by widespread reports of torture and brainwashing. In 1960, UK counterinterrogation methods used in the training of special forces were under serious public scrutiny. Yet these experiences were soon forgotten. In 1965, interrogation again became a controversial issue in the context of the fighting in Aden, with protests by Amnesty International and a subsequent UK inquiry. Although Aden prompted the Joint Intelligence Committee to issue firm guidelines on interrogation, often referred to as "The Bible," these were disregarded once the British army arrived in Northern Ireland. Between 1971 and 1972 there were several lamentable episodes, the most important of which was Operation Calaba. This focused on the deep interrogation of twelve high-value detainees selected from the 357 people subjected to internment in August 1971. The subsequent reports and inquiries hold significant lessons for those who wish to engage in policy learning, and accordingly are the focus of this chapter.[9]

The connected episodes of Aden and Northern Ireland triggered no less than three major inquiries in the space of seven years. They are especially interesting because they constitute early examples of the reverberation of investigative journalists, human rights organizations, and international courts, often working in collaboration, upon the practice of intelligence. During the 1960s and 1970s, the very idea that organizations such as Amnesty International or the *Sunday Times* Insight Team might probe these things was greeted in Whitehall with a mixture of horror and indignation. Yet, with hindsight, they perhaps constitute an early example of something that we are now more familiar with, namely a process in which intelligence is placed under the media spotlight and therefore subjected to what might be called regulation by revelation.[10]

Northern Ireland conjured up the familiar specter of emergencies and ad hoc procedures. The dramatic upsurge in political violence in Northern Ireland between 1970 and 1972 caught the UK government unawares and seemed to call for special measures. Although there had been intercommunal violence during 1969 and 1970, this became much worse during 1971. The violence peaked in 1972, when some 479 people died, mostly as the result of a wave of bombings. One factor contributing to this acceleration in violence was frustration among the Nationalists at the failure of the civil rights movement to deliver adequate social change. Unsophisticated security measures that had been used in colonial situations such as Cyprus, imported by the army, also proved counterproductive. The curfew imposed on the Nationalist Lower Falls area of Belfast was but one example. More dramatic was the introduction of internment without trial as a result of a decision by Edward Heath's cabinet, beginning on August 9, 1971. However, because of what Heath later called "hopelessly out of date" intelligence the majority were not current Republican activists, and so the more important figures soon fled south. Most internees were kept at Long Kesh internment camp and some also at Belfast prison.[11]

A further factor in the accelerating violence of the early 1970s was the formation of the Provisional Irish Republican Army or PIRA, a splinter group from the older official IRA. While the official IRA advocated passive resistance and nonviolent civil resistance, the Provisionals advocated military action. Formed in early 1970, they launched their military campaign in early 1971. By 1972, their activities were in full swing, with over 1,300 bombings focused on business and commercial premises. On July 21, 1972, there were no less than twenty-two bombs detonated in Belfast city center. Accordingly, the year of 1972 proved to be the most violent year of the Troubles. In January 1972, the events in Derry, which became known as Bloody Sunday, led to the shooting of some fourteen people in circumstances that are still heavily contested. Loyalist paramilitaries, such as the Ulster Volunteer Force and the Ulster Defence Association accelerated their campaign of sectarian killings. In these circumstances, there then followed a period of rapid population shifts in towns such as Belfast and Derry. Both Catholics and Protestants fled from mixed residential areas, either as a result of intimidation or because of their own well-founded anxieties. Understandably, the security forces felt that they now confronted an emergency.

The treatment of suspects and detainees during internment attracted a great deal of press attention. Complaints about violence during the implementation of internment and abuse during subsequent interrogations in August 1971 triggered the Compton inquiry, which reported within weeks. On reading the report, Cabinet ministers asked the Cabinet Office intelligence coordinator, Dick White, to look specifically at interrogation methods. The five interrogation measures that had caused controversy were wall-standing, hooding, subjection to noise, deprivation of sleep, and restrictions on food and drink. White had previously headed MI5 and then SIS, and so was highly experienced. His brief analysis, which is reproduced at the end of this chapter, defended coercive interrogation methods, but by the time his own internal report was complete, ministers were under renewed pressure from both the press and members of Parliament. As a result, White's own internal report was overtaken by a fuller investigation of interrogation methods by three privy counselors. This second investigation became known as the Parker inquiry and was completed in March 1972. Edward Heath disliked the Parker Report, but now felt he had no choice other than to ban coercive interrogation techniques. Accordingly, new guidelines were issued by the Joint Intelligence Committee in June 1972.

In the wake of internment, PIRA had created what were effectively no-go areas in both Belfast and Derry in which the writ of the security forces did not run. At the end of July 1972, the security forces launched Operation Motorman, which flooded these areas with large numbers of troops and police, rounding up suspects and searching houses for guns and explosives. One of the initial objectives of Operation Motorman when it was originally conceived was to try to net further individuals of interest for interrogation in the hope of improving the flow of intelligence. However, over the previous nine months, interrogation had become a live issue and the security forces were now extremely wary of this approach. Indeed, up until 1972, the British security forces had arguably been overdependent on interrogation for intelligence and now set off down a different path in terms of their overall intelligence strategy.

This was not the end of the matter. The government of Eire had already instituted legal proceedings in the European Court of Human Rights alleging torture, and although this proceeded at a snail-like pace, it worried officials in London. There were also individual claims for compensation lodged by those who had undergone deep interrogation, generating further unwelcome press attention.[12] Initially, the European Commission found that the combined use of the five coercive methods did amount to torture. However, this finding was later overturned on appeal. In 1978, the European Court decided that the controversial five techniques did not occasion suffering of the intensity implied by the word torture. Nevertheless, they ruled that UK interrogations in August 1971 had amounted to "inhuman and degrading treatment," and so contravened the European Convention on Human Rights.

British Interrogation in Historical Context

As the historian Richard Popplewell has discovered, British interrogation methods during the First World War were often innovative. British intelligence officers working in the Middle East would sit their own local intelligence agents on an "electric carpet" when questioning them. This was a large Persian rug with electrodes hidden underneath. If they suspected their agents of lying they would subject them to two or three electric shocks through the legs and pelvis.[13] Moreover, if paid local agents were considered to be persistent liars they were then subjected to another questionable technique. British intelligence officers would suspend the hapless individuals upside down and urinate into their nostrils. The effect of this was not dissimilar to modern water-boarding.[14]

One of the common presumptions about torture is the existence of coherent national styles, reflecting the idea of a centralized and coherent distribution of interrogation doctrine.[15] Instead, the British case demonstrates diversity, which is underlined by the Second World War. The most famous British example was Colonel Robin "Tin Eye" Stephens, an MI5 officer who wore a monocle and presided over Camp 020, where MI5 detained dozens of foreign spies during the Second World War. He was willing to use threats—but not force—because he claimed violence did not work. Very few spies held out against him. In fairness, while Stephens had an aversion to brutality, the threat of execution that could be dangled over those who refused to cooperate was an incentive that few other British interrogators have had at their disposal, before or since.[16] This episode contrasted with

British army practices in the "London Cage," where potential war criminals were interrogated by MI19. Here, detainees were sometimes beaten or else put under stress, using techniques such as a prolonged wall-standing that were later to surface in Aden and Northern Ireland. The British government intervened to censor published accounts of the London Cage by its chief, Lt. Colonel Alexander Scotland, and so the full story did not emerge until 2005.[17]

During the 1950s, the dominant narrative on the issues of interrogation and the torture issue was provided by North Korea, where Allied prisoners of war had not only been badly mistreated but also subject to brainwashing. The subject of brainwashing caught the public imagination and received extensive coverage in the press, something that was also reflected in spy films and spy fiction. On February 28, 1960, the *Observer* newspaper ran an excitable story on brainwashing. Its main source was a public lecture on the subject by Alex Kennedy, a professor at Edinburgh University. Kennedy's talk had focused on general scientific principles and also referred to well-known recent examples such as North Korea. Although Kennedy had not mentioned the United Kingdom, the *Observer* nevertheless claimed that recent exercises in "resistance to interrogation" run by the army's Joint Services Interrogation Wing for the Special Air Service (SAS) followed a similar pattern. There were further revelations in the *Daily Mail* on March 9, 1960.[18] John Profumo, the minister for war, prepared a lengthy refutation, insisting that there was no connection between brainwashing, "which takes months or even years," and the kind of training that was undertaken by the army's pathfinder units. Nevertheless, Profumo conceded that the resistance training had been sparked by the experiences of British POWs in North Korea.[19] The prime minister, Harold Macmillan, seemed to find the whole thing slightly amusing and thought his Cabinet colleagues would be "interested to hear about all this." Accordingly, in March 1960, Profumo's paper on brainwashing was circulated to the full Cabinet.[20]

Almost exactly a year later there were further private protests from the families of territorial SAS soldiers who had been subjected to the resistance training. These concerns were privately conveyed to John Profumo by Quentin Hailsham, the minister for science. Hailsham realized this was not his province and expressed his wish not to be seen to interfere. However, he was also alert to the potential dangers of these exercises and warned his colleague that "in view of the extremely sensitive nature of what is done I think you would be wise to control them very rigidly indeed."[21] Profumo insisted that his officials attached "very considerable importance to teaching parachute troops and the SAS the sort of treatment to which they might be subjected if they were captured." Nevertheless, Profumo was dismayed that after the "public rumpus" of 1960 there was now further trouble. With the agreement of the director of military intelligence, he had placed a ban on further resistance training until fresh instructions were issued. The lessons were already clear. Interrogation was a symbolic issue that was always likely to be held up as a test of civilized behavior.[22]

By February 1965, Britain could claim to have a fully fledged interrogation doctrine. With military interrogation teams providing assistance to internal security operations in Aden and British Guyana, together with advice to Malaysian forces during the confrontation operations against Indonesia, a doctrine was certainly needed. This doctrine advocated the highest standards of behavior on grounds of both morality and effectiveness. This was issued in February 1965 by the JIC on behalf of the director of military intelligence and its tone was unambiguous: "Successful interrogation depends upon careful planning both of the interrogation itself, and of the premises wherein it is conducted. It calls for a psychological attack. Apart from legal and moral considerations, torture and physical cruelty of all kinds are professionally unrewarding since a subject so treated may be persuaded to talk, but not to tell the truth. Successful interrogation may be a lengthy process." Among the activities prohibited were "cruel treatment and torture" together with "humiliating and degrading treatment." The JIC directive was commendably clear about achieving success through empathy and was normally referred to as the interrogator's "Bible."[23] This advice, which encapsulated what might be called a slow patient "cups of tea" approach, was echoed in other seminal documents, not least the advice offered to the South Vietnamese by the British Advisory Mission in Vietnam. Again, this emphasized the good treatment of surrendered enemy personnel in the hope that they might become regular informers or even counter-guerrillas.[24]

However, during 1965, it became increasingly clear that these guidelines were not always being followed on the ground in Aden. Amnesty International made inquiries about the condition of detainees there and dispatched Dr. Rastgeldi, a member of its Swedish executive, to investigate.[25] The UK government now made a further mistake, refusing to cooperate and insisting that the Red Cross alone was the proper investigative authority to consider the welfare of prisoners. The United Kingdom refused to grant Rastgeldi access to the detainees. Predictably, he not only visited Aden, where he quickly found many ex-detainees willing to give statements, but he also visited Cairo, the main external sponsor of the rebels in Aden. The subsequent Amnesty International report was very critical, and once it was published, the foreign secretary, Lord George-Brown, decided to appoint Roderic Bowen, Queen's Counsel, to conduct a British investigation. The Foreign Office explained that "it was important to set up an examination of a kind fully under our control."[26] The Bowen committee reported to Parliament in December 1965 and, to the dismay of officials, was sharply critical. Conditions at the interrogation center in Aden were described as "extremely grim" and its practices were deemed "highly undesirable."[27]

Despite the pain of the Aden experience, many lessons went unlearned. The Bowen Report recommended, among other things, that after Aden, all future interrogations in internal security situations should be undertaken by civilians. However, this was effectively ignored and instead the director of management and support for intelligence in the Ministry of Defence informed the Intelligence Corps in February 1969 that they would continue to undertake interrogation in internal security situations "as the FCO had NOT accepted responsibility." In reality, there was no other source of expertise and so the Joint Services Interrogation

Wing at Ashford in Kent remained the only official center for UK interrogation training, instructing not only military personnel but also the Metropolitan Police Special Branch and, at the request of the FCO, Special Branch officers from overseas.[28] Moreover, while the JIC guidance on interrogation was strengthened, the specific practices that Bowen had found repellent were not explicitly banned. This, too, was a mistake.

When the army was deployed to Northern Ireland in 1969, and then in increasing numbers during the violence of 1970, interrogations remained a mixed activity, employing both Royal Ulster Constabulary (RUC), Special Branch, and specialist army personnel from Ashford. Moreover, although the army personnel were required to operate under the Bible of 1965, in other words the JIC guidelines that counseled a gentle long-term approach to interrogation, in practice this was all but abandoned. Under the pressure of escalating violence in 1971, there was increasing pressure for short-term operational information and a rapid turnaround of suspects. This was especially true when confronted by internment in August 1971. From August 1971, alongside internment, the RUC deployed an approach termed "highly coercive interrogation," more commonly called "interrogation in depth," against suspected PIRA members. This was normally applied by RUC interrogators working under the guidance of the Army Intelligence Corps. They made use of five well-established techniques to wear their subjects down:

1. Wall-standing: forcing the detainees to remain for periods of some hours in a "stress position," described by those who underwent it as being spread-eagled against the wall, with their fingers put high above the head against the wall, the legs spread apart and the feet back, causing them to stand on their toes with the weight of the body mainly on the fingers.
2. Hooding: putting a black or navy colored bag over the detainees' heads and, at least initially, keeping it there all the time except during interrogation.
3. Subjection to noise: pending their interrogations, holding the detainees in a room where there was a continuous hissing noise.
4. Deprivation of sleep: pending their interrogations, depriving the detainees of sleep.
5. Deprivation of food and drink: subjecting the detainees to a reduced diet of bread and water prior to interrogations.

Amnesty International insisted that one prisoner was forced to remain wall-standing in this position for over forty hours and that there were at least six other recorded instances of prisoners being kept like this for more than twenty hours. Detainees were normally subjected to a combination of these techniques over the course of about a week. These techniques were hard to square with the cups of tea doctrine set out in the Bible issued by the JIC in 1965.[29]

One of the spin-offs of the introduction of internment was Operation Calaba, which took place at Hut 60 on Bally Kelly Airfield in Northern Ireland between

0532 hrs on Wednesday, August 11, to 1130 hrs on Tuesday, August 17. The operation dealt with the interrogation in depth of twelve of the higher value IRA suspects netted by internment. Hut 60 was in fact a complex of some two dozen rooms in an isolated block. The main role of the army personnel from the Joint Services Interrogation Wing (JSIW) was to advise on the overall approach to interrogation, together with technical support, including tape recording from a dedicated room. The RUC Special Branch took the lead on the questioning, while the RUC's Special Patrol Group undertook escort duties and security. The use of covert microphones seems to have been in evidence, since "Hut 60 at Bally Kelly had been examined by JSIW as early as March 1971 and detailed modifications and wiring had been carried out." The top priority for the questioners was PIRA operations that were planned for the near future. Operation Calaba was initially judged successful, producing details of safe houses and leading to an immediate operation which uncovered an arms cache. There were some thirty-eight pages of IRA Order of Battle material focused on Belfast, Derry, and Armagh. Some 500 personalities of Special Branch interest were also recorded and some forty previous incidents were cleared up. The suspects were taken to Hut 60 by helicopter by a circuitous route with a flight time of one hour "to simulate a long journey," and so "most suspects thought they were questioned in England." Intelligence officers felt they lacked the use of smaller discrete facilities which might accommodate individuals "who co-operate fully under interrogation" or those who offered to "actively assist the Security Forces" in the future.[30]

Accounts about general violence during the implementation of internment and specific information about the five techniques used during deep interrogation soon leaked out. The information was picked up by the *Sunday Times* Insight Team, and reports of ill-treatment, carried in some detail in the press, triggered the government inquiry by Compton during the autumn of 1971. Compton was hardly an impartial judge, being close to the Unionists; moreover, he was rather timid in drawing forth evidence. Although permitted to see some classified material, he was not even allowed to know the name of the RUC Special Branch officer overseeing the interrogation operations. Moreover, for security reasons he agreed to "say nothing of the interrogation process itself," which seemed to cut across the very remit of his inquiry.[31]

In late October, officials in the Ministry of Defence were agonizing over what approach they should take when they came to give evidence to the Compton inquiry. Their main problem was the so-called five techniques. After discussions with the secretary of the JIC, Brian Stewart, they came up with two possible approaches. The first was the idea that they should justify these by pointing to the accelerating violence, arguing that: "tough times and tough opponents require tough measures." The second alternative was to argue that the five techniques were actually defensive; in other words they would insist they were "designed essentially to provide security for guards, interrogators and detainees." They would insist that although they were useful in "softening up the detainees" this was not their main purpose. Brian Stewart preferred the second approach, but defense officials were skeptical. One of them observed: "I do not believe that this approach would be credible."[32]

Improbably, the latter approach was taken. Although almost all the detainees refused to cooperate with the inquiry, Compton drew on the detailed evidence gathered by the *Sunday Times* Insight Team and this made it impossible to deny that the techniques were primarily about softening up prior to interrogation. By October 25, 1971, with the Compton Committee still in session, Sir James Dunnett, the permanent undersecretary at the Ministry of Defence, discussed these developments anxiously with Dick White and the director general of intelligence at the MoD, Admiral Louis le Bailly, who now offered him more detail on Operation Calaba. On wall-standing, the best they could do was to assure the committee that it was never "more than six hours at a stretch," although it was clear to Compton that some of the detainees had fallen down with exhaustion. "If a detainee collapsed he was allowed to get his second wind and was not put back on the wall." They could plausibly claim that many detainees wished to be hooded to protect their own identity, but use of the noise machines was more difficult to explain. White and Le Bailly conceded that "the sensory deprivation aspect was indeed a spin-off which helped" in what they called "the breaking down process." The same was true of sleep deprivation, and Dunnett was informed that as a general rule "once a prisoner was cooperating he was allowed to sleep." Detainees were on a bread and water diet "until they started to talk."[33]

Achieving a clear sense of what really happened during Operation Calaba is difficult. Each side had an interest in minimizing or expanding their version of events and all these accounts are potentially biased. However, the principal account offered of interrogation at Bally Kelly given in the *Sunday Times* corresponds quite closely to the discussions chaired by James Dunnett on October 25. William Shannon, one of the twelve detainees, recalls: "On the same day I was put into a room with a fantastic noise like steam hissing through a pipe. I was completely disorientated from this. . . . I had nothing to eat for, I reckon, four days, except a cup of water and one round of bread each time. I got a sleep after three days. This went on and on. I had no idea where I was. I lost all track of time."[34]

The *Sunday Times* had not discovered the location of the interrogation center and believed it instead to be at Palace Barracks at Holywood in Belfast. However, they had identified all the men initially put through Operation Calaba and their reporting now focused on what they called the "pervasive noise." Their Insight Team claimed that the noise "literally drove them out of their minds." They had also identified that it was run by personnel from the Joint Services Interrogation wing and claimed that these activities were "among the most secret areas" of British defense activity. Most important was the way in which this practice was framed, recalling familiar worries derived from the Korean War. They asserted that it was all founded on "Russian brainwashing techniques" and had been refined for British use by an RAF wing-commander who later committed suicide.[35]

Compton delivered his report to government in early November. Edward Heath was furious. He had expected "a clean bill of health" for the security forces and instead it was critical of their behavior. "It seems to me one of the most unbalanced, ill-judged reports I have read." On the matter of interrogation, he felt that they had gone to "endless lengths to show that anyone not given 3-star hotel facilities suffered hardship and ill-treatment." What troubled him most was that while PIRA had ordered detainees not to participate in the inquiry, ensuring that Compton had almost no direct witnesses to substantiate their allegations, nevertheless media sources were given the same weight as official evidence.[36] As soon as Cabinet ministers saw the Compton Report they realized that there was likely to be a public fuss over deep interrogation. Accordingly, a fortnight before it was published, they decided to invite the intelligence coordinator, Dick White, to reassess methods of interrogation in Northern Ireland.[37] Somewhat anticipating this, a few weeks before, Brian Stewart, an SIS officer who was serving as secretary of the JIC, had already visited the province. Stewart argued that one of the main problems was the poor facilities. This meant that limited hooding was genuinely required to prevent individuals from seeing and being seen, in the interests of their own security and that of others. He argued that limited wall-standing was necessary to secure discipline when in transit. "White sound" at a non-offensive level was "essential" to prevent prisoners from overhearing or being overheard. However, Stewart was also frank in stating that these procedures were being used by interrogators to wear prisoners down. Stewart's suggested solution was to offer all concerned a stern reminder that these techniques "must be carefully restricted to conform with the spirit of the doctrine that these were security measures and not offensive techniques."[38] The White Report, prepared a few weeks later, and reproduced at the end of this chapter, took much the same line.[39]

Heath had always been greatly impressed by Dick White.[40] However, in this case both Stewart and White had miscalculated. First, the use of these techniques simply could not be reconciled with the spirit of the excellent guidelines produced by the JIC in 1965 known as the Bible. Second, in an operational context, it was unrealistic to try and separate out the use of these techniques for defensive and offensive proposes. Both Stewart and White accepted that there was huge operational pressure for short-term results in 1971, negating the long-term patient approach counseled in JIC(65)15. Most importantly, they had failed to recognize that given the interest of the press, the public, lawyers, and humanitarian organizations, measures like white sound would always look offensive, and so the cups of tea approach set out in 1965 was the only sustainable option. Indeed, White's attitude to the problem of public perceptions was to try to hide things. Indeed, White even questioned the wisdom of publishing the Compton inquiry, given that there was a possibility that there was "no legal basis for the interrogation processes and prisoner handling techniques in question."[41]

When the Compton Report was published on November 17, 1971, there was a public commotion and a lively debate in the House of Commons. Republicans inevitably argued that it was a whitewash, while others argued that it showed that RUC and army were restrained. Either way, it was the deep interrogation process which now became a matter of public debate. Chapman Pincher, the defense correspondent of the *Daily Express*, and himself a former interrogator, was interviewed on the BBC Radio 4 *Today* program. Pincher accused Compton of being "rather squeamish" and of not recognizing that intelligence was vital if lives were to be saved in the midst of a violent campaign of bombings and shootings. He insisted: "This intelligence can't be obtained by just giving people cups of tea. The people have got to be frightened into giving information."[42] There were now competing investigative activities. An inspection team from Amnesty International was on the ground in Northern Ireland; meanwhile the Irish government was bringing forward the cases of detainees in the European Court. Members of Parliament were also pressing for more details. Accordingly, after consulting with Harold Wilson, Heath felt he had little choice but to set up a committee of three privy counselors under Lord Parker to look specifically into the matter of interrogation methods.

By November 17, 1971, James Dunnett, the permanent undersecretary (PUS) at the Ministry of Defence, was already meeting with Dick White and other officials to prepare the ground for this second inquiry.[43] Dunnett felt they were "on pretty safe ground" in explaining why the various techniques used were necessary for the security of the interrogators and indeed the detainees. "Where we get onto more difficult ground is in explaining and justifying the methods used for the softening up of interrogatees." This, he added, was "the really crucial issue" on which the Parker committee had to advise. Dunnett suggested that White, who was to meet the committee early on, should emphasize operational pressures and the importance of obtaining the maximum amount of intelligence quickly "within the bounds of what is acceptable in a civilized community."[44] The army general staff went further, arguing that they should bluntly assert the right to use these techniques for making internees "more amenable to successful interrogation."[45] In his own evidence to the Parker committee, White tried to emphasize the "sense of utter urgency."[46]

The biggest problem for the government was the "noise machine." Operating against the background of the iconic 1965 film, *The Ipcress File*, in which Harry Palmer, played by Michael Caine, was subjected to mind-bending techniques using noise, the public felt that something nasty must be going on. Parliament took a strong interest and a member of Parliament, John Cunningham, asked to see an example of the machine. The noise machine was not a simple tape-recorder or a gramophone with amplifiers; instead it was an electronic sound generator that had no moving parts. Parliamentary questions from members of Parliament referred to a "noise torture machine" and this triggered further anxious investigations by civil servants. Experiments were conducted at the Joint Services Interrogation Wing at Ashford in Kent and the volume of sound was found to be 87 dB, slightly less than the noise encountered in a tube train in a tunnel with the windows open. The noise was likened to a radio that was not tuned in to a station, or to a railway engine letting off steam, and was sufficiently loud to prevent normal conversation. However, there was no discussion of the effects of prolonged exposure to such noise.[47]

Improbably, even in December 1971 Dick White believed that the use of the noise machine would be sustainable. He complained that they were the victims of the misrepresentation of interrogation techniques "by interested parties," which was expressly designed to interrupt the flow of information on the IRA. White was convinced that, with better regulation, the current techniques could be retained. He explained to James Dunnett: "I therefore believe it is in our best interests to clarify our rules of procedure in such a way as to remove all possibilities of charges being made in future that we are engaged in 'brainwashing and mind-bending.'" He accepted that these were real techniques "which the Russians and the Chinese use" but felt that it was possible to distance themselves from such things. However, he conceded that, ultimately, it was for the Parker committee to achieve a balance between "the severities needed to deal with violent men" and limitation imposed by human rights.[48]

Parker reported to the government on January 31, 1972, and was tougher than the government expected. Parker argued that there could be some debate as to whether the European Convention on Human Rights applied to emergency situations such as Northern Ireland. However, inescapably, the directive of 1965, which the security forces were operating under, exhorted them to abide by the Geneva Convention and in the committee's opinion this had not been observed. Some witnesses had even urged them that Britain should "set an example to the world" by improving on the standards set by the Geneva Convention. They argued that even though innocent lives could be and had been saved by the use of deep interrogation techniques, a civilized society should never use them since they were "a slippery slope" that might "lead to the deliberate infliction of torture. Indeed, some had argued it was better that innocent civilians should die than that the information which could save them should ever be obtained by these methods." This absolutist approach, the Parker committee noted, had the attraction of removing the most difficult aspect of their task, namely deciding where discomfort and hardship stopped and physical and mental torture began. Indeed, in the event, the task proved so difficult that the privy councillors could not agree and turned in majority and minority reports. The majority report by Parker and Boyd-Carpenter agreed that the five techniques could be used in exceptional circumstances, but only with explicit ministerial approval. The minority report by Lord Gardner called the events of the last year "a sorry story" and blamed the authorities for departing from what it called highly successful wartime techniques in favor of a program which was alien "to British democratic traditions." However all were agreed that the five techniques lay outside the Geneva Convention.[49]

Edward Heath was angered by the report, not least because the divided opinion offered no clear direction. Alec Douglas-Home, the foreign secretary, who was away at a summit, captured their dilemma. "I find this insoluble. Interrogation undoubtedly saves lives and on the evidence the interrogated does not suffer permanent harm. I will leave it to the lawyers at home." Douglas-Home was correct about the impact of the lawyers. Eyes were now cast forward towards the impending cases before the European Court brought by Dublin. Legal advisers in the Foreign and Commonwealth Office were mindful of the effect of Lord Gardner's minority report on the case being brought by the Irish government.[50] No less weighty was the recommendation that if coercive techniques were to be used, ministers would have to decide. Predictably perhaps, with this alarming ball bouncing into their court, ministers now decided to ban the five techniques outright.

Accordingly, in March 1972, Heath ordered the JIC to rewrite their directive on interrogation. As if to spur them on, in May 1972 there were further stories in the *Sunday Times* and ministers expressed "considerable concern about renewed allegations of brutality in the context of detention and interrogation in Northern Ireland." Trend asked the secretary of the JIC, now Michael Herman, to accelerate the work.[51] In fact, the JIC was already at an advanced stage with its new directive. The new JIC rules were robust. Interrogation was now to be a matter for the civil authorities and the participation of military personnel in interrogations required ministerial permission. The new directive put strong emphasis on both international and domestic law. It stressed compliance with the Geneva Convention and asserted that personnel should be aware of the Geneva Convention and added: "It is of paramount importance that they should not act unlawfully in any circumstances." The JIC also incorporated the so-called Parker prohibitions; it forbade the five techniques, namely, hoods, wall-standing, noise equipment, sleep deprivation, and restricted diet. Medical examinations were now mandatory on arrival and departure.[52] Michael Herman wisely advised Burke Trend that, while the document was secret for now, at some unforeseen point in the future it might well have to be published and so it should be drafted with public inspection in mind.[53]

On May 17, 1972, Trend was able to tell Heath that the new directive was ready.[54] On June 8, 1972, Edward Heath confirmed that all government departments were "content" with the new directive, and that both MI5 and SIS "will work at all times in conformity with the Directive."[55] In fact, this was not exactly the case, since Heath had overlooked a careful qualification. The new directive was to be observed "insofar as interrogations are conducted by or on behalf of MI5 and MI6 in British territory."[56] This had more significance for MI6, who mostly operated overseas and often in conjunction with foreign services who might be less choosy about interview techniques. The foreign secretary had chosen his words carefully, stating, "I confirm that the Directive will also be observed in the conduct of any interrogations which may be conducted by or on behalf of MI6 in British territory."[57] By contrast, the Ministry of Defence was anxious to see the new directive implemented universally, typically by the SAS personnel then on loan to Oman.[58]

Ultimately, there was an inescapable contradiction between the assurances that the British government was giving in public and their own private conviction that some softening up was necessary and justified. In April 1972, the Irish ambassador to London called on Willie Whitelaw, secretary of state for Northern Ireland, to bring forward further complaints of "physical maltreatment." Whitelaw assured him that "if there had been cases of physical maltreatment, this was strictly contrary to instructions." However, this could hardly be squared with the private conviction prior to May 1972 that a certain amount of pressure was essential to secure operationally valuable information quickly.[59] Belatedly, British ministers had recognized that interrogation was providing a field day for the press both at home and abroad. As if to underline the point, on May 9 the *New York Times* ran a story by Bernard Weinraub titled "New Torture Inquiry Is Set in Ulster."[60]

Privately, British officials remained divided. In April 1974, the General Office Commanding (GOC) Northern Ireland, General Frank King, wrote to Merlin Rees, who had succeeded Whitelaw as the secretary of state for Northern Ireland in the new Wilson government. He lamented the effects of the new restrictions and was "increasingly disturbed by the lack of intelligence forthcoming from the questioning of many terrorists that we have arrested." He argued that the current restrictions made no sense "in current insurgency conditions"; however, with the Strasbourg case still unresolved, he complained that civil servants were dragging their heels and insisting it was all "too difficult."[61] By late 1974, British diplomats were taking a "low profile defensive approach" as they confronted the embarrassment of the various court cases and their attendant publicity. J. B. Donnely of the Ireland department confessed that he had in any case found some of the previous guidance sent to him on how to present the Parker Report "offensive," and he added that it was now hard to square with the government's retreat on interrogation techniques. He predicted that the court settlements would have propaganda value for the IRA and would also be used widely by human rights bodies in international organizations. "These cases constitute a skeleton in our cupboard" he added, and unfortunately "the cupboard door is likely to be opened at regular intervals over the coming months as more of these cases are settled."[62]

In August 1975, Shivers and McClean, two of the detainees who underwent deep interrogation, were paid £15,000 and £14,000 compensation in out-of-court settlements, and some twelve other cases were pending.[63] In 1976, James Callaghan asked bullishly why the United Kingdom should not fight the other cases in court. However, defense officials had by now learned many of the lessons surrounding the dynamics of public and legal investigation of these matters, and offered a robust reply: "Fighting a deep interrogation case in court has the primary disadvantage that we would lose and that very heavy damages would be awarded. It is probable that a court would award exemplary damages to mark the improper use of executive power. A lengthy court hearing would generate considerable publicity and embarrassment for the government. The plaintiffs could produce medical witnesses who gave evidence before the European Commission of Human Rights to the effect that deep interrogation can induce both physical and mental illness and would compare the after-effects with those experienced by inmates of Nazi concentration camps." Officials added that the defense would require government to produce large numbers of classified and sensitive documents. In the event, the UK government chose not to defend any of the cases.[64]

NGOs, lawyers, and the press were now in the driving seat. By the autumn of 1977, the Ministry of Defence and Foreign Office were busy discussing an NGO Draft Convention on torture that had appeared at the United Nations.[65] Army lawyers worried over drafts. "I do not think MoD can be seen opposing any instrument abjuring torture," they concluded. However, they worried over phrases like "degrading treatment" that they felt gave "any evil-wisher the opportunity to make accusations in an international forum" attacking security procedures that "we regard as normal."[66] Some relief came in December 1977 when the European Court ruled that the notorious five techniques were not, in fact, torture, but only amounted to degrading treatment. In response the British government gave a firm assurance that the five techniques would be abandoned, and indeed, as we have seen, they have not been practiced since 1972.

Lessons Learned?

At least seven lessons might be distilled from the Northern Ireland case:

A. 'Cups of Tea'
Most importantly, the long experience of British interrogations confirms the wisdom of the biblical JIC(65)17. The most effective form of interrogation is one designed to achieve empathy with the subject by building up a relationship over time. This not only conforms to the requirements of law and morality, it is also the most effective way of extracting reliable intelligence.

B. Emergencies
Pressure for abandonment of sensible interrogation guidelines is most likely to occur in the context of unexpected emergencies. This is because of the underdevelopment of other sources of intelligence on a subject that hitherto has been a low priority. Agents of penetration typically take months, even years, to develop, and so in 1971, even routine intelligence gathering drew on what had been gained through interrogation.

C. Reverse Experience
One of the problems that repeatedly arises is that the knowledge of soldiers about interrogations is derived from what they have been taught that an unpleasant enemy might do to them. Few trainers expected them to draw on these resistance experiences and use the techniques themselves.

D. Lack of Secrecy
Interrogation measures rarely stay secret for long. Yet because interrogations are often conducted by secret or semisecret agencies in hidden locations, governments often operate under the illusion that this activity will also remain secret. In

reality, unless detainees are going to be detained forever, they will recount their experiences in detail and possibly elaborate on them.

E. NGOs
NGOs can be useful in countering false accounts of maltreatment. Therefore resistance to requests from NGOs to inspect facilities and to meet detainees is normally a bad idea. While NGOs sometimes have improbably high expectations, nevertheless their concerns can potentially act as a helpful warning light on a dashboard, alerting officials to emerging problems.

F. Framing
The press and the public are amateur intelligence watchers and not professionals. Their lexicon of reference for secret activities is unlikely to be sophisticated, and will often be shaped by a few mythologized cases, or even spy films and spy fiction. Presented with issues such as a noise machine, it is likely that the press and public will assume the worst.

G. Guidelines
Guidelines are there to ensure ethical practice and to keep people out of trouble. In both Aden and Northern Ireland, the biblical guidelines of JIC(65)15 would have been adequate if they had been followed faithfully. However, the guidelines as they stood failed to outlaw specific practices and had not received ministerial approval. These were both shortcomings.

H. Learning to Learn
Most importantly, officials are resistant to learning. Or else, if they learn they tend to draw on fanciful versions of past cases that amount to "bar stool history" rather than undertaking a serious review of past experience. Meanwhile, new events are often regarded as special or atypical, offering implicit reasons for departure from established norms and guidelines.

The experiences of 1971 point directly to more recent times. After 9/11, interrogation procedures were again driven by an overwhelming sense of emergency and specialness. During 2002 and 2003, the war on terror had produced many thousands of suspects, and yet there were few skilled interrogators. Detainees ended up being handled by the sort of personnel who worked at Abu Ghraib, including individuals with limited training and less intelligence. More alarmingly, the exigency of the moment also led senior officials in the Bush administration to approve methods such as water-boarding, which international bodies have universally categorized as torture. Here, at least, the CIA did display some modicum of learning, since the folk memory of the agency was, eternally, to be exhorted to undertake emergency measures by presidents and policymakers, and then to become the whipping boy when these things were uncovered. After 2001, both the CIA and the NSA were extremely careful to obtain direct instructions and approvals at the highest level for their activities. This, in turn, explains the reluctance of the Obama administration to probe these matters further, since it would likely involve the investigation of very senior figures.

Achieving adequate administrative and legal approval for alternative interrogation procedures was, however, as far as the CIA got with lessons learned. This was notably disappointing for an agency with a long history of sophisticated operations and clusters of remarkable skill sets. Although the CIA was the lead American intelligence agency in dealing with some of the most high-profile suspects, it had little experience in the field of interrogation, and could not be troubled to acquire this. Instead, the CIA officer called Martinez who was chosen to question Khalid Sheik Mohammed in a secret prison in Poland had no training in interrogation and spoke no Arabic. Indeed, until recently he had been a counternarcotics analyst. This stands in stark contrast to the FBI interrogator sent to question Saddam Hussein, a Lebanese American called George Piro, who was an experienced interrogator and one of the few FBI officers with fluent Arabic. Over months, Piro patiently established rapport with his subject and over many cups of tea, the fascinating inner story of Saddam's regime began to unravel.[67]

Proponents of torture often argue that time is a luxury, and tend to present the "ticking bomb" scenario, in which a greater evil can only be prevented though the use of torture. The idea of urgency underpins many of the arguments for robust treatment made by officials both in 1971 and also in 2001. Real examples of the ticking bomb are hard to find but are not unknown. Some of the intelligence that allowed the frustration of planned attacks on airliners in the United Kingdom in August 2006 may well have been secured through torture of a suspect in Pakistan. Ticking bombs may indeed have a counterpart in reality and certainly look less hypothetical now. Other proponents of torture tend to advance arguments of pragmatism. The Harvard lawyer Alan Dershowitz has argued that torture is such a widespread reality that we need to deal with this by regulating it through "torture warrants" in order to minimize the level of abuse. This has manifested itself in Israel, where the authorities have been required to go to courts to secure warrants for the application of what was termed "moderate physical pressure." The very idea of torture warrants is a fascinating example of modern government, which has arguably produced a climate of hyper-regulation.

Conversely, Sir Richard Dearlove, former chief of SIS, has advanced persuasive arguments for an absolute ban on maltreatment of any kind. For every person tortured, we lose other voluntary informants who do not come forward because they are frightened or disgusted. Trust, not fear, is the most valuable weapon for an intelligence officer. Torture is not only immoral and illegal; it is also ineffective. Proponents of torture also ignore the wider point that after 2001, incidents such as Abu Ghraib cost Western democracies the moral high ground. The strategic battle is essentially an informational one, in which competing truths advance claims to offer a superior way of life. In this realm, torture represents a disaster of the first order. We also need to bear in mind that more than ever before, counterterrorism depends on international cooperation. Philip Zelikow, a senior state department official, recounts that: "When I worked at the State Department, some of America's best European allies found it increasingly difficult to assist us in counterterrorism because they feared becoming complicit in a program their governments abhorred. This was not a hypothetical concern."[68]

Interrogation using torture or cruel and degrading treatment is prohibited by international law and by a welter of domestic legislation and regulation. However, the practice remains widespread. In the context of emergencies and special situations, those involved in operations will always be tempted by utilitarian justifications of torture. Typically, in the days and weeks after Operation Calaba, the interrogations were considered by intelligence officers to have been effective and successful. However, in short order these events came back to bite them. Accordingly, abstract arguments for established norms based on law and morality need to be buttressed by practical arguments for good behavior. Impatient interrogation not only produces weaker intelligence but also undermines the overarching strategic goals of counterterrorism and counterinsurgency.[69]

NOTES

I am indebted to the Cabinet Office, which kindly provided me with some declassified material from CAB 163 files to assist with this project.

1. Elizabeth Holtzman, "Torture and Accountability," *Nation*, July 18, 2005.
2. "September 11 Mastermind Khalid Sheikh Mohammed Waterboarded 183 times," *Times*, April 20, 2009.
3. Intelligence and Security Committee, *Rendition*, Cmnd. 7171, July 2007, 12, para. 28.
4. Major books on this subject include: M. Bagaric and J. Clarke, *Torture: When the Unthinkable Is Morally Permissible* (New York: State University of New York Press, 2007); M. Benvenisti (ed.), *Abu Ghraib: The Politics of Torture* (Berkeley, CA: North Atlantic Books, 2004); M. Danner, *Torture and Truth: America, Abu Ghraib, and the War on Terror* (London: Granta Books, 2005); A. M. Dershowitz, *Why Terrorism Works* (New Haven: Yale University Press, 2002); K. J. Greenberg (ed.), *The Torture Debate in America* (New York: Cambridge University Press, 2006); K. J. Greenberg and J. Dratel, *The Torture Papers: The Road to Abu Ghraib* (Cambridge: Cambridge University Press, 2005); Stephen Grey, *Ghost Plane: The Untold Story of the CIA's Secret Rendition* (London: Hurst, 2006); J. Jaffer and A. Singh, *Administration of Torture: A Documentary Record from Washington to Abu Ghraib and Beyond* (New York: Columbia University Press, 2007); S. Levinson (ed.), *Torture: A Collection* (New York: Oxford University Press, 2004); C. Mackey and G. Miller, *The Interrogators: Inside the Secret War against al Qaeda* (New York: Little, Brown, 2004); Alfred W. McCoy, *A Question of Torture: CIA Interrogation, from the Cold War to the War on Terror* (New York: Metropolitan Books, 2006); T. Paglen and A. C. Thompson, *Torture Taxi: On the Trail of the CIA's Rendition Flights* (New York: Melville House Publishing, 2006); D. Rejali, *Torture and Democracy* (Princeton:

Princeton University Press, 2007); K. Roth, M. Worden, and A. D. Bernstein (eds.), *Torture: Does It Make Us Safer? Is It Ever OK?: A Human Rights Perspective* (New York: Human Rights Watch, 2005); E. Saar, *Inside the Wire: A Military Intelligence Soldier's Eyewitness Account of Life at Guantanamo* (New York: Penguin, 2005); S. Strasser, *The Abu Ghraib Investigations: The Official Reports of the Independent Panel and Pentagon on the Shocking Prisoner Abuse in Iraq* (New York: Public Affairs, 2004).

5. The journal literature is vast and growing: F. Allhof, "Terrorism and Torture," *International Journal of Applied Philosophy*, 17 (2003): 105–18; T. E. Ayres, "'Six Floors' of Detainee Operations in the Post-9/11 World," *Parameters* 35 (Autumn 2005): 3–53; M. Bagaric and J. Clarke, "Not Enough Official Torture in the World? The Circumstances in Which Torture Is Morally Justifiable," *University of San Francisco Law Review* 39 (2005): 581–616 [see reply by Rumney below]; A. Bellamy, "No Pain, No Gain? Torture and Ethics in the War on Terror," *International Affairs* 82 (2006): 121–48; M. Bowden, "The Dark Art of Interrogation," *Atlantic Monthly*, 292 (2003): 51–76; R. Crelinsten, "The World of Torture: A Constructed Reality," *Theoretical Criminology* 7 (2003): 293–318; A. Danchev, "Accomplicity: Britain, Torture, and Terror," *The British Journal of Politics and International Relations* 8 (2006): 587–601; A. M. Dershowitz, "Reply: Torture without Visibility and Accountability Is Worse Than With It," *University of Pennsylvania Journal of Constitutional Law* 6 (2003): 326 [reply to Kreimer, see below]; A. M. Dershowitz, "The Torture Warrant: A Response to Professor Strauss," *New York Law School Law Review* 48 (2003): 275–94 [reply to Strauss, see below]; D. Forsythe, "United States Policy toward Enemy Detainees in the 'War on Terrorism'," *Human Rights Quarterly* 28 (2006): 465–91; G. Hook and C. Mosher, "Outrages against Personal Dignity: Rationalizing Abuse and Torture in the War on Terror," *Social Forces* 83 (2005): 1627–46; R. Jackson, "Language, Policy and the Construction of a Torture Culture in the War on Terrorism," *Review of International Studies* 33 (2007): 353–71; S. Kreimer, "Too Close to the Rack and the Screw: Constitutional Constraints on Torture in the War on Terror," *University of Pennsylvania Journal of Constitutional Law* 6 (2003): 278 [see reply by Dershowitz above]; A. W. McCoy, "Cruel Science: CIA Torture and U.S. Foreign Policy," *New England Journal of Public Policy*, 19, 2 (2005): 1–54; A. Meydani, "The Interrogation Policy of the Israeli General Security Service: Between Law and Politics," *International Journal of Intelligence and CounterIntelligence* 21 (2008): 26–39; A. Meydani, "Security and Human Rights Policy: Israel and the Interrogation Case of 1999," *Contemporary Security Policy* 28 (2007): 579–96; A. Roberts, "Torture and Incompetence in the 'War on Terror'," *Survival* 49 (2007): 199–212; P. N. S. Rumney, "Is Coercive Interrogation of Terrorist Suspects Effective? A Response to Bagaric and Clarke," *University of San Francisco Law Review* 40 (2006): 479–513 [see Bagaric and Clarke above]; H. Schue, "Torture," *Philosophy and Public Affairs* 7 (1978): 124–43; J. Slater, "Tragic Choices in the War on Terrorism: Should We Try to Regulate and Control Torture?," *Political Science Quarterly* 121 (2006): 191–215;

M. Strauss, "Torture," *New York Law School Law Review*, 48 (2004): 201–74 [see reply by Dershowitz above].

6. A. Field, "The 'New Terrorism': Revolution or Evolution?," *Political Studies Review* 7 (2009): 195–207.

7. Christopher Andrew, "Intelligence Analysis Needs to Look Backwards before Looking Forward," *History and Policy*, June 2004. www.historyandpolicy.org/papers/policy-paper-23.html.

8. Dan Reiter, "Learning, Realism, and Alliances: The Weight of the Shadow of the Past," *World Politics* 46 (July 1994): 490–526.

9. For a sophisticated analysis of Northern Ireland that connects with more recent conflicts, see Caroline Kennedy-Pipe and Andrew Mumford, "Torture, Rights, Rules and Wars: Ireland to Iraq," *International Relations*, 21 (2007): 119–26. On British intelligence and Northern Ireland more generally see Samantha Newbery: "Intelligence and Controversial British Intelligence Techniques: The Northern Ireland Case, 1971–72," *Irish Studies in International Affairs* 20 (2009): 103–19; Eunan O'Halpin, "'A Poor Thing but Our Own': The Joint Intelligence Committee and Ireland, 1965–72," *Intelligence and National Security* 23 (2008): 658–80.

10. R. J. Aldrich, "Regulation by Revelation?: Intelligence, Transparency and the Media," in R. Dover and M. Goodman (eds.), *Spinning Intelligence: British and American Intelligence and the Media* (New York: Columbia University Press, 2009), 13–37.

11. Edward Heath, *The Course of My Life* (London: Coronet, 1998), 429–30.

12. *Ireland v. United Kingdom*, 1976 Y.B. Eur. Conv. on Hum. Rts. 512, 748, 788–94 (Eur. Comm'n of Hum. Rts).

13. Richard Popplewell, "British Intelligence in Mesopotamia 1914–16," *Intelligence and National Security* 5 (1990): 139–72.

14. Additional information kindly supplied by Richard Popplewell. See also Rejali, *Torture and Democracy*, 329–30.

15. Ibid. See also M. Lazreg, *Torture and the Twilight of Empire: From Algiers to Baghdad* (Princeton, NJ: Princeton University Press, 2007).

16. Calder Walton, "Torture and Intelligence Gathering in Western Democracies," *History and Policy*, October 2008. www.historyandpolicy.org/papers/policy-paper-23.html.

17. Ian Cobain, "The Secrets of the London Cage," *Guardian*, November 12, 2005.

18. Memo, "The London Cage—Daily Mail Allegations," March 1960, WO 32/17501.

19. C(60) draft, "Brainwashing," Memo, by the Secretary of State for War, March 1960, WO 32/17501.

20. Macmillan (PM) to Profumo (Min War), M 60/60, March 10, 1960, WO 32/17501.

21. Hogg (Min Sci) to Profumo (Min War), March 28, 1961, WO 32/17501.

22. Profumo (Min War) to Hailsham (Min Sci), April 14, 1961, WO 32/17501.

23. This was JIC(65)15, "Joint Directive on Military Interrogation in Internal Security Operations Overseas," February 17, 1965, PREM 15/485. This was known as the

Bible and subsequently widely circulated as JIC/108/65, February 3, 1965, CAB 163/171.

24. Robert Thompson, British Advisory Mission Vietnam, "Notes on Treatment and Control of Surrendered Viet Cong," January 15, 1963, File 1570, Box 60, Lansdale Papers, Hoover Institute on War, Revolution and Peace, University of Stanford.

25. Stockholm to FO, "Amnesty International and Aden," Tel. No. 395, December 17, 1966, DEFE 24/252.

26. Crawford (FCO) to Trend (Cab Sec) November 1, 1971, enclosing, "Note on Events Leading up to the Preparation of the Bowen Report on Procedures for the Arrest, Interrogations and Detention of Suspected Terrorists in Aden (Nov. 16, 1966)" October 29, 1971, CAB 163/171.

27. Bowen Report, *Procedures for the Arrest, Interrogation and Detention of Suspected Terrorists in Aden*, Cmnd. 3165, (London: HMSO, 1965).

28. Stewart (JIC Sec), to White (Intell Co-ord), October 28, 1971, "Report on Interrogation Methods Used in Northern Ireland," Annex A, CAB 163/171. Brian Stewart handed over to Michael Herman as JIC Secretary in early January 1972.

29. In reality, other ad hoc techniques were sometimes used. In the late 1970s, it was not unusual for detainees to be threatened with being dropped from helicopters. Several hooded detainees would be put in a helicopter and flown around until they were disoriented. One would then be pushed out, somewhat disconcerting the remaining detainees. In fact this was a confidence trick, since the helicopter had only been a few feet off the ground when the detainee was ejected. Although no one was hurt during these escapades, the psychological effects were traumatic. A more mundane technique was simply to drive a Republican suspect into a Protestant area and threaten to hand him over to the local paramilitaries. All from private information.

30. Nicholson (DIS), "Report on Operation Calaba—August 1971," CAB 163/173. The Technical Staff were responsible for the installation and maintenance of tape recorders and noise generators; see "Standing Order No. 3: Order for Technical Staff," 1971, ibid.

31. Compton to Allen (Home Office), October 13, 1971, CAB 163/171.

32. AUS(GS) to PUS, "Northern Ireland—Interrogation," Oct. 23, 1971, DEFE 24/968.

33. Note of a meeting held by PUS, James Dunnett, to discuss interrogation procedures at 13.50 on Oct. 26, 1971, Oct. 28, 1971, DEFE 13/917.

34. John Whale and Lewis Chester, "Internees—New Cruelty Allegations," *Sunday Times*, October 24, 1971.

35. "How Ulster Internees Are Made to Talk," *Sunday Times*, October 17, 1971.

36. Heath (PM) to Trend (Cab Sec), M66/79, PREM 15/485.

37. Trend (Cab Sec) to Armstrong, "Interrogation Procedures," A0697, November 7, 1971, PREM 15/485. The request came from Cabinet subcommittee GEN 47.

38. Stewart (JIC Sec), "Report on Interrogation Methods Used in Northern Ireland," draft, October 1971, CAB 163/171.

39. Report by intelligence coordinator, "Prisoner Handling in Interrogation Centres in Northern Ireland," November 4, 1971, PREM 15/485. A further copy is at CAB 163/171.

40. Heath, *The Course of My Life*, 473–74.

41. Stewart (Sec JIC) to Trend (Cab Sec), October 28, 1971, ibid.

42. Transcript of Radio 4 Today program with John Timpson, November 17, 1971, "The Compton Report," CAB 163/171.

43. In preparation for the Parker inquiry, Brigadier H. M. Bremner, commandant of the Intelligence Corps, was asked to draw up a historical narrative of all interrogation operations since 1945. This would cover immediate postwar interrogations, Kenya, Cyprus, the Cameroon, Brunei, Swaziland, Aden, Guiana, Malaysia, and Northern Ireland. Interestingly, it was noted that: "Oman is such a special case that it should NOT be covered." See Levvis (BGS Int) to Bremner (Commandant IC), November 16, 1971, Annex A, CAB 163/172.

44. Dunnet (PUS MoD) to Defence Secretary, "Evidence to the Parker Committee," November 18, 1971, CAB 163/172.

45. LJD to SoS, "Papers for the Parker Committee," November 30, 1971, CAB 163/172.

46. Note by the intelligence coordinator, "Privy Councillors Inquiry," December, 1971, CAB 163/172.

47. Lewis (BGS Int DIS), "The Noise Machine: Sound Level Measurements Conducted at Ashford on Nov. 24, 1971," BGS (Int)/1/16, November 25 1971, CAB 163/172.

48. White (Intell Co-ord) to Dunnett (Cab), December 2, 1971, CAB163/172.

49. "Report of the Committee on Interrogation Procedures," Jan. 31, 1972, CAB 163/189. This was published in March 1972 as *Report of the Committee of Privy Councillors Appointed to Consider Authorised Procedures for the Interrogation of Persons Suspected of Terrorism*, Cmnd. 4901, (London: HMSO, 1972).

50. Goodall (PUSD) to Renwick, "Parker Committee Report on Interrogation Procedures," February 6, 1972, WCU13/2, FCO 87/157.

51. Trend (Cab Sec) to Herman (Sec JIC), A01791, May 8, 1972, CAB 163/189.

52. JIC, "Joint Directive on Interrogation in Operations by the Armed Forces," 3rd Draft, April 17, 1972, CAB 163/189. This later became JIC(A)72(21)(Final), "Directive on Interrogation by the Armed Forces in Internal Security Operations," June 29, 1972, WO 32/21726.

53. Herman (Sec JIC) to Trend (Cab Sec), "JIC (A) Directive on Interrogation," May 12, 1972, CAB 163/189.

54. Trend (Cab Sec) to Heath, A01828, May 12, 1972, FCO 87/157.

55. Heath (PM) to Trend (Cab Sec), "Interrogation—Revised Directive," June 8, 1972, CAB 163/189.

56. Trend (Cab Sec) to Heath, A01828, May 12, 1972, FCO 87/157.

57. Douglas Home (Foreign Sec) to Heath (PM), "Interrogation—Revised Directive," PM/72/19, May 23, 1972, PREM 15/1709.

58. The Defence Intelligence Staff decided that new directives should also be sent to the director of the SAS with regard to personnel in the Dhofar campaign who were on loan, even though the SAS only advised on questions to be put to detainees and "did not directly conduct interrogation." Bayley (Brig (Int) DIS), "Interrogation Directive," BGS(Int)/9/88A, August 3, 1973, WO32/21726. See also Bayley (Brig (Int) DIS), "Interrogation in Oman," ibid.

59. Douglas-Home (Foreign Sec) to UK Ambassador Dublin, April 25, 1972, CAB 163/189.

60. Washington Embassy to FCO, May 9, 1972, FCO 87/157.

61. GOC Northern Ireland, to Rees (NI Sec), April 16, 1974, DEFE 13/838.

62. Donnely, min, "Settlements in Deep Interrogation Cases," Dec. 17, 1974, FCO 87/410.

63. Head of C2(AD), "European Commission of Human Rights," August 21, 1975, DEFE 13/838; Nicolls to Def Sec, "Interrogation in Depth Cases," Oct. 18, 1974, ibid.

64. Fuller C2(AD) to APS/Sec of State, "Deep Interrogation Cases: William Shannon v MOD and Others," Dec. 8, 1976, DEFE 24/1612.

65. Edis (UK Mission to the UN) to FCO, "32nd General Assembly: Item 80: Torture," Oct. 19, 1977, DEFE 24/1612.

66. Morgan (Army Legal Services) to Gutterdige (DS11), 24 Oct. 1977, DEFE 24/1612.

67. Scott Shane, "Inside a 9/11 Mastermind's Interrogation," *New York Times*, June 22, 2008; David Connett, "From beyond the Grave, Saddam Reveals All (Nearly)," *Independent*, July 5, 2009.

68. Philip Zelikow, "A Dubious C.I.A. Shortcut," *New York Times*, April 23, 2009.

69. See especially Rod Morgan, "The Utilitarian Justification of Torture: Denial, Desert and Misinformation," *Punishment and Society*, 2 (2000): 181–96; Maureen Ramsay, "Can the Torture of Terrorist Suspects Be Justified?," *The International Journal of Human Rights*, 10 (2006): 103–19.

DOCUMENT 6.1: Prisoner Handling in Interrogation Centres in Northern Ireland: Report by the Intelligence Co-ordinator

CAB 163/171

TOP SECRET - PERIMETER

U.K. EYES ONLY.

SIR BURKE TREND

In accordance with the instructions I received at the Ministerial meeting on 18 October I attach my recommendations on interrogation procedures in Northern Ireland.

2   You will note that I am proposing some limitations on the use of those techniques which are likely to come in for some criticism in the Compton Report. In doing so I have, nevertheless, been mindful of the severe difficulties which face our Intelligence personnel in Northern Ireland and of the local conditions of the emergency in that country. I have not concerned myself with the legality or otherwise of the procedures themselves.

3   In preparing the attached paper I have been helped by the report I received from the Secretary JIC following his visit to Northern Ireland (19-22 October) and by the consultations I have had with the representatives of the MOD and the Home Office. The paper has also been cleared by the DGSS.

4   Since receiving my instructions, a recommendation has been made by Sir Philip Allen's Official Committee to the effect that following the publication of the Compton Report there should be an enquiry by privy Councillors into the whole question of interrogation methods. If this recommendations is approved by Ministers, I assume it will raise the question of whether my paper is required.

D.G.W

[D G WHITE]

4 November 1971

Enclosure

DOCUMENT 6.1:   Prisoner Handling in Interrogation Centres in Northern Ireland: Report by the Intelligence Co-ordinator *(Continued)*

TOP SECRET - PERIMETER

UK EYES ONLY

THIS DOCUMENT IS THE PROPERT OF HER BRITANIC MAJESTY'S GOVERNMENT

Copy No.12.

PRISONER HANDLING IN INTERROGATION CENTRES IN NORTHERN IRELAND

REPORT BY THE INTELLGENCE CO-ORDINATOR

Minutes of the meeting of Ministers (GEN.47(71)6th Meeting 18 October) instructed the Intelligence Co-ordinator "in consultations with officials of the Home Office, the Ministry of Defence and the Intelligence Services, to make an immediate assessment of the methods of interrogation suitable for use in northern Ireland."

In accordance with the above instructions the Intelligence Co-ordinator recommends as follows :

1.   That the handling of detainees and their subsequent interrogation in Northern Ireland should continue to be governed by the general principles laid down in JIC (65)15 and amendment dated 10 February 1967. [Annexes A and B respectively.]

2.   The responsibility for all prisoner handling and interrogation methods employed at the special interrogation centre should rest with the senior police supervising officer. The role of the military officers attached to the centre should be purely advisory.

3.   There should be substantial evidence of a detainee's involvement in terrorist activities before he is selected for protracted interrogation at the special interrogation centre.

4.   All prisoner handling and interrogation techniques referred to below should be subject at all times to medical scrutiny and advice.

5.   The three special techniques of "hooding", "wall-standing" and "white-sound" should be employed solely for the following specific purposes: -

DOCUMENT 6.1: Prisoner Handling in Interrogation Centres in Northern Ireland: Report by the Intelligence Co-ordinator *(Continued)*

(a) To protect the secrecy of the location of the special interrogation centre.

Providing the means of transport is such that only "hooding" will suffice to maintain secrecy, "hooding" should be permitted during the journey.

(b) To protect the identities of those selected for protracted interrogation.

Compulsory "hooding" should be permitted at the centre for the minimum period required for this purpose and in no circumstances for a period of longer duration than two hours at a time. If the prisoner asks to be hooded because he is fearful of his identity becoming known by other detainees, a record of his request and the time for which he remains voluntarily hooded must be kept.

(c) To protect guards and interrogators from sudden violent demonstrations.

The maximum time during which an individual may be kept wall-standing in the holding area, as opposed to an individual sound-proofed cell, should in future be defined. Subject to further medical advice, I recommend that no continuous period of wall-standing in a holding area (or elsewhere) between interrogation sessions should exceed two hours.

(d) To maintain absolute secrecy over the questioning of particular suspects and to prevent inter-communication between detainees.

"White sound" should be permitted for this purpose and for this alone.

6. Records should continue to be maintained throughout the detainee's period at the interrogation centre showing the exact time during which he has been hooded or has been ordered to wall-stand or has been subjected to "white sound".

7. The need for "hooding", "wall-standing" and "white sound" could be considerably reduced if the facilities, layout and construction (e.g., sound proofing) of the interrogation centre could be improved. There should be an immediate investigation into the possibilities of securing these improvements.

CHAPTER 7

The Value and Limits of Experience in the Early Years of the Northern Ireland Troubles, 1969–72

EUNAN O'HALPIN

Editors' Note:

This, the second of the book's Northern Irish chapters, focuses on the same period of time as the first, but with a markedly different object of attention. O'Halpin concentrates on the personality politics of intelligence in the turbulent province. By providing the contextual history behind key individuals in this story, and the general historical context of the moment, he provides greater awareness about the essentially personal dynamics behind government intelligence gathering and cooperation between agencies and the government. O'Halpin also provides valuable insights into the problems of researching such closed topics within the available archives.

The document selected for this chapter (Visits by the Secretary of JIC to Northern Ireland—January 10–12, 1972) and the accompanying commentary invite reflection on the limits as well as the benefits of the deployment of a high level of insight and expertise, gained in comparable but rather different conflicts elsewhere in the world, in one complex civil-military theatre of operations, Northern Ireland. It also confirms other evidence on the problems of interagency information sharing that bedeviled the British response to the growth of Northern Irish terrorism.

The document and associated high-level minutes also demonstrate the value of reputation and personal standing in getting access to the most senior decision makers: although couched as a purely personal perspective on the security challenges facing Britain in Northern Ireland rather than being a document solemnly passed through and mediated by the JIC machine, this crisp and uninhibited *nunc dimittis* by Brian Stewart, on the eve of his departure as secretary of the Joint Intelligence Committee (JIC), quickly reached Prime Minister Edward Heath, who not only read it but called for action to follow up the points made. Stewart was unaware of how high his parting shot had flown until I showed him Heath's handwritten comments in 2005.

Northern Ireland is an integral part of the United Kingdom. The insights into intelligence and security operations that Stewart brought to bear, however, were the fruits of long experience of counterinsurgency and intelligence gained in the Far East since the late 1940s, particularly during the Malayan Emergency of 1948–58 and the confrontation with Indonesia in Borneo in 1962–65, and demonstrate the transferability of lessons learned from one theater of operations to another.

Stewart evidently prepared the document as a valedictory informal and personal report just before he stood down after almost four years as JIC secretary. The JIC is a quintessentially bureaucratic entity. Anyone reading its minutes and papers—at least those available to the public eye—cannot but be struck by the measured, canonical style in which the committee recorded its response to papers and contributions outlining options and outcomes, triumph and disaster: heaven knows how many hundreds of times the "The Committee noted, with approval, ..." Papers reaching the JIC, like those that it sent onwards around Whitehall, were the product of meticulous and sometimes tortuous composition and redrafting within the JIC machine in the Cabinet Office and in customer departments; a "forward look" paper on Northern Ireland, commissioned early in 1971, had still not been finalized for presentation to the full committee a year later; the political and terrorist aftermath of Bloody Sunday on January 30, 1972, when the army shot dead thirteen unarmed civilians during efforts to quell rioting after an illegal civil rights march in Londonderry, made its draft prognostications irrelevant.[1]

Although adept at JIC usages when these were appropriate, Stewart's natural métier is direct, unequivocal English. This can be seen in his published essay "Winning in Malaya: An Intelligence Success Story," and in the foreword to his edited work *Operation Sharp End*, prepared "to ensure that police voices could . . . be heard," describing their experiences combating Communist guerillas.[2] It is also reflected in this document, which presented his own views in clear unambiguous prose. The redacted copy available in the prime minister's office papers in the National Archives does not show to whom his observations were formally addressed, but they were seized upon and endorsed by the cabinet secretary Sir Burke Trend.

Burke Trend was particularly mindful of intelligence issues and perspectives; he was regarded as a champion of the intelligence services in Whitehall, having dealt with their finances during his time as a treasury official.[3] In 1971 he congratulated "Dear Dick," the director of the American Central Intelligence Agency Richard Helms, on a recent public lecture: "I suppose . . . it would be tempting providence to say that little by little the intelligence community seems to be being accepted as both 'respectable' and worthwhile . . . in so far as this isn't an illusion, much of the credit must go to you and to people like yourself who are prepared to defend it with such vigour and conviction."[4] The only cabinet office predecessor with whom Trend can be compared in the weight which he attached to intelligence was Sir Maurice Hankey, the first cabinet secretary from 1916 to 1938. Hankey, a former Royal Marine, viewed government business predominantly in imperial and geostrategic terms, whereas Trend had a far broader and more rounded view of the role of government and the development of British society.[5] But he never lost sight of the significance of intelligence for policymakers, both as an early warning process and as an element in decision making. He oversaw the restructuring of the JIC in 1968, following the shock of the unexpected Soviet invasion of Czecho-slovakia, and also ensured the creation of the post of coordinator of intelligence in the cabinet office. The first holder of this appointment was his trusted friend and one-time schoolmaster Sir Dick White, who had been the head successively of MI5 and MI6.

Trend's attention to security issues relating to Ireland is reflected in the manner in which he personally oversaw precautions taken in the months leading up to the fiftieth anniversary of the Irish rebellion of Easter 1916, after the prime minister of Northern Ireland had made detailed—though in the event completely wrongheaded—predictions about Irish Republican plans and capabilities to make mischief in Northern Ireland. As feared, there were political killings during the fiftieth anniversary year, but the perpetrators were not the IRA, but a small group of Ulster loyalist paramilitaries, mainly ex-servicemen, intent on sectarian murder rather than on overthrowing Crown rule.[6] It is perhaps significant that Whitehall was untroubled by these harbingers of what was to come, arising as they did from a group committed to retaining rather than destroying the link with Britain. (It was a man convicted of one of those killings in 1966, Gusty Spence of the UVF (Ulster Volunteer Force), who was selected to make a public statement conveying loyalist acceptance of the 1998 Good Friday agreement and regret at the loss of so many lives. Spence had embarked on a remarkable journey of understanding two decades before, involving friendly contacts with successive Roman Catholic archbishops of Armagh.)[7]

In noting this endorsement of Stewart's document, we should point out that Edward Heath trusted Trend's judgment implicitly and relied very heavily on him. This is reflected in the fact that, most unusually for a former prime minister, Heath wrote the entry on Trend for the Oxford *Dictionary of National Biography*, making particular mention of the cabinet secretary's knowledge of the intelligence services.[8] We should also note that Trend's interest in addressing problems of security policy and operations in Northern Ireland was not simply one that arose for him *ex officio* as cabinet secretary: this is shown by the very different approach of his successor Sir John Hunt, secretary from 1973 to 1979. While Hunt was a competent and well-liked official, the available records indicate that where intelligence and security matters were concerned he ran the Cabinet Office more as a high-class secretariat than as a policy hub.

Edward Heath's personal role also deserves some consideration. Between the time of his election in June 1970 and his defeat in the May 1974 general election, this complex man, characterized by Henry Kissinger as an "erudite, highly intelligent" and socially awkward loner, changed his approach to the Northern Ireland issue radically.[9] Heath relied on his officials, trusted them, and was more at ease with them than with almost all his cabinet colleagues. Initially disposed to see matters largely in terms of a battle against Republican terrorism calculated to destabilize the northern state, he underwent a marked change in response to successive setbacks for British policy: the inability of the Ulster unionist leadership to secure the backing of the majority community for apparently modest political reform, the marked increase in Republican violence that followed the introduction of internment in August 1971, the problem of loyalist terrorism, the calamity for British policy and Britain's reputation that was Bloody Sunday, the unprecedented violence of 1972, which with 497 fatalities was the bloodiest ever during the conflict, and pressure from the Irish government.[10] Heath's official papers indicate that throughout his premiership he watched Northern Ireland closely, in terms of both security and wider political issues, despite the myriad other policy problems with which he had to deal. By the autumn of 1973, his views had so evolved that he concluded the Sunningdale agreement, under which the Irish and British governments, and representatives of Northern Ireland's constitutional political parties, agreed upon a formula to reconcile a role for the Catholic minority in the governance of Northern Ireland, through an elected power-sharing executive with measures calculated to reassure unionists that Northern Ireland's status within the United Kingdom could not be changed without their consent. One veteran of the Sunningdale experiment characterized the 1998 Good Friday agreement as being "Sunningdale for slow learners," albeit one in which the dominant domestic participants were those representing the extremes of Northern Irish politics, Provisional Sinn Fein and Paisleyite loyalism, as opposed to the moderate middle ground, which had shared power for a few months until deposed by a mass loyalist strike in May 1974.[11]

That the JIC secretary, together with the cabinet office coordinator of intelligence Dick White, became so involved in attempting to improve the Northern Ireland intelligence system from 1970 onwards is, consequently, most likely a reflection of the importance that both Heath and Trend attached to managing the Northern Ireland crisis after the disturbances of August/September 1969. As JIC secretary, Brian Stewart had plenty of other matters to work on and worry about, including Britain's crucial intelligence relationship with the United States, the "close ties" of which JIC chairman Sir Edward Peck wrote in a fulsome letter to CIA director Richard Helms in December 1968.[12] Indeed, Stewart made a strong impression in Washington: in 1969 Helms wrote to "Dear Jack" [Sir John Rennie, the chief of MI6] to say how pleased he was to see the names of a number of officials concerned with Anglo-American intelligence liaison in the New Year's honors list: "It was particularly gratifying to see Brian Stewart honored. We enjoyed having him with us for a few days in December." But from 1970 onwards the dreary matter of Northern Ireland consumed a lot of his time, although quite how much is impossible to determine due to extensive redaction of the available JIC records.[13]

Brian Stewart had fought in Northwest Europe in 1944–45, commanding an antitank platoon, and being wounded during a highly successful engagement with

German armor at Rouray in Normandy in July 1944. His wartime service gave him an appreciation of the workings and vagaries of the British military mind. His later experience working in a civilian role in the Malayan counterinsurgency, where he dealt with both police and military, convinced him of the need for police primacy wherever possible, on the basis that the police possessed far greater knowledge and understanding of local circumstances and culture, and were far better placed to gather and contextualize intelligence than army units moved into and out of hostile areas on rotation. He had also seen the importance of the development of a combined and sustained police/military interface, to ensure that each arm of the security forces understood the other's roles and priorities, and that all relevant intelligence and information was appropriately collated, contextualized, and pooled.

Brian Stewart had gained additional insights into the dynamics of irregular warfare and "wars of national liberation" from knowledge of other conflicts. During the early 1960s he had contributed to Whitehall analysis and discussion of how to thwart Indonesia's extensive campaign of infiltration and destabilization in Borneo, the so-called confrontation in which British forces fought a prolonged and successful border war with the Indonesian army. As British consul general and his country's sole diplomat in Hanoi at the height of the Vietnam conflict, he was a direct observer of one of the most controversial aspects of the war, the sustained bombing of North Vietnam. He reported on the galvanizing effect of the Tet Offensive of January 1968, concluding that the North Vietnamese clearly regarded this as a strategic turning point despite its short-term military cost to them. He spent most of his Foreign Office career in the Far East, and until he became secretary of the JIC in 1968, he had had no involvement with any aspect of the Irish question; his knowledge of Northern Ireland was limited to an agreeable stint of wartime training there. When the drift of events concerning Northern Ireland began to catch the JIC's attention in the autumn of 1968, Stewart could find no significant reservoir of experience or insight on which to draw. Instead he set himself a crash course in Irish history, and he also read selected Irish daily newspapers.[14]

Stewart was not alone in Whitehall in having to come to grips with Irish issues more or less from scratch: it was only in 1970 that the Foreign and Commonwealth Office established a Republic of Ireland department to manage Irish issues, and the Northern Ireland office was only created two years later, following the prorogation of the Northern Ireland government and parliament at Stormont some weeks after the catastrophe of Bloody Sunday. In the course of a fractious cabinet discussion during the first months of the crisis, home secretary James Callaghan explained his difficulties in determining what was happening in Belfast and what policy the British government should adopt: "I am working with a very small staff. I actually have only two men on Northern Ireland and we have nobody else dealing with it."[15]

In commending Stewart's report, Burke Trend "hesitated to inflict it on the prime minister, since it contains nothing very new," but he forwarded it nevertheless because "in [redacted: Stewart's] judgment (and he has been one of the sharpest critics of the intelligence arrangements in Northern Ireland in the past), we have now achieved a better and more efficient organization of the security forces than seemed possible a year ago." Trend highlighted certain aspects of Stewart's report, particularly evidence of newfound Home Office and Ministry of Defence willingness to supply specialist interrogators to assist the Royal Ulster Constabulary (RUC) Special Branch in handling detainees arrested since the introduction of internment on August 9, 1971: this, "if properly developed, should produce better intelligence," and might "enable detainees to be released earlier than would otherwise be possible." Trend concluded by noting that "the strain on the Director of Intelligence" at army headquarters in Northern Ireland "has now been relieved by additional administrative assistance." Stewart's report duly reached Edward Heath, who on January 25 wrote a minute: "Please ensure the points are followed up."

Intelligence during the Evolution of the Northern Ireland Crisis Up to January 1972

Stewart's document can only be appraised in the context of London's slowly evolving knowledge and understanding of the dynamics of the Northern Ireland crisis. It can be argued that, for a combination of reasons, the central machinery of British intelligence assessment was extremely slow to come to grips with what was happening in Northern Ireland from the late 1960s. The threat of Republican terrorism, specifically a campaign of assassination in Northern Ireland timed to commemorate the fiftieth anniversary of the Irish rebellion of 1916, had been taken very seriously in London, but that date had passed off without any significant IRA actions. In fact, as the Dublin authorities had told the British beforehand, the IRA leadership, then heavily penetrated in Dublin by the Siohâna (the Irish police) and in Belfast by the RUC, had decided against armed attacks.[16] Despite the appointment of Andrew Gilchrist, an ambassador with an unusual interest in irregular warfare and in radical movements internationally, to the Dublin embassy in 1966, no great alarm bells tolled in London about a serious Irish Republican threat to Northern Ireland until 1970. Gilchrist himself was placed under heavy Irish Special Branch guard in late June 1968 in light of intelligence indicating that a Republican splinter group intended to kidnap or attack him. Gilchrist had operated behind Japanese lines in Thailand in 1944–45, and more recently had stood armed alongside his defense attaché as an Indonesian mob attempted to storm the British embassy in Jakarta, where he was ambassador during the height of the confrontation over Borneo. He accepted this latest threat to his person with equanimity, remarking that his imposing bulk made him a good target, and wishing to be quickly rid of his Irish police escorts: "though these are much the nicest armed guards I have had in recent years, I would really rather be without them." He used the opportunity of the threat to get on good terms with the experienced head of the Irish Special Branch, Superintendent John Fleming, whom he thought highly efficient. Through this and other contacts Gilchrist was able to furnish London with an accurate picture of the mainstream Republican movement's increased absorption, through ill-digested Marxist influence, in social and economic agitation: this was achieved through creation or penetration of a range of protest groups, almost all of which focused on the failings of the independent Irish state rather than on the historic grievance of partition.[17]

In September 1969, by which time the perceived particular threat to his person had dissipated, Gilchrist was invited to attend the JIC to give his views. He emphasized his opinion that, with Irish passions inflamed by the unfolding events in Northern Ireland, the IRA was "a very real menace to [the] stability of Ireland, & therefore to ourselves." The JIC received Gilchrist's observations, particularly as regarded the impact of the Northern disturbances on the willingness and ability of the Irish government to deal firmly with the IRA, with an element of polite skepticism.[18] Neither Gilchrist nor the JIC explored the question of whether the southern IRA could pose a serious threat to Northern Ireland itself. Yet within a year, such a threat had emerged, following a split in the Republican movement that saw the formation of the breakaway Provisional movement, dominated by northern Republicans, in January 1970.

In succeeding months Gilchrist's star, already considerably tarnished by his habitual irreverence in his dispatches to London, waned further in the Foreign Office as he urged that greater heed be paid to the Irish government's views, saying that their "sabre-rattling" should be discounted as a necessary piece of playing to the gallery of Irish public opinion.[19] His successor, John Peck, who came to Dublin in April 1970, experienced much the same gradual diminution in influence in Whitehall. The more he urged greater consideration for Irish perspectives and sensibilities as the Northern Ireland crisis worsened, the less did his views count in the scales in London. His valedictory dispatch sent in March 1973 "played down, but has not concealed, the differences between the Department [Foreign Office] and himself."[20] But London's main problem in the first years of the Northern Ireland troubles was not that British representation in Dublin became unduly sympathetic towards Ireland; rather it was a lack of solid information from Belfast about political conditions and prospects. As early as November 1968, the Home Office asked MI5 for an independent assessment of the drift of affairs: the service observed that this would require "discreet handling," especially as they had long relied entirely on the RUC in respect of Northern Ireland and had no independent sources of information or analysis. An interdepartmental committee on Northern Ireland, chaired by the Home Office, was subsequently established, while at Burke Trend's prompting the JIC established an Ulster working group in April 1969. In the same week, an MI5 officer was posted for liaison duties to RUC headquarters in Belfast.[21] Confusingly, as the Saville inquiry into Bloody Sunday discovered, in 1970 two other MI5 officers were assigned to investigate links between mainland far right groups and loyalist extremists in Northern Ireland. While based in London, these traveled over to Northern Ireland fairly frequently. Only after some months had elapsed did they announce their presence and activities to the head of the RUC Special Branch, who was not best pleased to meet them. Almost by chance they took over the running of an important army informant on political conditions and opinion in both loyalist and Republican areas of Londonderry. In 2000, one of the officers concerned, "Julian," observed to the Saville inquiry:

> It may seem strange, but the IRA were not a prime target of ours. The RUC were running IRA informers, as were the Army. Nobody, however, was monitoring the extreme right so we were asked to do so.
>
> The three organizations involved in intelligence work in the Province . . . the Army, RUC Special Branch, and the Security Service, all operated independently of each other. It was up to each individual organization to tell the others what it thought appropriate. Some of our reports would therefore find their way to the Army and to [redacted] Head of RUC Special Branch. Others would go back to the office in London.[22]

This haphazard process, where individual agencies decided for themselves what information to share and what to withhold, appears symptomatic of London's chaotic response to the intelligence challenge posed by the Northern Ireland crisis. Despite Brian Stewart's best efforts, it was destined to endure for many years after 1971.

That the Home Office did not have a firm grasp of what was happening and what was likely to transpire in Northern Ireland was evident to some ministers quite early in the crisis. During a cabinet discussion on Northern Ireland in May 1969, the waspish social security secretary Richard Crossman noted that most of his ministerial colleagues were, like himself, at a loss to understand the nature of the crisis: he suggested that, as it appeared that "we were constitutionally bound to let our troops be used to defend law and order in Northern Ireland" if the situation deteriorated further, it might "be a good thing for us to have some political intelligence so that if we were faced with a civil war we should know what it was all about." This irked home secretary James Callaghan, responsible for Northern Ireland: "I don't think we really need that. After all I am seeing Chichester-Clark [the new prime minister of Northern Ireland] every day."

> He resisted the whole idea, saying it was absurd, and that the Northern Ireland Government would dislike our behaving in this way, though it would be all right if we were to ask them for ideas. But I was suggesting that we need political intelligence such as we had during the war and that if we have to know about Russia and every other country in the world, we should at least spend some money finding out something about Northern Ireland. The Prime Minister supported Callaghan but Denis Healey [the defense secretary] came in on my side, saying 'Frankly, Northern Ireland has completely different conditions from Britain and we shall be as blind men leading the blind if we have to go in there knowing nothing about the place.'

Crossman was not impressed by Callaghan's position:

> So there it is. After five years in which I and others have believed that we must have a basis of sound intelligence and sound information on which to base our policy, this is the way we prepared for the possibility that we might have to take over direct rule of Northern Ireland. As we went out of the room, Healey said to me: "You have no idea what it was like before you came on to the [cabinet Northern Ireland] Committee. The Prime Minister was always demanding active intervention early on, with this crazy desire to go out there and take things over, that we should side with the Roman Catholics and the Civil Rights Movement against the Government and the Royal Ulster Constabulary, though we know nothing at all about it.[23]

London's difficulties in securing a clear view of what was happening in Northern Ireland eventually led to the appointment of Sir Oliver Wright as UK representative in Belfast in September 1969. Wright's recollections are instructive. He had just relinquished his ambassadorship to Denmark to take up the post of deputy undersecretary for economic affairs at the Foreign Office, and was at home "up a ladder . . . wiping the orgies of my tenants off the walls when the telephone rang." It was a summons to go over to Belfast, preferably the next day. Wright knew nothing at all about Northern Ireland, but neither, it turned out, did anyone else whom he met in Whitehall: "one had to have a steep learning curve. . . . At the Home Office Mr. Callaghan was surrounded by a group of officials from permanent under secretary downwards and we sat in total silence for what seemed a very long time. Point number one was that the officials had no idea at all what to do." Wright "toddled off to Belfast almost on my own with one young official from the Home Office . . . and a secretary volunteer from the Foreign Office." A fortnight later, James Callaghan gave a bravura performance in Belfast which, along with the deployment of British troops, had a marked calming effect on all sides. But the relative calm which followed for some months was not to last. In the course of 1970 the newly formed Provisional IRA (PIRA) began to prepare a campaign based not simply on the street fighting and rioting seen in 1969, which was largely defensive in nature, but on systematic bombing. Wright regarded PIRA as one of two crucial factors which tipped the scales towards increased political violence, destroying any prospects for a quick political fix acceptable to the bulk of unionist and nationalist opinion and their leaders; the other was the Conservative victory in the general election of June 1970, which saw the appointment of Reginald Maudling as home secretary:

> Whereas Mr. Callaghan came from a slightly Celtic background and had a sort of empathy for the Northern Irish problem, not in a sense of having a solution to it but in having an understanding of the events leading up to it, I'm afraid Mr. Maudling did not. He was a strictly "south of Watford" man and couldn't begin to understand what these people were up to. . . . [The]

combination of the IRA and the change of government here led to a rapid deterioration in the whole situation which became an armed struggle.[24]

Wright was succeeded in Belfast by Sir Howard Smith, formerly British ambassador in Prague, who had begun his career as a wartime codebreaker before moving into the Foreign Office. Like Wright, he had no prior direct experience either of Irish matters or of security policy and operations, although he later became head of MI5, retiring in 1981. His deputy in Belfast, Frank Steele of MI6, is credited with establishing indirect and deniable channels of communications with the Republican movement that ultimately proved instrumental in the negotiations leading to the 1998 Good Friday agreement, which brought peace of a sort to Northern Ireland.[25]

Despite the sectarian riots in Belfast and the "Battle of the Bogside," the widespread disorder in nationalist areas of Londonderry in August, when Wright arrived in Northern Ireland in early September 1969 the underlying issue was, in his words, "still a civil rights problem." Catholic grievances were being "justifiably" articulated by the civil rights movement in an atmosphere of civil disobedience rather than of outright rebellion. The old bugbear of the IRA was conspicuous largely by its absence, although local units had played some part in the defense of Catholic areas from Protestant attacks in Belfast in August and September, as well as in retaliatory acts of ethnic cleansing against Protestants in some predominantly nationalist areas. The IRA leadership in Dublin, still partly under the sway of a half-baked Marxian analysis of Ireland north and south, exhibited uncertainty about how to respond to what was happening in Northern Ireland: as Derry rioted and parts of Belfast burned in August and July 1969, it was still devoting organizational resources and energy to such sideshows as arson attacks on foreign-owned farms in County Meath. In June it had been decided to switch from burning German-owned to British-owned properties, and in August it was agreed to fire warning shots at landowners who had not been sufficiently intimidated. The IRA leadership also pondered the possibility of mounting attacks on American targets in a gesture of solidarity with the Vietnamese people (a United States Navy sailor was shot and wounded on the Dublin docks in 1970, though this was probably the work of an IRA splinter group).[26]

Initially, the portents in Northern Ireland were encouraging following the deployment of British troops to restore order and to hold the line between Catholic and Protestant areas of Belfast and Londonderry: on a visit to Belfast, James Callaghan, "an instinctual politician, got it right at the very beginning," telling the two communities that he was there not to impose a solution, but to help them towards one. Over the next year various reforms demanded by the civil rights movement, most of which London had urged upon the Northern Ireland government for some time, were made in key areas such as housing, broadening the local government franchise (where Catholics had been systematically disadvantaged in some districts), employment rights, and antidiscrimination measures.

In the highly sensitive area of policing, the part-time and de facto wholly Protestant Special Constabulary was dissolved on the recommendation of the Cameron commission of inquiry, removing a very potent source of nationalist grievance while also unavoidably increasing unionist unease and sense of insecurity.[27] This arguably had the unintended impact of reducing opportunities for intelligence-gathering through well-informed local sources, although the 'Specials' had in fact had very little to do with the regular RUC, as a rule neither accepting RUC direction nor passing on information, and their relations with the nationalist community were at best strained and distant. In 1970 an opportunity was provided for both unionists and nationalists to contribute actively to security through the formation of the Ulster Defence Regiment (UDR). What at first seemed to Richard Crossman a stroke of genius ("If we can really get rid of these bloody "B" Specials and organize a regiment under the British Army it will be a tremendous achievement") turned out to have a downside as well.[28] Although recruitment from the Catholic community was initially encouraging, within a couple of years the UDR had become almost totally Protestant and unionist in composition. Due to inadequate vetting of applicants and poor control of weapons and security documents, problems also emerged of penetration by loyalist paramilitaries and their sympathizers (and even by some republicans: one ex-UDR soldier with IRA links was charged with the killing of RUC detective John Doherty in Lifford, County Donegal, in October 1973). The Ministry of Defence was inclined to downplay this issue: in 1974 Defence Secretary Roy Mason pointed out to the Northern Ireland secretary Merlyn Rees that the UDR "have good local knowledge and contacts," and supported the army's forceful argument for a discreet strengthening of the regiment's intelligence gathering capacity through the training of selected officers and men at battalion level. This was done in the knowledge that it involved at least a risk of increased leakage of information to loyalist paramilitary groups who might then use it for targeting of Republicans: "since the UDR is not regarded as an impartial force by most Catholics, any increase in its capability might be regarded with suspicion."[29] The UDR's perhaps exaggerated reputation for collusion with loyalist paramilitaries was to haunt the regiment until its final disbandment, although as Steve Bruce pointed out in 1995, "statistical evidence . . . does not support the general claim that the security forces have been of great assistance to the loyalist paramilitaries."[30]

Lessons Learned?

This document was lightly redacted before it was released to the National Archives, to remove among other matter its author's name (though not the JIC appointment that he held). This illustrates the difficulties that face ordinary mortals relying on records vetted before release to the National Archives. The picture available is necessarily incomplete. Researchers have also to resist the tendency to read too much into redactions, particularly in intelligence and security documents. On the other hand, secret records have an internal logic that sometimes obscures the bigger picture. Those fortunate to be appointed as official historians of intelligence, as of other arms of government, have the luxury of seeing far more uncensored records; but they face the danger that they may be so captured by the official mind as disclosed in secret documents that they lose their independent perspective.

Stewart's report deals with a range of issues. Readers will note its emphasis on practical measures, its focus on the police as the main protagonists in the struggle against terrorism, and its exclusive focus on the republican threat. There is not a mention of the problem of loyalist terrorism: it is as though republicanism was the solitary danger to the state. In one sense this was true, in that from late 1970 the newly formed PIRA had embarked on an escalating campaign of violence against the security forces, in combination with a series of bombings notionally aimed at commercial targets and infrastructure across the province. By the time that internment was introduced in August 1971 the British government was, in the words of an almost apoplectic Edward Heath, attacking the mildly critical tone of the Compton committee of inquiry into the treatment of detainees, "in the conditions of war with the IRA."[31] The tendency persisted in Whitehall to regard loyalist violence merely as reactive and without any autonomous political purpose. As Lieutenant Colonel Michael Dewar observed in 1985, "although both communities have contributed towards the present tragic situation, it is perhaps insufficiently highlighted to what extent the Loyalist community were responsible for leading Ulster over the precipice in 1969." We have already noted the three political killings carried out by loyalists in 1966. Loyalists also carried out the first significant attacks on Northern Ireland's water and electricity infrastructure early in 1969, actions initially attributed to the IRA; they were the main instigators of the sectarian riots and burnings in Belfast in August and September 1969; and in October 1969 they were responsible for the first killing of an RUC officer. They also attempted cross-border attacks on a limited scale: a UVF volunteer was fatally injured in a premature explosion in County Donegal in the Irish Republic in the same month.[32] Yet no matter how active loyalist paramilitaries were—and their level of activity waxed and waned markedly over the years—the army's and Whitehall's main focus was always on the IRA: as early as May 1969, over a year before PIRA launched its first campaign, the chief of the general staff spoke of the army's "accepted . . . anti-IRA role"; in 1976, the GOC Northern Ireland objected to a draft position paper which he felt gave undue weight to the problem of loyalist paramilitarism: "they are all killers and murderers, but PIRA is top of the league."[33]

Stewart's document makes passing reference to internment and to the opportunities for gathering intelligence through sustained interrogation that it afforded to the police and army. In retrospect, two aspects of this stand out: a lack of appreciation of the disastrous political impact on nationalist opinion in Northern Ireland of the unbalanced way in which internment was applied as a response to growing Republican terrorism, and directed entirely against the nationalist community; and a reluctance to acknowledge the political consequences of the controversial techniques, also known as the five techniques of hooding, white noise, wall standing, sleep deprivation, and minimal food provision, which were used in the interrogation of fourteen selected suspects. These techniques had been solemnly codified and approved for official use by the JIC in 1965, and again in 1967 when they were modified on legal advice. They had been used on insurgent suspects during the nationalist disturbances in Aden, where they and other aspects of British tactics had drawn some international criticism. Their use against untried British citizens in the United Kingdom created a storm of protest that might have been anticipated, and the intelligence benefits were at best debatable.[34]

Stewart's paper made passing reference to the problem of the Irish border. This was to become a major source of dispute between Dublin and London in terms of Republican terrorism. The British view was that, whatever the sincerity of Dublin's professions of intent to prevent PIRA from taking refuge and mounting attacks from across the border, at local levels the performance of the Irish police and military was at best hit-and-miss in the early years of the crisis, although by 1975 opinion in London was that the Irish security forces were doing a reasonable job.[35] The associated problem of PIRA acquisition of weapons and explosives proved equally difficult to address: PIRA, like other Republican and loyalist paramilitary groups, had a variety of sources inside and outside the British Isles. As early as 1971, the American authorities established an interagency task force in New York to investigate alleged smuggling of legally purchased weapons, after a consignment of hand grenades and weapons shipped on the liner *Queen Elizabeth II* was discovered in Ireland, although there remained considerable problems in securing convictions in federal courts.[36] British complaints about the allegedly dilatory attitude of the American government towards Irish Republican fund-raising and weapons smuggling were met in Washington with a combination of concern and mild irritation. In January 1975, Secretary of State Henry Kissinger told President Ford that, should British Prime Minister Wilson raise the question during a forthcoming meeting, he should stress the "great importance" which the United States attached "to ending the illegal flow of weapons to the IRA," while pointing out some of the complexities: of "the some 1300 US-manufactured firearms recovered by the British in Northern Ireland, more than 50 percent would seem to have been acquired from the international military surplus market." An accompanying Treasury memorandum, citing Bureau of Alcohol, Tobacco and Firearms intelligence on the international arms market, gave the example of 198 American firearms found among a weapons shipment from Libya seized by the Irish naval service on the MV *Claudia* in March 1973. The Treasury also reported that, contrary to British reports, most American weapons seized in Northern Ireland were "commercial versions of some US military weapons legally purchased in the United States" by "IRA sympathizers who are stockpiling and illegally exporting arms . . . to the IRA."[37]

No JIC papers relating to the decision to introduce internment and to use it as a weapon directed solely against the Republican threat have been traced in the National Archives. On the first anniversary of the introduction of internment, however, MI6's Frank Steele explored the arguments for and against maintaining it. Internment had become "a major cause of Catholic (and other) discontent and opposition to the Security Forces and the Government. To end internment would bring about a major change in feeling in the Catholic areas. It would be a serious and perhaps overwhelming blow to the influence of the IRA." Steele gave consideration to the argument that the ending of internment would provoke "the wilder and more extreme Protestants," but believed that this, like the danger of detainees returning to violence, was a risk worth taking: "As you know, my personal view, for what it is worth, is that we must sometime end the present internment (even if we have in future to use some form of selective and impartially applied form of detention). . . . I think that if we do not end internment, the Catholic areas will not in three months time be quiet and secure enough to allow the Army to leave."[38] How right he was.

We must contextualize Stewart's reference to "the festering Londonderry situation." By this he meant the impasse that had arisen following the Battle of the Bogside in August 1969, where "no-go areas" controlled by paramilitaries had been established in some nationalist and loyalist districts of Derry and Belfast cities. These were decisively dealt with on July 31, 1972, by the army's large scale Operation Motorman, reputedly "the biggest British military operation since Suez," involving thousands of troops and the use of tanks to deter republican and loyalist opposition while street barricades and obstacles were swept away for good.[39]

Stewart's document put emphasis on the need for more effective coordination of the security intelligence effort, noting that progress was still "regrettably slow" in some respects. The RUC Special Branch had always kept its cards very close to its chest. The force's founding chief constable Sir Charles Wickham (1922–45) had pursued a policy of keeping government ministers at arm's length from all operational and security matters, and even during the war MI5 had learned to tread carefully in dealing with Northern Ireland. When the chief of the general staff alluded delicately to evident weaknesses in RUC intelligence in May 1969 while on a visit to Belfast, the Northern Irish prime minister responded that "he was only too well aware of the sensitivities of the RUC to 'outsiders' and the possible damaging effects on their morale."[40] We should also recall the point made earlier that the RUC's deep-rooted reluctance during the early years of the Troubles to share information, and its mistrust of the intelligence-gathering activities of other agencies, was reciprocated by the army, MI5, and presumably also MI6 and the Metropolitan Police Special Branch.[41]

Despite Stewart's cautious optimism in January 1972, effective coordination of security force intelligence was to remain a significant problem for at least a decade because of deep-rooted institutional mistrust. We should, however, note that ultimately the accuracy of security force intelligence on both Republican and loyalist groups, and the consequent rate of attrition that paramilitaries experienced, was a decisive though often discounted element in the Republican and loyalist movements' decisions to contribute to a negotiated settlement of the Northern Ireland crisis in 1998.

NOTES

The research on which this paper is based has been funded by a project grant from the Irish Research Council for the Humanities and Social Sciences, whose support is gratefully acknowledged.

1. Eunan O'Halpin, "'A Poor Thing but Our Own': The Joint Intelligence Committee and Northern Ireland, 1969–1972," *Intelligence and National Security* 23, 5 (November 2008): 658–80.
2. Brian Stewart (ed.), *Operation Sharp End; Smashing Terrorism in Malaya 1948–1958* (1st ed. privately published, Newark, 2003); later published as *Smashing Terrorism in Malaya: The Vital Contribution of the Police* (Pendaluk Publications, Selangor Darul Ehsan, 2004); "Winning in Malaya: An Intelligence Success Story," *Intelligence and National Security* 14, 4 (Winter 1999): 267–83.
3. Information from Sir John Winnifrith (who served in the Treasury with Trend in the 1940s and 1950s), 1980.
4. Trend to Helms, April 26, 1971, Georgetown University Library, Helms papers, 8/14/423.
5. Stephen Roskill, *Hankey: Man of Secrets* (London: Collins, 3 vols., 1974–76).
6. Eunan O'Halpin, "Intelligence and Anglo-Irish relations, 1922–1973," in Eunan O'Halpin, Jane Ohlmeyer, and Robert Armstrong (eds.), *Intelligence, Statecraft and International Power: Historical Studies XXV* (Dublin: Irish Academic Press, 2006), 138–39; Steve Bruce, "Loyalist Violence," in Alan O'Day (ed.), *Terrorism's Laboratory: The Case of Northern Ireland* (Aldershot: Dartmouth, 1995), 117.
7. Spence to Cardinal Tómas Ó Fiaich, July 31, 1978, Tómas Ó Fiaich papers, Tómas Ó Fiaich Memorial Library, Armagh, "Prisoners 1980" folder, "An Tuaischeart" box.
8. Edward Heath, "Burke Frederick St John Trend," in *Oxford Dictionary of National Biography* (Oxford: Oxford University Press, 2004), vol. 55, 308–9.
9. Henry Kissinger, *Years of Renewal* (London: Phoenix, 1999), 602.
10. David McKittrick, Seamus Kelters, Brian Feeney, Chris Thornton, and David McVea, *Lost Lives: The Stories of the Men, Women and Children Who Died as a Result of the Northern Ireland Troubles* (Edinburgh: Mainstream Publishing, 1st ed., 1999, 2001), Table 1, 1494.
11. Seamus Mallon, MP, cited by James Downey in *Irish Independent*, September 23, 2002. The original source of this much-cited quotation has not been traced.
12. "Ted" Peck to Richard Helms, December 19, 1968, Georgetown University Library, Richard Helms papers, box 7/22/394.
13. Helms to Sir John Rennie, January 14, 1969, Georgetown University Library, Richard Helms papers, box 7/22/394.
14. Interview with Brian Stewart, 2005.
15. Entry for May 7, 1969, in Richard Crossman, *The Diaries of a Cabinet Minister: vol. 3. Secretary of State for Social Services 1968–70* (London: Methuen, 1977), 478.
16. Eunan O'Halpin, "A Poor Thing but Our Own," 658–80.

17. Gilchrist to Foreign Office, July 4–5, 1968, TNA: FCO 23/192.
18. Gilchrist's undated notes [? Oct. 1969] of talk with Taoiseach Jack Lynch, Churchill College Cambridge Archives, Gilchrist papers GILC 1 14B; annex to JIC minutes, Sept. 18, 1969, TNA: CAB 185/2.
19. Gilchrist to Foreign Office reporting conversation with Taoiseach Jack Lynch, Sept. 17, 1969, Churchill College Cambridge Archives, Gilchrist papers GILC 1 14 A.
20. Minute by Kelvin White, March 15, 1973, TNA: FCO 87/209.
21. Christopher Andrew, *The Defence of the Realm: The Authorized History of MI5* (London: Penguin, 2009), 602–603.
22. Statement by "Julian," Feb. 2, 2000, www.bloody-sunday-inquiry.org.uk/index2.asp?p=3, accessed Oct. 2, 2009.
23. Entry for May 7, 1969, *Crossman Diaries*, 478–79.
24. Interview with Sir Oliver Wright, Sept. 18, 1996, British Diplomatic Oral History Project, Churchill College Cambridge Archives.
25. Sir Howard Smith's obituary, in *Independent*, May 10, 1996; Jonathan Powell, *Great Hatred, Little Room: Making Peace in Northern Ireland* (London: Vintage, 2008), 66–67.
26. This is reflected in the most recent account drawn on Republican sources, Brian Hanley and Scott Millar, *The Lost Revolution: The Story of the Official IRA and the Workers Party* (London: Penguin, 2009), 125–38.
27. Michael Dewar, *The British Army in Northern Ireland* (London: Arms and Armour, 1985), 39.
28. Entries for Nov. 6, 1969 and April 5, 1970, *Crossman Diaries*, 719, 883.
29. Mason to Rees, Sept. 17, 1974, TNA: DEFE 24/151.
30. N. H. Nicholls to Secretary of State for Defence, April 18, 1974, TNA: DEFE 13/835; Steve Bruce, "Loyalist Violence," in Alan O'Day (ed.), *Terrorism's Laboratory*, 128–29.
31. Heath to Trend, November 8, 1971, TNA: PREM 15/485.
32. Michael Dewar, *The British Army in Northern Ireland*, 28–29; Paul Bew and Gordon Gillespie, *Northern Ireland: A Chronology of the Troubles, 1968–1993* (Dublin: Gill and Macmillan, 1993), 22.
33. GOC NI to Brian Cubbon, permanent secretary, Northern Ireland Office, May 23, 1976, TNA: CJ 4/1093.
34. Dewar, *The British Army in Northern Ireland*, 55. For recent analysis of issues arising from use of the five techniques, including Brian Stewart's retrospective views, see Samantha Newbery, "Intelligence and Controversial British Interrogation Techniques: The Northern Ireland Case, 1971–2," *Irish Studies in International Affairs* 20 (2009): 93–109, and Samantha Newbery, Bob Brecher, Philippe Sands, and Brian Stewart, "Interrogation, Intelligence and the Issue of Human Rights," *Intelligence and National Security* 24, 5 (October 2009): 631–43.
35. Briefing note for Sir Frank Cooper (Northern Ireland Office), June 3, 1975, TNA: CJ 4/1093.

36. Attorney General Levi to National Security Advisor Brent Scowcroft, Feb. 27, 1976, Presidential County File for Europe & Canada, box 7, folder Ireland (2), minifolder 3, Ford Library.

37. Memorandum for the President, Jan. 30, 1975, Presidential County File for Europe & Canada, box 7, folder Ireland (1), minifolder 2, Ford Library.

38. Steele to Woodfield (permanent secretary, Northern Ireland Office), Aug. 9, 1972, TNA: CJ 4/209.

39. Bew and Gillespie, *Northern Ireland*, 54–55.

40. Eunan O'Halpin, *Spying on Ireland: British Intelligence and Irish Neutrality during the Second World War* (Oxford: Oxford University Press, 2008), 109–10, 164, 261; report by Chief of the General Staff, May 19, 1969, TNA: CJ 3/55.

41. Statement no. 1 of "Julian," dated Feb. 2, 2000, accessed at www.bloody-sunday-inquiry.org.uk/index2.asp?p=1, Sept. 21, 2009.

DOCUMENT 7.1:   Visit by Secretary JIC to Northern Ireland, January 10–12, 1972

SECRET – PERIMETER

UK EYES ONLY

VISIT BY SECRETARY JIC TO NORTHERN IRELAND

[10–12 JANUARY 1972]

GENERAL

Morale in Security Forces is high. The Head of Special Branch appears to share the Army view that the IRA in Belfast are finding it increasingly difficult to maintain their original formations or the weight of their attack in the face of a steady and successful pressure by the Security Forces. The IRA are now short of experience officers: the use of less lethal chemical fertilisers instead of gelignite suggests that they are no longer able to supply themselves so readily with gelignite explosives: special batch markings of detonators and colouring of explosives should increase their supply difficulties. The rate of attrition measured in terms of recoveries of arms and arrests now seems to have levelled off: and it is possible that the law of diminishing returns is now operating. There is reason to expect that the IRA may have to abandon static bases in some parts of Belfast and to rely more on the use of crossborder or other rural sanctuaries for bases.

Relations between the Army and the Police appear to be good and the intelligence organisation is steadily improving although since all action has to be achieved by persuasion rather than by direct intervention, the rate of progress remains regrettably slow in some fields.

No promising solution to the festering Londonderry situation has yet presented itself.

2.   INTERROGATION AND COLLATION OF INTELLIGENCE

Preliminary interrogation continues to take place in Police Holding Centres in Belfast: this process produces useful information. Each centre is manned by a skeleton of RUC Special Branch supported by a Military Intelligence team which provides an immediate reference and collating service. At Police Headquarters Northern Ireland and Police Headquarters Belfast, other Military Intelligence teams are steadily ploughing through the backlog of uncollated

DOCUMENT 7.1: Visit by Secretary JIC to Northern Ireland, January 10–12, 1972 *(Continued)*

Special Branch records. There is a marked improvement in the closeness of Army-RUC collaboration in this field and current intelligence is now being collated immediately. The Army plans to bring a computer to bear on the mass of information now available and then to speed up tracing: the RUC has yet to accept the fact that CID records should also be brought into play in the Intelligence attack on the IRA.

The most significant development in the interrogation field is the plan now being canvassed by Northern Ireland Headquarters and supported by Ministry of Defence to recruit specialist interrogators [TWO AND A HALF LINES OF TEXT REDACTED]. Head Special Branch has indicated that he would be glad to have reinforcements in this field if they were under his command. The matter is under consideration in the Home Office.

Consideration is being given to the introduction of more prolonged interrogation at the Police Handling Centres within the existing rules and without the use of the controversial techniques. But unless specialist interrogators are supplied from Britain it is unlikely that the system will be developed beyond the present crash interrogation which takes place with[in] the 48 hours when the prisoners are held at the Police Holding Centre. It is however self-evident that the limited availability of skilled RUC interrogators and the short time currently spent on questioning each individual must reduce the chances of extracting information from recalcitrant prisoners.

3.   BRITISH INTELLIGENCE STAFFS

Apart from the possibility of recruiting a team of British interrogators, there does not seem to be any intelligence staff needs currently unfulfilled. The additional administrative assistance recently sent to reinforce the Director of Intelligence's staff has usefully reduced pressure on the Director of Intelligence himself: the Director of Intelligence continues to enjoy the fullest confidence of the GOC and of the RUC.

The Military Intelligence officers now deployed throughout the Province are well thought of by Head Special Branch. The massive injection of Military Intelligence staff over the past year is now paying high dividends not only in improving records and collation but also by providing a degree of continuity which was previously lacking in view of the constant changeover of battalions.

DOCUMENT 7.1:   Visit by Secretary JIC to Northern Ireland, January 10–12, 1972 *(Continued)*

4.   ARMS AND EXPLOSIVES

The most significant development in this field is the introduction of more bulky and less lethal agricultural fertiliser into the IRA bombs. The only valid explanation for this development seems to be that the IRA are finding it increasingly difficult to acquire gelignite in the quantities they require. It is thought that the IRA in Belfast are relying on one or two skilled bombmakers supported by untrained bomblayers, the latter being responsible for some of the misfires and premature explosions and other inefficiencies in current IRA operations.

5.   INTELLIGENCE REPORTING

I have suggested to the Northern Ireland Headquarters that some of the statistical presentations of the results being achieved in the anti-terrorist campaign should be made available to the JIC for possible incorporation in our central output. Although it is well recognised that the "numbers game" is not an infallible guide to the state of the campaign, graphic presentations on attrition rates, recovery of weapons and the numbers of incidents provide a useful clarification of the background against which the Northern Ireland Security Forces assess progress.

[REDACTED: Brian Stewart]

12 January 1972

PART IV

Avoiding Surprise

CHAPTER 8

Suez and the Threat to UK Interests Overseas

GILL BENNETT

Editors' Note:

This chapter, written by the former chief historian at the Foreign and Commonwealth Office, considers a well-trodden subject, the Suez crisis of 1956, but places it in a new context. Most accounts of Suez adopt a narrow focus and underestimate the influence of wider international events on British decision making. A number of lessons emerge, including the importance of clear lines of accountability between the intelligence community and the policymakers, and of liaison with close allies, as well as the pitfalls of using special operations as a way to influence events. Above all, however, the episode shows that while it is vital to see individual decisions against a wider international context, failure also to question the assumptions underlying such analysis can produce flawed policies and damaging consequences.

In the intelligence context, the Suez crisis of 1956 is usually considered either in relation to the secret arrangement between British, French, and Israeli ministers that led to the ill-fated Anglo-French military intervention in Egypt of November 1956; or in relation to the supposed activities, before and during the crisis, of intelligence agencies such as the British Secret Intelligence Service (MI6) and the American Central Intelligence Agency (CIA). This chapter, however, examines Suez from a rather different perspective, yet one that was in the forefront of the minds of both government ministers and the intelligence community in 1956: the implications of the crisis for Britain's global position, her security, and defense planning.

The document used for the focus of this chapter is a memorandum by the Joint Intelligence Committee (JIC), (JIC(56)104(Final) of October 18, 1956, titled "The Threat to United Kingdom Interests Overseas." The report had been commissioned on October 9, 1956 by the British chiefs of staff (COS), in order to "review the future world-wide strategic position, to appreciate what our essential military tasks might be in 1961, other than those for global war, and to suggest in broad terms the most suitable composition and location of our forces"; on October

11 the Joint Intelligence Staff (JIS, i.e., the JIC and the Joint Planning Staff (JPS) together) were invited accordingly to prepare a report setting out, area by area, the likely causes of trouble that would affect UK interests throughout the world, excluding Europe.[1] It was a forward planning paper of the kind prepared at regular intervals, and the terms of reference made no specific mention of the ongoing Suez crisis. In the final report, however, nearly all the trouble areas identified were considered likely to be affected adversely if matters were resolved in favor of Gamal Abdul Nasser, the Egyptian president whose announcement of the nationalization of the Suez Canal on July 26, 1956, precipitated a crisis that disturbed international relations on a global scale for the next six months and had long-lasting effects, not least on Britain's reputation and prestige.

The ten days in October 1956 between the commissioning and circulation of the memorandum coincided with crucial developments in and decisions on the Suez crisis, providing a useful opportunity to examine those developments and decisions in their wider context. This study does not attempt to provide a detailed account of events leading up to or during the crisis, which can be found both in the archives and in many good secondary works.[2] The object is to illustrate both the potential global ramifications of the Suez crisis for Britain, and to underline the important fact that Suez was only one (admittedly acute) problem out of many faced by the British government throughout the globe at that time.

British foreign and defense policy, like that of the United States and its Western European allies, had been dominated since 1945 by the Cold War, that is, the fight against Soviet Communism, in which a divided Europe constituted the front line. In June 1950 the chiefs of staff had defined as the principal aim of British global strategy "a stabilisation of the anti-Communist front in the present free world and . . . the intensification of 'cold' offensive measures aimed at weakening the Russian grip on the satellite states and ultimately achieving their complete independence of Russian control."[3] This remained a priority, and although in May 1956, less than three months before the Suez crisis began, the JIC judged that the Soviet Union did not want war and was unlikely to launch one before 1965, they stressed this might change in the case of heightened international friction, and that the rapid pace of Soviet rearmament meant the threat of global war remained.[4] Though the Suez crisis did not, as the Korean War had done in 1950, evoke the specter of a third world war—a JIC report of August 3, 1956, concluded that the Soviet Union was unlikely to embark on global war on behalf of Egypt[5]—the presence of this underlying threat was nevertheless an important factor for British policymakers.

Equally important was the fact that Britain remained a global power, and despite pressure after the end of World War II (not least from the United States) to shed her colonial possessions, she retained in 1956 both interests and responsibilities that transcended the Cold War context. In particular, the defense of the Middle East—the "land bridge" between Europe, Asia, and Africa—was seen as a key strategic priority, for three reasons: (1) it was a vital link in Commonwealth sea and air communications; and (2) a potentially important base for offensive action against the Soviet Union; in addition, (3) successive strategic studies underlined the "critically serious" situation that would be created if Russia gained control of Middle Eastern oil supplies. These priorities were shared by the United States, but the latter's understanding of and support for them was tempered by suspicion of British "colonialist" motives (not unrelated to US commercial interests in the region).

Both countries, however, were concerned by Soviet forward policy in the Middle East, combined with a rising tide of Arab nationalism antagonistic both to Anglo-American influence and to Israel, the young state whose creation in 1948 and subsequent military victories had placed Arab-Israeli conflict squarely at the root of regional tension. A JIC report of March 21, 1956, "Probable Soviet attitude to an Arab/Israel war," described "Soviet Cold War aims" in the Middle East as the destruction of the Bagdad Pact,[6] denial of Middle East bases and oil supplies to the Western powers, and "the undermining of Western, particularly British, influence in the area, replacing it by Communist influence."[7] This was a set of aims that seemed to be shared increasingly by Egypt, whose leader, Colonel Nasser, actively encouraged nationalist and anti-colonialist movements throughout the Middle East and beyond. Egypt's political leadership was not matched by economic strength, however, and of equal concern to Britain and the United States was the extension of Soviet influence through the provision of cash, credit, and armament supplies.

British interests in the Middle East were more than by-products of the Cold War. Commercial links, an actual or potential military presence, and embedded British populations in territories from Aden to Zanzibar meant that decolonization and Arab nationalism had serious implications for Britain's prestige, future position, and influence throughout the world. In July 1956 the Conservative government, led by Anthony Eden, already faced unrest and in some cases terrorism in a range of countries, including Ceylon, Cyprus, Malaya, and Singapore, often where the government was involved in difficult negotiations concerning the transfer of power. These global considerations, underpinned by the historic experience of British influence in the Middle East (and particularly in Egypt), were an important factor in the British government's response to the Suez crisis.[8] Nasser's nationalization of the Suez Canal in July 1956 was seen as an *existential threat*, not only to Britain's oil supplies and shipping routes, and her traditional political and military influence and interests in the region, but to her global interests, influence, and prestige. With hindsight, this may seem an exaggerated or unjustified reaction based on an imperialist outlook that was already outdated; but there is no doubt of its force at the time. Nor was it only the view of Eden, whose own long involvement with Egypt (he had personally negotiated both the 1936 and 1954 Anglo-Egyptian treaties), combined with ill-health, made him especially sensitive to Nasser's misdeeds.[9] It was an attitude widely understood and accepted by the government and Conservative party as a whole. As Chancellor of the Exchequer Harold Macmillan told the US secretary of state John Foster Dulles on August 1, 1956: "we just could not afford to lose this game. It was a question not of honour only but of survival."[10]

British Intelligence in the Middle East

Even before Suez, 1956 had been a difficult year for British intelligence. A series of "incidents," including the resurfacing of Burgess and Maclean in Moscow, the disappearance of Commander "Buster" Crabb in Portsmouth Harbour, and the discovery by Soviet and East German technicians of the Anglo-US tunnel under Berlin, provoked not just unwelcome publicity but organizational upheaval and review. The intelligence infrastructure was already overstretched. The United Kingdom's secret intelligence agencies (the Secret Intelligence Service (SIS) or MI6, responsible for overseas intelligence; the Security Service or MI5 (in respect of its overseas responsibilities in colonial territories); and the Government Communications Headquarters (GCHQ, formerly GC&CS), responsible for signals intelligence worldwide) had expanded greatly during World War II but had since been subjected to successive reviews by governments seeking budgetary savings, and were expected to limit their activities and cut staff while meeting the growing Soviet threat. The MI5/SIS relationship became more fractious globally in competition for scarce resources, complicated by turf battles in territories moving towards independence. Both relied considerably on GCHQ, whose reputation after its wartime triumphs remained high, but who also required increased resources to establish a robust global capability.

Since the government placed such a high premium on British interests and prestige in the Middle East, it might be supposed that it was well supported by solid intelligence on Nasser's capabilities and intentions, but this was unfortunately not the case. With the Cold War as a primary focus, resources for other overseas intelligence were distributed as efficiently—that is, as thinly—as possible. The Middle East, which in WWII had been a major intelligence hub, now had to be serviced from this residual capacity. With the Soviet bloc as the prime target, the limited intelligence effort in the Middle East (as in most areas of British interest from Africa to the Far East) was directed mainly against Communist parties and Soviet or satellite activities, with the aim of disrupting their influence and protecting British interests. This might have been expected to be effective in the Middle East, a much less secure environment than the Soviet bloc, but success in short-term objectives, such as intelligence on Soviet military aid to Egypt and other countries, tended to be at the expense of strategically important counterintelligence on long-term Soviet penetration.

Some elements were notably successful: for example, covert propaganda, coordinated with the military and, after 1948, with the Foreign Office's Information Research Department; the acquisition of intelligence on arms supply and orders of battle; and technical operations such as interception.[11] But the shortage of manpower on the ground made it impossible for British intelligence to keep on top of the complex and ever-changing developments in the region. Though reliable documentary evidence in the public domain is sparse, it seems clear that operational activity was a good deal less than anecdotal accounts suggest. In this situation cooperation with other friendly services in the region was vital, particularly with US intelligence, though French (and, increasingly, Israeli) links were also significant. Although differences in national (and commercial) interest, traditional areas of influence and obligation, and the shifting balance of power in the region made these links volatile, they were particularly important in view of the aggressive activities of the Egyptian Intelligence Services (EIS), reorganized after Nasser came to power and used for both internal security and counterintelligence purposes. The EIS's role in stirring up anti-Western sentiment was of concern to all powers with interests in the region (for example, to France in respect of Algeria).[12] Nevertheless, Nasser continued to retain links with both British and US intelligence, and was particularly close to the CIA.[13] After the SIS network in Cairo was wound up by the Egyptians in August 1956, the CIA were left in possession of the field, but while they may have shared some of their intelligence, the Americans did not share the British government's aim of getting rid of Nasser, to whom they saw little viable alternative.[14] This was a view in which senior British intelligence officials tended to concur, sharing also the view expressed by President Eisenhower on October 6 that any move to unseat Nasser could only be attempted at "a time free from heated stress holding the world's attention."[15]

Finally, a great deal has been made in some accounts of Suez, as well as in certain memoirs, of the individual activities of members of agencies like SIS and the CIA. Even though some of those involved were quite senior (and have been vocal on their role), it would be wrong to attach too much importance to them. In 1956 there were still many in politics, the military, the civil service, and in the intelligence community itself in Britain who had during WWII served in or on the periphery of the secret world. Memories of clandestine operations remained vivid: contacts had been maintained. Some found it difficult or impossible to accept what they saw as the decline of Britain's greatness, and felt that steps could and should be taken to arrest the trend, if necessary by force. On the whole their activities and arguments were peripheral: government ministers (even those like Churchill viscerally inclined to imperial glory) generally had a better understanding of the realities of power. During the Suez crisis, such maverick figures were certainly capable of causing at least a noisy distraction and at worst exercising a malign influence; but they were not the decision makers.

JIC(56)104(Final): The Threat to United Kingdom Interests Overseas

JIC(56)104 was commissioned when British ministers and their military advisers were experiencing intense frustration at the way the Suez crisis was progressing. Macmillan, an early advocate of strong action against Nasser, had written in his diary on October 4: "The Suez situation is beginning to slip out of our hands."[16] The initial decisive rush of late July and early August, when the Cabinet had ordered the preparation of a plan to force Nasser to accept international control of the Suez Canal, and if possible to unseat him, had soon turned to anticlimax as the realities of international consultation and military logistics were appreciated.[17] Conferences, meetings, and mediation seemed to the British to have moved matters little further on while increasing opposition within much of the international community—including, crucially, the Americans—to the use of force without further provocation by Nasser, who was playing his cards cannily and keeping Canal traffic moving. Meanwhile, backed by the Soviet bloc, he continued to build up Egypt's military strength, increase his influence in the Arab world, and foment anti-Western sentiment.

On October 5, the United Nations Security Council had begun to discuss the Suez Canal dispute, but Eden and his colleagues had little confidence that any United Nations solution would achieve the British objectives of guaranteed international access to the Canal *and* the defeat of Nasser. Indeed, the resolution adopted on October 13, setting out six principles on which any settlement of the Suez question should be based, included respect for the sovereignty of Egypt and allotted her a key role in the future of the Canal (and in any case the Soviet Union used its veto against implementation). The majority of ministers and the chiefs of staff still felt that military force would be required. This was also the view of the French government, who were, as Eden told the Cabinet on October 3 after a visit to Paris, "impatient at the obstacles which were preventing the Western Powers from imposing a satisfactory settlement."[18] Meanwhile, British military planning was subject to costly and debilitating delay, and the financial situation was worsening. Macmillan had just returned from the United States, where he had told the International Monetary Fund (IMF) Britain might need to call upon it to strengthen her monetary reserves.[19] On October 10, General Sir Gerald Templer, chief of the Imperial General Staff, told his colleagues it must be brought home "very forcibly to Ministers that we could either go to the aid of Jordan against Israel with sea and air power, or we could launch MUSKETEER; we could not do both."[20]

As drafting began on JIC(56)104, therefore, the British government faced unpalatable options in the Suez crisis. They were being warned *not* to use force against Nasser by the Americans (preoccupied with the forthcoming presidential election), by the "new" Commonwealth (where anti-imperialist sentiment ran high), by the United Nations, by the Labour party, and indeed by some Conservative elements. At the same time, the government was increasingly under pressure to *act*, from the Suez Group and other elements in the Conservative party, and from the French government, which had its own domestic political difficulties and wanted Egyptian support for the Algerian revolt derailed.[21] In addition, the Israelis were flexing their military muscles in regular border clashes with Jordan (raising the unwelcome prospect of British troops being obliged by treaty to defend Jordan against French-supported Israeli forces); and looked as if they might attack Egypt themselves (thereby creating a nightmare scenario whereby Britain might be obliged by treaty to defend the errant Egypt). It is not surprising, therefore, that the government felt desperate for a way out of the stalemate that would avoid the British fighting their friends, defending their enemies, or facing a catastrophic loss of position and prestige. It was in this atmosphere that the secret plan was hatched, during the same week that JIC(56)104 was drafted, for an Israeli attack on Egypt that would allow an Anglo-French invasion to "keep the peace."[22] Many studies have been devoted to examining why a small group of British, French, and Israeli ministers embarked on a scheme that seemed so inherently risky, guaranteed to incur the wrath of the international community and in particular of the United States. Few of these, however, pay sufficient attention to the British government's serious geopolitical concerns about the implication of a Nasser victory.

Given the timing of the report, the JIC were bound to consider the implications of two possible developments in the Suez crisis: that Britain would use force against Egypt, or that the crisis would be resolved peacefully but in Nasser's favor. In a shorter report circulated to the chiefs of staff on October 11, they had already raised some of these issues when considering "future courses which Nasser might adopt if the Suez crisis were settled on terms which were considered satisfactory by him and which left his prestige undiminished." They concluded that in maintaining the momentum of his success he would bring pressure on other Arab states to terminate arrangements with the Western powers, and use his influence against British interests in the Persian Gulf, Aden, and Africa.[23] A week later, the JIC's analysis had evolved to include the implications of British military action as well as of a settlement satisfactory to Nasser. In most cases, these implications were equally damaging to the United Kingdom.

Although the members of the JIC and JPS were not party to the secret discussions held during that week (the chairman of the JIC was not brought into the plot until October 24, and the chiefs of staff received only limited information), they were, nevertheless, aware both that the military considered it impossible to delay mobilization plans much longer and that the prime minister and some of his colleagues saw little hope of an acceptable outcome to UN-brokered negotiations.[24] The report's opening statement that "any concessions made by the United Kingdom under pressure are likely to have repercussions throughout the world," but that these might be avoided by "a successful demonstration of resolution and firmness" by the United Kingdom, was clearly a reference to Suez, but it also constituted a reminder from the committee to ministers that there was a lot more at stake than the Suez Canal, and even the position of Nasser.

The key to why this was so can be found in the arrangement of the report, which grouped "likely trouble spots" into four areas, in descending order of seriousness: the Middle East and North Africa; Asia; Africa; and the Americas. It is noteworthy that with the exception of the Americas, these groupings mirror the three "concentric circles" identified by Nasser in speeches (and later in his book *The Philosophy of Revolution*) as areas within which Egypt could play a significant role: the Arab, African, and Islamic worlds; underlining the global scale both of his ambitions and, from a UK standpoint, the extent of the threat posed.[25] Though the JIC's grouping did not consciously mirror Nasser's thinking in this way, it made the same powerful connections between potential trouble spots in different areas. Where troublesome territories fell into more than one category (for example, Arab and Islamic, or African and Islamic), the danger could be more acute. Thus, in Libya (Arab and Islamic), where there were both British military bases and a well-established and powerful Egyptian subversive apparatus, the JIC estimated that success for Nasser over the Suez dispute would increase the danger both of anti-British riots and of increased Soviet influence; while in northern Nigeria (African and Islamic), where the move to self-government was already turbulent, Moslem sympathies might be aroused if British troops were to fight in Egypt; and in Indonesia (Asia and Islamic), where an uneasy political situation and rumors of a *coup* prevailed throughout 1956, anti-British demonstrations were expected as a "gesture of Islamic and anti-Colonialist solidarity."

Of course, the United Kingdom's problems in many of the territories covered in the report began long before Suez. In some (like Singapore) they arose during negotiations intended to lead to independence or constitutional reform; in others (like Cyprus and Hong Kong, both long-running issues) important British defense and intelligence issues were involved; yet others were problems principally for other countries (such as France in respect of North Africa), but posed dangers nevertheless to British interests and citizens. There was, however, a common factor: the vulnerability of British authority, interests, and subjects to opposition and even attack in response to a combination of lessened prestige and nationalist or anti-colonialist propaganda. If Nasser, whose priorities—the security of his regime, the promotion of Egypt (and himself) as leader of the Arab world, and implacable opposition to Israel—brought him inevitably into conflict with Western interests, were perceived to have defeated those interests by agreeing an international settlement that recognized Egypt's authority over the Canal and independence from Western control, it would give encouragement to governments or interest groups throughout the world that they, too, could stand up to the British government and win. A closer look at some of the trouble spots identified in the JIC report reinforces the importance of this reasoning to British decision-making over Suez.

The group considered most threatening was, unsurprisingly, the Middle East and North Africa, which included the key foreign policy challenges of Anglo-Egyptian relations, Arab-Israeli conflict, and Cyprus, as well as Jordan, Libya, Aden, the Persian Gulf sheikdoms, Syria, Iraq, Algeria, Tunisia and Morocco, and Iran. In all these areas Egyptian influence was strong, and a common factor was the likelihood of anti-British demonstrations and, in some, a threat to oil supplies and military facilities. To take two examples: in Cyprus, a Crown Colony since 1925, and an important naval and intelligence-gathering base, British authorities faced tension between the Turkish and Greek Cypriot populations and the desire of the latter, under the leadership of Archbishop Makarios, for union (*Enosis*) with Greece. The United Kingdom was willing to move towards self-government while retaining a presence in Cyprus and control over security, but early in 1956 talks on a proposed constitution had broken down in the face of the increasingly violent campaign against the British waged by the pro-Enosis organization EOKA.[26] Makarios and others were deported on March 9, and an attempt on the Governor's life on March 21 led to punitive British measures including fines, curfews, and confiscations of property. On July 12, Eden had announced the appointment of Lord Radcliffe to draw up a constitution for self-government, but the restoration of law and order was a precondition for serious negotiation. Throughout, the Egyptian

Intelligence Services had been in close contact with EOKA, providing arms and money for their struggle against the British and taking every opportunity to stir up anti-colonialist sentiment. Nasser's support for EOKA was rewarded by information on British military and naval deployment in the region, both before and during the Suez crisis.[27] In this situation, the JIC's comment that a decline in British prestige would encourage terrorism and make a political settlement more difficult seems an understatement.

In Libya, where there were both British and American bases, Egyptian influence was also pervasive, as was the fear of attack by Israel. The Libyan government followed Egypt's lead in attempting to use the prospect of accepting Soviet aid to extract concessions from the West: the first Soviet ambassador arrived in Tripoli in January 1956; in February the British made a gift of armaments, including armored cars. In March the Libyan prime minister told the House of Representatives that Libya would help any Arab state which was the victim of Israeli aggression, and that the government would never allow foreign bases to be used in an attack on an Arab state; Libyan opposition to any attack on Egypt, therefore, was inevitable. That did not prevent their reaching an agreement with the United Kingdom in July for the creation of an air force and navy, and the supply of arms and equipment, 12 million dollars in aid, and 30,000 tons of wheat for famine relief. But Egyptian influence remained strong, and the JIC's prediction of anti-British riots and sabotage seemed likely whether Nasser were attacked or scored a success over Suez.

In the second group, Asia, which included Singapore, Hong Kong, Malaya, Korea, British Borneo Territories, Ceylon, Indonesia, and British obligations under SEATO, the common threat was perceived as Communist subversion rather than a direct attack on British interests or subjects.[28] These countries were unlikely to be directly involved with Egypt or the Suez dispute, but many were likely to welcome the nationalization of the Suez Canal as the prerogative of an independent state, and any retaliatory action towards Egypt would be seen as colonialist in nature and provoke opposition to Britain; similarly, Islamic sympathies lay with Nasser and would applaud his success. The JIC, however, clearly considered the principal danger to be that British military involvement in the Middle East would diminish her ability to intervene in the event of conflict occurring in Asia, and to fulfill her obligations as a member of SEATO. The report of the second annual meeting of SEATO, held in Karachi in March 1956, had stressed the need for collective action against infiltration and to promote the economic and social well-being of members, reflecting unease at the slow progress of regional governments towards what the West saw as stable democracy, and to stamp out Communist insurgency. These difficulties held up moves towards independence: in Singapore, for example, where continuing unrest had led in April 1956 to the breakdown of constitutional talks in London and a change of government, the inability to eliminate insurgency seemed likely to involve a continuing British military commitment to support civil power. In Malaya, on the other hand, where a constitutional commission had been announced under Lord Reid in March 1956 to work towards independence the following year, self-government was likely to restrict the employment of British troops unless invited by the Federation government. In both cases, possible British military action against Egypt, or a successful Egyptian challenge to British power, seemed equally damaging.

In relation to both Hong Kong and Korea, the identified threat involved Chinese as well as Soviet Communists, and was closely related to US policy (although that was not mentioned in the JIC report). In 1956 tension over Formosa (now Taiwan), the last stronghold of Chinese Nationalists regarded by Communist China (but not the United States) as part of the mainland, remained high, and on August 22 a US aircraft was shot down off the Chinese coast. As in Korea, it was unlikely that the Chinese or the Russians would take aggressive action in an area of prime importance to the United States, but from the viewpoint of the British government, which did not share the US view of Formosa, any conflict in the area raised the unwelcome prospect of increased Chinese pressure for the return of Hong Kong, a key staging post in British defense. In the Suez dispute Communist Chinese sympathies were firmly with Egypt (whose recognition of Communist China in May antagonized the Americans).

Although Africa (the Sudan, British Somaliland, Kenya, Tanganyika and Uganda, Zanzibar, the Federation of Rhodesia and Nyasaland, Mauritius, Nigeria, Sierra Leone, and the Gold Coast) was placed third on the list of the JIC's troublesome areas, it was, geographically, much closer to Egypt than Asia and would therefore seem more likely to be affected by the Suez dispute. There were, however, several connected reasons why it was perceived as less threatening. Decolonization in Africa was, on the whole, proceeding more quickly and smoothly than in the Middle East or Asia: in January 1956, for example, the British joint Anglo-Egyptian rule over Sudan had been terminated and independence granted, and though there was some concern over Nasser's plan for the Nile waters, the need for further British involvement was lessened. With the suppression of the Mau Mau, Kenya was also moving towards independence, as were Tanganyika and Uganda. Britain had less need to maintain troops or military facilities in Africa; and the territories were less important strategically. Most countries moving towards or achieving independence were making reasonable economic progress, reducing the potential for unrest. The British government was, on the whole, glad to divest itself of responsibilities in Africa. There remained serious concerns, indicated in the JIC report, that a gain in prestige by Nasser and a diminution in that of the United Kingdom would exacerbate existing tensions in all these countries, as well as in other African territories such as British Somaliland (threatened by Ethiopian territorial ambitions), by encouraging both anti-colonial and pan-Islamic movements. The loss of British prestige, and perceived triumph of Nasser, may have been perceived as of greater significance within the longer term, global context of British policy, but it was nevertheless potentially threatening.

In the case of the fourth group, the Americas (Falkland Islands, British Guiana, British Honduras, and the British West Indies), the JIC report did not identify any concerns as to the possible impact of Suez. The problems of Communist unrest in Guiana, and of internal dissension in Honduras fomented by propaganda from Guatemala, could not be laid at Nasser's door. There is no doubt, however, that in each of those cases lessons were taken from the Suez crisis about British strengths and weaknesses, and the possibilities of independence, that were to inform later developments.

Other Important Factors

Although the focus of this study is JIC(56)104, it would be incomplete without a brief reference to those elements of the global context to the Suez crisis that were *not* included in the report: in particular, European affairs, and relations with the United States and with the Soviet bloc in the European, rather than global Cold War context. The JIC report specifically excluded Europe, on the assumption that global war, that is war with the Soviet Union and satellites, was most likely to be triggered there, and the JIC had been asked to look at UK interests "in conditions short of global war." The report barely mentions the United States, and only deals with the Soviet Union in the context of countering its influence in the wider world. Yet a glance at the agenda of British Cabinet meetings in 1956 reveals how varied and challenging were the foreign policy issues faced by the government. The control of exports of surplus war materials, an important visit to Washington by Eden and Selwyn Lloyd to discuss European, particularly German, questions and atomic energy development, Soviet disarmament proposals, and a visit to the United Kingdom by Khrushchev and Bulganin, East-West trade, the sale of the Trinidad Oil Company to Texaco, the need for greater cooperation in NATO, demands from Malta for economic assistance, the cost of British forces in Germany, and the implications for Britain of standing outside European moves toward a common market are only a sample of the questions discussed. Some of these were clearly linked to events in the Middle East. More significantly, some were linked by Eden and his colleagues to the Suez crisis, while others (in particular moves towards European integration, and the threatening Soviet posture in Eastern Europe) were regarded, too readily, as entirely separate. In reality, Suez affected every area of British policy, but this was a lesson ministers were not yet ready to learn, despite the indications given in JIC(56)104.

Lessons Learned?

A small forest of books has been written about the consequences of the Suez crisis, and this chapter is not the place to rehearse them.[29] The term "Suez" is still shorthand for British decline, delusion, and ministerial duplicity, and often used (like "Munich") without much regard for the facts. Within the chosen focus of the JIC report of October 18, 1956, however, there are some observations that may be worth making.

Of course, no immediate lessons could be learned from the report, for there was no time to do so: on the same day that it was circulated, Eden reported to the

Cabinet on the Security Council's discussions of the Suez dispute, and was invited by his colleagues to agree with the French government terms of a communication asking Egypt to submit proposals for implementing the six principles agreed by the United Nations. The Cabinet minutes then record, however, that the meeting went on to consider "the general situation in the Middle East," when Eden spoke about his recent conversations with the French. He had, he said, told the French that if the Israelis were contemplating military operations against the Arabs, "it would be far better from our point of view that they should attack Egypt"; the Cabinet should be aware, Eden added, that "while we continued to seek an agreed settlement of the Suez dispute in pursuance of the resolution of the Security Council, it was possible that the issue might be brought more rapidly to a head as a result of military action by Israel against Egypt."[30] Even though the full details of the secret arrangement he had already made with the French and Israelis for the latter to attack Egypt at the end of the month were not divulged and were known only to a very few ministers and officials, Eden's statement made it very clear that the UN resolution was not the end of the matter and that a military solution of the Suez dispute remained firmly on the agenda; this very clarity led the minister of defense, Sir Walter Monckton, to resign.

The situation was explained even more clearly to the Cabinet on October 23 (while Patrick Dean and Foreign Office official Donald Logan were in Paris discussing the famous Sevres Protocol, the secret plan for an attack on Egypt), when they were told that "the military operation which had been planned could not be held in readiness for many days longer," and there was a full discussion of the implications of military action against Egypt.[31] Asked whether such an operation would not unite the Arab world in support of Egypt, Eden replied that while this was a serious risk it must be weighed against the greater risk "that unless early action could be taken to damage Colonel Nasser's prestige, his influence would be extended through the Middle East to a degree which would make it much more difficult to overthrow him." Even more starkly, he warned that if the dispute were brought to a head by diplomatic means, there was a danger that the Egyptians might comply with the Security Council resolution. There were, therefore, two options: either the British and French could "frame their demands in such a way as to make it impossible for the Egyptians to accept them," or they could seek a negotiated settlement in the knowledge that they would thereby "abandon their second objective of reducing Colonel Nasser's influence throughout the Middle East." This seemed pretty clear. When the discussion was resumed the following day, Eden told his colleagues that it "now appeared . . . that the Israelis were, after all advancing their military preparations," as they "evidently felt that the ambitions of Colonel Nasser's Government threatened their continued existence as an independent State and that they could not afford to wait for others to curb his expansionist policies." After considerable discussion, the Cabinet agreed in principle that if Israel attacked Egypt, the British and French governments should call on the two belligerents to "stop hostilities and withdraw their forces to a distance of ten miles from the Canal," and warn them that if either or both failed to comply "British and French forces would intervene in order to enforce compliance."[32]

These discussions have been set out at some length to show, first, that without revealing the details of collusion between the British, French, and Israelis, Eden left the Cabinet in no doubt that he preferred to provoke a military solution, that nothing less than the overthrow of Nasser was acceptable and that a negotiated settlement, with or without the United Nations, would not serve British interests. His colleagues endorsed this line. While there was undoubtedly an element of deception in what Eden did and said, there is a clear logical progression from the arguments set out in the JIC report to the policy agreed by the British government. Although military action against Egypt or the alternative of a Nasser success both threatened UK interests overseas, the latter outcome was considered more far-reaching in its impact, with the potential to inflict lasting damage on Britain's reputation as a world power—a reputation that, it must be remembered, was still taken for granted in 1956, despite setbacks, financial weakness, the loss of Empire, and exclusion from the US/Soviet superpower axis. And since the principle of deception is to "induce the adversary to make the wrong choice," and that surprise is best achieved by maintaining tightly held security over one's plans, it could be argued that Eden followed a course most likely to achieve British objectives in regard to Egypt.[33]

While this may have been true in relation to the JIC report, this policy failed demonstrably to take sufficient note of external factors and proved a serious miscalculation of the probable reaction of the United States and general international outrage. Following the Israeli invasion of the Sinai peninsula on October 29, British and French forces landed at Port Said on November 6 (the day of the US presidential election), but were forced by irresistible American pressure to withdraw on December 23. Nasser had, to that extent, won: he remained president of Egypt until his death in 1970, and retained control over the Suez Canal. Eden, whose health finally broke down at the end of 1956, resigned as prime minister and was replaced by Macmillan (who certainly learned a lot from Suez) on January 9, 1957. By May the British government was ready to lift its ban on passage by British ships, so could perhaps be said to have learned the lesson that Egyptian control did not mean closure of the Canal, and oil continued to flow (although Nasser too had learned lessons and was to use the power of closure to good effect in the Arab-Israeli conflict of 1967).

The British government learned other lessons, too, particularly the impossibility of any forward British foreign policy moves without American support (moral if not practical), while the military learned valuable lessons about readiness and flexibility.[34] In the context of JIC(56)104, the government also learned that a perceived success by Nasser in the Suez dispute did not bring the global catastrophe of which Eden, Macmillan, and others had spoken eloquently (invoking false analogies of Mussolini and Munich). It is true that many of the unfavorable developments anticipated in rather more measured terms by the JIC report did come to pass, in the sense that the road to independence for a number of former colonies was a rocky one, and may have been made more so by the government's humiliation over Suez, certain intractable problems (Cyprus and Hong Kong) remained so, and others appeared (Rhodesia). Though Britain's reputation internationally, politically, and economically suffered as a result of Suez, it is difficult to prove a definite causal link to her continuing foreign policy difficulties. Nasser was not solely responsible for the fomenting of nationalist unrest in the disappearing empires of the Western powers.

But just as before Suez British foreign and defense policy was dominated by the Cold War and the Soviet threat, so it remained both during and after the crisis. It may be coincidence that October 30, 1956, the day that the British and French governments issued their ultimata to Egypt and Israel to stop all warlike activity and withdraw ten miles from the Suez Canal, was the day that the Soviet leaders decided to overthrow the Hungarian government and use force against the uprising there; Dulles certainly did not think so.[35] Again, the link is not conclusive, though it seems only logical that the Soviet government would have welcomed the distractions of Suez as an international smokescreen to their own actions. And although there was a tendency for British politicians and, indeed, for the military and intelligence communities, to regard the threat of *global war*—that is, conflict between East and West, probably triggered in Europe—and the Soviet threat *in a global context*, that is, outside Europe, and particularly in the Middle East, as issues to be considered separately, the crisis did force the JIC, at least, to make the link.

On November 26, 1956, while British and French forces were fighting in Egypt, the JIS were invited to prepare a report that would "draw together all the indications of Soviet political, military and economic penetration of the Middle East," and consider the effect on Soviet aims of the Anglo-French intervention in Egypt and the likely future course of Soviet policy in the Middle East. The conclusions of the resulting JIC report, dated December 6, are worth quotation in the lessons learned context:

(a) The Soviet Union will continue to try to capture Arab sympathies, using rising Arab nationalism, hatred of Israel, and antagonism to the Western powers as its main instruments.

(b) The Soviet Union will maintain their control over the satellites. In doing this they will be prepared to make limited concessions to remedy popular discontent, but will not hesitate to use force to crush any radical undermining of their position.

(c) When the immediate crisis is past, the Soviet Union will no doubt maintain that the façade of "peaceful co-existence" remains the basis of Soviet Foreign Policy.

(d) In general, the Soviet Union will seek to drive wedges between the United Kingdom and the United States wherever opportunity offers.

(e) The situation is still too fluid to attempt any final assessment of Soviet gains and losses.[36]

While in some sense a statement of the obvious, these conclusions at least made tentative steps towards learning lessons. The same must be said for a further JIC report of December 13, 1956 (while British and French forces were still in Egypt), on the extent to which the present state of tension had increased the chances of miscalculation which might lead to global war, which concluded that "Soviet leaders do not want war, but that nevertheless the chances of global war arising through a chain of circumstances and miscalculations have somewhat increased." In the body of this report, the JIC expressed the view that while the present world tension arose from civil disturbance and war in two "unrelated" areas, the coincidence of timing had "had the effect of heightening the tension and hardening relations between the West and the Soviet bloc," creating an instability that could endanger peace. However, they added, comfortingly, that the Soviet Union had no vital interests in the Middle East for which they would go to war, and were unlikely to wish to see a situation develop where Soviet nationals fought against Western forces. But the Suez crisis had created conditions from which the Soviet Union was "likely to derive substantial political benefits," improve its position as the champion of the Arab world against the West and strengthen its ties with Egypt and Syria in particular. The Soviet dilemma, the report noted hopefully, was that "overt repression to maintain their position in the Satellites defeats their policy in the other countries of the world."[37]

At the end of 1956, after British and French troops had withdrawn from Egypt, the JIC undertook a further assessment of Soviet aims, the effect of the Suez crisis upon them and the likely course of future policy. In this report they now felt able to draw attention to the dangers Suez had presented to the Soviet Union, who might, if fighting had continued, "have had to choose between giving open military support to Nasser and letting his regime collapse"; the first would have risked global war, the latter would have been a "grave setback" to Soviet influence in the region. The cease-fire, which the Soviets probably attributed to "their own threats and the strength of 'anti-colonialist' feeling" in the region, had, the JIC opined, "saved the Soviet Union from this dilemma" and allowed them to think it justified their own policy. The report then drew up a balance sheet of the advantages and disadvantages of the Suez crisis to the Soviet Union, with the former outnumbering the latter by twelve to seven. The conclusion was that it was difficult to assess how far the Soviet Union might go to pursue its aims in the Middle East, but that it seemed unlikely that these aims had any urgency at present, "while current policies are proving so effective." The final clause is, perhaps, the best proof of lessons learned.[38] The Suez crisis had proved a traumatic experience for every part of the British government, and the principal lesson learned was not to let such a thing happen again: but as far as foreign policy, military planning, and intelligence gathering were concerned, the constant nature of the Soviet threat meant that in many respects it was business as usual.

Finally, what lessons did the British intelligence community learn from Suez, and from the JIC's contribution to the crisis? There were several lessons that one could argue *should* have been learned, and these fall into the category of what might be called "intelligence constants": that it is important to try and avoid false analogies (such as seeing Nasser as a new Mussolini); to avoid "mirror imaging," that is, projecting the British government's priorities and strategy on to others—many misperceptions arose from assumptions about both Egyptian and Soviet policies, for example; and finally, that the coordination of intelligence and use of liaison contacts are vital. As to what the intelligence authorities *did* learn, this is of course difficult to pin down, as the views expressed by and in secret organizations are necessarily confidential, as are the details of any changes of procedure or practices that may be adopted. Nevertheless, it is possible, by looking at changes in government and official policies and procedures, to draw some general conclusions as to the kind of lessons that were learned. First, there was a need for a greater degree of coordination between ministers, officials, and the intelligence community (though it must be said that this is a conclusion that is always drawn in the aftermath of a crisis or disaster). Second, there was a need for better formulation of requirements, tasking, and collation, and for closer policy coordination, whether between the Foreign Office and the JIC, the JIC and the chiefs of staff, between SIS and its parent department, the Foreign Office, or between SIS and the Security Service.

More specifically, the intelligence community learned that the policy of containing nationalism in the Middle East by supporting existing regimes and their security services did not work. Special operations, already inhibited by the requirement to obtain prior Foreign Office sanction before any action, were an unreliable way of affecting the course of events, particularly in view of the scarcity of manpower. Rather, the crisis underlined the value of technical intelligence, particularly SIGINT, and the importance of liaison, in particular with the Americans but also with friendly Middle Eastern powers, such as Israel, who could supply information on Soviet activities in the region. More generally, both the intelligence agencies and their departmental taskmasters in Whitehall learned the lesson that it might be profitable to devote greater effort countering political and economic subversion, although Suez had also demonstrated that detailed tactical intelligence was essential, and that Soviet reactions to the crisis, as well as their reaction to unrest in Eastern Europe, underlined the continuing need for information on Soviet order of battle and strategic intentions. In the end, it was Cold War business as usual for the British intelligence community as well.

NOTES

1. Terms of reference, JIC(56)104 of 11 October 1956, TNA: CAB: 158/26.
2. The most balanced and comprehensive account of Suez, and the one most mindful of the global context, remains Keith Kyle, *Suez* (New York: St. Martin's Press, 1991). Also useful are Wm. Roger Louis and Roger Owen (eds.), *Suez 1956: The Crisis and Its Consequences* (Oxford: Clarendon Press, 1989), W. Scott Lucas, *Divided We Stand: Britain, the US and the Suez Crisis* (London: Hodder and Stoughton, 1991), and Richard Aldrich, *The Hidden Hand: Britain, America and Cold War Secret Intelligence* (London: John Murray, 2001).
3. COS report on Defence Policy and Global Strategy (DO(50)45) of June 7, 1950, TNA: CAB 131/9, printed in *Documents on British Policy Overseas (DBPO)* (London: HMSO, 1985), Series II, Volume IV, as Appendix I.

4. JIC(56)21(Final), "Likelihood of Global War and Warning of Attack," May 1, 1956, TNA: CAB 158/24.
5. JIC(56)80(Final)(Revise) of August 3, 1956, "Egyptian Nationalisation of the Suez Canal Company," TNA: CAB 158/25.
6. The agreement signed between Turkey and Iraq on February 24, 1955, mediated by the British but rejected by Colonel Nasser as compromising Arab solidarity.
7. JIC(56)36(Final) of March 21, 1936, TNA: CAB 158/24.
8. For a detailed documentary study of British policy towards Egypt throughout this period, see John Kent (ed.), *Egypt and the Defence of the Middle East*, Parts I–III (London: The Stationery Office, 1998), part of the *British Documents on the End of Empire Project (BDEEP)*. All the BDEEP volumes are worth consulting on specific territories mentioned in this study: for a full list see www.commonwealth.sas .ac.uk/british.htm.
9. Anglo-Egyptian Treaty of Alliance, August 26, 1936, Cmd 5270 (see also *Documents on British Foreign Policy 1919–39* (London: HMSO, 1977), Second Series, Volume XVI, Appendix V; Anglo-Egyptian Treaty of October 19, 1954, Cmd 9586.
10. Diary entry for August 1, 1956, Peter Catterall (ed.), *The Macmillan Diaries: The Cabinet Years 1950–1957* (London: Pan, 2004), 580.
11. See Paul Lashmar and James Oliver, *Britain's Secret Propaganda War 1948–77* (Stroud: Sutton Publishing, 1998); also James R. Vaughan, *The Failure of American and British Propaganda in the Arab Middle East, 1945–1957: Unconquerable Minds* (Basingstoke: Palgrave, 2005).
12. On the pervasive activities of the EIS see Yaacov Caroz, *The Arab Secret Services* (London: Corgi, 1978). There is also some interesting documentation attached to Guy Laron, "Cutting the Gordian Knot: The Post-WW II Egyptian Quest for Arms and the 1955 Czechoslovak Arms Deal," available on the website of the Cold War International History Project (www.wilsoncenter.org).
13. On CIA activities in Egypt at this time see Miles Copeland, *The Game Player: Confessions of the CIA's Original Political Operative* (London: Aurum, 1989); Laura M. James, *Nasser at War: Arab Images of the Enemy* (Basingstoke: Palgrave, 2006), which also considers the possibility of CIA involvement in the Free Officers' coup of 1952 that led to Nasser's rise to power.
14. See Kyle, *Suez*, 219–24.
15. Ibid., 275, quoting from papers in the Eisenhower Library.
16. Catterall (ed.), *The Macmillan Diaries*, 607.
17. See CM(56)54th Conclusions, July 27, 1956, TNA: CAB 128/30; and the Cabinet secretary's notes of the same meeting, now open in TNA: CAB 195/15, in which it is made clear that the British objective would be "to unseat Nasser," rather than merely returning the Suez Canal to international control.
18. CM(56)68th Conclusions, October 3, 1956, TNA: CAB 128/30.
19. See G.C. Peden, *Arms, Economics and British Strategy* (Cambridge: Cambridge University Press, 2007), 303–4.
20. COS(56)98th meeting, October 10, 1956, TNA: DEFE 4/91. MUSKETEER (later MUSKETEER (Revise)) was the code name for the British military operation against Egypt: see Kyle, *Suez*, chapters 9 and 13.

21. On the Suez Group, see Sue Onslow, "The Suez Group," in *Oxford Dictionary of National Biography* (Oxford: Oxford University Press, 2005).

22. The essentials of this plan, usually known as collusion, are in Kyle, *Suez*, chapters 16 and 17; on the emergence of further details in later works and in the light of documents made public more recently, see Christopher Baxter and Stephen Twigge, "Clearing the Canal: the Whitehall Review Process and the Release of Suez Records," *Archives* XXXII:117 (October 2007).

23. JIC(56)97(Final), "Probable Actions by Nasser in Certain Circumstances," October 11, 1956, TNA: CAB 158/25.

24. See Sir Patrick Dean's account of these events, written in May 1978, and now open at TNA in FCO 73/205.

25. G. A. Nasser, *The Philosophy of Revolution* (Washington, DC: Public Affairs Press, 1959): on Nasser's political philosophy see also James, *Nasser at War*, and Caroz, *Arab Secret Services*, 50–51.

26. *Ethniki Organosis Kyprion Agoniston*, led by General George Grivas.

27. Caroz, op. cit., 28.

28. The South East Asia Treaty Organization, created by the Manila Pact in September 1954 and established formally in 1955 by the US, UK, Australia, France, New Zealand, Pakistan, the Philippines, and Thailand. It provided for collective action against aggression, and was aimed at preventing further Communist advances in the region.

29. See most recently Simon C. Smith (ed.), *Reassessing Suez 1956: New Perspectives on the Crisis and Its Aftermath* (Aldershot: Ashgate, 2008); a more general perspective is given in Martin Woollacott, *After Suez: Adrift in the American Century* (London: IB Tauris, 2006).

30. CM(56)71st Conclusions, October 18, 1956, TNA: CAB 128/30.

31. On the meetings in Paris and Sèvres, see Kyle, *Suez*, chapter 17; also the revealing archival detail in Baxter and Twigge, "Clearing the Canal."

32. CM(56)73rd and 74th Conclusions, October 24 and 25, 1956, TNA: CAB 128/30.

33. See *Anticipating Surprise: Analysis for Strategic Warning*, an instructive work by Cynthia Grabo, who was a senior US intelligence analyst from 1941 to 1979 (Lanham, MD: University Press of America, 2004); she notes favorably the fact that "the entire British military staff from the Allied CinC on down" were kept from knowledge of the Anglo-French-Israeli collusion plan (22).

34. Interesting material on military lessons learned after Suez can be found in TNA: WO 32/126731. See also works by Eric Grove on Suez, including his essay in Smith, *Reassessing Suez*.

35. See Kyle, *Suez*, 376–77.

36. JIC(56)133 (Terms of Reference), November 26, 1956 and JIC(56)123(Final) (Revise), December 6, 1956, TNA: CAB 158/26.

37. JIC(56)136(Final), December 13, 1956, TNA: CAB 158/26.

38. JIC(56)133(Final)(Revise), January 1, 1957, TNA: CAB 158/26.

DOCUMENT 8.1:   The Threat to United Kingdom Interests Overseas, October 18, 1956

TOP SECRET: UK EYES ONLY

J.I.C.(56)104 (Final)

18th October, 1956

CHIEFS OF STAFF COMMITTEE

JOINT INTELLIGENCE COMMITTEE

THE THREAT TO UNITED KINGDOM INTERESTS OVERSEAS

REPORT BY THE JOINT INTELLIGENCE COMMITTEE

Introduction

As instructed* we examine in this report the likely trouble areas throughout the world (exclusive of Europe) where United Kingdom interests would be affected in conditions short of global war. The report covers the period up to 1961 but it is emphasised, with particular reference to the Colonies, that any forecast of the situation prevailing at the end of the period cannot take account of many imponderable factors, such as the pace of political development and the extent of the movement towards self-government, and is, therefore, at best only a general estimate.

2.   We have examined likely trouble spots listing the general areas and the individual countries within them in the approximate order in which we believe British interests would be most seriously affected. We have only stated the general type of trouble anticipated and have noted in certain cases the consequential effect of troubles elsewhere. In the latter connection it should be emphasised that any concessions made by the United Kingdom under pressure are likely to have repercussions throughout the world, encouraging further claims and exacerbating potential points of friction. Conversely, a successful demonstration of resolution and firmness by the United Kingdom would have the effect of discouraging similar pressure throughout the world.

TOP SECRET: UK EYES ONLY

DOCUMENT 8.1: The Threat to United Kingdom Interests Overseas, October 18, 1956 *(Continued)*

TOP SECRET: UK EYES ONLY

Middle East and North Africa

EGYPT

3. Until the outcome of the present Canal dispute is known, any forecast about Egypt is impossible. However, if Nasser remains in power, he can be expected to intensify his present expansionist and anti-colonial policy and thus to continue his present hostility to the United Kingdom.

ARAB-ISRAEL WAR

4. In the present very tense situation, the possibility of an Arab-Israel war cannot be excluded. Hostilities might arise out of:

   i.   a series of retaliatory border incidents;

   ii.   a decision by the Israeli Government to attack before the Arabs get stronger and better organised, e.g. the move of Iraqi troops into Jordan;

   iii. a decision by the Arabs to attack when they are eventually satisfied with their strength and organisation.

5. If Nasser emerges successfully from the Suez dispute, a triumphant surge of Arab nationalism might lead him to act against Israel earlier than he would wish.

CYPRUS

6. Whatever progress is achieved against terrorism, it will persist to some extent until a political settlement is reached. The Governor estimates that it will take several months to eliminate the terrorists as a major factor. The restoration of law and order has been declared a condition precedent to the introduction of the new and liberal Constitution now being drafted.

7. If British prestige in the Middle East declines, the terrorists will be encouraged, and a political settlement made more difficult. If however the latter can be achieved, there is prospect of a period of peace in Cyprus during which United Kingdom interests would be fully safeguarded.

TOP SECRET: UK EYES ONLY

DOCUMENT 8.1: The Threat to United Kingdom Interests Overseas, October 18, 1956 *(Continued)*

TOP SECRET: UK EYES ONLY

JORDAN

8. If Israel attacks Jordan the United Kingdom is committed to go to the latter's assistance under the terms of the Anglo-Jordan Treaty. In the present very tense situation, the possibility of an Israeli attack cannot be excluded. In addition, Egyptian influence is considerable and might be used to instigate riots against the Anglo-Jordan Treaty and the British connection in general and attacks on British military installations and airfields. If the King and his advisers opposed this, the Egyptians might attempt the overthrow of the monarchy thus creating a situation of internal chaos which Israel might use as a pretext for occupying at least part of the country. The lives of British subjects and the British bases would be endangered.

9. This dispute would be greatly increased by an Egyptian political success over the Suez dispute.

LIBYA

10. Egyptian propaganda against the United Kingdom is powerful and Egyptian subversive organisation has been established capable of endangering British lives and sabotaging British property, especially the military bases. Anti-British riots and sabotage are to be expected, particularly in the event of our engaging hostilities with Egypt.

11. Moreover this danger would remain after an Egyptian success over the Suez dispute. The existing Soviet influence would also be increased.

ADEN

12. Trouble, both internally and on the frontiers, is to be expected, but, unless exacerbated by external factors, should be manageable with the existing garrison and police.

13. Egyptian success over the Suez issue, resulting in greatly increased prestige of Nasser, a flare-up of Pan-Islamism and a loss of British prestige could lead to a rapid and serious deterioration of the whole situation in Aden.

TOP SECRET: UK EYES ONLY

DOCUMENT 8.1:   The Threat to United Kingdom Interests Overseas, October 18, 1956 *(Continued)*

TOP SECRET: UK EYES ONLY

PERSIAN GULF SHEIKDOMS

14. Disturbances are likely from time to time due to dynastic squabbles, labour unrest, &c, and to Egyptian and Saudi subversion, particularly over the problem of Buraimi which remains unresolved. Reinforcements for the inadequate or unreliable police forces would be needed, except in Kuwait where the comparatively large local security forces should be able to cope with any situation, unless they themselves became disaffected.

    If the Suez dispute is settled on terms which the Egyptians can plausibly represent as a victory over Western pressure, nationalised elements opposed both to the Ruling Families and the British connection, will be encouraged. But the traditional attachment of the Rulers to their treaties with Britain will probably not be seriously shaken. Internal stresses might, however, increase and possibly involve the need for further reinforcements.

SYRIA

16. Syria is the closest of Nasser's allies. Her alliance with Egypt combined with local xenophobia may lead to riots endangering British lives and property, particularly the pipe-lines, though there is evidence that the Syrian authorities at least realise the advantages to Syria of keeping the oil flowing.

17. This danger would be greatly increased by an Egyptian success over the Suez dispute.

IRAQ

18. Iraq is Egypt's principal rival for the leadership of the Arab world. Nasser may try to overthrow the present régime, deposing, the King and assassinating Nuri. In present circumstances, the Government can probably cope with this threat. The situation could change, however, for the worse if Nuri disappeared from the political scene or if the United Kingdom failed to give adequate support in the face of Egyptian pressure.

TOP SECRET: UK EYES ONLY

DOCUMENT 8.1:   The Threat to United Kingdom Interests Overseas, October 18, 1956 *(Continued)*

TOP SECRET: UK EYES ONLY

19. If prolonged hostilities occur between the West and Egypt, riots may occur in which the lives of British subjects and the oil installations would be endangered.

ALGERIA, TUNISIA AND MOROCCO

20. Local xenophobia might give rise to anti-Western riots in which the lives of British subjects would be endangered.

21. This danger would be greatly increased by an Egyptian success over the Suez dispute.

IRAN

22. Extreme nationalism and social unrest may combine with xenophobia to cause agitation directed against the monarchical régime and the United Kingdom, which is supposed to support it.

Asia

SINGAPORE

23. Communist subversion is a constant threat. A potential commitment for British troops to support the civil power will remain for as long as the United Kingdom retains defence responsibilities in the Colony.

HONG KONG

24. The Chinese Communists regard this colony as territory to be recovered. They are unlikely to use military force in the period under review except possible as a consequence of hostilities elsewhere or should the internal situation get completely out of hand when they might be temped to move in nominally to restore order. Internal troubles are probable, requiring the intervention of police and troops.

25. Fighting in the Straits of Formosa or against the offshore islands would increase Chinese Communist pressure on Hong Kong. In the unlikely event of the United Kingdom becoming involved in such fighting the threat to Hong Kong would be greatly increased.

TOP SECRET: UK EYES ONLY

DOCUMENT 8.1:   The Threat to United Kingdom Interests Overseas, October 18, 1956 *(Continued)*

TOP SECRET: UK EYES ONLY

MALAYA

26. It is unlikely that an external threat will develop in the period under review in conditions short of global war—see also paragraph 32 on SEATO. Internal Communist terrorism seems likely to continue after self-government is attained. The extent of British troops' participation in anti-terrorist operations will depend on agreement with the Federation Government. Subversion, apart from terrorist activities, may also lead to civil disorders: but the extent of any possible United Kingdom commitment on this account in an independent Commonwealth country in defence treaty relations with the United Kingdom cannot be forecast.

KOREA

27. The USSR will still have the paramount influence in North Korea. The Russian and Chinese Communists will continue to support the North Korean Communists in their attempts to subvert the Republic of Korea and thus obtain control of the whole of the country. The Chinese and North Koreans are unlikely to resort to overt aggression and attempts at subversion are unlikely to succeed while the United States continues to be firmly committed to the Republic of Korea. There is an increasing sense of responsibility among the influential senior officers of the Republic of Korea and the dangers of a South Korean 'march to the North' have receded accordingly. However, if President Syngman Rhee were replaced by an even more irresponsible politician the risk of a renewal of hostilities by the South Koreans might increase.

28. Intervention by SEATO in Indo-China or Thailand could lead to a heightening of tension in Korea.

BRITISH BORNEO TERRITORIES

29. A situation is looming up in Brunei as a result of growing nationalism and anti-feudalism which may lead to troubles during the later years of the period under review. These might have repercussions in Sarawak and Borneo.

TOP SECRET: UK EYES ONLY

DOCUMENT 8.1: The Threat to United Kingdom Interests Overseas, October 18, 1956 *(Continued)*

TOP SECRET: UK EYES ONLY

CEYLON

30. There is a chance of an upsurge of local agitation for the removal of British bases, but it is unlikely that this will reach such proportions as to require the intervention of British forces.

INDONESIA

31. In the event of the United Kingdom using force in the Suez dispute, there would probably be anti-British demonstrations as a gesture of Islamic and anti-colonialist solidarity. In view of the inefficiency of the police, the lives of British subjects might be endangered.

OBLIGATIONS UNDER SEATO

32. The primary threat to the SEATO area is one of subversion; British troops are not required for the purpose of countering this threat, but should subversion not succeed in some or all of the states of Indo-China and Thailand, overt aggression becomes a possibility. Present SEATO planning is that overt aggression would be reduced to manageable proportions by the use of allied nuclear weapons and meeting the residual threat from a pre-planned defensive position. The protocol States of Laos, Cambodia and South Vietnam are under the treaty permitted to invoke SEATO protection if attacked. The possibility of SEATO expeditionary forces being despatched to the aid of any of these countries cannot therefore be ruled out. The possibility that Laos and Cambodia will come under Communist domination through subversion is real. Such events would weaken Thailand's determination to resist, and would leave South Vietnam more open to overt aggression.

Africa

SUDAN

33. If the Sudan does not fall in with Nasser's plans for the use of the Nile waters, he may attempt to overthrow the Sudanese régime by subversion. If law and order breaks down in the process, he may send troops into the Sudan, ostensibly to maintain the peace, against the wishes of the Sudanese Government. In this event the latter might appeal to the United Kingdom, as the other former *co-dominus*, to intervene too.

TOP SECRET: UK EYES ONLY

DOCUMENT 8.1:   The Threat to United Kingdom Interests Overseas, October 18,
1956 *(Continued)*

BRITISH SOMALILAND

34. Ethiopian ambitions to achieve the incorporation of all Somali territories in
    an Ethiopian empire and Somali dissatisfaction with the Anglo-Ethiopian
    Agreement of 1954 could lead to serious troubles which could not be
    dealt with by the forces in the territory.

35. A gain of prestige by Nasser, and a loss of British prestige, following a
    settlement of the Suez dispute in Egypt's favour, would give great impetus
    to Anti-Colonialism and to Pan-Islamism, and would thus exacerbate our
    difficulties with the Somalis.

KENYA, TANGANYIKA, UGANDA

36. After the final suppression of Mau Mau internal troubles in Kenya should
    be manageable with local troops and police. In addition to any internal
    troubles there may well be trouble on the Northern Kenya Frontier from
    Ethiopian expansionism. Local forces could, as hitherto, deal with sporadic
    raids, but anything more than this (particularly if the general situation in
    the Horn of Africa deteriorated) would call for reinforcements.

37. Any internal troubles which might occur in Tanganyika and Uganda
    should be manageable by local forces.

38. As in the case of Somaliland a settlement of the Suez dispute in Nasser's
    favour would tend to increase troubles in all these territories.

39. In the unlikely event of fighting between Pakistan and India there would
    be heightened racial tension in colonies where these two communities,
    or where both Hindus and Mohammadans are both found in numbers,
    notably in East Africa.

ZANZIBAR

40. No serious trouble is foreseen, except as a consequence of external Pan-
    Islamic influences. An increase in the prestige of Nasser would be such an
    influence.

DOCUMENT 8.1: The Threat to United Kingdom Interests Overseas, October 18, 1956 *(Continued)*

TOP SECRET: UK EYES ONLY

FEDERATION OF RHODESIA AND NYASALAND

41. Any internal troubles should be manageable with local troops and police.

MAURITIUS

42. Racial friction will continue, but really serious internal troubles are not expected.

NIGERIA

43. Internal troubles during the remaining constitutional phases before full self-government is reached are not unlikely. The extent to which British troops might be involved would depend upon the situation and the constitutional position at the time. The Northern Region is Mohammadan, and, although the Government has so far cold-shouldered Egyptian approaches, Moslem sympathies where Egypt is concerned could change this situation.

SIERRA LEONE

44. The internal situation is at present uneasy and is exacerbated by trouble with foreign Africans in the diamond fields, which might have wider security repercussions. Troubles should normally be manageable by local forces, but more serious disturbances, in which local troops might need reinforcement from outside, cannot be ruled out.

GOLD COAST

45. Internal troubles can not be ruled out in the early days of independence, but at present it seems doubtful whether any situation would reach such a pitch that action would become necessary to protect British lives.

Americas

FALKLAND ISLANDS

46. Argentina claims this colony. Propaganda will continue but the use of force is most unlikely. The dispute with Argentina and Chile over the status of the Dependencies will continue, and may be complicated by claims in

TOP SECRET: UK EYES ONLY

DOCUMENT 8.1: The Threat to United Kingdom Interests Overseas, October 18, 1956 *(Continued)*

TOP SECRET: UK EYES ONLY

Antarctica by other nations including possibly the USSR and United States particularly during the International Geophysical Year of 1957-58: the use of force is, however, unlikely.

BRITISH GUIANA

47. The avowed Communists who caused the breakdown of the previous Constitution remain a potent factor in the local political scene. The situation will continue to call for the presence or immediate proximity of troops to support the police, if necessary.

BRITISH HONDURAS

48. Internal political dissensions, fomented by external propaganda, is [sic] a likely cause of trouble. Guatemala claims the territory, but is unlikely to use force while British troops remain in the colony or are immediately available to go there.

BRITISH WEST INDIES

49. Serious trouble is not foreseen but local trouble in Trinidad, and perhaps in Jamaica, is possible.

> (Signed) P.H. DEAN
> J.G.T. INGLIS
> W.M.L. MACDONALD
> K.W.D. STRONG
> W.H.A. BISHOP
> C.Y. CARSTAIRS
> C.H. TARVER (for DMI)

Ministry of Defence, SW1

18th October, 1956

---

* C.O.S.(56)97th Meeting, Minute 5.

TOP SECRET: UK EYES ONLY

CHAPTER 9

Oleg Penkovsky, British Intelligence, and the Cuban Missile Crisis

LEN SCOTT

Editors' Note:

One of the world's leading experts on the Cuban missile crisis tackles the use, value, and impact of human intelligence. Oleg Penkovsky has been described by some as the "spy who saved the world," but is this a fair label? In considering the role of the information he provided, Len Scott raises some pertinent questions about the utility of human intelligence, not least when it is compared with other methods of intelligence gathering. As he concludes, human intelligence is but one source and its value often cannot be assessed in isolation from other sources.

The Cuban missile crisis is generally accepted as the most dangerous event of the Cold War and, indeed, the most dangerous event in human history. Intelligence played a variety of roles, some of which were crucial to the unfolding and outcome of the crisis. The American intelligence community did not believe that the Soviets would deploy nuclear weapons in Cuba, reinforcing views within the Kennedy administration. When the missiles were discovered, President Kennedy's immediate reaction was that a military attack on Cuba was necessary. However, the discovery of the missiles before their deployment was complete gave Washington time to consider a response more carefully. This discovery owed everything to intelligence, and in particular to clandestine aerial photography of the U-2 spy planes. As the crisis developed, intelligence played crucial roles in assessing capabilities and intentions. One aspect of the role of intelligence is that of Oleg Penkovsky, a colonel in the Chief Intelligence Directorate of the Soviet General Staff (GRU) who, from the spring of 1961 to the autumn of 1962, spied for the British Secret Intelligence Service (SIS) and the American Central Intelligence Agency (CIA).

The view that Penkovsky's espionage was of crucial importance in the missile crisis has received wide circulation on both sides of the Atlantic.[1] The Chief of SIS, Sir Dick White, is reported to have told SIS officers shortly after the crisis that the CIA believed in the "absolutely crucial value of the Penkovsky intelligence" which "was largely instrumental in deciding that the United States should not make a preemptive nuclear strike against the Soviet Union" in October 1962.[2] Gordon Brook-Shepherd argues that "with the enigmatic figure of . . . Penkovsky . . . for the first, and so far, the only recorded time in postwar history, human intelligence, supplied directly to the enemy, helped to tilt the course of world events."[3] According to John Le Carré, "The information which Penkovsky provided . . . led, there is little doubt, to the greatest moral defeat suffered by either side in the Cold War: Khrushchev's decision to withdraw his rockets from Cuba."[4] Baroness Daphne Park, a former senior SIS officer, has written that Penkovsky "averted war in Cuba."[5] And the most authoritative study of Penkovsky's espionage reaches a similar conclusion: "During the Berlin crisis of 1961 and the Cuban missile crisis in 1962, Penkovsky was the spy who saved the world from nuclear war."[6]

Yet, very different views have also emerged. Some historians dispute the significance of Penkovsky's espionage for Western policymaking.[7] McGeorge Bundy, then Kennedy's special assistant for national security, argues that "Penkovsky had no discernible relation to the real assessments and actions of the United States government in the missile crisis,"[8] and his own account of October 1962 makes no reference to the spy.[9] Similarly, Raymond Garthoff, then a CIA analyst responsible for appraising Penkovsky's material, describes the "tremendous amount of important military information," but argues that this was merely "useful background information during the crisis."[10] A special issue of *Intelligence and National Security* devoted to the role of intelligence in the Cuban missile crisis relegates Penkovsky to passing references.[11] More controversially, works drawing in particular from disaffected insiders within British intelligence have questioned whether Penkovsky was working for the West or against it.[12] And in the words of one American writer, Penkovsky was "a Soviet postman at the time of the missile crisis."[13]

So any lessons that might be drawn from Penkovsky's espionage clearly depend on our interpretations of his role. Lessons about his espionage need to be set alongside lessons about writing on his espionage. So how do we know about Penkovsky's intelligence? In 1963, Penkovsky went on trial in Moscow alongside British businessman, Greville Wynne, who had acted as contact and courier, and who was eventually imprisoned (before being freed in a swap for Soviet agents). Penkovsky pleaded guilty to the charge of treason and was sentenced to death. He had conducted over forty meetings with his SIS and CIA case officers on official trips to the West, and these were recorded and transcribed. The information provided in this way formed the basis for a book whose publication was organized by the CIA, titled *The Penkovskiy Papers*.[14] After he returned from Moscow, Greville Wynne published several accounts of his role, which also describe aspects of SIS's involvement.[15] British attitudes to secrecy and declassification precluded official comment, though by the 1980s authoritative accounts by respected writers had appeared that clearly reflected access to officialdom.[16]

In the United States, interest in the Cuban missile crisis began to accelerate with the twenty-fifth anniversary of the crisis and the declassification of US archival material. A key element in reviewing the history of Penkovsky's role was the material released by the CIA both as a result of the US Freedom of Information Act and through its own declassification program. The credit for the former rests with Jerrold Schecter, an American writer, and Peter Deriabin, a KGB defector and CIA consultant, whose 1992 book, *The Spy Who Saved the World*, drew upon this material to present an absorbing, if contested, interpretation of Penkovsky's significance.[17] From 1992, the CIA declassified, and has now published, nearly two hundred key documents on their website.[18] They include transcripts of Penkovsky's meetings in Britain and France with his SIS and CIA case officers, and in general provide unprecedented documentary insights into CIA tradecraft. More importantly, the documents illuminate how Penkovsky's material was assessed, evaluated, and integrated into the US intelligence analytical and policy processes.

One further dimension concerns intelligence collaboration between the British and the Americans. SIS ran a joint operation with the CIA to collect materials from Penkovsky in Moscow and debrief him on his visits to Britain (in April/May and July/August 1961) and Paris (in September/October 1961). These visits were under his Soviet cover as a civilian official of the State Committee for the Coordination of Scientific Research Work (GKKNIR). Back in Moscow, Penkovsky communicated via Wynne and then through SIS channels using Ann Chisholm, the wife of the head of station, Rauri Chisholm. SIS records have not yet been released to the National Archives, though in the early 1990s the government did cooperate in declassifying CIA records, discussed above, that helped Schecter and Deriabin construct parts of their account. These CIA records contain details about senior SIS officers, including Maurice Oldfield, senior liaison officer in Washington; Harry Shergold, the senior SIS case officer; and Sir Dick White. CIA and SIS officers, and other officials, including the former British ambassador to the USSR, Sir Frank Roberts, have also written or spoken on the record about the operation.[19]

There are two sets of documents appended to this chapter.

(1) Document 4: JIC(62)93(Final), "Cuba: Threat Posed By Soviet Missiles," October 26, 1962.[20] This document is an assessment by the Joint Intelligence Committee of US photographic evidence of Soviet deployments in Cuba.

(2) Document 5: CIA: Meeting 1 (London) April 20, 1961. This is an extract from the transcripts of debriefings of Oleg Penkovsky by his SIS and CIA case officers in London in April 1961. Both documents illuminate different stages of the intelligence cycle (gathering and analysis). They also provide insights into the UK–US relationship in the intelligence field.

Missiles in Cuba

The discovery of Soviet missile bases in Cuba in October precipitated the most intense and dangerous crisis of the Cold War. The chronology of Soviet decision making is now clear. On May 24, the presidium approved the plan for Operation Anadyr, drawn up by the Soviet General Staff to deploy 36 R-12 medium-range ballistic missiles (MRBMs) (NATO designation SS-4) and 24 R-14 intermediate-range ballistic missiles (IRBMs) (NATO designation SS-5) in Cuba.[21] Both carried thermonuclear payloads. The R-12s would be within range of Washington as well as many air bases, ICBM complexes, and command and control centers. The R-14s could reach virtually all US territory. Eighty Frontovye Krylatye Rakety (FKR) Meteor Ground Launched Cruise Missiles (GLCMs), with a range of 90–110 miles and armed with yields of up 12 kilotons were also sent. A further aspect of the plan was to establish a Soviet naval base that would accommodate surface ships, ballistic missile–armed submarines, and diesel-electric torpedo submarines.[22] In September, Khrushchev shelved the surface ships and ballistic missile–carrying submarines. However, the diesel-electric submarines did proceed, and a decision was taken to equip each of them with a nuclear-armed torpedo.

In exploring Penkovsky's role in the crisis it is helpful to draw the distinction, frequently made by students of intelligence, between intentions and capabilities. Penkovsky failed to provide *any* indications that Khrushchev was preparing to deploy MRBMs or IRBMs in Cuba. Indeed by September, the CIA was increasingly anxious to learn whether the Soviets were sending missiles to Cuba, and the last message from his CIA case officers specifically requested "concrete information as to military measures being undertaken by the USSR to convert Cuba into an offensive military base. In particular we would like to know if Cuba is to be provided with surface to surface missiles."[23] Despite several attempts to make contact in Moscow, these urgent requests failed to reach Penkovsky before his arrest.

By October 22, 1962, when President Kennedy appeared on television to announce the discovery of the missiles, Penkovsky had been arrested by the KGB. Until his last contact with Western intelligence in August, Penkovsky had supplied some 10,000 pages of testimony and classified material from general staff files.[24] In addition, the colonel was a confidant and protégé of the chief marshal of Soviet artillery, Marshal Sergei Varentsov, responsible for Soviet tactical missile forces, and had cultivated a relationship with the head of the GRU, General Ivan Serov. He was therefore able to supply "gossip and reports of the leadership's private meetings."[25] This provided Kennedy with useful insights into Khrushchev's approach to Berlin in 1961 (though Penkovsky was unable to pass on a warning that the Berlin Wall was about to be erected).[26] He also passed information about the Soviet ICBM program, which suggested that far from moving ahead in a missile gap, the Soviets were lagging well behind. The relative importance of Penkovsky's intelligence against photographic and electronic intelligence remains a matter of adjudication, though it is increasingly clear that intelligence from the US Corona satellite program (therefore not Penkovsky) was the principal reason for dispelling the missile gap.

However, although Penkovsky did not alert the West to the deployment of missiles, he did supply technical information, including the field manual for the R-12/SS-4. Richard Helms, then CIA deputy director of plans, believed that Penkovsky's material on the MRBM enabled American decision makers to know exactly when the missiles would become operational, which in Helms's view gave Kennedy three extra days: "I don't know of any single instance where intelligence was more immediately valuable than at this time. Penkovsky's material had a direct application because it came right into the middle of the decision-making."[27]

British Assessments

When Robert Kennedy saw the photographic evidence from the U-2 overflights he remarked that "what I saw appeared to be no more than the clearing of a field for a farm or the basement of a house."[28] In other words, assessment depended upon the expertise of the photo-interpreters. The British Joint Intelligence Committee (JIC) assessment of October 26 was based on "the immediate advice of staff officers working in the field who have had a brief opportunity to study some of the more significant original photographic cover."[29] It generally concurred with the US appreciation, though some points of comparison are clear. The British assessment was based on more limited access to the raw data and adopted a more cautious view, including on the question of an IRBM base. On the critical issue of whether MRBMs were present, the British agreed with the Americans, though some caveats were entered. It was noted that the sites 50 miles southwest of Havana could be for the 650-nm range R-5/SS-3. This was indeed something the Americans had considered but discounted.[30] The British also thought it possible that the sites 100 nautical miles (nm) east of Havana could be for 300-nm range missiles. The JIC assessment provides no clues as to whether or how Penkovsky's material had been used in these assessments.

The JIC assessment did not disagree with the Americans, "but in view of the apparently limited site preparation there is the possibility that these are sites for the 650-nm missiles."[31] Presumably the information that the Americans possessed was also available to the British, though whether it was available to the analysts who worked on JIC(62)93 is another matter. The information in the R-12/SS-4 manual was helpful to analysts at the National Photographic Intelligence Center (NPIC) in identifying the missiles, as the deputy director of central intelligence, General Marshall Carter, told the president and his advisers on October 16.[32] Yet other sources were important, in particular photographs taken by military attachés at Red Army parades. As the head of the NPIC, Arthur Lundahl told the president on October 16, the CIA knew that the missiles were MRBMs because of their length.[33]

Identifying the type of missile was important: the R-5/SS-3 had a range estimated by US intelligence at 630 nautical miles, enabling coverage of seven Strategic Air Command (SAC) bomber/tanker bases; the 1020-nm R-12/SS-4 was within range of 18 bomber/tanker bases (plus one ICBM complex),[34] and some 58 cities each with a population of over 100,000, including Washington, accounting for some 92 million people.[35] These calculations reflected estimates of the range of the Soviet missiles that were shared by American and British intelligence, although it has recently been suggested that US intelligence underestimated the range of the Soviet MRBMs and IRBMs by over 20 percent.[36]

Richard Helms's claim that Penkovsky's intelligence gave the president "three extra days" (between October 16 and 19) is central to the argument that Penkovsky's intelligence was of vital importance during the crisis. An implicit assumption is that Kennedy might have launched a military attack on Cuba had he not understood the readiness state of the missiles. Certainly, the president's initial reaction on October 16 reflected his anger at Khrushchev's behavior, though this quickly gave way to a more sober and pragmatic disposition.[37] Some senior officials believed that the operational status of the missiles would determine when a decision to destroy them had to be taken and felt indeed that the readiness of the missiles was an indicator of Soviet intent. Within the White House, on October 16, there was disagreement over the implications of the operational condition of the missiles. Secretary of Defense Robert McNamara argued that if an air strike was to be launched it had to take place "prior to the time these missile sites become operational."[38] Secretary of State Dean Rusk, however, questioned whether the Soviets would automatically retaliate with their surviving missiles in Cuba against the United States.[39]

The JIC considered separately the likely Soviet responses to an American attack on Cuba.[40] They were clear that "on the basis of the evidence at present available we cannot assess when the missiles will be operational."[41] This raises the question of whether the British assessment reflected access to the R-12/SS-4 field manual. It should also be noted that regardless of Secretary McNamara's opinion, US consideration of an attack on, and invasion of, Cuba continued after the missiles began to become operational. Indeed, the joint chiefs of staff were still keen for an invasion of Cuba *after* all six MRBM sites were reported to be operational by October 27. Debate remains about whether Kennedy would have opted for military action if Khrushchev had not agreed to the withdrawal of the missiles (though McNamara believed the president would have "gone the extra mile for peace" to avoid escalation). How far Penkovsky's information was vital depends on contested assumptions about how President Kennedy and his senior officials saw the issues. Similarly, it is surely worth noting the conclusion of the president's national security assistant. McGeorge Bundy was present at all the ExComm meetings (whereas Richard Helms was present at none). His view was that Penkovsky had no "discernible relation" to the assessments and actions of the US government during the missile crisis.

Tactical Nuclear Missiles

The Cuban missile crisis occurred when missiles were discovered in Cuba that could strike the United States. Yet unbeknownst to the Americans (or the British), the Soviets had also deployed nearly a hundred tactical nuclear weapons. These went undiscovered until, in 1992, a Soviet general first began to disclose the existence of tactical nuclear weapons in Cuba intended for use against an American invasion.[42] These and subsequent revelations generated concern and debate about the risk of inadvertent nuclear war. The most conspicuous intelligence lapses concerned the 12 Luna (NATO designation FROG-7) short-range ballistic missiles and the 80 Meteor ground-launched cruise missiles (GLCMs). The latter were deployed at two sites, near Mariel in western Cuba and overlooking the US naval base at Guantánamo Bay.[43]

US intelligence had photographed Soviet cruise missiles, which were all taken to be Sopka coastal-defense systems. These were known not to be nuclear-capable. However, some of the missiles were in fact Meteor GLCMs that were nuclear-capable, and it has recently been revealed that they were armed with nuclear warheads.[44] Similarly, some of the Luna missiles were mistakenly assumed to be in conventional rather than nuclear configuration. These were first photographed on October 25, and there is no indication that the photography was shown to the British. The JIC were shown photographs of the cruise missiles and these appear to have included missile bases 400 miles east of Havana, near Mariel.[45] However, it is now clear that these were nuclear-capable land-attack missiles. The British accepted the US assessment that the missiles were anti-ship, and so shared in the error. The Meteors were in fact intended for use against Guantánamo Bay and against invading US forces. The GLCMs near Mariel would have been within range of where the US First Armored Division was planning its amphibious assault in the event of an invasion.

Penkovsky no more provided intelligence on Soviet tactical nuclear deployments than he did on the M/IRBMs. Despite his relationship with Marshal Varentsov, who was responsible for Soviet tactical missile forces, he provided no warning of Soviet tactical deployments. Yet he did provide intelligence which, in retrospect, was of potential significance to Western intelligence. Penkovsky had made reference to short-range rockets at his first meeting with his SIS and CIA case officers in London on April 20, 1961, when he said it was possible that there were "small-caliber rockets" there.[46] As noted above, Khrushchev only decided to install nuclear missiles, including a significant number of GLCMs, in the spring of 1962.[47] The decision to send short-range ballistic missiles was taken in September 1962.[48]

Perhaps more significantly, Penkovsky also warned his CIA and SIS case officers about Soviet tactical nuclear missiles in East Germany. At his first debriefing in London in April 1961, he explained that with the exception of Albania, all "People's Democracies" were being provided with ballistic missiles, including the R-11 missile."[49] Moreover, he stated that "in the DDR we now have four [rocket] brigades, and of these two brigades already are equipped with nuclear warheads."[50] Further details were provided at this and subsequent meetings.[51] Aside from the military significance to NATO, this challenged the existing belief that the Soviets had never deployed nuclear warheads outside the USSR.

The American intelligence community believed that because the Soviets had never deployed offensive nuclear weapons outside their own territory, they would not do so in Cuba.[52] It is not clear whether the British Joint Intelligence Committee was tasked with evaluating the subject. In September, however, British officials told the Pentagon that the Soviets probably did not have sufficient confidence in the future of Cuba to commit themselves to supply surface-to-surface missiles, in particular because of "the very serious repercussions which the supply of offensive weapons would have on United States policy."[53]

There is evidence that in October 1962, the director of the Joint Intelligence Bureau, Sir Kenneth Strong, and the Cabinet secretary-designate, Sir Burke Trend (who were attending a conference at CIA headquarters), told Ray Cline, the CIA deputy director for intelligence, that the Soviets would not put missiles into Cuba. This was shortly before he explained to them what the Americans had discovered.[54] It therefore seems clear that Penkovsky's information on Soviet nuclear deployments outside the USSR did not materially affect assessments of the likelihood of Soviet deployments in Cuba. Without close scrutiny of precisely how material from Penkovsky's debriefings was integrated into the American and British analytical processes, it is difficult to assess whether his information could have facilitated more accurate assessments of Soviet behavior.

Whether or not Penkovsky was crucial to averting war in October 1962, there is some reason to believe he may have tried to start one. In October 1961, Penkovsky was briefed on a procedure to enable him to provide the West with emergency warning of a Soviet attack.[55] This involved voiceless telephone calls to the American embassy that were to be followed by use of a dead letter box to give details (although the telephone calls were themselves sufficient to constitute emergency warning). Penkovsky was arrested on October 22. The emergency procedure was activated by the KGB on November 2.[56] The director of the CIA, John McCone, was told and he briefed President Kennedy on November 3.[57] This was after Khrushchev announced that he would withdraw the missiles from Cuba. Nevertheless, Soviet-American agreement had still not been formalized, and moreover, American (and British) nuclear forces remained at high states of readiness. The alert state of the US Strategic Air Command remained at the unprecedented Defense Condition 2, with its intercontinental ballistic missiles prepared for launch and a proportion of the B-52 strategic bomber force on airborne alert.

Why the KGB acted in this way is unclear, but the most plausible explanation is Raymond Garthoff's suggestion that Penkovsky deliberately tried to provoke a nuclear attack on the Soviet Union.[58] This would be consistent with his repeated suggestions to his handlers that they provide him with atomic demolition charges to plant at strategic points in Moscow to "decapitate" the Soviet system at the necessary moment.[59] Certainly one useful lesson to be drawn from the incident is never to start a nuclear war on the basis of heavy breathing on the telephone.

Value and Limits: Intentions and Capabilities

The case of Oleg Penkovsky provides instructive lessons in assessing the value and limitations of intelligence as well as in exploring how intelligence is represented by various kinds of authors. It should be clear from the above discussion that the lessons we draw depend on the interpretations we make. Several lessons are matters of robust and sometimes acrimonious debate, so conclusions drawn here may well be contested by other commentators. What is clear is that interpretations reflect, and in many cases are driven by, availability of sources. Here the study of intelligence parallels the practice of intelligence, and as with the practice, the study of intelligence is beset by various obstacles in accessing and interpreting the data. Evidence from British archives about intelligence and the Cuban missile crisis is limited and often fragmentary, whereas even understanding of the US intelligence cycle (of gathering/analysis/dissemination) is partial.

For those who believe that Penkovsky's intelligence was vital in the crisis, the key information concerned Soviet missile capabilities. It is clear, however, that Penkovsky provided no intelligence on Khrushchev's intentions or on any aspect of Operation Anadyr, the huge Soviet military effort to transport some 160 nuclear weapons, including 36 MRBMs and 24 IRBMs, as well as over 50,000 troops, across the world to Cuba. Penkovsky was capable of the deepest penetration that Western intelligence had achieved at that time, and was one of the most significant spies run by Western intelligence during the Cold War. This illustrates the limits of, and challenges to, the conduct of espionage against the Soviet Union.

One clear lesson concerns the importance of secrecy and the effective compartmentalization of information. Security in Moscow matched the security surrounding the movement of missiles across land and sea. Conversely, the case of Penkovsky demonstrates that the fact that an organization may have been penetrated by enemy agents does not mean that all their secrets are betrayed. When agents are caught (or flee), the business of damage assessment assumes a particular importance. What Khrushchev was told about Penkovsky's treachery is potentially of great significance in the crisis. Although public pronouncements from the Kennedy administration in October 1961 made clear that Washington knew that the missile gap was very much in America's favor, Khrushchev did not know how far the Americans understood Soviet strategic weakness.

Penkovsky provided testimony that was of potential significance concerning the deployment of Soviet tactical nuclear weapons. The suggestion that short-range rockets could have been deployed in Cuba by April 1961 was in fact in error. The evidence now shows that Khrushchev decided to send GLCMs in April 1962 and short-range battlefield missiles in September 1962. Penkovsky's revelations about "nuclear rockets" in East Germany do have a potential relevance not only to the question of deployments of short-range weapons in Cuba, but also the deployment of longer-range missiles. American officials appeared to believe that the Soviets had never deployed any nuclear weapons outside their own territory.[60] By October 1962, the British intelligence community said that they had "every reason to believe that shorter range tactical missiles are deployed in East Germany and possibly in Poland."[61] It remains unclear how the CIA assessed the material from Penkovsky's debriefing and how it was integrated into the analytical process.

In September 1962, the US intelligence community carefully considered whether the Soviet Union would deploy nuclear weapons in Cuba, but concluded that it "would be incompatible with Soviet practice to date and with Soviet policy as we presently estimate it. It would indicate a far greater willingness to increase the level of risk in US–Soviet relations than the USSR has displayed thus far, and consequently would have important policy implications with respect to other areas and other problems in East–West relations."[62] The assessment of CIA analysts that the Soviets would be unlikely to put nuclear weapons into Cuba was informed by the view that the Soviets had not deployed nuclear weapons outside Soviet territory. This suggests that the information Penkovsky supplied about the missiles in the DDR was not integrated into the assessment process. Most pieces of intelligence come in the guise of clues rather than answers. Invariably, it is through the analysis of all sources (including nonsecret sources) that assessments are made. As yet, we have an incomplete picture of how US (and a barely discernible picture of how UK) assessments were made, and of the role in this of material supplied by Penkovsky. Whether knowledge that the Soviets had put nuclear weapons into Eastern Europe would of itself have challenged the assumption that Khrushchev would not confront the US in Cuba is far from certain. Putting nuclear weapons on to Warsaw Pact territory raised different questions from putting them in Cuba. Most obviously, putting missiles within range of the USA would entail a greater provocation to Washington than anything in Eastern Europe.

Liaison

One area illuminated by the Penkovsky operation concerns intelligence liaison. Various commentators have suggested that the recent increase in international intelligence cooperation constitutes the most significant change within the world of intelligence over the previous decade which has wrought major qualitative changes in the nature of intelligence.[63] From the Western point of view, the need for such cooperation after 9/11 reflects the fact that other services may be better placed or better equipped to gather intelligence, particularly human intelligence. So it was with Penkovsky. In 1961, the CIA's capabilities in Moscow were at a fledgling stage of development. Operationally, the CIA had to rely on SIS.

Although Penkovsky was run for some seventeen months from the heart of the Soviet defense and security establishment, there was some recrimination when he was caught. In 1963, the director of the CIA told the president's Foreign Intelligence Advisory Board (PFIAB) that the CIA "thought the case was blown because of a penetration in the British government" who saw Penkovsky with Greville Wynne.[64] And Joseph Bulik, one of Penkovsky's two CIA case officers, later reflected that the "big lesson on the Penkovsky case is never to enter into a joint operation with another service."[65]

The CIA told the president on October 19 that two MRBM sites were operational, though they could not confirm whether the warheads were present (or were even in Cuba).[66] The British intelligence estimate of October 26 was based on what the British believed was original photography. However, the American assessment referred to two MRBM bases being operational. The original U-2 photography had identified the missiles before the missiles were adjudged operational. It was not until October 19 that the CIA concluded (and reported to Kennedy) that the MRBMs were operational. So the photographs that the British officials were shown (which have not been declassified) may not have corresponded with the American assessments they were given. The intelligence that the Americans were sharing may well have already been out of date.

It seems clear that the purpose of intelligence sharing was not designed to provide British input into American assessments; instead it was to help persuade the British of American judgments. This is consistent with evidence that when Ray Cline briefed Sir Kenneth Strong about the MRBMs, the American official misled him about when the missiles in Cuba were identified. By October 15, the US intelligence community was clear that MRBMs were present and Kennedy was briefed by the CIA the following morning. Strong was told, however, that it was not until October 20 that Kennedy "was presented with a great deal more material which was then generally accepted as demonstrating that there were offensive missiles in Cuba."[67] The issue of when the missiles were discovered and when the British were told was potentially sensitive. Although the British learned earlier than America's other allies, it is clear that the UK government was not consulted during the period in which Kennedy was making up his mind about how to react. Although the closeness of the intelligence relationship remains apparent, one lesson is that intelligence liaison can be a vehicle to influence or manipulate, rather than an exercise in sharing sources or assessments.

Lessons Learned?

If the lessons we draw inevitably reflect our interpretations, then we should also explore the foundation of those interpretations. In seeking to understand intelligence we should examine how sources inform arguments, and how agendas inform analyses. The case of Penkovsky provides rich material for such an undertaking and for scrutinizing the agendas of various writers and protagonists. Writing without access to archival sources, both academics and journalists are wholly dependent on the willingness of those with inside knowledge to provide explanation and information. Those who provide such information invariably have reasons to do so. Some are more obvious than others. Those who wish to present espionage as an important and legitimate activity of the state have an interest in emphasizing the importance of success, and as the remarks of Sir Dick White to his officers suggest, one specific reason for emphasizing the value of espionage operations is to praise and motivate those involved in mounting them.

One particular aspect of the Penkovsky case concerns the suggestion that far from being a prized Western asset, he was in fact a Soviet-controlled agent, disseminating disinformation to the West. Here, the literature on Penkovsky illuminates the realm of counterintelligence and what has commonly been termed "the wilderness of mirrors." The initial source of the claim that Penkovsky was a Soviet-controlled agent came from the controversial KGB defector, Anatoly Golitsyn. He persuaded some senior Western intelligence officials that Penkovsky was working for the Soviets.[68] James Angleton, the CIA's head of counterintelligence, initially endorsed Penkovsky's *bona fides*,[69] but came to believe that Penkovsky may have been a double agent. Edward Jay Epstein publicly expounded Angleton's doubts and suspicions about Soviet success in penetrating and deceiving Western intelligence, asserting, *inter alia*, that Penkovsky was "a Soviet postman at the time of the missile crisis."[70] In Britain, Angleton's doubts were shared by some British officials, whose views became public. This involved provision of information to selected specialist journalists, and then publication of the book *Spycatcher* by Peter Wright, a former officer of the Security Service (MI5).

What remains so difficult to explain is why, if Penkovsky was a conduit of disinformation, he would have been discontinued at the precise moment in October 1962 when communication channels between the leaderships were so crucial. The available evidence overwhelmingly suggests that Penkovsky was genuine. As Schecter and Deriabin argue: "he told too much, and what he provided was too damaging to Soviet interests."[71] Nevertheless, without access to the records of Soviet intelligence, for some there will always be a margin of doubt, even though the KGB defector, Oleg Gordievsky, is reported to have "told his debriefers quite categorically that Penkovskiy was a genuine defector-in-place."[72] Yet, surely, if Penkovsky had been an agent of disinformation he would have been used to reinforce the efforts of the Soviet leadership to project the illusion of strength rather than to expose the reality of weakness.

It is easy to disparage the views (and motives) of those who believed Penkovsky was a double agent. But the question of whether Penkovsky was (and remained) genuine was a necessary concern for the US and UK intelligence communities. CIA records indicate that the British were convinced perhaps more wholeheartedly, and at an earlier stage, than their American counterparts, though fear that their agent might be turned was an inevitable concern.[73] Tom Bower recounts that Sir Dick White believed Penkovsky might have been turned by the spring of 1962.[74] The most plausible explanation for the claims that Penkovsky was an instrument of disinformation lay not in Moscow conspiracies but in the personal and political agendas of his doubters in the West. Key to this are various claims and fears about Soviet deep penetration agents, and in particular the allegation that MI5 was penetrated at a very senior level. Several candidates emerged in both internal "molehunts" and public accusations, most notably the director-general, Sir Roger Hollis, and the deputy director, Graham Mitchell.[75] Penkovsky was important to these claims because if MI5 (or SIS) were penetrated at the highest levels, then the Soviet authorities would certainly have learned of his activities. Conversely, Gordon Brooke-Shepherd argues: "If it is accepted that Oleg Penkovsky was not a Soviet plant, then it must follow, as night follows day, that Roger Hollis, then head of MI5, was not a Soviet agent."[76] This logic, respective internal British government inquiries, and most notably revelations from Soviet archives and sources, including Oleg Gordievsky, all reinforce the view that the key assumptions and conclusions of the molehunters were simply wrong and that MI5 was not penetrated at a senior level at this time.[77]

One important lesson here is that we cannot fully assess intelligence without access to the adversary's files. Such arguments should not be taken to mean that history can be reduced to the simple distillation of information. And as Richard Aldrich has warned, archives cannot be taken to represent "an analogue of reality."[78] Historians and intelligence analysts are in the same business of converting evidence into judgments. Access to archives does not expunge bias, conscious or otherwise. Perhaps one of the more significant insights into the study of the Penkovsky case is that the study of intelligence presents enduring challenges of interpretation that, happily for historians, can benefit from archival and other disclosures but nevertheless remain fertile ground for reinterpretation and reevaluation.

One other important lesson to note concerns the fact that Penkovsky was a "walk-in." His recruitment as an agent had not been actively sought by Western intelligence. Indeed he had experienced considerable difficulty when offering his services to the CIA. Since 9/11 Western intelligence services have been greatly exercised about penetrating al-Qaeda and related terrorist groups. Penkovsky shows that the best spies may be volunteers, and that the existence of an adequate system for running and supporting these may be at least as important as active attempts at recruitment.

The case of Oleg Penkovsky is widely acclaimed as one of the most significant examples of espionage in history. His role in the Cuban missile crisis looms large in these claims. Some of what he provided illustrates the potential value of human intelligence as a source (though much of what he passed to the West has not been declassified and its importance remains difficult to assess). Penkovsky did provide a great deal of information about Soviet military capabilities as well as about debates within the Soviet military and the Soviet leadership. He provided some information about Soviet intentions at a time when most Western appreciations were based on induction or deduction. Yet not everyone would agree that Penkovsky's information was crucial to the outcome of the events of October 1962, and some would argue that the treatment of his case illustrates a tendency to exaggerate the significance of espionage in general. Certainly, human intelligence is but one source and its value often cannot be assessed in isolation from other sources. Moreover, what is clear from the discussion above is that however significant the intelligence that is provided, its value depends on how it is fed into the analytical process and then how any assessment is presented to decision makers.

NOTES

1. Christopher Andrew, *For the President's Eyes Only: Secret Intelligence and the American Presidency from Washington to Bush* (London: HarperCollins, 1995), 267–71, 273, 274, 290; ibid., *Secret Service—The Making of the British Intelligence Community* (London: Sceptre, 1986), 691–92; Tom Bower, *The Perfect English Spy: Sir Dick White and the Secret War, 1935–90* (London: Heinemann, 1995), 280–81; Gordon Brook-Shepherd, *The Storm Birds—Soviet Postwar Defectors* (London: Weidenfeld and Nicolson, 1988), 135–62; Ray S. Cline, *Secrets, Spies and Scholars, Blueprint of the Essential CIA* (Washington, DC: Acropolis Books, 1976), 198; Alastair Horne, *Macmillan 1957–1986, Volume II of the Official Biography* (Basingstoke: Macmillan, 1989), 369–70; Loch Johnson, *America's Secret Power: The CIA in a Democratic Society* (Oxford: Oxford University Press, 1989), 32, 84; Thomas Powers, *The Man Who Kept the Secrets: Richard Helms and the CIA* (New York: Alfred A. Knopf, 1979), 283; Anthony Verrier, *Through the Looking Glass—British Foreign Policy in an Age of Illusions* (London: Jonathan Cape, 1983), 193–233; Clarence Ashley, *CIA Spy Master* (Gretna, Louisiana: Pelican Publishing Co., 2004), 219–20, 225–26; Tennent H. Bagley, *Spy Wars: Moles, Mysteries, and Deadly Games* (London: Yale University Press, 2007), 52–55.

2. Verrier, *Through the Looking Glass*, 193; the accuracy of the quotation is questioned by Andrew, *Secret Service*, 786n. There is certainly no evidence that President Kennedy ever considered a preemptive nuclear attack on the USSR at any stage during the crisis.

3. Brook-Shepherd, *The Storm Birds*, 135.

4. John Le Carré, *Sunday Times*, October 1965.

5. Baroness Park of Monmouth, Letter to *The Times*, February 8, 2004.

6. Jerrold L. Schecter and Peter S. Deriabin, *The Spy Who Saved the World* (New York: Charles Scribner's Sons, 1992), 3.

7. For discussion, see Len Scott, "Espionage and the Cold War: Oleg Penkovsky and the Cuban Missile Crisis," *Intelligence and National Security* 14,3 (Autumn 1999): 23–47, and Charles Cogan and Len Scott, "The CIA and Oleg Penkovsky, 1961–63," in R. Gerald Hughes, Peter Jackson, and Len Scott (eds.), *Exploring Intelligence Archives: Enquiries into the Secret State* (London: Routledge 2008), 141–71.

8. Bruce J. Allyn, James G. Blight, and David A. Welch, *Back to the Brink: Proceedings of the Moscow Conference on the Cuban Missile Conference, January 27–28, 1989*, CSIA Occasional Paper No. 9 (Lanham, MD: University of America Press, 1992), 40.

9. McGeorge Bundy, *Danger and Survival: Choices about the Bomb in the First Fifty Years* (New York: Random House, 1988), 391–462.

10. Raymond L. Garthoff, *Reflections on the Cuban Missile Crisis* (Washington: The Brookings Institution, 1989), 63.

11. James G. Blight and David A. Welch, *Intelligence and the Cuban Missile Crisis*. Special Issue of *Intelligence and National Security* 13, 3 (Autumn 1998). Raymond

Garthoff's discussion of US intelligence and the crisis makes only two references to Penkovsky, Raymond L. Garthoff, "US Intelligence in the Cuban Missile Crisis," in Blight and Welch, *Intelligence and the Cuban Missile Crisis*, 53, 57n.

12. Edward Jay Epstein, *Deception: The Invisible War between the KGB and the CIA* (London: W. H. Allen, 1989), 79–80; Chapman Pincher, *Their Trade Is Treachery* (London: Sidgwick and Jackson, 1981), 183–89; idem, *Too Secret Too Long* (London: Sidgwick and Jackson, 1984), 341–45; idem, *The Secret Offensive: Active Measures: A Saga of Deception, Disinformation, Subversion, Terrorism, Sabotage and Assassination* (London: Sidgwick and Jackson, 1985), 72; Peter Wright (with Paul Greenglass), *Spycatcher* (Richmond, Australia: Heinemann, 1987), 204–12.

13. Epstein, *Deception*, 79.

14. Oleg Penkovskiy (Trans. Peter Deriabin), *The Penkovskiy Papers* (New York: Doubleday and Co. 1965).

15. Greville Wynne, *The Man From Moscow* (London: Hutchinson, 1967) and *The Man from Odessa* (London: Robert Hale, 1981); for challenges to the veracity of these accounts, see Nigel West, *Seven Spies Who Changed the World* (London: Mandarin, 1992), 178–212.

16. Brook-Shepherd, *The Storm Birds*, 135–62; Verrier, *Through the Looking Glass*, 193–233; see also Bower, *Perfect English Spy*, 280–81.

17. Schecter and Deriabin, *The Spy Who Saved the World*.

18. www.foia.cia.gov/penkovsky.asp.

19. The most notable 'source' was Sir Dick White, erstwhile head of SIS (and MI5), who was interviewed on the subject by Schecter and Deriabin, and by Bower.

20. The National Archives (TNA): CAB 129/111, J.I.C. (62)93(Final), "Cuba: Threat Posed By Soviet Missiles," October 26, 1962.

21. Aleksandr Fursenko and Timothy Naftali, '*One Hell of a Gamble': Khrushchev, Castro, Kennedy, and the Cuban Missile Crisis, 1958–1964* (London: John Murray, 1997), 188.

22. Svetlana V. Savranskaya, "Soviet Submarines in the Cuban Missile Crisis," in Lyle J. Goldstein, John B. Hattendorf, and Yuri M. Zhukov, special issue of *Journal of Strategic Studies* 28/2 (April 2005), 233–59: Fursenko and Naftali, '*One Hell of a Gamble*', 188–89; Anatoli I. Gribkov and William Y. Smith, *Operation Anadyr: US and Soviet Generals Recount the Cuban Missile Crisis* (Chicago: Edition Q, 1994), 27–28.

23. Schecter and Deriabin, *The Spy Who Saved the World*, 328; Andrew, *President's Eyes Only*, 285.

24. For details of the operation, see Schecter and Deriabin, *The Spy Who Saved the World*, passim. The first materials Penkovsky passed to the West, in August 1960, were to establish his bona fides. He was run as an agent or defector in place from April 1961.

25. Ibid., 104.

26. Aleksandr Fursenko and Timothy Naftali, *Khrushchev's Cold War: The Inside Story of an American Adversary* (London: W. W. Norton, 2006), 380.

27. Schecter and Deriabin, *The Spy Who Saved the World*, 334–35.
28. Robert F. Kennedy, *13 Days: The Cuban Missile Crisis October 1962* (London: Pan Books, 1969), 28.
29. JIC(62)93(Final), 1.
30. Albert Wheelon, Memo for Chairman, US Intelligence Board, Evaluation of Offensive Missile Threat in Cuba, October 17, 1962, Mary S. McAuliffe (ed.), *CIA Documents on the Cuban Missile Crisis* (Washington: Central Intelligence Agency, 1992), 176; see also "Joint Evaluation of Soviet Missile Threat in Cuba, 18 October 1962," McAuliffe, ibid, 187–91. The CIA knew, presumably assisted by Penkovsky's material, that the R-5/SS-3 was an early generation liquid-fueled missile, requiring radar guidance, compared to the R-12/SS-4, which possessed inertial guidance and could be configured with storable propellant; the absence of fuel tankers and radar equipment was an indicator that the R-12/SS-4 was being deployed. See Ernest R. May and Philip D. Zelikow (eds.), *The Kennedy Tapes: Inside the White House during the Cuban Missile Crisis* (Cambridge, MA: Harvard University Press, 1997), 78. The 73-feet-long R-12/SS-4 was compared with the 68-feet-long R-5/SS-3, and positive confirmation that some R-12/SS-4s were present was made on this basis by October 17, Wheelon, memo for Chairman; for discussion of length; see also May and Zelikow, *Kennedy Tapes*, 48–49.
31. JIC(62)93(Final).
32. May and Zelikow, *Kennedy Tapes*, 81–82; see also Dino A. Brugioni in *Eyeball to Eyeball, The Inside Story of the Cuban Missile Crisis*, ed. Robert F. McCort (New York: Random House, 1991), 199. For details of the NPIC's work during the crisis see Brugioni, ibid. 190 et seq.
33. May and Zelikow, *Kennedy Tapes*, 48.
34. Annex: Strategic Considerations, CIA Memo. Probable MRBM Sites in Cuba, October 16, 1962, McAuliffe, *CIA Documents*, 143.
35. May and Zelikow, *Kennedy Tapes*, 338.
36. Norman Polmar and John D. Gresham, *DEFCON-2: Standing on the Brink of Nuclear War during the Cuban Missile Crisis* (Hoboken, NJ: John Wiley and Sons, 2006), xxiii.
37. See Mark J. White, *The Cuban Missile Crisis* (Basingstoke: Macmillan, 1996), 115–34; May and Zelikow, *Kennedy Tapes*, 47–117.
38. Ibid., 57.
39. Ibid., 59.
40. TNA: JIC(62)99, October 27, 1962. "Possible Soviet Response to a U.S. Decision to Bomb or Invade Cuba."
41. JIC(62)93(Final).
42. James G. Blight, Bruce J. Allyn, and David A. Welch, *Cuba on the Brink: Castro, the Missile Crisis and the Soviet Collapse* (New York: Pantheon Books, 1993); and Gribkov and Smith, *Operation Anadyr*.
43. Fursenko and Naftali, *Khrushchev's Cold War*, 473; Steven Zaloga, *The Kremlin's Nuclear Sword: The Rise and Fall of Russia's Strategic Nuclear Forces 1945–2000* (Washington, DC: Smithsonian Institution Press, 2002), 84. For detailed

discussion and important new evidence, see Michael Dobbs, *One Minute to Mid-night: Kennedy, Khrushchev, and Castro on the Brink of Nuclear War* (London: Hutchinson, 2008).

44. Dobbs, ibid, 124–27, 178–81.
45. Ibid, 177.
46. CIA: Mtg. No. 1 (London), April 20, 1961, para. 110; see also Schecter and Deriabin, *The Spy Who Saved the World*.
47. Richard Ned Lebow and Janice Gross Stein, *We All Lost the Cold War* (Princeton, NJ: Princeton University Press, 1993), 72–77; Garthoff, "US Intelligence," 6–42; Fursenko and Naftali, *'One Hell of a Gamble,'* 166–83.
48. Fursenko and Naftali, ibid., 210, 211–12.
49. CIA: Mtg. 1, 20 April 1961, paras. 40–41; see also Schecter and Deriabin, *The Spy Who Saved the World*, 68. The R-11 was a 150 km 'operational-tactical missile'; the ground forces version (NATO designation: SS-1) became known as the SCUD, David Holloway, *Stalin and the Bomb: The Soviet Union and Atomic Energy 1939–56* (New Haven, CT: Yale University Press, 1994), 324.
50. CIA: Mtg. 1, April 20, 1961, para. 42; Schecter and Deriabin, *The Spy Who Saved the World*, 68.
51. CIA: Mtg. 1, April 20, 1961, paras. 101–2; Mtg. No. 4 at Leeds, April 23, 1961, para. 36; Mtg. 12, London, May 1, 1961, paras. 19, 25, 62; see also Schecter and Deriabin, *The Spy Who Saved the World*, 149–50.
52. For discussion of US intelligence and the crisis, see Blight and Welch, *Intelligence and the Cuban Missile Crisis*; Brugioni, *Eyeball to Eyeball*; Charles C. Cogan, "A Surprise, Surprise et Demie: Le Role du Renseignement," in Maurice Vaisse (ed.), *Europe et la Crise de Cuba* (Paris: Armand Colin, 1993); Peter Usowski, "John McCone and the Cuban Missile Crisis: A Persistent Approach to the Intelligence-Policy Relationship," *International Journal of Intelligence and CounterIntelligence*, 2, 4 (Winter 1988); David Welch, "Intelligence Assessment in the Cuban Missile Crisis," *Queen's Quarterly* (Summer 1993); Jonathan Renshon, "Mirroring Risk: The Cuban Missile Estimation," *Intelligence and National Security*, 24, 3 (June 2009).
53. TNA: FO 371/162374, I.J.M. Sutherland, minute, September 12, 1962, AK1201/20/G.
54. Richard Deacon, *'C': A Biography of Sir Maurice Oldfield* (London: Futura, 1984), 135.
55. Schecter and Deriabin, *The Spy Who Saved the World*, 262–63, 284–87, 347–48.
56. When the episode was first disclosed by Garthoff, his source had suggested that the phone call had been made on October 22. Raymond L. Garthoff, *Reflections on the Cuban Missile Crisis* (Washington: The Brookings Institution, 1987), 39–41. For details, see *The Spy Who Saved the World*, 337–52.
57. CIA: John A. McCone, Memorandum, November 5, 1962 (courtesy of the US Information and Privacy Coordinator); Schecter and Deriabin, *The Spy Who Saved the World*, 346–47.
58. Garthoff, *Reflections on the Cuban Missile Crisis*, 64–65.

59. Schecter and Deriabin, *The Spy Who Saved the World*, 74 et seq.; Ashley, *CIA Spymaster*, 194, 203, 232–34.

60. It is also now clear that Soviets had previously stationed medium-range missiles in East Germany. See Matthias Uhl and Vladimir I. Ivkin, "Operation Atom: The Soviet Union's Stationing of Nuclear Missiles in the German Democratic Republic, 1959," *Cold War International History Project Bulletin*, Issue 12/13, Fall/Winter 2001, 299–307.

61. TNA: CAB 182/11, JIC Missile Threat Co-ordination Subcommittee, JIC (MT) (62) 7th Meeting, October 30, 1962.

62. *FRUS, 1961–1963, Volume X*: Document 433, Special National Intelligence Estimate, SNIE 85-3-62, "The Military Build-up in Cuba," September 19, 1962, 1070–80.

63. Stephen Lander, "International Intelligence Co-operation: An Inside Perspective," *The Cambridge Review of International Affairs*, 17, 3 (2004), 481–93; Richard Aldrich, "Global Intelligence Co-operation versus Accountability: New Facets to an Old Problem," *Intelligence and National Security* 24, 1 (February, 2009): 26–56.

64. CIA: Penkovsky Case, June 26, 1962.

65. Schecter and Deriabin, *The Spy Who Saved the World*, 35; see also Bower, *Perfect English Spy*, 273. According to his fellow CIA case officer, George Kisevalter, however, Bulik had an indifferent relationship with his SIS counterparts. This was in contrast to Kisevalter, who retained a very positive view of the British. Ashley, *CIA Spy Master*, 221–22, 227–28.

66. Ibid., 173; see also Joint Evaluation of Soviet Missile Threat in Cuba, October 19, 1962, McAuliffe, *CIA Documents*, 203–8.

67. TNA: PREM 11/3972, Note for the Record [of a meeting between Prime Minister, Foreign Secretary and General Strong, Director of the Joint Intelligence Bureau], November 19, 1962.

68. For Golitsyn on Penkovsky, see Anatoliy Golitsyn, *New Lies for Old—The Communist Strategy of Deception and Disinformation* (London: Bodley Head, 1984), 54.

69. Schecter and Deriabin, *The Spy Who Saved the World*, 204–205; Tom Mangold, *Cold Warrior—James Jesus Angleton: The CIA's Master Spy Hunter* (New York: Simon and Schuster, 1991), 77–78.

70. Epstein, *Deception*, 79.

71. Schecter and Deriabin, *The Spy Who Saved the World*, 194.

72. Mangold, *Cold Warrior*, 78.

73. CIA: Memorandum for Record: Assessment of [Penkovsky], July 13, 1961.

74. Bower, *Perfect English Spy*, 282.

75. For an account of the molehunts, see Bower, *Perfect English Spy*, 311–40; for an account of how they became public, see Richard V. Hall, *A Spy's Revenge* (London; Penguin, 1987); see also Chapman Pincher, *The Spycatcher Affair: A Web of Deception* (London: Sidgwick and Jackson, 1988).

76. Brook-Shepherd, *Storm Birds*, 62; Mangold makes the same argument for both Hollis and Mitchell, *Cold Warrior*, 77–79. It is conceivable that Soviet intelligence might have learned of Penkovsky's activities from a mole but calculated that moving against him would risk their source. The KGB had apparently chosen not to close down the Western signals intelligence operation in Berlin in 1954–55 presumably to protect their source in SIS, George Blake, even though this was at considerable cost to the Soviet military. Joseph C. Evans, "Berlin Tunnel Intelligence: A Bumbling KGB," *International Journal of Intelligence and CounterIntelligence* 9, 1 (Spring 1996).

77. For Gordievsky's views on Penkovsky, see Christopher Andrew and Oleg Gordievsky, *KGB: The Inside Story of Its Foreign Operations from Lenin to Gorbachev* (Hodder and Stoughton, 1990), 389–90, 393–95.

78. Richard Aldrich, *The Hidden Hand: Britain, America and Cold War Secret Intelligence* (London: John Murray, 2001), 6.

DOCUMENT 9.1:   TNA: CAB 129/111, JIC(62)93(Final), 'Cuba: Threat Posed By Soviet Missiles', October 26, 1962

TOP SECRET

C. (62) 166

26th October, 1962

CABINET

CUBA: THREAT POSED BY SOVIET MISSILES

Note by the Acting Secretary of the Cabinet

The attached report by the Joint Intelligence Committee is circulated for the information of the Cabinet.

(Signed) A.L.M. Cary

Cabinet Office, S.W.1

26th October, 1962.

TOP SECRET   Copy No. 37

J.I.C.(62)93(Final)

26th October, 1962   IMMEDIATE

UK EYES ONLY

CABINET

JOINT INTELLIGENCE COMMITTEE

THE THREAT POSED BY SOVIET MISSILES IN CUBA

Report by the Joint Intelligence Committee

Object

The object of this short study is to comment on the US assessment of the Soviet offensive build-up in Cuba.

Basis of Assessment

2.   The assessment is based entirely on photographic evidence so far released to us by the US authorities. A firm UK assessment is difficult until more basic data is available for detailed study by our own photo-interpreters. Our preliminary comments below are based on the immediate advice of staff officers working in this field who have had a brief opportunity to study some of the more significant original photographic cover. We would like to record here our appreciation of the US authorities for permitting this.

DOCUMENT 9.1:   TNA: CAB 129/111, JIC(62)93(Final), 'Cuba: Threat Posed By Soviet Missiles', October 26, 1962 *(Continued)*

Surface-to-Surface Missile Launch Sites

3.   IRBM

   (a)   US Position: There are two launch areas located about 25 nm West of Havana, each of four pads, under construction, which might be ready for
   operational use by early December 1962.

   (b)   Comment: If these are IRBM they will have a range of 2200 nm, extending from Hudson Bay through California to Lime, and be capable of striking a
   selection of strategic targets in the USA. We are satisfied that these two launch areas represent surface-to-surface missile sites capable of launching missiles with nuclear warheads. On the basis of the evidence available we cannot positively identify the sites as being associated with the 2200 nm missile.

TOP SECRET

If they are not associated with this missile we would expect them to be associated with a missile with a range of up to 1100 nm. In the case of these being 1100 nm missiles they would still be capable of covering an arc from Washington to the Panama Canal, which would include many significant strategic targets in South East USA. On the basis of the evidence available we cannot assess when the missiles will be operational.

4.   MRBM

   (a)   US Position: There are three launch areas located some 50 nm South-West of Havana, each of four pads. These are of a simple type involving the minimum site preparations. Two are judged to be operational, with missiles and transporter/erectors in position. In each case four missiles are on the pads and four more are in a holding position.

   (b)   Comment: If these are MRBM sites with a range of 1100 nm, they could strike targets from Washington to the Panama Canal, as described in para. 3(b)
   above. We do not disagree with the US assessment but in view of the apparently limited site preparation there is the possibility that these sites are for the 650 nm missile. If this were the case they would cover the whole of the Florida peninsula including Cape Canaveral. On the basis of the evidence at present available we cannot assess whether the missiles are already operational.

DOCUMENT 9.1:   TNA: CAB 129/111, JIC(62)93(Final), 'Cuba: Threat Posed By Soviet Missiles', October 26, 1962 *(Continued)*

(c)   US Position: There are two more launch areas located about 100 nm East of Havana. These are a field type which require no permanent site preparation. They are judged to be operational, with missile trailers and erector/launcher equipment present.

(d)   Comment We do not know the range allocated by the US to missiles associated with those areas. In view of the nature of the site, we consider that these may be for missiles with a range of' about 300 nm and able therefore to strike at installations in Key West. Because of the limited photography available to us we are unable to see the missiles themselves. However, it must be assumed that they are there, in view of the associated equipment present; although on the basis of the evidence at present available we cannot assess whether the missiles are already operational

Shore-to-Ship Missiles

5.   (a)   US Position: There are four launch areas: two 400 nm East of Havana, one at Cabo Lucrecia and one on the Isle of Pines. These also each contain at least two launchers for cruise-type missiles and are to judged to be operational, with missiles on site.

(b)   Comment: We accept this assessment. These weapons are believed to be anti-ship and to have a range of at least 30 nm.

- 2 –

TOP SECRET

Surface-to-Air Missiles

(a)   US Position: 24 SA-2 sites each with six launch positions are deployed, with their
acquisition and guidance radars, throughout the length of Cuba, providing
continuous cover of most of the island. 17 of' these sites are judged to be operational now. Two SAM support facilities have also been seen.

(b)   Comment: We accept this assessment.

Naval Missiles

(a)   US Position There are 12 KOMAR-type patrol vessels, each mounting two launchers.

(b)   Comment: These are primarily anti-ship missiles with a range of 10-15 nm. They could also be used in support of land operations but the missile is believed to be limited to an H. E. warhead.

DOCUMENT 9.1:   TNA: CAB 129/111, JIC(62)93(Final), 'Cuba: Threat Posed By Soviet Missiles', October 26, 1962 *(Continued)*

Air-to-Air Missiles

  (a)   US Position: The presence of least 39 FISHBED fighters has been reported.

  (b)   Comment: These could be a version capable of carrying air-to-air missiles. The
range of this aircraft enables them to operate over the Florida peninsula.

Nuclear Warheads

  (a)   US Position: Some sites which are probably for storing nuclear warheads are at present under construction.

  (b)   Comment: We have no evidence on which to base a firm <u>conclusion</u> but we agree that these sites may be for storing of nuclear warheads. Neither we nor the US authorities have any evidence on which to judge whether nuclear warheads have or have not reached Cuba.

Conclusions

Our conclusions at this stage are:-

  (a)   We are in agreement with the US authorities that a Soviet MRBM capability is being built up in Cuba which could, in our assessment, be up to 1100 nm. Based on the evidence available we are not in a position to assess whether the capability extends (as the US authorities believe) to the IRBM i.e. 2200 nm.

  (b)   Provided nuclear warheads are available, missile units in Cuba could be allocated certain strategic targets on the American Continent at present allocated to other Soviet forces. If all known sites are completed, we estimate that the overall Soviet initial launch capability against the US will have increased significantly by the end of 1962.

(Signed) Hugh Stephenson

DOCUMENT 9.2: CIA Memo: Meeting No. 1 (London) at Mount Royal Hotel, 20 April 1961

Document can be found at www.foia.cia.gov/penkovsky.asp, docs. 141-50. Underscoring in the document indicates the redaction of still classified material.

Meeting #1 (London), 20 April 1961

1.   The meeting was held at the Mount Royal Hotel. Participants in the meeting were:

   _____   Harold Hazlewood

   _____   Michael Fairfield

   _____   Joseph Walk

   _____   George McAdam

2.   By means of a prearranged meeting set up through Mr Greville WYNNE as organised by Mr _____ (details of which are recorded elsewhere), Subject was expected at any time convenient for him to take leave of his companion under the pretext of turning in for the night. This was expected to occur at any time after 2100 hours. Subject's instructions were to report to Room 712 which was engaged by Mr Hazlewood. Since Room 360 appeared to be far superior as a meeting place because it was much larger, with adequate seating and capacity and, more important, it was an interior court thus avoiding street noises and in addition since a clandestine recorder could be more conveniently concealed in this room, it was decided to move to Room 361. Mr Hazlewood, hereafter referred to as H. and Mr _____, hereafter referred to as J., waited for the arrival of Subject in Room 712 for the purpose of escorting him to Room 360 where the other two members of the party waited. Subject arrived at Room 712 at about 2140 hours and after being greeted by H. and J. was told that a more adequate meeting area was set up in Room 360, to which room Subject was conducted. Subject arrived in Room 360 at 2150 hours. Upon entering Subject was introduced to G. and N. and all persons sat in a circle with a small serving table in the middle.

3.   G: Would you prefer to speak Russian or English? S: I would much rather speak Russian because I can express myself much better in Russian. G: Very well, then. S: I graduated from the Military-Diplomatic Academy in 1953. In 1955 I went to Turkey. My working language there was English. I had many difficulties there and during the past four years I simply forgot much of my English by disuse. Well, Gentlemen, let's get to work. We have a great deal of important work to do. G: You have already introduced yourselves

DOCUMENT 9.2:   CIA Memo: Meeting No. 1 (London) at Mount Royal Hotel, 20 April 1961 *(Continued)*

upstairs. S: Yes. G: Therefore you do know now that you are in good hands. S: Yes, and I have thought about this for a long time and I have attempted to make this contact taking a very devious path about which I feel I must report to you in full. G: You must know that we are in receipt of your original letter. S: You mean the one I gave to the two teachers (the two American tourists). If you knew how many grey hairs I have acquired since that time; if you had only marked the signal just so I would have known that the message got into the proper hands. I worried so much about this. (To reassure Subject J. pulled out the original copy of Subject's first letter referred to above including the photograph he enclosed of Colonel Charles PEEKE, US Military Attache, Ankara, at the time Subject served his tour there.) S: Yes, that is the photograph I sent and Colonel PEEKE was then Military Attache there. G: This was shown you to reassure you and in two words I can tell you why a response was not made to you immediately after. . . ...

. . . Committee and our OTDEL consists of officers who are working under cover in Moscow. We have a total of 58 officers including myself. In all ministries which have any foreign relations, there are strategic intelligence officers. As members of these ministries and committees thereof they have contact with and conduct intelligence against visiting foreign delegations, tourists, lecturers, etc.

40. S: There is also a Fifth Directorate. The chief of this directorate is the former chief of the MDA of whom you (G.) have reminded me – Gen. Leit. KOCHETKOV. This directorate is concerned with the placement of REZIDENTURAS in all countries including the countries of People's Democracies, and the preparation of diversionists groups. This directorate studies all critical targets such as bridges, tunnels etc. and analyses drop zones for large scale operations for General Staff use as well as small group operations for behind-the-lines sabotage groups. G: Are they now engaged in sabotage activities? S: No, they are not placed in critical areas where they will set when the order is given. G: In all countries, including the Democracies? S: In all countries, but in the Democracies it is of a different nature, like stay-behind, because we do not conduct active intelligence against the Democracies. We have a Tenth Directorate of the General Staff which deals with all matters of a military nature with the People's Democracies through the military attaches and this Directorate controls the delivery of all rocket weapons, in the countries of People's Democracies.

41. S: In this year all countries of People's Democracies must be furnished rocket weapons. VARENTSOV and his people are also working on the development of bases, storage areas, launching sites, and the training of cadres for the countries of People's Democracies. The rockets which we are now delivering to these countries are those which are now being mass-produced such as the R-11 about which I gave you a report. This one, and in addition all those which are on production lines, are being given to China and all other countries of People's Democracies. (Note: later Subject emphasised that Albania was the one exception, due to the recent 'revisionistic' attitude of Gen. Enver Hoxha.)

42. S: In the DDR we now have four brigades and of these two brigades already are equipped with atomic warheads. They also have special storage facilities and the engineers of the Artillery Academy Dzerzhinskogo are working on this. This Academy is now in the hands of MOSKALENKO, which occurred after the accidental death of Marshal NEDELIN due to a rocket disaster. That was not an aircraft accident. The report was a big lie deliberately reported to the world. But I will give you all details of this separately. I wrote a little about this but I must add to it because it is impossible to write all details.

43. G: Let me fill out the GRU organisational chart. S: I have given you five directorates, and there is no Sixth Directorate so designated. There is a separate Eighth OTDEL called the Coding Section and there are Rear Service unites (SLUZHBY TYLA) which provide logistical support such as clothing and even diamonds and gold for agent operations.

CHAPTER 10

Avoiding Surprise

The Nicoll Report and Intelligence Analysis

MICHAEL S. GOODMAN

Editors' Note:

As the official historian of the Joint Intelligence Committee (JIC), Michael Goodman uses the files that have been released into the public domain to discuss the Nicoll Report, an innovative study that has been underexplored in the extant literature. Goodman highlights the timeless problems faced by intelligence analysts, the attempts of governments to combat the major pitfalls, and the success of the Nicoll Report as a critique of government intelligence over the past twenty-seven years.

S itting at the top of the intelligence pyramid is the Joint Intelligence Committee (JIC). Created in 1936, it rose to prominence during World War II. Since that time it has been central to every aspect of British intelligence, from allotting requirements and priorities to the collectors, through the process of strategic assessment and analysis, to the dissemination of intelligence reports to policymakers. At various points in its existence chairmen of the JIC have tried to evaluate their product: How well are JIC assessments written? Are they produced on the right subject? Do they satisfy the demands of their customers? At similar points in the past, efforts have been made to review previous assessments and check their accuracy and veracity. The most important of these, but one that has hitherto received scant attention, is the Nicoll Report.[1]

In 1980, Douglas Nicoll, a veteran of the British intelligence community, was asked to produce a series of case studies involving foreign acts of aggression, and to assess how well the intelligence community had done in predicting and monitoring the progress of events. Nicoll was well suited to the task: he had worked at Bletchley Park for most of the wartime years (1941–45), and following a short spell in Oxford to attain a master's degree, he joined the infant Government Communications Headquarters (GCHQ), remaining there until 1980 and his commission for the Cabinet Office.[2]

Nicoll's work was not the first study that the JIC had commissioned to look into its past efforts. Following its meteoric rise in stature toward the end of WWII, the JIC began to consider why prewar intelligence had often been lacking, and what might be done to ensure that intelligence was sufficient for any future crisis. The central issue was, of course, the Soviet Union. Arguments in the mid-1940s between the relatively hawkish chiefs of staff, and the more dove-like Foreign Office, often left the JIC trapped in the middle. The result, as the JIC readily admitted, was that there were intelligence gaps in the coverage of the Soviet Union that were extremely difficult to fill.[3]

The response was an innovative and extremely interesting review, produced by the JIC in 1951, reexamining their past assessments of Communist intentions since 1947. The rationale behind the study was made clear in its introduction: "in order to determine to what extent they have been proved correct by subsequent events and, in cases where their conclusions have been proved wrong, to discover why false conclusions were drawn."[4] In the period 1947–51, the study concluded that thirty-three different assessments had either proved to be correct, or at least not yet proven to be incorrect. In comparison, only three had proved to be wrong, and for these the JIC considered what had caused the error.

Despite the favorable statistics, in a frank statement it was conceded that "our assessment of Communist intentions has not, however, been as good as the small number of our miscalculations suggests. In the first place we failed altogether to forecast the blockade of Berlin in 1948 and the attack on South Korea in 1950." Furthermore, a comment was also made on the nature and tone of the assessments themselves: "we have also, in many cases, drafted our conclusions somewhat equivocally and so allowed ourselves a fairly wide margin of error. The present tendency is to make the conclusions more definite."[5]

So what had gone wrong? In the example of the Korean War the JIC had concluded that the Chinese would not "embark on operations."[6] The reasoning behind this, supposedly not based on intelligence but rather on a reading of the Communist leadership, was that the Chinese would not dare risk war with the United Nations. In reality, just a few weeks after the assessment was approved, the Chinese army swept into Korea and attacked the UN forces based there. How had the JIC managed to get their assessment completely wrong? Once more the 1951 review is very honest in its examination of the intelligence community's failings, and in which two factors are prevalent:

a. That our intelligence about Communist intentions in the Far East is even less adequate than our intelligence about the Soviet Union, largely due to the fact that we obtain less SIGINT on China; and
b. That we do not yet understand the mind of the Chinese Communist leaders.[7]

The report was approved by the JIC in December 1951, and the Secretary of the Committee was tasked with circulating it "for examination in Departments, in order that study should be made of the lessons to be learnt from previous intelligence appreciations and of measures to improve future estimates."[8] Unfortunately, such optimistic aspirations were never fully realized: despite efforts to improve the quality and quantity of collected intelligence, and with various revisions to the analytical process, no in-depth study was commissioned to follow up on such changes. Indeed, it would not be until almost thirty years later, with the assignment of Douglas Nicoll, that the JIC would entertain such a large-scale review again.

Unlike the 1951 effort, Nicoll's study was unique in its scope, breadth, and depth. The report, officially titled "The JIC and Warning of Aggression," had, as it states at the outset, four main aspirations:

a. to describe the actual sequence of events in the light of the information now available;
b. to consider the JIC's performance in reporting the crisis and assessing the likelihood of war;
c. to summarize the use made of the intelligence; and
d. to consider the sources used.[9]

In examining these four elements, Nicoll focused on seven detailed case studies: the Soviet invasion of Czechoslovakia (1968); the Egyptian/Syrian invasion of Israel (1972–73); the Chinese attack on Vietnam (1978–79); the Soviet invasion of Afghanistan (1979); the Iraqi attack on Iran (1979–80); the Soviet attack on Iran (1980); and Soviet intervention in Poland (1980–81). The full report is the length of a monograph and remains classified. Each case study follows the pattern above, which, perhaps unintentionally, replicates the various stages of the frequently cited "intelligence cycle." Each section, therefore, includes a vast amount of detail on how information was collected in each instance, what it comprised, what assessments were produced, and what the policymaking departments did as a result. The declassified extract, reprinted below, is the conclusion to the report. In fact, this is the more interesting component of the study, because it is in these pages that Nicoll attempts to extract the lessons from the case studies. The Nicoll Report was discussed by the JIC at its meeting on March 4, 1982, and considered itself, in Lawrence Freedman's words, "alert to the lessons to be learnt." Within a few weeks a copy of the report had been sent and received by the prime minister, Margaret Thatcher. The timing was critical: just a few days later the Argentine military junta authorized the invasion of the Falkland Islands.[10]

Before an examination of the Nicoll Report can take place, it is worth pausing briefly to outline the different constituent elements of the British intelligence machinery as they existed in the early 1980s prior to the Falklands war. Spinning in the center, as it were, was the JIC. This organization comprised a deliberate and disparate mix of people: a Foreign Office chairman, the heads of the intelligence agencies, and representatives from policy departments in the shape of the Foreign Office, Ministry of Defence, and the Treasury.[11] The JIC was responsible for several aspects: it was involved, in consultation with policymakers, for setting the intelligence community's requirements and priorities; but above all, its role was to provide assessments for senior policymakers incorporating all relevant information, be it from diplomatic reporting, covert sources, or open media. It therefore provided a top-down function, in looking after the health and well-being of the intelligence agencies; and also a bottom-up function, in producing intelligence assessments for senior readers.

Functioning in tandem were the intelligence agencies. Less relevant in this context was the Security Service, MI5, responsible for counterespionage. Far more important was the Secret Intelligence Service (SIS) and GCHQ. The former of these was created to garner human intelligence, usually operating out of British embassies abroad. GCHQ complemented this function by the interception of communications intelligence and the provision of signals intelligence. Both, therefore, were collection agencies, with limited analytical functions. Much of this latter work was done within the Defence Intelligence Staff (DIS), part of the Ministry of Defence but responsible for providing assessments on a wide array of topics, many nonmilitary in nature.

The majority of assessments, at a strategic level, were, however, within the Joint Intelligence Organization, a broad outfit that included the JIC, but also the assessments staff and the current intelligence groups (CIGs). These two bodies were the engine rooms, boilers, and stokers of the British intelligence machinery. The Assessments Staff, then a group of approximately twenty civil servants, were transferred to the Cabinet Office (in which the JIC resided) for two to three years. Each was assigned a topic or "desk," and was therefore responsible for producing assessments. To this end they wrote the papers, using all available information, both classified and unclassified, and then the information was discussed and dissected in CIGs, essentially mini-JICs, with all the relevant experts from across Whitehall. Once a paper had been approved by the experts, it was passed to the JIC for comment, discussion, and final approval, and then disseminated to policymakers.

Central to everything, then, was the JIC; it is for this very reason that one former chairman has called it the "final arbiter of intelligence."[12] Given the nature of the declassified record, we cannot access the JIC's terms of reference as they existed in the early 1980s. We can get a recent glimpse, though, from its 1974 incarnation. At this time, the JIC had various responsibilities:

a. To give direction to, and to keep under review, the organization and working of intelligence as a whole at home and overseas in order to ensure efficiency, economy and prompt adaptation to changing requirements;
b. To present at agreed intervals statements of intelligence requirements and priorities;
c. To assemble, evaluate, and present such joint intelligence on events, situations and problems in the field of external affairs and defense as may be required;

d. To coordinate the activities of the United Kingdom joint intelligence organizations overseas;
e. To supervise and maintain liaison with appropriate intelligence agencies;
f. To keep under review threats to security at home and overseas and to deal with such security problems as may be referred to it.[13]

The JIC's remit, then, was a broad one. The Nicoll Report was commissioned by the prime minister and it fell to the JIC to commission it. Thus, within the structure of the case studies, the four aspects to deal with, and the JIC's terms of reference, Douglas Nicoll set out to examine how well the JIC had done.

The JIC and the Warning of Aggression

From the outset Nicoll identified the central role of the JIC in both intelligence and its wider governmental responsibilities: "the provision of warning of possible aggressive action by the USSR against the West must be the highest priority requirement laid upon the JIC" (para. 2). In stating that the JIC should act as the first and last watchdog of aggression, the report immediately calls into question the standard role of the committee, something that Lord Franks would subsequently discuss in his inquiry into the Falklands invasion. Since its creation in 1936, the JIC had been a body designed to assess strategic intelligence. In other words, its major preoccupation in the Cold War was identifying trends in Soviet behavior (intentions) and monitoring their advances in research and development of weapons (capabilities). This long-term role was a major factor identified by Nicoll, yet should the committee act as the body to warn that an attack was imminent?

Its terms of reference were rather vague on this, but the JIC was tasked with "keeping under review threats." The question was, how should this work in practice? As it happens this had been a problem that had been discussed as far back as the 1940s, when, according to its secretary, the JIC was unofficially and informally made responsible for monitoring foreign threats. There is no question that this was the JIC's function, but as became clear with the Franks review, if a country or subject like the Falklands is low on the list of priorities, how in practice should the JIC be responsible for monitoring a threat presented to it? This question is never answered.

In considering the preparations by various countries to launch acts of aggression, the JIC had to distinguish between intentions and capabilities: that is, whether a country had the political will to launch an attack, and whether it had the practical means to do so. Nicoll clearly identifies this in stating that JIC reports should include such information in advising ministers whether or not an attack is imminent. However, there are differences between the two, and in particular what intelligence can reveal about them. In this way, it is far easier to spot and count the number of tanks than it is to gauge whether or not an attack will take place. There is a relationship between capabilities and intent, but it is not a linear or simple one, and the two are usually only joined when considering the "threat."[14]

In many ways, then, such ideas can be related to the nature of collected information itself, and what the relative strengths and weaknesses are of, for example, human intelligence as opposed to photographic reconnaissance. It is these areas that can only be hinted at in the report, primarily because they are the areas that have been redacted. However, there are some allusions to this when, for instance, Nicoll states that "intelligence on the preparation of the aggressor force has been reasonably good, though . . . the evidence of preparation is liable to come late in the process" (para. 9). This relates not only to what intelligence can realistically reveal, but also highlights something of the difference between estimating capabilities (in this case physical military preparation) as opposed to intent (the decision to go).

Given the inherent difficulties in gauging intentions Nicoll concludes that it is "quite essential . . . to handle the intelligence on political and military developments together, and to understand if possible the developing outlook and policy of the potential aggressor in political/military terms, right from the beginning" (para. 11). Related to this are the enemy decision-making processes, as identified by the JIC, which would be followed in the build-up to an attack. Thus, to provide a useful warning function—in other words to be able to provide evidence of the threat before it is too late—the JIC, in Nicoll's mind, had to be convinced of three factors: "a) that the country would have the political will to undertake political action; b) that military action would achieve a desired political end; and c) that specific military preparations to that end have begun" (para. 3).

To highlight just how difficult a task the intelligence agencies faced, Nicoll emphasized that "the essential point to note is that while planning, preparation and training may last for up to a year from the initial order to the armed forces to prepare, the period of readying, mobilization and deployment of forces may be quite short" (para. 16). In this context, through the detailed analysis of several case studies of Soviet aggression, the evidence was taken to indicate that there was a "21–30 day Soviet system of reaching full combat readiness" (para. 17). The implication inferred from this and the detailed examination of the case studies was that "wars scarcely ever happen by accident, and that they almost always take place because a potential aggressor plans, prepares, deploys, and decides to attack" (para. 25). Put another way, it was clear that the process of planning and preparation took many months, but that deployment and mobilization were comparatively short: using Nicoll's examples the former could take months, whereas the latter might take just days. To further confound matters, the actual decision to "go" might be in the hands of a small number of people, and the final choice to do so might be made in a matter of minutes. Two factors emerge: that each stage, therefore, posed different problems to the intelligence community, and that war had to be a conscious decision. It is fascinating to compare this latter point to the conclusion reached in the early parts of the Cold War, when it was felt that the Soviets would only launch a nuclear attack on the West by miscalculation.[15]

Nicoll stated that it should be possible to spot preparatory acts in time to inform ministers as to what was in the offing, and that this should be the real aim of the JIC (para. 20). Thus, for instance, in the case of Poland (1980–81), once the Soviet build-up had started the JIC "attempted to estimate how many days or hours warning could be given of a possible Soviet move" (para. 21). This raises the question whether the JIC—a body designed to deal with strategic estimates— could cope effectively with what, in essence, was tactical information? Nicoll's conclusion was that the JIC was neither organized nor equipped to carry out such a warning role.

In the wake of Lord Butler's report into pre-Iraq war intelligence, the government accepted his recommendation that the size of the assessments staff be increased. This is something that twenty years earlier Nicoll, too, had addressed, but that despite his advice was never acted upon. His view was that because preparations for attack take time, the most important role of the JIC was to provide "cumulative collation" of evidence, as this is "the only way in which a country's aggressive intent can be discovered other than very late in the day" (para. 27). The issue, as he put it, was whether this could be done effectively with such a small assessments staff (para. 51). More important, though, was whether the Ministry of Defence, which had an "effective 24-hour watch for the study of Soviet indicators" could marry their information with the longer-term developments monitored by the JIC and the Foreign Office. Both of these factors were confounded by the growing role of open source information in intelligence estimates (para. 28).

On balance, Nicoll concluded that "the JIC has been able to assess the military capability of the potential aggressor with a fair degree of accuracy. On two occasions, however, the wrong deduction was drawn from these assessments" (para. 7). These were to prove fatal: in the context of the Yom Kippur war the JIC correctly forecast that Sadat was planning to attack but concluded that he would not actually do so because of the inevitable likelihood of defeat. This, therefore, raises the question of the connection between collected information and analyzed intelligence, particularly with a focus on the assessment function.

In considering the performance of the JIC, Nicoll observed that the committee had "found it difficult to believe that the potential aggressor would indeed find the use of force politically acceptable" (para. 4). This in itself is a sensible conclusion, yet by looking at the estimates with the benefit of hindsight, Nicoll discovered that "there has been a tendency to assume that factors which would weigh heavily in the United Kingdom would be equally serious constraints on countries ruled by one-party governments and heavily under the influence of a single leader" (para. 5). This is now a well-known trap, known in the jargon as mirror-imaging; interestingly it was a trap that the United Kingdom would fall into with the Falklands just a short time afterwards.

The major parts of the report that have been retained deal with the section "Sources of Warning Intelligence." Those parts of the section that are still extant deal almost exclusively with open source intelligence. In particular, Nicoll stated that the main sources of information on political intelligence come from open sources (para. 33), but that these need to be carefully weighed against information from closed sources and information on military preparedness (para. 38). Once more, then, this reveals the differences between estimating intent and capability, and how, perhaps, the former can be revealed best through open means, the latter through closed means.

The final aspect that Nicoll focused on is how intelligence estimates should be presented to those whose job it was to act upon them. In doing so he concentrated on the usage of language in assessments, something that Lord Butler later discussed in detail, as the Americans have done in their National Intelligence Estimates.[16] In particular, Nicoll emphasized the importance of phrases such as "no evidence," and how it should be made clear to readers that this meant "an absence of information" (para. 58). Similarly, the fear of composing reports in such a way that the "cry-wolf" syndrome could be averted was also highlighted (para. 59). A related factor was the way that different questions on the same subject could lead to totally different assessments. The corollary of this is the way in which the assessment is compiled: should it be written as a forecast based on the evidence, or should it provide the evidence itself with additional comments? To Nicoll this latter method was better suited to the "requirements of Ministers and the Chiefs of Staff" (para. 61).

Of the final recommendations that Nicoll makes, only four have been revealed in the document, though we can infer that there were at least eight different ones. Three of these concern the composition of the assessments staff and how it deals with estimates. In particular Nicoll suggested having more dedicated intelligence professionals in the assessments staff, as opposed to people seconded from customer departments. The fourth recommendation looks at the role of open source information. In concluding, Nicoll stated that given the timetable for action, there is no reason why warning should not be discovered. That the JIC had had "varying success" owed as much to its own virtues as it does to the "inherent difficulty of the task" (para. 62).

Lessons Learned?

The major importance of Nicoll's study was his examination and depiction of the various traps awaiting analysts, of which they needed to be constantly aware. In doing so he highlighted six different traps that could lead to errors of assessment or judgment:

1. *Mirror-Imaging*—the assumption that any factors that would affect the formation of policy in the United Kingdom would be equally constraining on decisions made by one-party states. Such factors could include the weight of public opinion or the unwillingness to use military force.

One of the big issues here was Nicoll's view that the JIC had, in some cases, overestimated "the value placed by the USSR on world opinion" (para. 4). Thus, for instance, from March to August 1968, the JIC had repeatedly stated that the Soviet Union was unlikely to invade Czechoslovakia because of the effect it would have on the worldwide Communist movement. Mirror-imaging is now a well-known problem, yet that does not mean that it is one that is easily overcome. As Sun Tsu wrote in fourth century BC in his famous treatise *Art of War*: Know your enemy.

2. *Transferred Judgment*—the assumption that a foreign aggressor would make the same calculation of the military balance, and therefore of their chances of victory, as the United Kingdom would in the same position.

This relates to mirror-imaging but is, perhaps, more specific. Once more it is an attempt to understand the situation through the eyes of your opponent. To cite an example, in the case of the Iran/Iraq war, the JIC had predicted that the Iraqis could not maintain an invading force much beyond the border, and that, as a result, an Iraqi attack was unlikely. This is a classic case of what they would have done, had they been in Iraqi shoes, yet without a proper understanding of the situation, it is all too easy to come to the wrong conclusion.

3. *Perseveration*—the likelihood that assessments made in the first stages of an event will affect subsequent judgments, even when evidence to the contrary is discovered.

There are several related problems here. The first is the difficulty of keeping a constantly open mind as to what the intelligence is suggesting. One possible impact of this is that an estimate will have to be reversed in the face of new evidence, and this can have obvious implications for the assessor involved. It also suggests a bigger point, that often trends will need to be monitored over a long period of time, and so the question is who is best placed to do this: the expert who potentially has a particular mind-set on the situation, or a newcomer who may not understand the context and background?

4. *War as a Deliberate Act*—this is the idea that war, or indeed an attack of any kind, is a deliberate act and rarely ever the result of an accident or chance.

The implications from an intelligence perspective are clear: in the preparation stage there will be ample opportunity to gather information; by contrast in the "decision to go" stage, intelligence could be much harder to come by; not only will the period of time be shorter, but often, as in the cases of one-party leaderships, the decision will reside with a very small number of people.

5. *Coverage*—Assessments are invariably difficult to produce in regard to areas where the priority is low.

This is a more subtle point and one that becomes increasingly clear if we examine Nicoll in the context of the subsequent Falklands war. Put simply, the order to which a target is prioritized will have a direct impact on its intelligence coverage. This may be stating the obvious, but it is an important point. Related, and perhaps most crucially, is the question of where responsibility lies with raising the priority of a threat. In the case of the Falklands, its low priority status meant that insufficient means were spent on it, yet should the responsibility have lain with the intelligence agencies to raise this, with the Foreign Office, or with ministers?

6. *Deception*—An aggressor will almost certainly do everything in his power to deceive the country he intends to attack, and perhaps third nations too, as to his real intentions.

This is an overarching point, that if it were not hard enough already, intelligence analysts should expect there to be false flags along the way, intended to deliberately throw them off the scent.

The Lessons of Nicoll

The Nicoll Report was approved by the JIC on March 4, 1982. Just twenty-nine days later the Falkland Islands were invaded by Argentina. The subsequent review by Lord Franks as to what had gone wrong led to considerable criticism of the JIC for its failure to warn of possible Argentine intentions. The Franks Report contained, for the first time, a public description of the structure and role of the JIC; it also included, in some detail, the assessments made in the run-up to the invasion. Franks made several criticisms, and it is interesting to compare these to Nicoll's lessons:

- that there were several principal factors that underlay the assessments produced by the assessments staff (para. 308)
- that the assessments staff had not been aware of the weight of the Argentine press campaign (para. 316)
- that the JIC had not fully understood how the actions of the British Government might affect Argentine thinking (para. 316)
- that the assessments staff did not take into account relevant diplomatic and political developments, or foreign press reporting (para. 317)
- in a low-priority area like the Falklands, the JIC were too passive in what was really a rapidly changing situation (para. 318).[17]

Despite these criticisms the JIC were essentially absolved of blame because the Falklands had been considered a low priority. The collection of intelligence, therefore, had been focused elsewhere, with the result that not enough effort had been spent on accurately gauging Argentine intentions; furthermore, even when the priority had been raised, no further resources had been diverted. Just as Nicoll discovered, and as Franks reported, the actual Argentine decision to go was taken "at a very late date," and coupled with its relatively low priority, there could be no reasonable expectation that the JIC could have predicted such a decision.[18]

Can the lessons of Nicoll be applied to the post–Cold War world? We need to consider this on two levels: state and nonstate conflict. At the state-to-state level, then Nicoll's lessons are clearly relevant. Whether we are referring to a behemoth like the Soviet Union or smaller, developing nations, the essential basis will stay the same. For nonstate actors, too, the same six lessons will apply, though the situation is not quite so clear-cut. For starters nonstate actors do not obey state rules; furthermore, the implications of intelligence will be harder when considering the decision when to intervene to stop an attack. Thus, while the target may change, and the means by which intelligence is procured will alter, the analyst will remain crucial. The declassified extracts of the Nicoll Report focus largely on the assessment side of the intelligence picture; we cannot know what he prescribed for the collection phase, other than inferring that different types of intelligence will be revealing at different stages in the build-up to a crisis. The importance of Nicoll is to focus the analytical mindset, for assessors to be aware of the potential pitfalls and traps that await them. In this Nicoll has concentrated on perhaps the most important aspect of the intelligence cycle, for as history has shown us, even the most advanced intelligence machineries cannot overcome the propensity to be surprised.

NOTES

This paper is drawn only from released official records and published sources and the views expressed are mine in my capacity as an academic historian. They do not represent the views or carry the endorsement of the government.

1. This chapter is partly based on an earlier work, Michael S. Goodman, "The Dog That Didn't Bark: The Joint Intelligence Committee and Warning of Aggression," *Cold War History* 7 (November 2007), 529–51.

2. These details are taken from the *Who's Who* entry for Nicoll, Douglas Robertson.

3. For further details see Richard J. Aldrich, *The Hidden Hand: Britain, America, and Cold War Secret Intelligence* (London: John Murray, 2001). Also see Julian Lewis, *Changing Direction: British Military Planning for Postwar Strategic Defence, 1942–47* (London: Frank Cass, 2003).

4. JIC(51)87(Terms of Reference), "Review of Assessments Made since January 1947 by the Joint Intelligence Committee on Communist Intentions," September 20, 1951. The National Archives (TNA): CAB 158/13.

5. JIC(51)87(Final), "Review of Assessments Made of Communist Intentions since January, 1947 by the Joint Intelligence Committee," December 12, 1951. The National Archives (TNA): CAB 158/13.

6. JIC(50)88, "Chinese Communist Military Intentions and Capabilities in the Non-Communist States Bordering China," October 11, 1950. TNA: CAB 158/11.

7. JIC(51)87(Final), "Review of Assessments Made of Communist Intentions since January, 1947 by the Joint Intelligence Committee," December 12, 1951. TNA: CAB 158/13.

8. Ibid.

9. "The JIC and Warning of Aggression," November 1981. The report was obtained in 2007 by the author through the Freedom of Information Act, and is reprinted below.

10. Lawrence Freedman, The Official History of the Falklands Campaign: Volume I, The Origins of the Falklands War (London: Routledge, 2007), 219.

11. Cmnd.8787. Falkland Islands Review: Report of a Committee of Privy Counsellors. January 1983. (London: HMSO), 95.

12. Percy Cradock. Know Your Enemy: How the Joint Intelligence Committee Saw the World (London: John Murray, 2002), 261.

13. JIC(74)(SEC)1, "Composition and Terms of Reference," October 1, 1974. TNA: CAB 163/212.

14. For more, see Michael S. Goodman, "Jones' Paradigm: The How, Why and Where fore of Scientific Intelligence," Intelligence and National Security 24 (April 2009): 236–56.

15. For more, see Michael S. Goodman, Spying on the Nuclear Bear: Anglo-American Intelligence and the Soviet Bomb (Stanford, CA: Stanford University Press, 2007).

16. See HC 898. Review of Intelligence on Weapons of Mass Destruction (London: TSO, 2004).

17. Cmnd. 8787. Falkland Islands Review: Report of a Committee of Privy Counsellors. January 1983 (London: HMSO).

18. Cmnd.8787. Falkland Islands Review: Report of a Committee of Privy Counsellors. January 1983 (London: HMSO), 73.

DOCUMENT 10.1:   "The JIC and Warning of Aggression," November 1981

This is a partial document. This extract is the portion of the document that has been declassified to date. The full document is a book-length study.

The JIC and Warning of Aggression
[redacted version May 2007]

Cabinet Office
London

PART	TITLE	PAGES
I	INTRODUCTION	1-2
II	THE JIC IN ITS WARNING ROLE	2-6
III	DECISION MAKING PROCESSES IN ACTS OF AGGRESSION	6-10
IV	JIC PROCEDURES IN HANDLING WARNING INTELLIGENCE	10-11
V	JIC PROCEDURES AND THE ROLE OF THE ASSESSMENTS STAFF IN THE PROVISION OF WARNING	12-14
VI	SOURCES OF WARNING INTELLIGENCE	14-20
VII	SOME POSSIBLE WAYS OF IMPROVING OUR CHANCES	20-24
VIII	CONCLUSIONS AND RECOMMENDATIONS	24-27

INTRODUCTION

1. In accordance with proposals made last year by the then Co-ordinator of Intelligence, Sir Brooks Richards, and with requirements laid down by his successor, the present Co-ordinator, Sir Antony Duff, studies have been made of a number of periods of crisis in which preparations for war have been made by the USSR and by other countries. The aim of these studies has been -

    a. to describe the actual sequence of events in the light of the information now available;

    b. to consider the JIC's performance in reporting the crisis and assessing the likelihood of war;

    c. to summarise the use made of the intelligence and

    d. to consider the sources used.

The subjects studied have been -

    a. Soviet preparations for intervention in Czechoslovakia, March to August 1968.

    b. Egyptian/Syrian preparations for the attack on Israel, October 1972 to October 1973, and related Soviet activity.

    c. i.   Chinese preparations for the attack on Vietnam, June 1978 to February 1979.

DOCUMENT 10.1:   "The JIC and Warning of Aggression," November 1981 *(Continued)*

---

      ii.   The Soviet response, February to March 1979.

    d.   Soviet preparations for intervention in Afghanistan, March to December 1979.

    e.   Iraqi preparations for the attack on Iran, November 1979 to September 1980.

Page 1

    f.   possible Soviet preparation for action against Iran, April to September 1980;

    g.   Soviet preparations for intervention in Poland, August 1980 up to 15 April 1981.

I.   THE JIC IN ITS WARNING ROLE

2.   The provision of warning of possible aggressive action by the USSR against the West must be the highest priority requirement laid upon the JIC: the provision of warning of possible aggressive action by the USSR, or by other countries which could damage vital United Kingdom interests, is clearly likewise among the JIC's very high priority requirements. The provision of this warning is not only its highest priority, but undoubtedly its most difficult task. The reasons have been well demonstrated in the course of these studies.

3.   To be able to present Ministers with an assessment that there is a serious possibility that a country is preparing for war, the JIC must be convinced -

    a.   that the country would have the political will to undertake political action;

    b.   that military action would achieve a desired political end; and

    c.   that specific military preparations to that end have begun.

Assessment of Political Will

4.   In a number of cases studied, the JIC has found it difficult to believe that the potential aggressor would indeed find the use of force politically acceptable. In the case of the USSR, this has been because the JIC has tended in some cases -

    a.   over-estimate the value placed by the USSR on world opinion;

Page 2

    b.   to take the view that because the USSR has demonstrably wished to avoid nuclear confrontation with the USA, and to obtain the benefits of détente, it will for that reason avoid high-risk policies.

5.   More generally, there has been a tendency to assume that factors which would weigh heavily in the United Kingdom would be equally serious

DOCUMENT 10.1:   "The JIC and Warning of Aggression," November 1981 *(Continued)*

constraints on countries ruled by one-party governments and heavily under the influence of a single leader; thus -

a.   In March to August 1968 the JIC consistently took the view that the USSR was unlikely to invade Czechoslovakia because of the effect a move would have on world opinion (not least in the world Communist movement) and on détente.

b.   In 1978/1979, in the face of growing evidence of Chinese military concentrations on the Vietnamese border, the JIC took the view until just over a week before the invasion, that such a move was unlikely because the Chinese would fear both possible Soviet military reaction and danger to their developing economic ties with the West, and generally the effects on world opinion.

c.   In the 9 months from March to December 1979, when there was growing evidence of Soviet military interest in Afghanistan, the JIC until mid-December consistently took the view that direct involvement was unlikely and that, insofar as there was evidence by September of possible Soviet planning for military action, it must be contingency planning to rescue their own nationals should they be in danger from eternal Afghan fighting.

6.   Indeed, in several of these studies, it has appeared that the JIC made up its mind very early, and either did not change it at all (as with USSR/Czechoslovakia) or only later, in the face of very strong

Page 3

evidence of military preparations. This belief in the virtue consistency I have described as "perseveration", which is I understand the term used for the psychological phenomenon whereby certain data, such as telephone numbers and the spelling of names, if learned incorrectly the first time, are very difficult subsequently to learn correctly.

Military Capability and the Achievement of the Political End

7.   In almost all the cases studied, the JIC has been able to assess the military capability of the potential aggressor with a fair degree of accuracy. On two occasions, however, the wrong deduction was drawn from these assessments. The first case was in the lead up to the Yom Kippur war. The estimate was that the Arab forces were militarily inferior to the Israelis. Although the JIC correctly forecast in May/June that: Sadat was planning a limited attack across the Suez Canal, by October the assessment was that he would not do this in view, inter alias of the likelihood of defeat. Similarly, in the lead up to the Iraqi/Iranian war, what proved to be a correct assessment was made that the Iraqis had only a limited capability to sustain an invasion of   to any distance beyond their boundaries. This was considered to be a, factor likely to constrain Saddam Hussein from attacking Iran, and together with his assumed fear of super power

DOCUMENT 10.1:   "The JIC and Warning of Aggression," November 1981 *(Continued)*

involvement and of the likely effect on the Shias in Iraq if he went to war, it led to the conclusion that an Iraqi attack was unlikely.

8.   Thus, though our assessment of military capability may be broadly accurate, it does not follow either that the potential aggressor will make the same assessment, or if he does that he will draw the same conclusions from it.

The Preparation and Assembly of a Military Force

9.   In all the cases except one, intelligence on the preparation of the aggressor force has been reasonably good, though as will be disc below, the evidence of preparation is liable to come late in the process. The exception was that of the Iraqi preparations against Iran. The primary reason for this was that Iraq

Page 4

[RETAINED/REDACTED]

was of lower priority than the USSR or China,

[RETAINED/REDACTED]

In most of the other cases studied the detection of these military preparations enabled the JIC to give a varying degree of warning for example -

a.   "Not to exclude" the possibility of an Arab attack on Israel in October 1973, some 18 hours before it happened.

b.   To indicate the possibility that the Chinese "might-be tempted" to launch punitive operations against Vietnam, 9 days advance.

c.   To give about a week's warning of the possibility of Soviet intervention in Afghanistan.

10.   The extreme difficulty of making deductions from military preparations is shown by the JIC handling of the evidence of the build up on the borders of Czechoslovakia in 1968. The Committee had come to the conclusion as early as March 1968 that intervention was probably a politically unacceptable option for the Russians and remained committed to that view. To cover the assembly of 27 divisions round the Czechoslovak borders, the Russians announced first a large-scale mobilisation and logistic Exercise Neman, from 24 July to 10 August 1968; and followed this with the announcement of a Warsaw Pact "Staff and Signals" exercise, i.e. a Command Post exercise, which lasted from 11 August until 20 August, the date of the invasion. The JIC explanation for these 2 announced exercises, and the build up of forces, was that they were part of the psychological warfare being waged against Czechoslovakia.

11.   This incident, like the Arab preparations for the Yom Kippur war, on which our knowledge is now very good, brings home the point that an aggressor will normally do his best, to keep his build up secret and will seek to mislead the victim and others by producing alternative explanations for

DOCUMENT 10.1: "The JIC and Warning of Aggression," November 1981 *(Continued)*

that which he thinks cannot be concealed. It is, therefore, quite essential in dealing with a centrally controlled, one-party State

Page 5

To view its attitude to a crisis as a unified whole and to handle the intelligence on political and military developments together, and o understand if possible the developing outlook and policy of then potential aggressor in political/military terms, right from the beginning.

12. We know from Heikal's account that Sadat personally directed the preparation of his country and forces for the war against Israel from October 1972 onwards. The preparations for intervention in Czechoslovakia in 1968 and Afghanistan in 1979, we knew that as one would expect, Brezhnev was personally involved at critical decision-making stages. To enable effective United Kingdom diplomatic and military action to be taken in response to a military build up, it seems to me that our Ministers and Chiefs of Staff need to know, if possible, where the potential aggressor stands in the decision-making process, and if possible the length of time that this implies to a possible D-day. In the following paragraphs, therefore, the crises studied are reviewed in that light.

III. DECISION-MAKING PROCESSES IN ACTS OF AGGRESSION

13. In some of the cases, the Governments concerned are known to have gone through, and in the rest, I believe they can be deduced to have gone through, the following stages in making their decisions -

   a. Order by the top-most Government authority to its armed forces consider and put forward military options.

   b. Top Government approval of a military plan.

   c. Order to the armed forces to prepare a military force.

   d. Order by the armed forces for deployment to begin.

Page 6

   e. The decision to 'go'.

   f. The launch of the attack.

In the table at Annex, the relevant dates are shown where known or deducible. In addition, the traditional indicator of preparation for war, mobilisation of reservists, is included though on the evidence from these studies, at least for the USSR, I am convinced that mobilisation is not a separate decision from that at c. above. For the USSR, the call-up of reservists and of civilian transport is an essential process in bringing a large part of its forces, including a substantial number of its divisions, to readiness. It is almost certain that Brezhnev took the decision to authorise mobilisation of reservists on 20 July 1968 as part of his

DOCUMENT 10.1:   "The JIC and Warning of Aggression," November 1981 *(Continued)*

decision to order the Minister of Defence, Marshal Grechko, to prepare a force, and the same procedure would appear to have been adopted in the Soviet preparation of their force on the Chinese border in March 1979 and for the intervention in Afghanistan in October–December 1979.

14.   There is considerable variation in the above time-scales. Sadat originally intended his attack to be launched in May or June 1973, but the months allowed between his order to make plans given in October 1972 and the first intended date of attack, May 1973, proved too short – his forces were not ready – and he postponed again in June. In the run up to the Soviet invasion of Afghanistan, the 9 months between March arid December 1979 included intensive studies by 2 top-ranking Soviet Generals with supporting staffs, Epishev in April and Pavlovsky from August to October, and no doubt a variety of options for Soviet action were presented to the General staff and Politburo during that period.

15.   It may be suggested that some military contingencies are so obvious that will be exercised over and over again and therefore a Government, may be in a position to launch its forces totally without warning. One example is the Turkish invasion of Cyprus in 1974. However,

Page 7

it should be remembered. that on a previous occasion, in 1967, though the Turks had been exercising over the years for the invasion of Cyprus, there were enough anomalies in the pattern of their military activity identified in 1967 **[RETAINED]** to reveal. that what they were doing was different from their normal exercising and that invasion was almost certainly what was intended; which led I believe directly to the successful Vance mission to Cyprus, and years without partition. The 1974 Turkish attack was a response to the coup in Cyprus. When a Government and its armed forces' leaders prepare an attack, they will go to considerable lengths to try to ensure success. Hence, the months of study, discussions and training which cleanly preceded the Soviet decision to prepare their forces for the invasion of Czechoslovakia and of Afghanistan; the 4-5 months' build up for the Chinese invasion of Vietnam, preceded by intensive study by the armed forces of the "Vietnamese/Soviet hegemonists" over the previous 3 months: and from the establishment of the joint Egyptian/Syrian planning group in January 1973, the 9 months planning and preparation for a Yom Kippur war.

16.   But the essential point to note is that while planning, preparation. and training may last for up to a year from the initial order to the armed forces to prepare, the period of readying, mobilisation and deployment of forces may be quite short. In the case of Czechoslovakia, we know that the relevant military leaders were recalled to Moscow on 19 July 1968 almost certainly for a meeting of decision on 20 July; that they had deployed

DOCUMENT 10.1: "The JIC and Warning of Aggression," November 1981 *(Continued)*

the bulk of their forces by 10 August, i.e. within 3 weeks, and that they exercised for 10 days before the invasion on 20 August. The deployments were in this case no doubt simplified because a number of units had already been deployed around Czechoslovakia in connection with the earlier Warsaw Pact exercise Sumava. In the case of Afghanistan, the decision by the Politburo to prepare for invasion was probably made on 17 October 1979 and deployments began in early December for the invasion on 25th. There has, indeed been some evidence over several years, that the Soviet Armed Services act under a directive that from the order being given, they should be able to reach Full Combat Readiness, ie the highest state of readiness, within

Page 8
21-30 days. This period is what was described by President Sadat as the countdown, ie the period in which preparations were liable to be detected. Heikal tells us that, when the final plan produced by the Egyptian and Syrian Chiefs of Staff was submitted at the end of August 1973, Sadat approved it in every detail except for the "countdown" which was scheduled to be 20 days. He ordered it to be reduced to 15 days with the aim that coupled with the political deception measures in the plan, it would provide a reasonable chance that the attack could be launched before full Israeli mobilisation; and the United Kingdom, indeed, had the first **[RETAINED]** evidence of the Egyptians readying their forces on 22 September, 14 days before the attack.

17. It can be argued that in the case of Czechoslovakia and Afghanistan, the Russians could choose their own time for the attack and that the period of the "countdown" of 21-30 days might be generous if assumed for a Soviet attack elsewhere. However, I would suggest that in the Soviet preparations and assembly of their forces in the Far East in March 1979, it is likely that the Soviet armed forces were ordered to prepare their forces in the period 1-4 March. The main large-scale field training phase of the activity took place between 20-25 March. We do not know whether the Russians would have moved on to a diversionary action against China had the Chinese not withdrawn their forces from Vietnam; nor how much longer it would have taken the Soviet forces to prepare if they had. But the Soviet action earl, I think, be taken as an example of a Soviet-response, and once the order was given, of the Russians moving at best speed.

18. I believe that the studies made support the earlier evidence. for a 21-30 day Soviet system of reaching full combat readiness. I am encouraged in this view after reading a subsequent study **[RETAINED]** On the basis of° evidence from Soviet intervention in Czechoslovakia and Afghanistan, and from the Soviet build-up in the Far East in March 1979, with evidence also from preparations on the Iranian border in August 1980

DOCUMENT 10.1:   "The JIC and Warning of Aggression," November 1981 *(Continued)*

Page 9

[RETAINED] and around Poland in 1980/83, it deduces that the period laid down for Soviet forces to reach Full Combat Readiness must be 25-30 days.

IV.   JIC PROCEDURES IN HANDLING WARNING INTELLIGENCE

19.   The studies tabled in paragraph 1 above strongly support the thesis that ware very rarely happen by chance; and that they scarcely ever happen as the result of an escalation of border incidents, except in the sense that such incidents may provoke one of the participants into preparing for war. Neither the Chinese/Vietnamese border incidents in.1978 nor the Iraqi/Iranian border incidents in 1979/80, escalated into war. War came because Deng and the Chinese leadership, and Saddam Hussein, respectively, prepared for war and launched their attacks.

20.   If therefore the JIC is to provide early warning of preparation for war, should if possible provide evidence in the planning stage, before the "countdown"" has started. At the very least, it should if possible be in a position not to discount evidence of a military build up in the first part of the "countdown" on grounds of political improbability.

21.   In my study on USSR/Poland, I have. suggested that this has been something of a model of JIC work in this field, since -

   a.   the JIC from the first assessed that the USSR might use force f the Polish party seemed to be losing control of the situation;

   b.   it was therefore ready to accept immediately the evidence of an "intervention contingency force";

   c.   the provision of intelligence very rapidly in the building up late-November 1980 and in late-March 1981, enabled sustained and high-level diplomatic action to be taken.

Page 10

One aspect of the JIC's work on Poland I find particularly attractive is that on this occasion it has normally presented evidence rather than attempted to forecast the future; and when the Soviet-build-up began, attempted to estimate how many days or hours warning could be given a possible Soviet move. It could however be argued that the circumstances were particularly favourable in this case since the Polish crisis came so soon after the intervention in Afghanistan. and therefore the readiness of the USSR to use force in pursuit of its-objectives was in the forefront of everyone's mind. It is also possible that if the Russians do not use force in Poland, it is this which will be widely remembered a few years hence rather than the specific evidence of military preparations, which after all came from highly classified sources of which the. details are not widely known.

23.   In the study of Soviet intervention in Afghanistan, I have suggested that it was a combination of **[RETAINED]** high-level Soviet military interest

DOCUMENT 10.1:   "The JIC and Warning of Aggression," November 1981 *(Continued)*

in Afghanistan over the period March to August 1979, including special training by Soviet forces on its borders, backed up by **[RETAINED]** intensive training by the nearest Airborne Division, which led the JIC for the first time in September that, to suggest that the USSR might be planning some form of intervention. (It was suggested that this might be contingency planning for the protection of its own nationals).

24. Had the evidence for Egyptian preparations for war **[RETAINED]** in March to June 1973, been collated in detail, I have little doubt but that the phenomena of late-September/early-October would have been identified as a virtual repeat of preparations of April to June 1973, and earlier and more positive warning of the Arab attack would have been given, the present Soviet /Polish crisis, **[RETAINED]** preparation for intervention in November/December 1980 has already been summarised, and a further report has been written on the second "countdown" in March/April 1981. These reports should greatly facilitate JIC appreciation of Soviet preparations should the Soviet Armed Forces once again be called upon to prepare for intervention in Poland in the future.

Page 11

V   JIC PROCEDURES AND THE ROLE OF THE ASSESSMENTS STAFF IN THE PROVISION OF WARNING

25. It is then, I believe, the lesson of history and certainly of the cases studied, that wars scarcely ever happen by accident, and that they almost always take place because a potential aggressor plans, prepares, deploys and decides to attack. The phase of planning and preparation is likely to take several months. The deployment phase is likely to take 3-4 weeks and to be concealed as far as possible. The question must therefore be asked whether our JIC and Assessments Staff procedures are ideal for the appreciation of evidence of such planning.

2b. Reading again a good deal of the JIC's weekly output during this study, I am struck again by the range and richness of the JIC's Weekly Surveys of Intelligence. They represent, I believe, a very high quality periodical. If, therefore, the warning provided in some of the cases of aggression studied has been non-existent or ambiguous, or late, and if our sources on military preparations have been generally good, the fault must lit in part in our procedures.

27. Where the JIC considers a longer term subject, such as Soviet military capabilities, or the outlook for the Middle East, a paper is prepared by the MOD or the FCO or the Assessments Staff; is, studied by members of departments; considered probably in more than one draft by the CIG; and finally reaches the Committee itself in a form acceptable at least to the staff _urn member departments. This is possible because the subjects

DOCUMENT 10.1:   "The JIC and Warning of Aggression," November 1981 *(Continued)*

are essentially long-term. If, however, one looks at the JIC's assessments over the months on the subjects studied, they are almost always in the Weekly Surveys of Intelligence except in the final stages when, necessarily, Immediate Assessments are produced. Admittedly, some of the weekly surveys like the specially classified survey on Afghanistan in September 1979, make use of earlier material. But the weekly system is not designed to allow of that highly detailed collation, and cumulative collation, of evidence which I believe to be the only way in which a country's aggressive intro tan be discovered other than very late in the day.

Page 12

28. I have discussed this problem with [**RETAINED**] the two members of the Assessments Staff who have so successfully shared the work on USSR/Poland. The latter both stressed to me that the kind of medium-term collation worn am describing would be beyond their resources given the volume of both open source and secret intelligence input which they must handle week by week. They are dependent, therefore, upon discussion with the FCO, the MOD and the Agencies for the discovery of trends.. But in discussion with those who contribute to and take part in CIGs, it has struck me that to a considerable extent the work of the current intelligence staff in member departments is essentially geared to the provision of input to the CIGs for the Weekly Surveys, and that although the MOD has an effective 24-hour watch for the study of Soviet indicators, it is only in the Assessments Staff and the JIC machinery, that that collation of political and military developments can be done which is so essential if early warning is to be given.

29. It has been suggested to me that the Assessments Staff should perhaps not indeed be the place where detailed collation of the type I believe to be necessary should be done; that the role of the Cabinet Office as a whole is in essence that of a high-level co-ordinating secretariat; and that, the role of the Assessments Staff may be considered to be broadly analogous, ie it should depend on detailed collation work done in the MOD and FCO and the agencies. My firm belief is that there is a need for central collation work in addition to the necessary work done by the MOD and the producers. In the field of political developments, the FCO would not claim in any way to be a detailed collator of intelligence; its role, as the Chairman of the JIC has pointed out, is essentially policy formulation and it is the first user of indicator and warning intelligence. The FCO Research Department is a user of secret intelligence and an important contributor of staff to the Assessments Staff but it is not analogous to the intelligence collation staff in the United States State Department. Logically and practically, therefore, I believe that there must be enough highly detailed collation work done in the Assessments Staff., in co-operation with the

DOCUMENT 10.1:   "The JIC and Warning of Aggression," November 1981 *(Continued)*

MOD, FCO geographical departments and the producer Agencies in this most important field to ensure -

Page 13

    a.   that the JIC has the best possible chance of <u>early</u> detection of planning for aggression;

    b.   that to that end the evidence from all sources - some of which is highly complex - is fully understood and taken into account at the centre, and <u>cumulatively</u>.

I believe that our chances of achieving early detection could be improved without substantial change in the number of staff. I shall come back to some suggestions after first discussing our sources.

VI   SOURCES OF WARNING INTELLIGENCE

    A.   The Planning and Preparation Phase

[RETAINED]

Page 14

33.   Detailed analysis of political developments and particularly of Governmental pronouncements by the potential aggressor, is particularly important in this planning and preparation phase, and especially the analysis of the timing of such pronouncements against the evidence of military developments. For example, the Warsaw Letter enunciating the Brezhnev Doctrine on 15 July 1968 was followed by the recall of Grechko and Yakubovsky to Moscow on 19/20 July, and the beginning of deployments from about 27 July. The importance will be clear of the compilation of a detailed and cumulative comparative chronology. The main source for this political intelligence is the Press, radio and TV of the aggressor country, received direct eg by BBC monitoring; through our Embassy analysis and reporting; and through the Western Press. A study of this material is already an essential but formidable task for the Assessment Staff, and I make some suggestions for simplifying this task in my recommendations.

    B.   The Count-Down Phase

[RETAINED]

Page 15

Page 16 omitted

38.   As in the planning and preparation phase, open source political information requires careful collation against the military data during the "count-down". For example, Saddam Hussein's abrogation of the Algiers Iraqi/Iranian Treaty on 17 September 1980 was clearly related to his move of divisions to the Iranian frontier.

[RETAINED]

DOCUMENT 10.1:   "The JIC and Warning of Aggression," November 1981 *(Continued)*

Page 17

[Pages 18-19 omitted]

VII.   SOME POSSIBLE WAYS OF IMPROVING OUR CHANCES

Staffing of the Assessments Staff

50.   The Assessments Staff has been, I believe, from the beginning intended to be a mix of FCO and MOD, and other generalist intelligence users, and intelligence collators and producers. Intelligence most clearly revealing possible military planning/preparation for aggression, tends to come from sources that are complex and require considerable background for their weight to be understood.

[RETAINED]

Page 20

51.   It is not appropriate for this study to suggest the precise number of people who should be allocated to the Assessments Staff or how they should be organised, though it is my impression that the staff has been pared rather closely and that there is now little margin to take the strain in crisis periods. But I would urge that the mix between intelligence user and intelligence collator/producer should be carefully looked at, both in numbers, and in level, to ensure as far as possible that the appropriate weighting is accorded in the Assessments Staff work to the complex evidence likely to produce warning intelligence.

52.   I would also suggest that there should always be sufficient members of the staff with knowledge of Soviet affairs and intelligence collation experience to allow work on the Soviet side to be increased in times of crisis – even if some have to turn their attention to Belize or Anguilla for part of their stay.

53.   I have said above that I regard it as crucial to improving our chance, of deducing the intentions of a potential aggressor that there should be detailed collation of relevant. political and military activities on the part of the possible suggested aggressor, over a period of months. This implies the designation of a member of the Assessments Staff to do precisely this when necessary; to work in close collaboration both with members of the Assessments Staff handling the current input for the Weekly Survey and with the analysts **[RETAINED]** and to produce summaries of the developing actions and attitudes of the country concerned for presentation to the JIC as medium-term reports.

Technical Aids and Procedures

54.   The Assessments Staff is not at present equipped for cumulative collation. The type of collation work I am suggesting requires ready access to relevant intelligence end-product reports up to one-year-old.

Page 21

DOCUMENT 10.1: "The JIC and Warning of Aggression," November 1981 *(Continued)*

[RETAINED]

Open Source Information

56. I have pointed out above the importance of the study of open source information, and the burden which this imposes on the members of the Assessments Staff. It seems to me that there are 2 possible requirements here; one to reduce the volume of material handled by the Assessments Staff in the normal way, and the other to facilitate the type of medium-term study I am proposing. For the first, there are already two London firms, Finsbury Data Services and Fintel, which offer computer-based services of UK Press extracts by subject. There may be others.

Page 22

57. For the second, Keesing's Contemporary Archives, which is not mechanized, might be prepared to speed up its service of summaries in particular cases. There may be other solutions. I recommend that the handling of open source material should be investigated in the light of modern methods of information handling.

JIC Presentation of Evidence

58. The Chairman of the JIC has made the point that readers of JIC reports may sometimes read more than is intended into a JIC report of "no evidence". In this field of indicator and warning intelligence, where aggressors will do their best to conceal their preparations, it is especially important for the JIC to make it clear how far we would expect to receive evidence, and how far "no evidence" simply means an absence of information.

59. One persistent concern of the members of the JIC over the years has been the fear of "crying wolf". It may well be that this underlay the committee's reluctance to accept the evidence from Sadat's preparations in September/October 1973 after his failure to move in June. I believe this fear is overdone. Analysts and reporters **[RETAINED]** are trained from the start to look for the norm and where their evidence produces something unusual, to look for the simple, not alarmist, explanation.

60. There has been a tendency in several of the cases studied for the JIC to view a military build up as intended to exert psychological pressure. This tendency was most marked in the JIC's handling of the Soviet preparations for intervention in Czechoslovakia, and was present in its consideration of Sadat's preparations in 1973 and the Chinese build up
On the Vietnamese border in 1973/79. It is the classic dilemma which faced both the JIC and Stalin in their assessments of the German build up along the Soviet Frontier in 1941. There is no simple answer, but I would suggest that in presenting the evidence, the JIC should attempt to answer questions of the following kind -

Page 23

DOCUMENT 10.1:   "The JIC and Warning of Aggression," November 1981 *(Continued)*

---

   a.   How far is our knowledge of the build up intended to be seen by a
        potential victim and how far is our knowledge of it from secret and
        unintended sources? (The Czechs could not possibly have had any
        idea of the size of the build up round them in July/August 1968).
   b.   If only psychological pressure is intended, would it be applied in this
        way? (Exercise SUMAVA in June/July 1968 looks to be a clear example
        of Soviet psychological pressure.)
   c.   What will be the effect if the force prepared is dispersed to its bases
        without action being taken?

61. In several earlier crises the JIC has tended virtually to produce a forecast on
    the basis of a combination of the evidence and of our own judgments of
    the attitude of the country concerned. I very much favour the procedure
    adopted in the Soviet/Polish crisis in which in essence it is evidence which
    has been presented together with comment. It seems to me that this has
    been effective in allowing diplomatic action to be taken in this case, and
    it seems to me likely to be more effective in meeting the requirements of
    Ministers and the Chiefs of Staff.

VIII. CONCLUSIONS AND RECOMMENDATIONS.

62. Conclusions

   A.   The pattern of aggressive action revealed by these studies is of careful
        planning, preparation over many months, followed by comparatively
        short periods of deployment and mobilisation which lasted 15 days in
        the case of Sadat's 1973 attack on Israel, about 2 months in the case
        of the Chinese build up against Vietnam, and probably normally last
        21-30 days in the case of the USSR (paras. 13-18).
   B.   The JIC has had varying success in the provision of warning. Among
        the complex reasons for this are the inherent difficulty of the task; a
        tendency to assume that, the constraints such as world opinion

Page 24

[RETAINED]

and economic factors which would be critical for the UK, would be equally
limiting in the case of a centrally directed one-party-Government such as
the USSR or China; and a tendency on the JIC's part to overvalue the virtue
of consistency – "perseveration". Nevertheless the JIC was able to give about
a week's warning of the Soviet move into Afghanistan, and to provide
clear evidence of Soviet military preparations for intervention in Poland in.
November/December 1980, and March/April 1981 (paras. 2-11).

[RETAINED]

   E.   In both these phases, the importance of careful collation of the evidence
        with the largely open source evidence of the political attitudes and
        pronouncements of the country, cannot be overestimated (paras. 33-38).

DOCUMENT 10.1: "The JIC and Warning of Aggression," November 1981 *(Continued)*

[RETAINED]
Page 25
- H. The key to earlier provision of warning is careful and cumulative collation of the evidence. (paras. 27-29, 53)
- I. Though such collation could be undertaken without substantial changes in numbers of staff, it would be greatly facilitated by easier access to source material and by modern methods of information handling. (paras. 54-57)
- J. The JIC's performance in the warning field has been effective in the Soviet/Polish crisis where it has essentially concentrated on the provision of evidence and of warning times. (paras 61)

63. Recommendations
[RETAINED]
- C. The balance between generalist and specialist intelligence staff in the Assessments Staff, both in numbers and level, should be kept under careful review.
- D. The Assessments Staff should include enough people with knowledge of Soviet affairs to ensure that work on the Soviet side can be stepped up in times of crisis.
- E. When a country begins to show signs of possible aggressive intent a member of the Assessments Staff should be detailed to undertake cumulative collation of the evidence.

Page 26
[RETAINED]
- H. The handling of open source material should be examined in the light of modern methods of information handling.

Page 27

DOCUMENT 10.1: "The JIC and Warning of Aggression," November 1981 *(Continued)*

ANNEX

	1. Order to prepare military options	2. Govt approval of military plan	3. Order to prepare force	4. Order to mobilize reserves	5. Mobilization of reserves	6. Beginning of employment	7. Action
USSR/Czechoslovakia 1968	Probably March '68	U/K	7.20.68	By 7.22.68	24.7-1.8 (in Exercise NEMAN) By 5.1.73	7.27.68	8.17.68
Egypt and Syria/Israel 1973	Oct 72	Late March 73 Probably 5.19.73 Between 28.8 & 9.19.73	March/April 73 By 5.22.73 As at 2.	April 73 U/K Probably as at 2.	U/K 9.27.73	March-early May 1973 3-6.10.73 By 9.22.73	Postponed 5.9.73 Postponed for political reasons 10.3.73
China/Vietnam 1979	June 1978	Final approval 9.2.1979	Probably by 9.1978	–	–	Mid December 78	2.9.1979
USSR/China 1979	U/K	U/K	Probably 3.1-4.79	By 3.7.79	3.8.79	3.6-14.79	Chinese withdrawal 3.16.79
USSR/Afghanistan 1979	March 1979	U/K	Probably 10.17.79	U/K	12.15-18.79	Early December	U/K Possibly 9.17.80
USSR/Iran 1980 Iraq/Iran 1980	April–July 1980	–	U/K Between 11.25.80 and 11.27.80	–	–	–	Decision against 12.5.80
USSR/Poland 1980	Possibly April 1980	U/K	3.20-25.81	–	Early Dec	Mid August- early Sept. 1980	Decision against probably 4.3.81
USSR/Poland 1981	Early Sept 1980	U/K		U/K	Early April	11.27-early December 25.3-early April	

CHAPTER 11

Lessons Learned

What the History of British Intelligence Can Tell Us about the Future

ROBERT DOVER AND MICHAEL S. GOODMAN

F ailing to appreciate historical lessons is a widespread problem in all aspects of political and social life. It appears that our political masters and elites in other spheres (particularly in the economic arena) are doomed to repeat the mistakes of their forebears. In our recent history, and in the aftermath of the Iraq war and the intelligence fiasco that contributed to it, the British government authorized Lord Butler, a former Cabinet Secretary, to look at both what had gone wrong, and what the wider implications for the intelligence community were. In his report Lord Butler concluded that historical lessons had been forgotten, and that a regular review process should be instigated. The "Implementation Group" created following Butler's recommendations and chaired by David Omand, who contributed the introduction to this book, also emphasized the necessity to review past judgments. The rationale for this book was to attempt to ameliorate this situation. We aimed to bring to the fore an awareness of what has gone on in the past, and the lessons that it is crucial to learn from historical precedents.

Intelligence is often a difficult subject from which to draw lessons. Most intelligence successes go unreported and unremarked in the public realm. Public inquiries held into intelligence and particular operations or events are almost always those concerning intelligence failure. Those outside the intelligence community are, therefore, always drawing on visible errors or "perfect storms" to generate key lessons, on those moments where the agencies or their political masters can be seen to have lapsed. They are not drawing on what we assume to be the vast wealth of best practice and conspicuous successes the agencies have had, or the methods they have used to achieve these successes, and the evidence of the degradation of the capabilities of adversaries as a result. It is fiendishly difficult to judge that which we cannot observe—the prevention of a terrorist act, for example—but part of the assessment of the effectiveness of intelligence has to be the vast majority of the agencies' output, which is successfully monitoring, containing, and rolling back threats to national security.

Identifying lessons learned is not new: the military has been doing it for centuries; indeed, the rationale behind the creation of an official history program at the start of the twentieth century was an attempt to identify the lessons from the Boer War for the benefit of future conflict. In the intelligence world it is, however, a new approach. Various attempts to extract the wider lessons have been utilized at various points in the past, but their common problem is that they are forgotten as fast as they appear. This is partly because of the time pressures on intelligence officers—they simply do not have the time to sit back and reflect on these lessons, and partly a problem of selection—how to select someone to conduct the research necessary to construct these historical case studies. There is, of course, the additional problem of where the histories are going to be published, be it for internal agency consumption or wider academic and public consumption. But what is clear from the range of the case studies that have been presented here is that today's intelligence targets are neither new nor original: in one way or another there are common links with the past, and if we are truly to progress, then those lessons need to be heeded and built upon. As the old maxim goes, if one does not learn from history, one is certain to repeat it.

What was noticeable about the case studies that the eleven authors contributed to this book was the timeless quality of some of the lessons. Big questions about "how we know what we know" inform all of them, from the sanctity of sources, the effectiveness of technology, the believability of double agents, or the politicization of the process, which includes, for example, whether intelligence and analysis had been withheld. The use of intelligence by government ministers features prominently in the chapters by Mark Phythian and Rob Dover, who deal with the intelligence behind the Iraq War and the Scott Report, respectively. The relationship between politicians (and government politicians in the main) and intelligence officers also comes through strongly. The presence of David Omand and Michael Herman in the list of authors brings to the fore the perspective of high-ranking former government officials involved in intelligence; and both are strongly supportive of the excellent work that intelligence officers do, both in "speaking truth to power" and in providing an excellent intelligence product. In contrast, the authors from the civilian side offer a greater level of criticism and questioning about this relationship.

Michael Goodman and Gill Bennett bring the perspective of historians with a measure of insider access (although neither can be assumed to provide an official perspective), and they encapsulate the tension between intelligence agencies learning accurate lessons and the dangers of releasing too much information into the public domain; the law of unintended consequences. Richard Aldrich, with his chapter in this volume and his recent unauthorized examination of GCHQ, demonstrates the role of the outsider historian, and also his considerable skill at piecing together open source information into compelling narratives. These are skills that Len Scott, Eunan O'Halpin, and Matthew Jones also brought to this book; but in their respective cases they drew out historical echoes to the present day, which is essential if we are to learn that many of the "new" phenomena in the international system have their antecedents in our past. And finally, Peter Gill provided the legal-bureaucratic basis of intelligence oversight, something that we have been told successively, since 9/11 particularly, is crucial for the effective operation of intelligence in democratic political systems.

Ultimately, we want our intelligence agencies to learn from history for very practical reasons. We want them to continue to be effective at what they do, and in learning from history they can avoid the pitfalls and errors of the past (or put in place operating procedures to help them avoid them, or at least identify the potential for these errors), to create greater forward capability—the ability to predict the behavior of adversaries through a large body of collected observations, and finally, to continually reinforce the core mission of intelligence agencies in western democracies, which is to protect a particular way of life and political vision without unduly impacting on it themselves. It is this last function of lessons learned that has received the most attention in Western Europe and the United States since 2005. The vast improvements to electronic intelligence and methods of surveillance have opened up the potential for agencies to collect intelligence on a larger proportion of the population than ever before; but in doing so there is a sense in which the relationship between the civilian population and the agencies has changed. One of the key lessons from history that has yet to be fully worked through is the role of intelligence in society, and the relationships between intelligence agencies and their governments, and the people they serve and protect. Until we can learn from and understand the past, what hope do we have for the future?

Contributors

Richard J. Aldrich is professor of international security at the University of Warwick and is the author of several books, including *The Hidden Hand: Britain, American and Cold War Secret Intelligence* and *GCHQ: The Uncensored Story of Britain's Most Secret Intelligence Agency* (Harper Press, 2010).

Gill Bennett is the former chief historian of the Foreign and Commonwealth Office (FCO) and senior editor of the FCO's official history of postwar foreign policy, *Documents on British Policy Overseas, 1995–2005.* Her most recent book is *Churchill's Man of Mystery: Desmond Morton and the World of Intelligence* (Routledge, 2007).

Robert Dover is a senior lecturer in international relations at Loughborough University and coeditor of the Intelligence and Security Series for Hurst and Columbia University Press. He has published *The Europeanisation of British Defence Policy* (Ashgate, 2007) and is coauthor (with Michael Goodman) of *Spinning Intelligence: Why Intelligence Needs the Media, Why the Media Needs Intelligence* (Columbia University Press, 2009).

Peter Gill is honorary fellow at the University of Liverpool. He is author of *Intelligence in an Insecure World* (Polity, 2006) and is coeditor of the *PSI Handbook of Global Security and Intelligence: National Approaches,* two volumes (Praeger, 2008) and *Intelligence Theory: Key Questions and Debates* (Routledge, 2009).

Michael S. Goodman is a senior lecturer in the Department of War Studies, King's College London. His publications include *Spying on the Nuclear Bear: Anglo-American Intelligence and the Soviet Bomb* (Stanford University Press, 2008) and as coauthor with Robert Dover, *Spinning Intelligence: Why Intelligence Needs the Media, Why The Media Needs Intelligence* (Columbia University Press, 2009). He is coeditor of the Intelligence and Security Series for Hurst and Columbia University Press.

Michael Herman served from 1952 to 1987 in Britain's Government Communications Headquarters, with secondments to the Cabinet Office (as secretary of the Joint Intelligence Committee) and to the Ministry of Defence. He has published two books: *Intelligence Power in Peace and War* (Cambridge University Press, 1996) and *Intelligence Services in the Information Age* (Frank Cass, 2001).

Matthew Jones is a professor in the School of American and Canadian Studies at the University of Nottingham. He is the author of several books, including *Conflict and Confrontation in South East Asia, 1961–1965: Britain, the United States, Indonesia and the Creation of Malaysia* (Cambridge University Press, 2002), and *After Hiroshima: The United States, Race and Nuclear Weapons in Asia, 1945–1965* (Cambridge University Press, 2010).

Eunan O'Halpin is professor of contemporary Irish history at Trinity College, Dublin. Among his works are *Defending Ireland: The Irish State and Its Enemies since 1922* (Oxford, 1999), and *Spying on Ireland: British Intelligence and Irish Neutrality during the Second World War* (Oxford, 2008).

David Omand is a visiting professor in the Department of War Studies, King's College, London. He spent his earlier career in the civil service, including as the director of GCHQ and the intelligence and security coordinator in the Cabinet Office. He recently published *Securing the State* (Hurst, 2010).

Mark Phythian is professor of politics and head of the Department of Politics and International Relations at the University of Leicester. He is the author or editor/coeditor of nine books, including *Intelligence in an Insecure World* (Polity, 2006); *Intelligence and National Security Policymaking on Iraq: British and American Perspectives* (Manchester University Press, 2008); and *Intelligence Theory: Key Questions and Debates* (Routledge, 2008).

Len Scott is professor of international politics at Aberystwyth University. He is also director of the Centre for Intelligence and International Security Studies. His recent publications include *The Cuban Missile Crisis and the Threat of Nuclear War: Lessons from History* (Continuum Books, 2007); *Exploring Intelligence Archives: Enquiries into the Secret State* (Routledge, 2008); and *Intelligence, Crises and Security: Prospects and Retrospects* (Routledge, 2008).

Index